LATINX REVOLUTIONARY HORIZONS

Latinx Revolutionary Horizons

FORM AND FUTURITY IN THE AMERICAS

Renee Hudson

FORDHAM UNIVERSITY PRESS   NEW YORK   2024

Copyright © 2024 Fordham University Press

All rights reserved. No part of this publication may be reproduced, stored in a retrieval system, or transmitted in any form or by any means—electronic, mechanical, photocopy, recording, or any other—except for brief quotations in printed reviews, without the prior permission of the publisher.

Fordham University Press has no responsibility for the persistence or accuracy of URLs for external or third-party Internet websites referred to in this publication and does not guarantee that any content on such websites is, or will remain, accurate or appropriate.

Fordham University Press also publishes its books in a variety of electronic formats. Some content that appears in print may not be available in electronic books.

Visit us online at www.fordhampress.com.

Library of Congress Cataloging-in-Publication Data available online at https://catalog.loc.gov.

Printed in the United States of America

26 25 24   5 4 3 2 1

First edition

for my parents

Contents

Introduction: Forming Revolutions   1

PART I – LATINX REVOLUTIONARY CONSCIOUSNESS

1 Captive Revolutions: Revolutionary Consciousness as Racial Consciousness in Ruiz de Burton and Cisneros   33

PART II – LATINX REVOLUTIONARY PEDAGOGIES

2 Romancing Revolution: The Queer Future of National Romance in Rizal, Rosca, and Hagedorn   69

3 Teaching Revolution: The Latinx Bildungsroman in Alvarez and Díaz   100

PART III – LATINX REVOLUTIONARY IMAGINARIES

4 Retconning Revolution: The Solidarity of Form in García, Barnet, and Avellaneda   133

5 Speculative Revolutions: Otrxs Latinidades in Delany and Silko   159

Coda: Is the X a Commons? 191

ACKNOWLEDGMENTS 201

NOTES 205

BIBLIOGRAPHY 255

INDEX 281

LATINX REVOLUTIONARY HORIZONS

Introduction
Forming Revolutions

"Latinidad is cancelled": so declares Tatiana Flores, riffing on Alan Pelaez Lopez's Instagram graphic of the same proclamation.[1] Using Lopez's work as the anchor for her article on the cancellation of latinidad, Flores outlines the white roots of the conceptualization of a specifically "Latin" America before turning to a discussion of mestizaje and an exploration of how Afro Latinx artists engage with notions of racial mixture. Flores historicizes how the invention of Latin America arose in the nineteenth century as, according to Walter Mignolo, "*latinidad* is a construct created by 'White Creole and Mestizo/a elites, in South America and the Spanish Caribbean islands, to create their own postcolonial identity.'"[2] In tracing this genealogy of the term, Flores argues that, fundamentally, "'Latin America' is a white supremacist construct."[3] For Flores, because Latin America is a white supremacist construct, so is the designation "Latin American and its derivations" (68). She ends the article by writing that "anti-Blackness is unacceptable, and if *latinidad* cannot embrace a platform of antiracism and speak out against sexism, gendered violence, homophobia, transphobia, family separation, migrant criminalization, white supremacy, Indigenous invisibility, geographic segregation, and cultural erasure—in short, if it cannot decolonize—it deserves to be canceled" (79).

I want to observe a couple things here: one, how we go from Latin America to Latin Americans to latinidad. In other words, how we move from a geographic imaginary to a form of identification to the sense of what it means to be Latinx or Latinx-ness. We also move from the strident claim "Latinidad is Cancelled" in the title to the significantly modified claim that, if latinidad cannot do certain kinds of political work, "it deserves to be canceled." The list of political stances latinidad must take quickly expands beyond combating anti-blackness to a host of other actions, such as speaking out against "family separation" and "migrant criminalization." I single out these two issues in particular because, even though they are no doubt present in other countries, Flores's list looks tellingly like a list of concerns for people of Latin American descent living in the U.S. Although Flores's historical reclamation of the various projects of latinidad in Latin America are cogent, her takedown of latinidad is rooted more in current U.S. political projects than on historical trends. It is fair to say, as Mignolo argues, that Latin American history helps to establish the contours of latinidad in the U.S., but I would point out that the very concerns that preoccupy Flores are still—and tellingly—rooted in the U.S. After all, while Mexico might also be the site of family separation and migrant criminalization, this is due in no small part to the pressures the United States puts on countries south of the border.

The gap between Latin America and latinidad, between the call for cancellation and the hesitation about enacting such cancellation, is where my project *Latinx Revolutionary Horizons: Form and Futurity in the Americas* comes in. My book argues that Latinx revolutionary horizons are a hemispheric project in which contemporary Latinx authors return to earlier moments of revolution to theorize a liberatory latinidad that is not yet here. I pair nineteenth-century authors such as Gertrudis Gómez de Avellaneda who reflect the Latin American revolutions of the nineteenth century with contemporary Latinx literature to historicize how our literature is one that emerged well before conventional periodizations that locate it as stemming from the Civil Rights Movement. In turning to these earlier works, I demonstrate the shifting imaginaries of what latinidad could mean across authors and centuries. In this way, I examine how a nascent conceptualization of Latinx identity emerges in nineteenth-century novels such as María Amparo Ruiz de Burton's *Who Would Have Thought It?* (1872).

Nineteenth-century works in particular speak to an emergent revolutionary consciousness. For example, in my reading of Ruiz de Burton's *Who Would Have Thought It?*, I investigate the very trajectory Flores traces in charting the whiteness of latinidad. However, in contrast to Flores, I argue that Ruiz de Burton's emphasis on Latin whiteness is a way to combat the hegemonic Anglo-Saxon whiteness of the U.S. Although Ruiz de Burton's possessive investment in whiteness is problematic, to say the least, I turn to such controversial figures in the archive of Latinx literature to explore how glimmers of revolutionary horizons emerge in even the most unlikely places. In short, we may take it for granted that Latinx literature is a literature of resistance, but that resistance does not always take the form one would expect. Instead, Latinx revolutionary horizons emerge out of fraught histories and reveal themselves in disruptions and departures from generic conventions. Through such departures, Latinx revolutionary horizons catch us unawares, underscoring ties between the center and the so-called periphery.

One of the contentions of my project is that such revolutionary horizons, within the Latinx context, can best be apprehended in literature. This is in part because of the specifically literary quality of revolution within both Latin American and Latinx frameworks. Simón Bolívar's insistence on speeches and pamphlets for his revolutionary campaigns speaks to the importance of the literary to the revolutionary imagination in the Americas, especially given Angel Rama's argument regarding Spain's orchestration of literacy and political administration in the colonies.[4] José Martí's "Our America" (1891) takes up the tradition begun by Bolívar to imagine revolution via the literary.[5] Moreover, as evidenced by the Nuyorican Poets Café more broadly and famous Chicano poems such as Rodolfo "Corky" Gonzalez's "I am Joaquín" (1967) more specifically,[6] Latinx resistance is imagined into existence through the literary, from poetry to manifestos. Yet, even though poetry, essays, and manifestos have played important roles for Latinx and Latin American resistance, they often speak to the concerns of the present, even when they seem to engage with history. As "I am Joaquín" and "El Plan Espiritual de Aztlán" (1969) illustrate,[7] such works engage with Mexican history to raise a *mythic* homeland, often at the expense of communities in the present, as evidenced by the Chicano Movement's problematic relationship to indigeneity, as Aztlán makes clear.

Latinx Revolutionary Horizons, then, turns to Latinx novels specifically because they are historical—and preoccupied by history—in a way that other Latinx cultural productions are not.[8] The narrative registers of the novel speak to the historical past and contemporary meditations on it in a way unavailable in other forms. Further, given that the central preoccupation of *Latinx Revolutionary Horizons* is the relationship between latinidad and race, focusing on novels allows me to examine race "beyond the priority of the already visualized body."[9] Drawing on Mark Jerng's work, rather than only attending to "the recognition of racial ideologies" (8), analyzing novels allows me to explore "*participation* in race" (8, emphasis Jerng's), particularly as Latinx authors grapple with revolutionary legacies in which race is a dividing factor—as we can see in the Cuban context—as well as when issues of race are papered over—in the case of the Mexican Revolution—to offer a faux sense of unity. For Jerng, operating outside of visual registers and within literary ones allows for a better understanding of how "we are taught to notice race not just on bodies but as social facts embedded in our temporal organization of experience" (8).

Novels, then, allow for attending to the very issues of race that plague current conversations about the cancellation of latinidad and illuminate how the complexities of latinidad are not reducible to cancellation. A key claim I make in *Latinx Revolutionary Horizons* is that reading across centuries underscores that latinidad is far from a static concept: it has always shifted and branched out, such that the presumed whiteness of latinidad today ignores other conceptualizations of latinidad not grounded in whiteness. Examining a range of latinidades across texts allows me to also investigate the shifting terrain of utopian imaginaries and longings that necessarily point to the limits of liberatory movements and imaginations while exploring the speculative potential of latinidad. Additionally, in staging a conversation between contemporary Latinx authors and nineteenth-century authors from across the hemisphere, I point to an ongoing conversation on a decolonization that has yet to come but has also been continuous. This conversation is a recognition of historicity, of the openness of history, with the resistance of borders that are nevertheless assessed for the damage they imply and the complicity with imperial nationalisms that independence movements became.

To that end, *Latinx Revolutionary Horizons* examines a range of genres to apprehend the various forms that resistance takes; to do so, I analyze captivity and conversion narratives, Latinx dictator novels, neo-slave narratives, and testimonios. I also consider several revolutions, including the Mexican Revolution, the Filipino People Power Revolution of 1986, resistance to the dictator Rafael Leónidas Trujillo Molina in the Dominican Republic, the Cuban Revolution, and imagined Latinx revolutions. Focusing on such foundational writers as Sandra Cisneros, Julia Alvarez, and Cristina García allows me to investigate how the history of the hemisphere is one of revolution. Each author represents a larger phenomenon of revolutionary contact and exchange as well as how Latin American revolutions have been a generative force for imagining resistance in the U.S. It remains a paradox of actually existing latinidad that in many ways Latin American–descended people in the U.S. most consistently choose to align their interests with whiteness, despite the fact that our ancestors are African, Indigenous, Asian, and white. Our people would seem uniquely positioned to join such groups together, but, as evidenced by the legal fiction of Mexican whiteness and the Latinxs who voted for Trump, the hope of accessing rights via proximity to whiteness consistently disrupts the potential for solidarity and coalition-building. I agree that our current liberatory imaginaries do not live up to the task of latinidad that Flores outlines; that said, I also contend that before we can make claims about what comprises "Latinx-ness," we must first determine what to call ourselves, as well as understand the political conceptualizations that attend such namings.

The Revolution to Come

I have thus far used the term "Latinx" in the way it is typically understood—as a gender-inclusive form of identification for people of Latin American descent in the U.S.—but moving forward, I want to reserve it for a political formation in much the same way that the term "Chicano" came to signify a people with a particular politics. Importantly, Flores clues us into resolving the whiteness of latinidad in her own formulation of Latinx, which she argues "is useful as an operative construct because I visualize the term *Latinx* as Latin X-ed out."[10] Here, I read Flores as suggesting that the "x" in Latinx has the power to cross out the "Latin" that precedes it and, in so doing, serves as a visual marker of opposition to the very genealogy of whiteness that Flores details.

Revolution as discussed in *Latinx Revolutionary Horizons*, then, draws upon the revolutionary potential of Latinx as a political formation as well as the history of Latinx resistance. However, while theorists of revolution largely focus on how revolutions come to be, my project is less concerned with a theory of revolution or even its representation.[11] In fact, my focus here is on texts in which revolutionary consciousness irrupts in contemporary Latinx novels in which revolution is not the explicit raison d'être, but where revolutionary imaginaries find their way in, nevertheless. Latinx revolutionary horizons emerge, then, sideways. Such a sidewise surfacing allows us to see how revolution haunts Latinx novels even when—perhaps especially when—revolution seems beside the point. The structuring principle of revolutions in these texts is analepsis, as authors look to past revolutionary histories to imagine Latinx futurities. Even when we get explicit mentions of revolution as we do in Sandra Cisneros's *Caramelo* (2002), the novel is even more preoccupied with Emperor Maximilian than the Mexican Revolution (1910–20) itself. Similarly, in Cristina García's *Monkey Hunting* (2003), we learn of the protagonist Chen Pan's participation in the Ten Years' War only briefly as he delivers machetes to Commander Sian and only tells his wife, Lucrecia, short tidbits of his time during the war.

Although critics often contest definitions of revolution, James DeFronzo offers a serviceable definition in which revolutions are "social movement[s] in which participants strive to drastically alter or totally replace existing social, economic, or political institutions."[12] A key aspect of contention in discussions of theories of revolution is the role of violence, which DeFronzo mediates by noting that "although revolutionary social change (change in the structure of basic institutions) can be brought about through nonviolent means such as peaceful labor strikes or democratic elections, most successful revolutionary movements have been accompanied by some level of violence emanating from both movement participants and governments and groups opposing revolution" (10). As these definitions and elaborations show, the realities of revolution differ markedly from their literary legacies as the question of revolution in the texts that I discuss is less about the how and the why and more about other revolutionary imaginaries that never came to be—the unrealized revolutions that are resurrected to imagine a liberatory latinidad that is yet to come.

To that end, I turn to Jacques Derrida's theory of revolution as "a radical caesura in the ordinary course of History."[13] Derrida's conceptualization of the caesura resonates with Ricardo Ortiz's contention that the "x" in Latinx is "a suspension in time's unfolding."[14] Reading the caesura alongside the "x" as a suspension underscores the revolutionary potential of the "x" as it marks the ever-shifting horizon of latinidad. Questions about what should come after Latin—should it be "a/o," "@," "x"—underline the ongoing issue of who belongs in latinidad as each ending pierces the previous horizon of latinidad. For Derrida, revolution is the only true event, the one that punctures—and extends—the horizon. As Rodolphe Gasché explains, "Now since, within the horizon, an event can only take place on the condition that the horizon master it as something possible in advance (thereby precluding any surprise), Derrida proclaims the need to exceed, pierce, perforate, puncture, or even burst open the horizon."[15]

Derrida observes, "As the only event worthy of the name, [revolution] exceeds every possible horizon, every *horizon of the possible*—and therefore of potency and power."[16] To this formulation, Gasché adds, quoting from Derrida's *Rogues: Two Essays on Reason* (2005), that "for an event to happen not only is the end (*la fin*) of the horizon required, but also—implicated by the latter—the end of 'teleology, the calculable program, foresight, and providence.'"[17] Thus, for Derrida, revolution and horizon are deeply entangled, as only revolutions are capable of piercing the horizon and revealing new ones outside of teleological notions of progress. Although Derrida refers to actually existing revolutions, as do I, the x's metaphorical piercings also signal a revolution in thought where revolution is not only a form of resistance, but also a turn, a revolving and evolving idea of a people that becomes a politics. As Derrida remarks of a revolution to come, "if we want to save the Revolution, it is necessary to transform the very idea of revolution."[18]

Gasché's work on Derrida cues us to two conceptualizations of horizon: one as infinity and one as finitude. For Derrida, revolutions puncture the horizon, bringing another world and another horizon into being. Along similar lines, the novels I discuss reveal Latinx revolutionary horizons by puncturing the text and the existing boundaries around latinidad to make other worlds possible. A common pattern that emerges in these novels is how moments of revolution interrupt and shift the plot, revealing *revolutionary* horizons by remembering the "radical caesura[s] in the ordinary course of History" that comprise Latinx histories and enacting such ruptures on the level of the text.

Genre reveals the generative force of revolution through the friction between dominant and minor histories that preoccupy Latinx literature. Latinx revolutionary horizons emerge out of these fraught histories and reveal themselves in disruptions and departures from generic conventions, such as when a novel like *Caramelo*, which is a multigenerational historical fiction, suddenly incorporates a lengthy footnote about the French colonization of Mexico. Through such opaque references, Latinx revolutionary horizons reward the curious reader who wonders at the significance of the French colonization of Mexico and why it becomes a point that Cisneros returns to throughout the novel. By creating hemispheric connections, Latinx revolutionary horizons draw attention to the interdependence between the U.S. and Latin America as well as how the U.S. often binds Latin American countries together through shared histories of colonization and occupation. Latinx revolutionary horizons create temporal reverberations, as narrative events rarely unfold contemporaneously and meditations on these rebellions often result in temporal displacements—as, for example, when the Awful Grandmother of *Caramelo* takes over the second part of the novel to tell her story, which is also a story of the Mexican Revolution (1910–20). This is how the Awful Grandmother—and the Mexican Revolution—interrupt the temporality of the text, illuminating how such temporal displacements signal the earlier ruptures and limits that create the possibilities for more expansive Latinx revolutionary horizons in the future.

To apprehend such revolutionary futures, I read contemporary Latinx writers back into earlier revolutionary histories to show how they are part of a hemispheric tradition of revolution that builds on transnational connections to decenter the U.S. as the key site of revolution. As we will see in Chapters 3 and 5, even though the legacy of the Haitian Revolution is often contested, it still emerges as a site of revolutionary potential that is much more generative than the U.S. By comparing colonialisms, *Latinx Revolutionary Horizons* explores alternate revolutionary histories that foreground the centrality of Latinx revolutionary genealogies to U.S. literature. Although such resistance to revolution would seem to be antithetical to the U.S.'s advocacy of liberation and democracy, celebrating a revolutionary tradition while advancing an imperialist agenda marks the paradox of U.S. policies.

Similarly, the U.S.'s narratives of the American Revolution are ironically coupled with its disavowal of anti-colonial revolutions. As Emily García observes, conventional narratives "regard U.S. revolutionary rhetoric as originary and all that follows as secondary,"[19] which prevents any understanding of how "the U.S. national imaginary was dependent on Latin American independence for its own development in the early nineteenth century."[20] The contradictions and erasures that inform contemporary understandings of the American Revolution underscore the U.S.'s conflicted relationship with such forms of resistance beyond its borders and demonstrate how it exercises hemispheric hegemony. While scholars have begun to address Latinx literature in the nineteenth century, *Latinx Revolutionary Horizons* examines how nineteenth-century texts inform contemporary Latinx literature. By exploring how contemporary texts engage with revolutionary genealogies, I uncover how the question of revolution has been suppressed as the U.S. disavows revolutionary history in the hemispheric sense by co-opting the language and history of revolution, thus limiting the imaginaries and tactics of Latinxs by obscuring the long history of Latin American and Latinx resistance in the Americas. Ultimately, by turning to the revolutionary histories that inform Latinx America, I aim to demonstrate that, contrary to ongoing political discourse, Latinxs are not newcomers to the U.S.; in fact, as Latinx literature testifies, we have a long and storied history here.

Puncturing the Horizon

To conceive of the resonances between revolution and horizon, I also build upon the work of María Josefina Saldaña-Portillo, who, in observing the disturbing resonances between discourses of development and discourses of revolution in the U.S. and Latin America, argues that revolutionaries subscribed to a "meliorist theory of subjectivity"[21] in which revolutionary agency is "figured as the leaving behind of one's own particularity, as leaving behind the feminized ethnos of Indigenous, peasant, or urban black cultural identity" (7), a move that Saldaña-Portillo sees as "contribut[ing] to the 'failure' of decolonization and liberation struggles in Latin America and the United States in the late twentieth century" (7).

Against this meliorist theory of subjectivity, Saldaña-Portillo analyzes how "insurgent subalterns challenge a model of revolutionary subjectivity and a theory of agency not from a position of Indigenous purity but from an Indigenous and peasant subject position simultaneously produced by modernity and in reaction to its developmentalism" (12). In this way, "the peasants of Guatemala and Cuba constituted the revolutionary horizon of [Mario] Payeras's and [Che] Guevara's guerrilla errand" (269). For Saldaña-Portillo, "the formation of revolutionary consciousness [that] was predicated on the transcendence of a premodern *ethnos*" (7) is what limits revolutionary possibilities, while "insurgent subalterns" expand those limits by offering revolutionary horizons not dependent on notions of purity. Rather than "leaving behind the feminized ethnos of Indigenous, peasant, or urban black cultural identity," Saldaña-Portillo offers a basis for conceiving of Latinx revolutionary horizons as well as how such horizons rely on a celebration of particularity as a generative force for imagining not only revolution, but also the unrealized potential of latinidad, which I assert has been limited by its confinement to the U.S. context.[22] Reading expansively across continents and through the lens of colonization—which paradoxically reveals the unfulfilled horizons for solidarity—brings more liberatory Latinx imaginaries to the fore.

In thinking about what "Latinx" could mean and the political imaginaries that such a formation could make possible, I consider the not-yet-here of latinidad—the places where, I argue, we hope to arrive—as a speculative fiction. As Catherine S. Ramírez reminds us, "Chicanafuturism articulates colonial and postcolonial histories"[23] and centers Chicanxs in the future, a future from which we are often excluded and erased.[24] As her reliance on Afrofuturism to theorize Chicanafuturism shows and the title of her article "Afrofuturism/Chicanafuturism: Fictive Kin" testifies, Chicanafuturism and Afrofuturism are fictive kin; moreover, I would add, theorizing futurity necessitates speculations about kinship and belonging. For me, the "x" in Latinx points to this kind of futurity and symbolizes the horizon as the deferred site of arrival and knowledge. The capaciousness of latinidad is marked and held by the "x"—if "x" indicates an unknown variable, then the "x" also invites us to embrace unknown possibilities and to work toward a more just future. To theorize Latinx revolutionary horizons, then, I draw on José Esteban Muñoz's concept of the horizon as "imbued with potentiality,"[25] which signals the then and there of a liberatory future beyond the here and now which he calls a "quagmire" and "a prison house" (1). As Simón Ventura Trujillo remarks in his own theorization of the horizon, "While horizons offer orientation and perspective, they are not in themselves definitive places of arrival or knowledge."[26]

Although scholarship on horizons mostly stems from phenomenology, particularly the work of Edmund Husserl, I focus on the affective and temporal registers of the horizon. For me, a return to the past is necessary to excavate viable futures out of the ruins. As Helmut Kuhn reminds us, "The very terms by which we explained the significance of the horizon, such as anticipation, actualization of the potential, explication, involve an element of time."[27] This element of time, I argue, also signals how Latinx authors and their kin relate to past and future horizons. As Andrea Davis observes in *Horizon, Sea, Sound: Caribbean and African Women's Cultural Critiques of Nation* (2022), the horizon speaks to how "the trope of the horizon both encapsulates and frustrates Caribbean and African women's demand for autonomous life not as a delayed future possibility but as a necessity to their *being* in the present."[28] Davis's comments resonate with Didier Maleuvre's contention that horizons are about "dissatisfaction"[29] as "the horizon teases the thirst for resolution but never satisfies it" (xiv). Such dissatisfaction, along with the past "failure of the horizon to deliver the promise of a better future,"[30] encourages us to examine the archive of Latinx literature to explore how authors reckon with their revolutionary histories. In so doing, we can see how contemporary Latinx authors look to the past to resolve previous failures of imagination, of inclusion, and of independence. My project also argues that Latinx literature becomes an archive of revolutionary thought in which Latinx revolutionary horizons offer a vision of what Reinhart Koselleck calls "former futures" (or, alternately, futures past or superseded futures)—those futures that were imagined in the past but never came to be. Latinx revolutionary horizons point to alternate temporalities as the horizon at times seems to recede; at other points it seems to form a double helix in which competing revolutionary horizons twist around each other. Returning to futures past and untangling such intertwined temporalities, as Latinx revolutionary horizons show, can reinvigorate our revolutionary imaginations.

While the discussion of how the horizon elicits anticipation and dissatisfaction replicates the ongoing discussion of horizon as an opening and a limit, I argue that it is also useful for considering latinidad as a process of frustrated desires and limited imaginations, but also radical potential. As Derrida explains,

> Horizon is the always-already-there of a future which keeps the indetermination of its infinite openness even though this future was *announced* to consciousness. As the structural determination of every material indeterminacy, a horizon is always virtually present in every experience; for it is at once the unity and the incompletion for that experience—the anticipated unity in every incompletion.[31]

If we view this horizon from latinidad, then we can see how the future potential of latinidad is already present within its existing forms. An open-ended loop, this project reaches for "the anticipated unity" of latinidad's current incompletion.

The notion of latinidad as an incomplete project resonates with how its roots lie in the Wars of Independence, which, I argue, actually forestalled the formation of a liberatory latinidad. Turning toward revolution, then, allows Latinx authors to revisit key revolutions that ultimately sought to resolve the fractures instituted by the Latin American independence movements. However, whatever successes may have been achieved during twentieth-century revolutions such as the Mexican Revolution and the Cuban Revolution are ultimately still tied to the fractures created in the nineteenth century. Even though each chapter of *Latinx Revolutionary Horizons* revolves around a central revolution, the concerns that crop up across texts are often preoccupied not only—or not always—with such revolutions, but also with earlier moments of revolt or disturbance that point to a history that could have unfolded otherwise.

Failed Solidarities

In cueing us to the ways that latinidad itself is a speculative, collective project, Latinx revolutionary horizons also encourage us to foreground shared histories of colonization as well as collective struggles rather than simply a shared culture. Latinx revolutionary horizons point to how the political can never be extricated from a full accounting of latinidad; to imagine an apolitical or hegemonic latinidad is itself a political project that has historically suppressed Black-, Indigenous-, and Asian-inflected latinidades. Reaching for a latinidad with an explicit politics around shared histories of struggle—which I argue is not yet here—is exactly the kind of latinidad that Latinx scholars have been theorizing, as exemplified by Ortiz's theorization of it "as desire, as wish, and as *project*."[32]

Latinx revolutionary horizons reanimate history to show how Latinx literature remembers our histories even as the U.S. figures Latinxs as new to the U.S. and obscures its own history of interventions in Latin American countries. In this way, Latinx revolutionary horizons displace U.S. hegemony and imagine possibilities for revolution that do not depend on the nationalist formations foundational to Latinx Studies. Instead, Latinx revolutionary horizons point to a latinidad that embraces the transnational potential made possible by Latinx as an anti-national category of difference. I argue that Latinx revolutionary horizons illuminate how latinidad can signal a politics grounded in shared struggles and histories rather than merely as a mode of identification; a doing rather than a being.[33]

Latinx revolutionary horizons also help us apprehend such a project, specifically through what author Simón Ventura Trujillo calls "disappeared relations." Although Trujillo uses this formulation to describe the relationship between Mexicans and Indigenous people specifically, I suggest that we can extend the notion of disappeared relations as structuring current conceptualizations of latinidad. In many ways, such relations are intentionally disavowed and disappeared as Flores's discussion of anti-blackness illustrates. The task of contemporary scholars is to excavate that history. Latinx revolutionary horizons emerge from such excavations as forgotten rebellions and alliances surface, however opaquely, in contemporary Latinx novels. Resurrecting such pasts opens up space for Latinx authors to create their own imagined histories—literary and otherwise—to conceive of the futures of latinidad that, as Saldaña-Portillo argues, refuse decolonization's "future-perfect temporality [that] marks a firm commitment to the developmentalist time of linear progress in which history will have been perfected"[34] and instead offers *futures*-perfect that point to many possibilities.

Uncovering disappeared relations also underscores how these failed revolutions ultimately stem from failures of solidarity, which have a long history in both Latin America and the United States. These have been failures to imagine a revolution that would also uplift Black, Indigenous, and Asian Latinxs rather than simply consolidating power among elites. While *The Afro-Latin@ Reader*[35] and the "Critical Latinx Indigeneities" special issue of *Latino Studies*[36] make inroads in imagining a more capacious latinidad in the present, we must still reckon with the legacies of the nineteenth century. Many of these nineteenth-century texts actually demonstrate hegemonic, conservative forms of both revolution and latinidad, which demonstrate how contemporary novels are tasked with grappling with the contentious, uncomfortable aspects of the past that current regimes—and even current scholarship—would prefer to gloss over.

As Saldaña-Portillo notes in her examination of nineteenth-century policies toward Indigenous people in Mexico, "The Indian is the horizon of inclusion," and this inclusion into, for example, a Mexican national identity was a violent process, as Indigenous people "existed in landscape, as we shall see, not to be obliterated, but to be convinced, cajoled, coerced, and included, by force if necessary."[37] This violent inclusion did not extend to Afro Latinxs and Latin Americans of African descent. As Benedict Anderson observes, it was *"creole* communities that developed so early conceptions of their nation-ness,"[38] conceptions that also relied on foundational exclusions. Indeed, twenty years after beginning his fight for independence in 1808, Bolívar would comment that "a Negro revolt was 'a thousand times worse than a Spanish invasion.'"[39] Thus, even though Bolívar freed his own enslaved people and advocated for abolition, "he shared the fear of a Haitian-style slave uprising that consumed other members of his class."[40]

Given this history, I would argue that the potential for hegemonic impulses in contemporary latinidades stem from this foundational moment in the history of the Americas, which also extends into Bolívar's views on Indigenous people, who were mostly "out of sight and out of mind" (xlv–xlvi). Moreover, "during his final dictatorship Bolívar reverted to the unequal, formally paternalistic, approach of colonial legislation, placing the Indians under the care of special 'protectors' yet at the same time restoring the recently suppressed Indian tribute" (xlvi). As John Lynch remarks, after effectively winning Venezuelan independence in 1821, "the new Venezuela reproduced the essential features of the old";[41] all that changed were the people in power. In other words, even though Latin Americans began to consolidate their national identities, they did so with the ruling class in mind. In doing so, they disenfranchised Latin Americans of African and Indigenous descent and also promoted racial mixture as a whitening project, as Doris Sommer reminds us.[42]

At the same time, recent work on nineteenth-century Hispaniola and Cuba by Lorgia García Pena and Carmen E. Lamas, respectively, uncovers earlier forms of latinidad based on blackness. For example, in *Translating Blackness: Latinx Colonialities in Global Perspective* (2022), García Peña "remind(s) us that Latinidad was grounded, imagined, and founded through blackness—specifically, the possibility of anti-colonial freedom and Black citizenship in Hispaniola, in contradistinction to US hegemony and expansionism."[43] García Peña cues us to an insurgent latinidad centered on blackness. Lamas, meanwhile, analyzes the writings of Martín Morúa Delgado to show "that the black experience in the Americas could serve as a cultural and political model for the US itself—one that could redeem the US from its own racist origins."[44] Although Morúa is a markedly different figure of Black resistance than those García Peña discusses, my intention here is to point to two forms of latinidad that center blackness and emerge in the nineteenth century.[45]

Within the field of Latin American Studies, Enrique Dussel and Edmundo O'Gorman map how the construction of Latin America as Latin was a relatively new development, one that can be traced to the nineteenth century.[46] As O'Gorman reminds us, in *The Invention of America* (1958), Columbus did not discover the Americas because he could not identify it; Columbus thought that the Americas were Asia for the remainder of his life.[47] Further, because America as a concept did not exist until Europeans created it based on what they already knew, in O'Gorman's view, no one actually discovered the Americas. Dussel critiques O'Gorman's argument by observing that America was not invented in the image of Europe, but that the invention of America was that it was conceptualized as Asian. By not reflecting on how indigeneity became subsumed under the category of Asian, Dussel contends that O'Gorman perpetuates the Eurocentric act of domination that he attempts to decenter. Both scholars articulate another foundationational erasure, that of Asian Latinxs. To my knowledge there has yet to be a reader or special issue on Asian Latinxs, but the work of Evelyn Hu-DeHart and Lisa Lowe points to the colonial histories that made such formations possible. That said, as texts like *Alternative Orientalisms in Latin America and Beyond* (2007), edited by

Ignacio López-Calvo, demonstrate, there is work being done on Asians in Latin America;[48] however, Asian Latinxs remain at the margins of conceptions of latinidad, demonstrating how latinidad, as it's currently constituted, remains a fairly narrow imaginary.[49]

In short, what currently constitutes latinidad is not the latinidad I trace in my project. I have pointed out the foundational exclusions of latinidad as it is currently constructed; however, I do not advocate an inclusive model of latinidad, nor do I think that is where Latinx revolutionary horizons orient us. Instead, Latinx revolutionary horizons reveal multiple, competing latinidades that forecast a future latinidad capable of not only acknowledging Latinx complicity in U.S. imperialism, but also realizing its radical potential as a formation that is not constricted by national formations. For instance, for me, it is significant that Latinx Studies and earlier formations such as Chicano Studies and Puerto Rican Studies all manage to keep "American" out of their titles, thus resisting U.S. claims to the term.

Chicano Studies is especially relevant for my work, as, rather than naming a geographic formation, it describes a political position. Despite the fact that there are many critiques to be made about Chicano Studies, it can be an inspiration for a politically positioned Latinx Studies and conception of latinidad. To make this claim for the future of latinidad, I draw on Ortiz's formulation of the "x" in Latinx where "the *x* in this case isn't an alternative ending to *Latina/o* that refuses a conclusion in and as binary gender, but instead acts as refusal to allow *Latin_* an ending at all, in either or any gender."[50] While Ortiz centers the importance of gender in formulations of Latinx, here I signal the importance of race by adding that in refusing to allow Latin_ an ending, we also leave open the possibilities for a heterogeneous sense of Latinx and the work it can do as not only a term of identification, but also as a term that signals a particular politics around race as well as gender.

By considering a range of genres, I shed light on how Latinx literature is deeply preoccupied with how history is told and how the unique historical circumstances of the Americas lent themselves to the formation of new genres as novel ways of narrating history.[51] What emerges in the texts I investigate are three patterns that, combined, illustrate Latinx revolutionary horizons: Latinx revolutionary consciousness, pedagogy, and imaginaries. Latinx revolutionary consciousness explores how Latinxs come to understand themselves as racialized subjects, which in turn radicalizes them into developing revolutionary consciousness. Latinx revolutionary pedagogies shed light on how authors imagine people shifting from revolutionary consciousness to political action. Finally, Latinx revolutionary imaginaries contemplate the potential futures offered by Latinx revolutions—both those that have already occurred and those that will happen in the future. My project untangles how genres of the Americas foreground colonial violence as the formative experience that shapes them; the revolutionary ruptures that emerge in these texts become de-formations that point to futures past as well as unrealized forms of futurity. I argue that Latinx literature becomes a repository for revolutionary thought, both for the possibilities that not only remain unfulfilled in the past, but also continue animating Latinx struggles in the present.[52]

Speculative Latinidad

Imagining a latinidad that is not yet here requires a turn to the speculative, the site of future possibilities. Building on Kirsten Silva Gruesz's exploration of Latinx as a "fiction,"[53] I assert that a speculative turn to latinidad is also a hailing into being as it is the revolutionary horizon that keeps trying to be born as latinidad increasingly signals a class for itself rather than simply a class in itself.[54] The "x" in Latinx is uniquely capable of signaling not only forms of Latinx futurity but also apprehending the shifting latinidades that inform the histories that lead to such futures. I turn to the speculative possibilities of the "x" as it signals how latinidad is not yet here—the "x" signifies this future potential. The "x" in Latinx symbolizes the horizon as the deferred site of arrival and knowledge.

In cueing us to the ways that latinidad itself is a speculative, collective project, Latinx revolutionary horizons also speak to the anti-identitarian turn in Latinx Studies, in which Latinx Studies scholars parse out the unique ability of latinidad for theorizing collectivity exactly because it reaches across ethnic and national boundaries. Building on the work of scholars who have discussed Latina/o/x as a pan-ethnic term, such as Marta Caminero-Santangelo, Raphael Dalleo, Elena Machado Sáez, Ylce Irizarry, and David Vázquez, I argue that reaching for a latinidad with an explicit politics around shared histories of struggle—the latinidad I argue is not yet here—is exactly the kind of latinidad that Latinx scholars have been theorizing.[55]

In many ways, my book is a response to the question Caminero-Santangelo asks at the end of *On Latinidad: U.S. Latino Literature and the Construction of Ethnicity* (2007): "What if we saw *latinidad* as commitment—not just to an exploration of conditions that encourage pan-ethnic collectivity but also to an exploration of those conditions (including differences) which potentially inhibit it?"[56] Viewing latinidad as commitment—and a particular political commitment at that—encourages us to imagine what those kinds of political commitments might look like. As my earlier reference to Ortiz's theorization of latinidad "as desire, as wish, and as *project*" emphasizes,[57] Ortiz's formulation prompts us to consider how the field's future orientation depends on how we grapple with Latinx literary studies' relationship to this repository of revolutionary thought. In other words, Ortiz invites us to consider Latinx Studies as a field that does not necessarily describe Latinxs as they currently are, but how Latinx Studies continues to wrestle with who—and how—we could be. However, to do the important work of who we could be, we must figure out who we are, which is where Latinx revolutionary horizons come in to underscore such shared histories, histories that refuse to be forgotten or contained by nationalist formations that further segregate along racial lines.[58]

While the horizon articulates an expansive arena in which latinidad can manifest, it also speaks to the limits that have bounded notions of latinidad not only along racial lines, but also those of citizenship status and migration. Robert McKee Irwin and Ortiz posit a capacious latinidad that exceeds such limitations in their conceptualizations of the "almost Latino" and the "always-already" Latinx. In Irwin's formulation, the "almost Latino" describes "one whose process of becoming Latino is thwarted" by deportation, for example, leading to "truncated, disrupted, obstructed Latinidades."[59] In *Latinx Literature Now: Between Evanescence and Event* (2019), Ortiz describes how "always-already" Latinxs are those who are already enmeshed with the U.S. because of mixed-status families and/or the need to flee their home countries because of U.S. exports like the MS-13 and 18th Street gangs. The "almost Latino" projects a future orientation, albeit one whose future is disrupted. Yet, the hope that undergirds the almost Latino's journey to the U.S. surely speaks to the dream of a better future. The always-already Latinx formation, on the other hand, looks backward to analyze the historical conditions at the place of origin and how U.S. economic and political interventions have led to an entanglement with U.S.-based latinidad, even if one is not within the U.S. By expanding the definition of who is Latinx and thus who is included, Ortiz's "always-already" Latinx formation outlines the contours of an already existing latinidad that, in its expansive reach, also indicates the work that needs to be done for the future project of latinidad. To imagine this future project, we must account for the potential latinidades that are erased by an emphasis on arrival and how definitions are limited by only naming those who live in the U.S. Taken together, both Irwin's and Ortiz's formations push the boundaries of latinidad by showing how it exceeds the borders of the U.S. and nations as a whole.

Central to *Latinx Revolutionary Horizons* is how notions of latinidad unfold over time and how in this unfolding new possibilities emerge for realizing its speculative potential. As Irwin's and Ortiz's theorizations suggest, latinidad is just as much about time—*when* one is—as it is about space, or *where* one is. The issue of the *when* of latinidad permeates both the field and public discourse around Latinxs as Latinxs are hyper-identified with the future, for better or worse. As numerous scholars have pointed out, but that is perhaps crystallized best in Elda María Román's notion of demographobia, or the fear of demographic change, Latinx futurity is often tied to the mid-twenty-first-century projection that Latinxs will become a majority population (an anxiety rendered visible by Trump's rhetoric around a so-called invasion at the U.S.-Mexico border).[60] These fears are predicated on the idea that Latinxs will achieve a kind of "Reconquista" or re-colonization of the U.S.

That said, I'm more interested in the *promise* of a Latinx future that has yet to arrive. As Gruesz points out in "The Once and Future Latino: Notes Toward a Literary History *todavía para llegar*," there are two conflicting forms of Latinx futurity that have yet to manifest. In the first instance, she notes how Latinx scholars point out that "the truest forms of latinidad have yet to appear. The future will reveal new, utopian forms of the single-group meaning of the term, as Latinos reverse the initial intentions of the 'government fiat' and expend it as political capital."[61] Against this utopian vision, Gruesz points to "a progressivist vision of the development of Latino identity in which the separate histories of long ago are now in the process of melding into one (better, finer) *latinidad*" (123). Although the two visions are not necessarily antithetical to one another, the first example indicates an alignment of political interests and goals, while the second applies the melting pot metaphor to latinidad, suggesting the loss of specific identities within it. In examining how latinidad unfolds over time, I suggest that we can apprehend how to maintain particular political alignments without assimilating into the latinidad melting pot Gruesz describes.

In fact, I argue that Latinx revolutionary horizons invite us to project a future for latinidad. We can see this in the turn to the future perfect that Gruesz's comments render visible as well as how Latinx authors create their own imagined histories—literary and otherwise—to theorize the futures of latinidad.[62] My project builds on Ortiz's contention, mentioned earlier, that the "x" in Latinx is "a suspension in time's unfolding, a pause to consider and to accommodate what might take place next in the place of and as an alternative to gender, especially heteropatriarchal, binary cis-gender";[63] and, finally, Raúl Coronado's formulation of nineteenth-century revolutionary imaginaries as "a world not to come" or a past future that remains unrealized in the present.[64] Embracing the potential of the future perfect and resurrecting the specters of former futures are how Latinx revolutionary horizons grapple with the contentious and contested histories of our home countries while also carving out a space for Latinxs in the U.S. that does not rely on proximity to whiteness.[65]

Exploring how contemporary Latinx authors return to the nineteenth century in their work allows us to see how they incorporate the diversity of their histories rather than the absorption of their racial differences into national identities, thus offering a model for the kind of latinidad that Latinx revolutionary horizons point us to. Moreover, as Esmeralda Santiago's 2012 novel *Conquistadora* demonstrates, turning to the nineteenth century requires the speculative to excavate erased histories, particularly the erased history of blackness in Puerto Rico.[66] As Ileana M. Rodríguez-Silva argues, issues of race, particularly blackness, are sublimated under "idioms of labor" in the post-emancipatory period of 1873 as Puerto Rican "government institutions, academic studies, and cultural organizations reproduced the idea that Puerto Rico is a unified nation" where "races mixed harmoniously" and "racial conflict has never existed on the island."[67] Therefore, Puerto Rico is a useful example of how the problems that some scholars ascribe to latinidad are also problems that structure nationalist formations; we cannot think one without the other.[68]

Conquistadora exemplifies the engagement with the past that Latinx revolutionary horizons foster as, in this novel, Santiago speculatively imagines a past not only for herself, but for all Puerto Ricans. *Conquistadora* tells the story of Ana Larragoity Cubillas, a Spanish woman who decides to go to Puerto Rico and follow in the footsteps of her conquistador ancestors. The novel begins in 1826 and ends in 1865, which allows Santiago to discuss the number of laws that were enacted to ensure the subjugation of enslaved peoples. For example, *Conquistadora* covers the slave codes of 1842, which outlined the many ways enslaved people were expected to be obedient. The novel also discusses the laws that were put in place to manage people of color, not just enslaved people, on the island more broadly. The Bando Negro of 1848 outlined the punishment people of color would receive for crimes and "minor transgressions (like not ceding the way to a *blanco* on a narrow path)."[69] Even as Santiago adopts the perspective of the hegemonic conquistador, she also layers this history with the suppression of people of color that made the success of the conquistadors possible.

To that end, *Conquistadora* tells the story of some of the enslaved people on Ana's plantation, underscoring how we cannot learn one history without the other. One such figure is Flora, who we learn was captured in the Congo region (she's Mbuti) by Portuguese enslavers; it's implied that she's sold in the Dominican Republic, since later Flora attempts to escape with other enslaved people "over the mountains toward the setting sun, to a place called Haiti, where there were no masters" (98). Here Haiti signals a revolutionary imaginary that the Wars of Independence were incapable of imagining as

Creole elites feared a revolution that centered the emancipation of enslaved people. Flora is once again captured, but this time she is sold in Puerto Rico, where she's eventually bought by Ana's overseer, Severo. The brief background Santiago offers on Flora proves instructive, as Flora is the aperture through which we learn that Spaniards fleeing "the revolutions in Hispaniola and South America" (100) land in Puerto Rico, where they stifle the independence movement "because independence and abolition were spoken in the same whispering breath" (100).

The issue of enslaved people's role in revolution was an ongoing point of contention, as Creoles were reluctant to incorporate them because of their fear of another Haiti, but they also could not win the Wars of Independence without them, as evidenced by the fall of the First Republic in Venezuela (1811–12). During this initial foray into independence, many enslaved people fought on the Spanish side because Creoles wanted to maintain slavery (as codified in the Venezuelan constitution of 1811)[70] and rejected earlier attempts by the Spanish crown to improve enslaved peoples' conditions (193). In contrast to Venezuela's paradigmatic example, Flora reveals that in Puerto Rico, independence and slavery are tied to the same revolutionary imaginary.[71] Flora's story disrupts Ana's narrative of conquistador nostalgia and foregrounds how Puerto Rican independence cannot be achieved without the emancipation of enslaved peoples. In this way, Flora offers a vision of a Latinx revolutionary horizon that acknowledges how blackness signifies revolution and independence. However, this is a revolutionary horizon that has yet to be fully realized in the present, given the continued need to assert the blackness of latinidad in the face of its presumed whiteness.

This sort of racial reckoning informs the context of the writing of the novel as Santiago acknowledges the need to invent a past that colonization and occupation have erased. In so doing, she also remarks upon the need for new imaginaries in a *PBS News Hour* interview. When the interviewer asks her about the genesis of the book, Santiago replies, "I come from poor, landless peasants who left no records. And so I began to read the story of Puerto Rico, and the more I read the story the more I realized I would never find my own ancestors, but I could make my imaginary ancestors. And so the book emerges as a result of my trying to create them, to create the people that might have been."[72] *Conquistadora* is explicitly an attempt by Santiago to create a history for her people, but also to acknowledge the violence of her history. As she notes later in the interview,

> I come from African decedents at some point. My dad is very dark, my mom is very fair. So I know that somewhere along the lines, on

my father's side at least, there would have been Africans. And so I wanted to know who they were and how they lived and what happened to them. It was difficult. I have to admit that when I was reading the history and then when writing about it, I went through the entire gamut of emotions, from shame, embarrassment, to rage, anger, to also just admiration that they survived under the circumstances, that they actually lived.[73]

Yet, at the same time that Santiago wants to write about her Black heritage in Puerto Rico, her comments illustrate her reluctance to identify as Black—she states that on her father's side "there would have been Africans," but refuses to identify him as Afro Puerto Rican or to identify herself as such. Accordingly, it is no surprise that Santiago chooses a white protagonist of the novel in Ana. That said, Santiago is unrelenting in her portrayal of the violence it takes to run a plantation, which demonstrates how she takes her enslaver ancestors to task. In short, while writing the history of slavery in Puerto Rico—and her family's role as both enslaver and enslaved—clearly causes Santiago discomfort, she still reaches for the possible futures that Latinx revolutionary horizons make possible by highlighting overlapping and entangled histories.

In *Conquistadora*, that entanglement is the result of a choice, of Ana's decision to become an enslaver. And this is where Santiago's interrogation of her past via speculative history is important for understanding Latinx revolutionary horizons—in examining the past, Latinx revolutionary horizons force us to acknowledge our role in it, how the present is made up of decisions we and our ancestors made along the way. In *Conquistadora*, Santiago emphasizes how in becoming the kind of person who can enslave other people, Ana takes on a dehumanized view of people in general, including her own son. After the death of her husband, Ramón, Eugenio, Ana's father-in-law, wants to take Miguel, Ana's son, back with him to San Juan. Ana agrees, but only after suggesting using Miguel as collateral so she can mortgage the plantation from Eugenio. Eugenio initially declines, to which Ana says that the mortgage would be "'secured by Miguel.'"[74] After then suggesting a "straight barter"—Miguel for Los Gemelos—Ana and Eugenio agree that Los Gemelos will stay in Eugenio's name with Miguel as heir, but that if he should decide to sell, Ana will be able to buy the plantation.

This discussion leads Eugenio to reflect, of his twin sons, "What did it take for his sons, living and working alongside them, to accept their roles as slave owners?" (218), thus illuminating the toll it takes to dehumanize people, a toll that Ana does not express because "she didn't see them as human beings [. . .] They were tools" (218). Eugenio's questions—what did it take for his sons to accept their roles as slave owners—is the question that drives the novel as Santiago interrogates the motivations of her enslaver ancestors. Yet the possibility that *Conquistadora* holds for us is that if one can choose to become an enslaver, one can also choose otherwise. What Latinx revolutionary horizons tell us is that as Latinxs, we have always had ancestors who chose to be enslavers and ancestors who chose to fight for independence and freedom. Unlike in the United States, in Latin America and the Caribbean, creoles like Bolívar contended with what it would mean to fight for independence even as they still enslaved large swaths of the population. Although the results were mixed and the legacies are still fraught, Latinx revolutionary horizons encourage us to turn away from the hegemonic white latinidad that includes the Anas of the world and reach for the horizon that Santiago can't quite reach, one in which she identifies with her Black heritage and also acknowledges the privilege that her skin color affords.

Revolutions in Form

Building on readings of texts like *Conquistadora*, *Latinx Revolutionary Horizons* makes four paradigm-shifting contributions to traditional discussions of the role of resistance in Latinx literature and discussions of genre more broadly. First, in tracing a longer history of resistance, it analyzes how the race, class, and colonial relations that were unique to the Americas gave shape to genres that are both new and original, revolutionary in content and form. In demonstrating how revolution and genre are mutually constitutive and shape Latinxs' orientation to the U.S., I also show how revolutions are both a concept and a form; revolutions are concepts that take specific forms. *Latinx Revolutionary Horizons* also shows how race, colonization, and imperialism in the Americas are the crucible out of which new genres emerged. For example, of the genres I survey, only one—the conversion narrative—had a history before the conquest of the Americas. The first dictator novel, Sarmiento's *Facundo: Civilization and Barbarism* (1845),[75] emerged out of the political instability that followed the Wars of Independence and laid the groundwork for the dictator novels that characterized the Latin American Boom of the 1960s and 1970s and, more recently as Jennifer Harford Vargas has shown, the Latinx dictator novel. As Yogita Goyal demonstrates, slave narratives are "a new world literary genre" of which neo-slave narratives are a part.[76] Miguel Barnet, meanwhile, established testimonio as yet another genre of the Americas in his *Biography of a Runaway Slave* (1966);[77] Rigoberta Menchú secured this legacy in *I, Rigoberta Menchú* (1983).[78] In short, in response to John Beverley's question, "Do social struggles give rise to new forms of literature . . . ?,"[79] *Latinx Revolutionary Horizons* responds with a resounding "yes."

Second, I argue against genre studies' tendency toward deracination and reorient literary analyses of revolution toward a consideration of aesthetic form. While it might seem odd to focus on the bourgeois form of the novel, I build on Edward Said's argument that, within the Western (especially British) context, "imperialism and the novel fortified each other."[80] Where Latinx literature differs is in its incorporation of nonfictional forms such as the captivity narrative and testimonio to imagine what an insurgent literature could look like. Moreover, as Goyal, in *Runaway Genres*, explains, "Formalist analysis often presumes a kind of universalism, leading to the suspicion that focusing on the taxonomy or circulation of genres may displace historicist modes of inquiry more clearly tied to political and ethical agendas."[81] Yet, as Goyal continues, "What such polemical understandings often conceal is that race has always been entangled with form. Not only are all aesthetic categories deeply racialized, identity itself has a form" (31). One of the most compelling implications of Goyal's work is that we understand the world *through* genre.

As Jerng argues, "We *participate in genres* in order to form and organize our sense of the world."[82] Such a view of genre, with all its taxonomizing implications, also informs our understanding of race, which Jerng describes as an entangled relation where we can apprehend "race at the level of its genre-like organizing force and genre formations in their dependence on the capacities of race" (9). Moreover, as Colleen Lye has persuasively argued, "a focus on form may provide an initial bridge between the notion of race as a representation and the notion of race as constitutive of literary and other social formations"[83] A turn to genre, I suggest means thinking about "race as construed as form rather than as formation" (99), which, for Lye, offers the ability to think past identity and argue for how centering form encourages "wider intellectual reaches and more radical political prospects" (99).[84] Within a specifically Latinx context, I argue that when Latinx writers turn to genre to give their histories—and themselves—a particular form, they're also calling upon specific histories of colonization and occupation as well as distinct literary traditions. Latinx revolutionary horizons and considerations of aesthetics are therefore two sides of the same coin, as the latter gives form to the revolutionary possibilities of latinidad uncovered by Latinx revolutionary horizons.

In this way, my work is in conversation with Ralph E. Rodriguez's *Latinx Literature Unbound*.[85] Rodriguez's book marks a turning point in Latinx literary scholarship toward a consideration of form and aesthetics, which we also see in works like Harford Vargas's *Forms of Dictatorship*.[86] Rodriguez usefully turns to genre because, for him, it operates at "a scale that might allow us to understand better the complexities and nuances of what we have heretofore considered Latinx literature."[87] I would hazard to say that the anxiety around what constitutes a Latinx body, on both an individual level and as a collective, elicits a turn to issues of aesthetics and form. In other words, what can the form of literature tell us about the form of latinidad?

To that end, where I depart from Rodriguez is in his insistence on the primacy of genre over identity. Rather, I argue that form, politics, and identity mutually inform each other. Concerned with taxonomies and boundaries, Rodriguez views identity as a limitation. Reducing Latinx to "a strategic category—a fiction employed to effect political outcomes" (3), Rodriguez argues that "there are more satisfying taxonomies and heuristics for grouping and analyzing literature than what scholars now recognize as the biological fiction but social reality of race" (3). Viewing racial and ethnic categories as political and biological fictions, Rodriguez introduces a paradox—if race and ethnicity are political and biological fictions, then wouldn't they be useful apertures for apprehending... well, fiction? And isn't our literary training what allows us to recognize fictions as fictions, particularly when they occur outside the realm of literature? Such are the considerations that preoccupy *Latinx Revolutionary Horizons*.

Rather than focus on Latinx literature within taxonomic terms, I see it as an invocation and an invitation. Like Vázquez, I'm interested in how genres help us see the forms of relation that arise "*between* the insufficiencies of traditional identity categories."[88] Moreover, rather than policing the boundaries through taxonomies and heuristics, I'm interested in the messiness of Latinx literature. I see the entanglement of genres with each other—such as testimonio and slave narrative—as signaling the broader instabilities around Latinx identities. Thus, for me it is significant that in a novel like *Monkey Hunting* (2003), Cristina García invokes Esteban Montejo's testimonio to describe the experiences of figures who are often absent from the archive, like Chinese indentured servants in Cuba.[89] She also invites us to continue thinking about Asian Latinxs by including them in her later work, such as *The Lady Matador's Hotel* (2010).[90]

Third, *Latinx Revolutionary Horizons* reads against nationalist constructions of literary canons as it obscures the historical, racial, and ethnic connections across national boundaries produced by a colonialism that wasn't national to begin with. To make this argument, I join together recent work on the Latinx nineteenth century and Latinx literary recovery projects with contemporary Latinx literature. In so doing, I build on scholars whose work emphasizes the hemispheric nature of Latinx literature, which allows me to highlight previously unrecognized connections.[91] While hemispheric dynamics are widely acknowledged in Latinx literature from the nineteenth century, they have yet to fully take hold in accounts of contemporary Latinx literature, which still largely rely on nationalist models of literary formation.

As Caminero-Santangelo points out, "Interactions between characters from the author's own ethnic group and other 'Latino' groups have been represented infrequently or not at all. (Literary critics have generally followed suit by dealing with the separate ethnicities separately, even in critical texts that wrap them together under the broader term 'Hispanic' or 'Latino' in the title)."[92] Although the issue Caminero-Santangelo outlines continues to plague Latinx literature, reading hemispherically does allow one frame for investigating the transnational possibilities revolutions open up. This is in contrast to how market aesthetics silo Latinx authors.[93] Even if I use José Rizal to talk about the Filipino People Power Revolution and José Martí to talk about the Cuban revolution, reading them alongside each other illustrates how both late nineteenth-century men were revolutionary thinkers who were tackling similar problems—namely, the issue of independence—at the same time.[94]

Finally, my project insists on reading transhistorically as a reading methodology that puts ethnic and area studies in conversation with one another and asks us to read across periods. By focusing on the conventional ways that our fields are organized—by nation (or at least geographically) and by time period, our current reading practices miss the richness that transhistorical reading offers. One way to read transhistorically, I suggest, is to identify formal similarities as a way of uncovering previously unrecognized connections that depict literature not as a monolithic, mononational project, but as a messy, tangled network of influences and exchanges. Paradoxically, this messiness offers a more coherent view of how literature shapes our historical and political understanding of Latinxs. My project therefore contributes to both Latinx and Hemispheric Studies in addition to ethnic and area studies. By focusing on colonization over continent, I emphasize the colonial histories that inform our present and trace transnational connections that defy literary studies models and render visible such tangled networks. In thinking transhistorically, I reveal similar preoccupations about revolution and liberation that manifest on the level of genre. Further, by underscoring the porous revolutionary histories that unfold hemispherically, I demonstrate how Latinx literature emphasizes a shared heritage that unearths new sites of revolutionary thought and more liberatory relations between the idea of "America" and Latinxs in the U.S.

To responsibly theorize a latinidad that is not yet here, I engage with Latin American scholarship and literature in addition to Latinx authors. This means that I have often had to work with Spanish-language texts; while Shelley Fisher Fishkin called for a transnational American Studies that foregrounds the need to be able to work in multiple languages in 2004, I can attest to the difficulty of doing such work, particularly as a heritage speaker who has tried multiple times to become fluent in Spanish. The legacy of my family's assimilation into the U.S., exemplified by my mother's refusal to speak Spanish to me growing up, has had a greater psychological impact on my relationship to Spanish than I anticipated. In fact, I only learned that my difficulty with Spanish was unique because taking a year of Italian in college and a French translation class in graduate school showed me that the issue isn't that I can't grasp other languages easily, but that Spanish is a special case. In my courses, I often talk to my students about how to be Latinx means loss — loss of language, loss of culture, loss of history. Even though *Latinx Revolutionary Horizons* speaks to the recovery of culture and history, language still eludes me. And it's not for lack of trying: I took a semester of Spanish in seventh grade, four years of Spanish in high school (including A.P. Spanish), a summer at the Middlebury Language School during graduate school (the first time I started to think in Spanish; that said, all my memories remain in English), and continuing education classes during my postdoctoral fellowship at UCSD. Doing this work responsibly has been a painful process that illustrates the difficulty of this kind of project; however, without engaging with Spanish language texts, the revolutionary potential of latinidad would be severely curtailed.

The layering of Spanish colonization and U.S. occupations that informs this project guides the method for selecting the ethnic groups and authors that appear within these pages. I focus on revolutions such as the Mexican Revolution and the Cuban Revolution because of their outsized impact on the field of Latinx Studies as well as how their success has been overshadowed by the institutionalization of revolution in their respective countries, which have successfully forestalled future revolutions, a point made most clearly by Mexico's Partido Revolucionario Institucional (the Institutional Revolutionary Party, or PRI). The failure of revolutions necessarily undergirds *Latinx Revolutionary Horizons*, a point made even more clearly by the Philippine Revolution in 1896 (which was folded into the Spanish-American War) and the 1986 People Power Revolution in the Philippines. The Philippine Revolution speaks to a period in which literature — specifically José Rizal's novels — could instigate a revolution. Jessica Hagedorn's and Ninotchka Rosca's returns to Rizal, coupled with their refusal to portray the People Power Revolution beyond the event that instigated it — the murder of Senator Benigno "Ninoy" Aquino Jr. — illuminates how both authors seek out moments of revolutionary potential rather than depict the failure of the 1986 revolution. Along similar lines, rather than focus on the 1965 Revolution in the Dominican Republic, I focus on how in Dominican American literature this particular revolution has been suppressed because of a preoccupation with the dictator Rafael Trujillo, the movements against him, and the events that led to his rise. Finally, given the failures of these revolutions, I consider how authors who do not identify as Latinx grapple with the question of revolution and choose Cuba and Mexico specifically to animate their revolutionary imaginaries.

Given the structuring principle of revolution, then, in some ways I have been unable to escape the issue that plagues projects that focus on Latinxs more broadly rather than individual groups within latinidad: "dealing with the separate ethnicities separately."[95] This is largely because authors preoccupied with their own revolutionary histories tend to be the ones who write novels such as the ones in this project. In short, since I am tracing a particular *textual* phenomenon in which the ghost of revolution haunts, derails, and interrupts the narrative of the novels I discuss, authors are often haunted by the revolutionary histories that inform their own personal histories. After all, a key part of the methodology of *Latinx Revolutionary Horizons* is reading authors back into their national literary traditions as a way to excavate what is lost when we append "American" to authors' identities—Cuban American, Mexican American, etc.[96] *Latinx Revolutionary Horizons* foregrounds the tension between the national identity marked by "American" and the nation-state that precedes it: for example, Cuban. This also raises the question of the terms that guide ethnic studies as exemplified by the uneasy fit between the Philippines and Asian America and the resonances between the Philippines and Latinx America. In highlighting these tensions, *Latinx Revolutionary Horizons* transcends the nation-state formation to think about the potential that exists for solidarities based on colonization and shared colonial histories rather than the nation-state. Such an approach underscores the racialization processes that colonial regimes enforce as a tool of white supremacy.

That said, the method of selection for *Latinx Revolutionary Horizons* does blur the neat compartmentalization of ethnicities through its transnational framework. For example, it expands the notion of Latinx futures by including the Philippines with Latinx imaginaries. Along similar lines, in looking at Martin R. Delany and Leslie Marmon Silko, *Latinx Revolutionary Horizons* examines how revolution is a transnational phenomenon in which revolutionary movements turn to other revolutionary histories to imagine their own. Finally, by including Julia Alvarez's *In the Name of Salomé* (2001), rather than *In the Time of the Butterflies* (1994), I foreground the exile and displacement that accompanies revolution as Salomé Ureña's husband, Francisco Henríquez y Carvajal, must flee the Dominican Republic because of his revolutionary activity, and her daughter, Camila Henríquez Ureña, spends more time in the U.S. and Cuba than her homeland, the Dominican Republic. Additionally, while

Caminero-Santangelo conceives of different Latinx groups as ethnicities, this project questions the idea of ethnicity altogether by emphasizing the Asian, Black, and Indigenous heritages that inform the literatures of the groups I discuss. In sum, *Latinx Revolutionary Horizons* reads across not only race, but ethnos, to elucidate the limits such frameworks place upon Latinx revolutionary horizons and, more significantly, the question of latinidad.

The category of Latinx dissolves ethno-national barriers and foregrounds the arbitrariness of Latinx identities as well as their unsettled quality. The shared sovereignty struggles that link the groups I discuss together speak as well to the artificial boundaries of Latinx Studies that often seem to be intent on taxonomizing Latinx populations as a way to add an artificial coherence to latinidad. Rather than subscribe to such artificial boundaries, the horizon encourages us to pierce them and, in so doing, embrace the incoherence of latinidad because such incoherence is what gives it its power: the power to think beyond both the racial categories that compartmentalize ethnic studies and the nation-state categories that cordon off Latinx populations from one another.

And yet, as the boundedness of the chapters by nation attest, the nation has proven to be the central revolutionary formation of Latin American countries as they fought against colonization and occupation.[97] As Vázquez reminds us, although in our contemporary moment the nation is itself a hegemonic framework, this is because the force of the nation as a revolutionary formation has been erased: "As a result of the younger and more frequently foreign-born population of U.S. Latina/os that have no living memory of the cultural nationalist period, the touchstone of the nation has in many ways become a historical anachronism."[98] Consequently, the nation remains a driving force in some of the chapters as, for example, Mexican American and Chicanx authors sought to cohere around an identity in opposition to the U.S. in light of land loss. Or we can think of how the framing of Filipinx American literature divests a people of a nation and thus erases the revolutionary tradition that contemporary Filipinx American authors operate in. However, I would add that the decision to frame each chapter by nation does not always signal a boundary, but a site of revolutionary potential. After all, Cristina García's *Monkey Hunting* is a transnational novel preoccupied with Cuba, while my final chapter on imagined revolutions looks at how two authors have turned to separate revolutionary contexts—Cuba and Mexico—to theorize what revolution means for their own (non-Latinx) people.

Additionally, even though the authors I discuss may be surprising, as they are not necessarily the people who have been oppressed the most (Julia Alvarez comes to mind) or who have unproblematic politics (Junot Díaz exemplifies how one's stated politics do not align with one's practice of politics), their works nevertheless speak to where and how our notions of latinidad have been limited and how they can be expanded. Although they may be inadequate to the task of imagining a truly liberatory future of latinidad, the very ways they have failed to do so (by prioritizing elite families, in the case of Alvarez) and the ways they try to do so (by focusing on Afro Latinxs in *Salomé*) offer us both the horizon as limit, as something that must be punctured, and the horizon as an opening, an expansion of a previously delimited world.

With revolution as the staging ground for investigating the shifting nature of who belongs in latinidad, each chapter of *Latinx Revolutionary Horizons* analyzes how contemporary representations of revolution respond to the legacy of failed revolutions to reckon with the past failures of latinidad but also its potential for more liberatory futures. Part 1 focuses on revolutionary consciousness as a form of *racial* consciousness as I consider how issues of race and ethnicity both racialize and radicalize the characters in the novels I discuss. Chapter 1, "Captive Revolutions," considers how emergent and solidified notions of mestizaje hold the idea of revolution captive by juxtaposing how María Amparo Ruiz de Burton narrates the U.S.-Mexico War (1846–48) in *Who Would Have Thought It?* (1872)[99] against Sandra Cisneros's ruminations about Mexican history in her novel *Caramelo* (2002).[100] I argue that Cisneros marks the shift to brownness that allowed for the absorption of a generalized indigeneity into chicanidad in a move that replicates how the Mexican state absorbed indigeneity into its national identity. In this reading, brownness flattens difference because it cannot help but impose a false unity that attempts to elide colonial complicities, which is an attempt that fails miserably, as such a project creates a revolutionary persona that sutures over real differences.

Part II turns to revolutionary forms of relationality to explore how such revolutionary relationships encourage the development of political consciousness and offer an alternative to the hegemonic romance paradigm Sommer describes.[101] Chapter 2, "Romancing Revolution," considers how José Rizal revised the conversion narrative into one of guerrilla conversion that operates on a model of revolutionary education. Building on scholarship that situates the Philippines within a Latin American context, I read Rizal's *Noli Me Tangere* (1887)[102] and *El Filibusterismo* (1891)[103] alongside Ninotchka Rosca's and Jessica Hagedorn's treatment of the Filipino People Power Revolution (1986) in *State of War* (1988) and *Dogeaters* (1990), respectively.[104] Both Rosca and Hagedorn extend the literary tradition of the guerrilla conversion narrative Rizal inaugurates. Where Rizal suggests homosociality as the basis for nationalism, Rosca and Hagedorn modify the guerrilla conversion narrative to include women as political subjects who can also convert to the cause. Operating outside the national romance paradigm allows Rosca and Hagedorn to imagine the possibility of a future, successful revolution that incorporates the guerrillas' vision of kinship into a nonfamilial notion of the nation.

In Chapter 3, I turn to a discussion of revolutionary pedagogy in the Dominican Republic. "Teaching Revolution" looks toward the larger pedagogical project of the conversion of the reader to political consciousness. To do so, I investigate how Julia Alvarez's *In the Name of Salomé* (2001) and Junot Díaz's *The Brief Wondrous Life of Oscar Wao* (2007) contend with the history of revolutions and dictatorships in Latin America by reading these texts alongside the poetry of the Dominican nineteenth-century poet Salomé Ureña.[105] By resisting the totalizing narrative of the Latin American dictator novel, Alvarez and Díaz write against the legacy of the dictatorships in the Caribbean by theorizing the Latinx bildungsroman. Because both texts address themselves to U.S. readers, I suggest that the novels align these readers with a Dominican perspective, thus exposing and seaming up the hemispheric divide to illustrate the entangled political and personal histories between the U.S. and the Dominican Republic. Both authors suggest that contemporary literature must revise national history and aesthetic form to open the way for more liberatory, literary futures.

Finally, in Part III, I turn toward revolutionary imaginaries to explore the utopian possibilities of Latinx revolutionary horizons. Chapter 4, "Retconning Revolution," considers how, in *Monkey Hunting* (2003), Cristina García breaks the mold of writing the immigrant bildungsroman and expands notions of U.S. latinidad by analyzing Asian ancestry and history. Even though writing in English, she focuses on Cuba within a transnational framework that also incorporates China, the U.S., and Vietnam. This chapter also takes up the issue of revising national literary histories by examining how *Monkey Hunting* draws upon Miguel Barnet's *Biography of a Runaway Slave* (1966). In reimagining Montejo's narrative as her protagonist Chen Pan's, García reveals solidarity on the level of form, particularly as *Monkey Hunting* writes against the historiography of the Cuban Revolution (1953–59). I then read Gertrudis Gómez de Avellaneda's *Sab* (1841) in light of García's work and analyze how Avellaneda relies on testimonio, or first-person accounts of significant events, to argue for the rights of enslaved people and women.[106] García extends Avellaneda's tactics by using testimonio to grapple with the Cuban Revolution's failure to eradicate racism in Cuban culture, implying that contemporary novels are tasked with testifying to the controversial aspects of the past that current regimes would prefer to ignore. García also demonstrates the shared experiences of oppressed peoples in the Americas and offers new imaginaries for liberation that succeed through retroactive continuity (retconning), in which past events are altered to fit within new narratives.

In Chapter 5, "Speculative Revolutions," I read Martin Delany's *Blake* (1859) alongside Leslie Marmon Silko's *Almanac of the Dead* (1991) to investigate how the turn to the speculative more broadly informs their construction of revolutionary imaginaries.[107] An African American writer, Delany revises the history of revolution in the Americas by underscoring the importance of Cuban revolutions to African American revolutionary imaginaries. I end by discussing how Leslie Marmon Silko offers an Indigenous perspective of what liberation would look like for all people, thus demonstrating how Silko, like Delany, revises Latinx revolutionary imaginaries by positing latinidad as a politics that creates a community capable of rising up.

As these chapters show, *Latinx Revolutionary Horizons* traverses centuries and continents to shed light on the sustained conversation Latinx literature has had regarding the concept of revolution. This conversation reveals how upheavals in kinship structures attend revolution and remake, for example, the relationship between mentor and mentee, teacher and student. *Latinx Revolutionary Horizons* also theorizes a new methodology for how we read literature by illuminating the value of reading hemispherically to see the complex negotiations that happen when authors reckon with the politics, canons, and genres of their home countries and juxtapose them with those of the U.S. In considering the future potential of latinidad, *Latinx Revolutionary Horizons* suggests alternate methods for theorizing the history and geography of Latinxs such that former affinities are resurrected and new affinities can come to light.

PART I
Latinx Revolutionary Consciousness

1

Captive Revolutions

Revolutionary Consciousness as Racial Consciousness in Ruiz de Burton and Cisneros

On December 23, 2016, the day that Carrie Fisher was hospitalized, Lalo Alcaraz posted a print to Facebook titled "Princess Lupe" in which he depicts Princess Leia of the *Star Wars* franchise as the Virgin of Guadalupe.[1] In so doing, he created a fictional, revolutionary Mexican background for Princess Leia, thus demonstrating the power of Latinx revolutionary imaginaries. During a moment when Latinx futures seemed foreclosed following the election of Donald Trump as president, Alcaraz's post both commemorated Fisher and created an aperture through which to imagine Latinx futurity by turning to a speculative past a long time ago, in a galaxy far, far away. My claim is further underscored by Alcaraz's posting a second version of the image that he published on *Pocho*, a website that specializes in Latinx news and satire, on December 27, 2016, the day Fisher died. In this second image, Princess Leia features much darker skin than the image on Facebook. In darkening Princess Lupe's skin color, Alcaraz underscores both the Virgin and Princes Leia as potentially brown, Indigenous figures of resistance.[2] In both images (see Figures 1a and 1b), instead of a cherub, an Ewok holds the crescent moon at the Virgin's feet. Princess Lupe wears the iconic star-covered mantle worn by the Virgin as well as the buns and blaster pistol of Princess Leia. The differing skin tones emphasize the relationship between the Virgin of Guadalupe and her Indigenous counterpart, the earth goddess Tonantzin. Ten years before the Virgin of Guadalupe presumably appeared to Juan Diego on the Hill of Tepeyac in 1531, the Spanish destroyed a temple of Tonantzin in the same place. Consequently, when the Virgin spoke to Juan Diego in his native Aztec language, Nahuatl, dressed in Indian clothing, it rendered visible the connections between the Virgin and Tonantzin, which in turn made the Virgin into a key figure in Mexican culture. By creating a genealogy that joins together the Virgin of Guadalupe with Princess Leia, Alcaraz imagines Latinx futures that do not rely on a "Hispanic past,"[3] but suggest a speculative past to imagine a future in which latinidad embraces its Indigenous origins and reclaims Tonantzin as a figure of resistance. Reworking the Princess Leia image into Princess Lupe transforms Princess Leia into a figure of resistance in the age of Trump.

Yet Alcaraz's transformation of the Patroness of the Americas, as the Virgin is also known, is not the only signifier of Latinx revolutionary horizons in the piece. Rather, I contend that Princess Leia's iconic buns also show how her iconography signals revolution by echoing the iconography of soldaderas during the Mexican Revolution, therefore highlighting the captivating appeal of the revolution and Latinx revolutionary imaginaries more broadly. We know from interviews with George Lucas that he based Princess Leia's iconic buns on soldaderas during the Mexican Revolution. More specifically, Lucas based the costume on Clara de la Rocha, a colonel in the revolution, as well as the traditional dress of Hopi women living in present-day Arizona. As *Remezcla* reports, George Lucas told *Time* magazine in a 2002 interview that "in the 1977 film, I was working very hard to create something different that wasn't fashion, so I went with a kind of Southwestern Pancho Villa woman revolutionary look, which is what that is," and "the buns are basically from the turn-of-the-century Mexico."[4] To prove the veracity of the claim, Eric Tang, an associate professor at the University of Texas Austin, posted a photo of Clara de la Rocha wearing buns.[5] Significantly, Tang found this picture in the Denver Art Museum's exhibit *Star Wars and the Power of Costume* (2018). The exhibit in turn led to another debate, as the whole display (as reported by *Remezcla*) also presents Indigenous Hopi women next to the soldadera.[6] The buns of Princess Leia represent not only revolutionary women, but also indigeneity via the Hopi women who inspired the hairstyle.

I read the possible narrative that "Princess Lupe" implies as one that allows us to see the revolutionary possibilities of Princess Leia—already a figure of anti-imperial resistance—as a figure of specifically Latinx resistance. "Princess Lupe" browns *Star Wars*. We can then read Princess Leia's buns—as symbol of both soldaderas and Hopi women—as akin to the vulnerability that Galen Erso builds into his plans for the Death Star.[7] In *Rogue One* (2016), his daughter Jyn Erso seeks the schematics to the Death Star so that she can send them to the Rebel Alliance, who will be able to exploit this vulnerability. Similarly, Princess Leia's buns are a vulnerability in the *Star Wars* universe that, rather than erasing the Mexican and Indigenous influence on Princess Leia's look, highlights the importance of these revolutionary imaginaries in the *Star*

Figure 1a. Lalo Alcaraz, Princess Lupe (2016)

Figure 1b. Lalo Alcaraz, Princess Lupe (2016)

Wars universe and suggests that Latinx revolutionary horizons stretch well beyond Latinx cultural productions, which I discuss in more detail in Chapter 5.

While *Rogue One* in particular was singled out by white supremacists for its diverse, female-led cast, Princess Leia's buns reveal a Mexican, Indigenous revolutionary history. The connections Alcaraz creates among Princess Leia and the Virgin, soldaderas, and Indigenous women reinforce Princess Leia as a figure of decolonial resistance. In reading the split narrative that Princess Leia's buns and Alcaraz's print invites, a soldadera becomes Princess Leia, who in turn becomes Princess Lupe, suggesting that the narrative of revolutionary education is one in which a princess from another planet takes up the mantle of resistance from the Mexican Revolution and is in turn commemorated as an intergalactic, Mexican, and Indigenous figure of resistance. Although the history of Princess Leia's buns seems resigned to a history of forgetting—as George Lucas's forgotten 2002 interview demonstrates—Carrie Fisher's death becomes another opportunity to recover a Latinx presence, as excavating these connections reveals an expansive, speculative network of resistance that spans the First World, the Third World, and the *Star Wars* universe as a whole.

Star Wars films famously open with "A long time ago, in a galaxy far, far away," which underscores both temporal and spatial distance. Yet Princess Lupe's buns imply that the events of *Star Wars* are closer than they appear, as they signify the Mexican Revolution. The *Star Wars* universe is not so far away, after all, if we route it through Princess Lupe, who recalls Mexico and reminds us of George Lucas's Central Valley upbringing, which in turn serves as the inspiration for Luke Skywalker's home planet of Tatooine, as Curtis Marez reminds us.[8] According to Marez, on Tatooine, "the figure of the white farm boy occupies a position that more closely resembles that of a migrant farm worker" (138). Whereas *Star Wars* whitens farm worker labor and migration, "Princess Lupe" browns *Star Wars* and emphasizes the material realities Chicanxs face.

In also potentially signifying Tonantzin, Princess Lupe offers an alternative to a "Hispanic past," one in which the through line from 1531 to the future does not begin with the Virgin of Guadalupe and Juan Diego but with Tonantzin. Rather than a Hispanic past, Princess Lupe represents an imagined Indigenous past that carries through to the Mexican Revolution, which centered indigeneity, however problematically, in a way that it had never been before. Princess Lupe also projects forward as she represents revolution in the future. Even though viewers are asked to imagine the events of *Star Wars* as in the past, I suggest that we posit Princess Lupe as a figure of resistance in which the Latinx and Indigenous figure is simultaneously past, present, and future. She saturates the very boundaries of temporality itself, moving from the ephemeral and coded to the eternal and omnipresent. My reading of "Princess Lupe" underscores the importance of an imagined past to the project of creating a more liberated future.

I detail this history to illuminate how U.S. cultural productions are imbued with Latinx revolutionary imaginaries such that even someone like George Lucas could draw on this iconography to create his own revolutionary imaginary. That said, Lucas's revolutionary imaginary is ultimately an imperial one, as Marez makes clear: rather than offer up an imaginary that seeks the liberation of actually oppressed people, Lucas's transubstantiation of the brown migrant farm worker into a white farm boy "rearticulate[s] civil rights rhetoric in order to argue that state efforts to redress prior histories of inequality violated the rights of white men" (138), making Lucas's revolutionary imaginary a counterrevolutionary one that participates in "an emergent neoconservative and neoliberal reaction of tactical reversals" (138). Indeed, while Darth Vader would appear to be a dictator, Marez provocatively argues that he "condenses a variety of racialized or Third World movements for social transformation" (138) that are part of the legacy of 1968.

It is only in Alcaraz's hands, then, that *Star Wars* illuminates a Latinx revolution horizon. Given that both *Star Wars* and Juan Diego's sighting of the Virgin of Guadalupe happen in the past, Latinx revolutionary horizons extend as much behind us as they do in front of us. As we see in "Princess Lupe," such Latinx revolutionary horizons appear as traces and residues that are difficult to apprehend because of ongoing processes of forgetting, such as Lucas's comment about Princess Leia's buns. Alcaraz's browning of Princess Lupe makes these connections more explicit as his focus on pigmentation and indigeneity recalls the complicated relationship between revolution and brownness in Mexican and Chicanx revolutionary imaginaries.

This, then, is the problem that Alcaraz clarifies: what is the relationship between brownness and latinidad? Is brownness subsumed under latinidad or vice versa? As with the novels I discuss in this chapter, "Princess Lupe" is another cultural production from a mestizx, not an Indigenous perspective. I focus on mestizx imaginaries in this chapter to examine how mestizxs represent indigeneity, and, in so doing, how they fail to imagine an Indigenous present, much less an Indigenous future, which is one of the ongoing challenges latinidades must face to be a viable framework for thinking outside of the nation toward liberation. Moreover, the "Princess Lupe" image emblematizes the hegemonic white latinidad that emerged in the nineteenth century as well as the browning of revolution in both the Mexican Revolution (1910–20) and the Chicano Movement in the mid-twentieth century.

Indeed, Mexico allows us to think of Mexican *revolutions*, or the many attempts made in Mexico to imagine a liberatory national identity and how these imaginaries impacted those of Mexican Americans and Chicanxs. While Michael Rogin famously coined the phrase "the American 1848," aligning it with the global revolutions that took place that year, Shelley Streeby points out that this framing "implicitly constructed the United States-as-America and stopped short of addressing the broader hemispheric significance of 1848,"[9] which was the year that established "the United States [as] a major player in the battles for influence and control of the Americas" (8), in large part because of the U.S.'s victory in the U.S.-Mexico War. Although 1848 may not signal a revolution in either Mexico or the U.S., it does lay the foundation for the Mexican Revolution as well as the U.S. Civil War (1861–65). Scholars such as Rogin and David Potter trace the connections between the U.S.-Mexico War and the Civil War, particularly how U.S. expansion — its Manifest Destiny — brought the issue of slavery to a head. That said, the U.S.-Mexico War would have repercussions in Mexico as well, since it continued to experience instability through civil wars, the Second French Intervention (1861–67), and the increased foreign influence (especially the U.S.) on the country under Porfirio Díaz's dictatorship (1877–1911).

The novels I discuss in this chapter, María Amparo Ruiz de Burton's *Who Would Have Thought It?* (1872) and Sandra Cisneros's *Caramelo* (2002),[10] illuminate how authors such as Cisneros engage with these past histories and authors like Ruiz de Burton underscore how even after the Wars of Independence, national identity was far from solidified. While *Who Would Have Thought It?* is ostensibly a novel about the U.S. Civil War, it's really about competing forms of whiteness.[11] Significantly — and strangely — the Second French Intervention arises as a nodal point in the conception of national identity in the novel, thickening the Franco-Latin connections Ruiz de Burton makes, particularly as a way to theorize a hegemonic latinidad grounded in the idea of a Latin form of whiteness in contrast to the Anglo-Saxon whiteness of the United States. As Rosaura Sánchez and Beatrice Pita argue, Ruiz de Burton's "view of the French enterprise in Mexico was colored on the one hand by her resentment in the face of what she saw as the onslaught of Anglo-Saxon imperialism, and, on the other, by her cultural allegiance to a sense of latinidad, much influenced by French writings of the period."[12]

In taking up the French influence on Ruiz de Burton, I trace an earlier, elite form of latinidad that offers an alternate form of whiteness circuited through France to counteract the hegemonic whiteness of the Anglo-Saxon U.S. To make this argument, I draw on Walter Mignolo's discussion of two distinct forms of latinidad in *The Idea of Latin America* (2005).[13] Here, Mignolo discusses an elite, hegemonic latinidad as conceptualized by light-skinned and white mestizxs in Latin America and its opposite within a U.S. context: a decolonial latinidad that Mignolo reads as "closer to the ethical and political projects of Black and Indigenous people in South America and the Caribbean than to Creoles of 'Latin' descent" (145). In exploring the pan-Latin frameworks espoused by French intellectuals and taken up by the white creole and mestizx privileged classes, Mignolo argues that "white Creole and Mestizo/a elites, in South America and the Spanish Caribbean islands, after independence from Spain adopted 'Latinidad' to create their own postcolonial identity. Consequently, I am arguing here, 'Latin' America is not so much a subcontinent as it is the political project of Creole-Mestizo/a elites" (59). As Mignolo elaborates, this conception of latinidad would come "to displace and replace Simón Bolívar's 'Confederation of Spanish American Nations'" (60), which in turn would be supplanted by the form of latinidad espoused in the U.S. that Mignolo describes as "an ideology for the colonization of being that Latinos/as in the US are now clearly turning into a decolonizing project" (64). In short, whereas in Latin America the political project of the Creole-Mestizx elites was to consolidate power, often at the expense of darker-skinned Latin Americans, the decolonial project of latinidad in the U.S. is one that increasingly diffuses power, moving horizontally across different racial groups.

As I will discuss in this chapter, the elite form of latinidad Ruiz de Burton theorizes would find itself ostensibly replaced by the kind of chicanidad authors like Cisneros exemplify. Within this context, I use "chicanidad" to signal not only Cisneros's commitment to the Chicano Movement, but also how her chicanidad exists in tension with the latinidad we see in Ruiz de Burton; while there are a number of critiques to be made in terms of chicanidad, the point remains that it features an embrace of indigeneity rather than the embrace of whiteness Ruiz de Burton advocates. However, central to my argument is how *Caramelo* is in conversation with this kind of whiteness, as my discussion of the brief footnote in *Caramelo* on the Second French Intervention makes clear. I argue that the footnote stands in for how this earlier white latinidad continues to inform conceptualizations of presumably non-hegemonic latinidades—in this case chicanidad—even in the period following the Mexican Revolution, when mestizaje presumably became the ascendant category of difference. Regardless, as I argue in my discussion of *Caramelo*, in many ways mestizaje operates in a manner similar to Ruiz de Burton's notion of latinidad; even if mestizaje signals a turn to brown and an embrace of Indigenous heritage, it ultimately relies on a romanticized notion of indigeneity that does not imagine Indigenous Mexicans as part of the Mexican nation.

I read *Who Would Have Thought It?* alongside Cisneros's *Caramelo* to examine how the protagonist of the novel, Celaya Reyes (Lala), revises Ruiz de Burton's protagonist, Lola. Here I focus less on *Caramelo*'s explicit discussion of the Mexican Revolution in the short chapter that details how Narciso Reyes, Lala's grandfather, joined the revolution, only to be given the task of burning dead bodies, which led to him returning home and, ultimately, fleeing to the United States for the duration of the war. Instead, I'm more interested in how the Mexican Revolution haunts the text, particularly through discussions of race. Indeed, Celaya's name speaks to the broader ways that *Caramelo* signifies the revolution, given that the Battle of Celaya was where Pancho Villa incurred his first defeat at the hands of Álvaro Obregón. To explore the revolution as the key moment for the creation of Mexican American identity after the U.S.-Mexican War and Chicanx subjectivity during the Chicano Movement, I focus on Lala's preoccupation with Candelaria, the house servant who Lala later learns is also her half-sister.

Lala's fascination with Candelaria's caramelo skin echoes José Vasconcelos, the scholar and politician credited with the founding ideals of the Mexican nation-state after the revolution.[14] More specifically, Cisneros recalls Vasconcelos's notion of la raza cósmica from his eponymous essay, published in 1925. In drawing upon Vasconcelos and the commitment to brownness that his ideas recall, I read Cisneros as illuminating how the ideas that undergird the Chicano Movements' notions of brownness actually stem from the same thinking that produced Ruiz de Burton's theorization of Latinx whiteness. In other words, Cisneros responds to the politics of the Chicano Movement by aligning the racial thinking of the latter with the thinking around the so-called Latin race in the nineteenth century. In *La raza cósmica*, Vasconcelos theorized a fifth race, a bronze race, that would be the product of the mixing of all the races—European, African, Indigenous, and Asian—and feature the best aspects of each. Although Vasconcelos's theory depended on eugenicist thought, he developed the idea of la raza cósmica to combat the presumed inferiority of the Mexican people and to advocate for a Mexican national identity grounded in the cultures indigenous to Mexico. In this way, Vasconcelos presumably uplifted Mexicans' Indigenous heritage; still, he did so by relegating it—and therefore, containing it—to a romanticized past based on the erasure of the multiplicity of living Indigenous peoples of Mexico, most of whom are not of Aztec descent, the group most centered by both Vasconcelos and the Chicano Movement.[15]

Cisneros's use of the term "caramelo" also echoes the descriptions of Chicanxs as a bronze race in key texts of the Chicano Movement, such as the

Chicano manifesto "El Plan Espiritual de Aztlán," thus illuminating how the idea of "la raza" (the race) indexes the problems associated with latinidad that I have discussed so far. The origins of the term "la raza" are unclear; what we do know is that it was a key racial concept that arose during the Chicano Movement. B. V. Olguín traces the use of "la raza" from Vasconcelos to the poet Alurista's concept of la raza de bronce (or the bronze race). However, Olguín also notes that "various syntheses of 'raza' reveal that its hegemonic and proposed counterhegemonic syntheses remain inseparable";[16] indeed, Olguín's tracing of these syntheses point to such a paradox as he grounds his discussion of la raza in the history of the casta system in New Spain as well as the various ways that Latin Americanists have theorized race, from José Enrique Rodó's theorization of Ariel in his essay of the same name (1900)[17] to Roberto Fernández Retamar's conceptualization of Caliban in his essay that bears the same title (1974).[18] As we can see in the way that Alurista takes up Vasconcelos, the latter would go on to inspire the Chicano Movement's embrace of Indigenous heritage, particularly through the idea of a mythic Aztec homeland, Aztlán.[19]

While both *La raza cósmica* and "El Plan Espiritual de Aztlán" demonstrate a desire to reclaim Indigenous identity and heritage, as *Caramelo* illuminates, this desire still perpetuates anti-indigeneity by relegating Indigenous people to the past.[20] At the same time, such a view of mestizaje participates in the continued denial of Black lineage, illustrating how it is tied to a project of whitening—given that in Vasconcelos's formulation, the bronze race emerges through the dilution of blackness—which aligns with the hegemonic latinidad found in nineteenth-century Mexico.[21]

Reading *Caramelo* against the backdrop of *Who Would Have Thought It?* shows the complicity between mestizaje and the hegemonic latinidad Ruiz de Burton champions, a complicity that Cisneros attempts to undo by critiquing how the privileging of whiteness in the present of the novel echoes this earlier formation of latinidad in the nineteenth century. In this way, I see Cisneros as doing two things: first, she expands on the glimpses of Latinx revolutionary horizons in Ruiz de Burton even as she exposes the limits of the imaginaries mestizaje makes possible; and second, she revises Ruiz de Burton's arguments by focusing on the limits of the logic of inclusion through her discussion of skin color and beauty. Although Cisneros would seem to be part of a longer lineage of scholars and activists who theorize a mexicanidad and a chicanidad that center indigeneity vis-à-vis Vasconcelos, her critique of mestizaje in the period after the Mexican Revolution reveals Indigenous inclusion as a failed project of the revolution.[22]

Captivity in *Who Would Have Thought It?*

To explore Ruiz de Burton's hegemonic latinidad, I reevaluate Chicanx literary history in light of the "Recovering the U.S." Hispanic Literary Heritage project, which was founded in 1992 "to locate, preserve and disseminate Hispanic culture of the United States in its written form since colonial times until 1960."[23] As the Recovery Project's first publication, Ruiz de Burton's *The Squatter and the Don* (1885), republished in 1992, makes clear, Latinx literature published before canonical texts like Jose Antonio Villarreal's *Pocho* (1959) track a literary genealogy at odds with Chicanx literary studies' former grounding in novels by Villarreal and Ernesto Garza.[24] As José Aranda remarks, writing on Ruiz de Burton, the recovery project illuminates how "the emergent archive of nineteenth-century Mexican America had collided with the counternationalist, Marxist-leaning, activist archive of the Chicana/o movement,"[25] which has resulted in nothing less than "the transformation of a Mexican American archive that no longer solely revolves around a Chicana/o movement politic or set of poetics to organize the critical identities or keywords of the field" (148). Additionally, Aranda's comments suggest that the first novels published by the Recovery Project illuminate a much more conservative literary history that runs counter to the narrative of Chicanx literature—and Latinx literature more broadly—as a literature of resistance exemplified by key Chicano Movement texts such as Oscar Zeta Acosta's *Revolt of the Cockroach People* (1973) and canonical Chicana texts like Cherríe Moraga's *Loving in the War Years* (1983) and Gloria Anzaldúa's *Borderlands/La Frontera* (1987). Indeed, while Ruiz de Burton is an important figure for the project of recovery, given that not only is she the first author to be published by the Recovery Project but also the first Mexican American author writing in English (that we know of), she also exemplifies how the Recovery Project's first foray into this kind of work begins with a fairly conservative writer. After all, Ruiz de Burton would eventually withdraw her support for Benito Juárez, the first Indigenous Mexican president, as her discussion of the Second French Intervention in *Who Would Have Thought It?* suggests. She also held positivist viewpoints, a line of thought shared by the Científicos, who were advisers and supporters of Díaz, the Mexican dictator who fled to Paris shortly after the Mexican Revolution began.

In this way, Ruiz de Burton, despite her importance for the genesis of Mexican American literature and the work of recovery, is also a controversial entry in the archive of Chicanx literature, which her background further reinforces.[26] Born in Baja California, Ruiz de Burton was from the class of elite Californios who were often white-identifying landowners. Born in 1832, Ruiz de Burton was one of several thousand Mexicans who saw their country transition into U.S. hands, especially once she moved to Alta California in 1847. In 1849, she married Captain Henry S. Burton, the man responsible for the capture of her hometown, La Paz. Notably, Henry S. Burton was a key figure in several U.S. campaigns that focused on Indigenous removal and the acquisition of lands as part of the U.S.'s belief in Manifest Destiny, such as the Second Seminole War, the U.S-Mexico War, and the Civil War. In fact, during the Civil War, Henry S. Burton was in charge of Jefferson Davis's imprisonment, and, during this time, Ruiz de Burton befriended Davis's wife.

This brief biography illustrates that Ruiz de Burton is hardly the figure of Chicanx literature that one would imagine if one traces the conventional lineage I outlined at the beginning of this chapter. However, it is exactly Ruiz de Burton's uneasy entry into the Chicanx canon that interests me here, particularly in her novel *Who Would Have Thought It?*, which contends with the subjugated status of Mexican Americans after the U.S.-Mexico War. While *Latinx Revolutionary Horizons* argues that such revolutionary horizons are sites of rupture that reveal forgotten revolutionary histories and, in doing so, resurrect them, turning to nineteenth-century texts sheds light on not only the conflicted legacy of the Wars of Independence but also the emergent revolutionary and counterrevolutionary imaginaries that later Latinx texts would draw upon to grapple with the past and imagine better futures. As *Who Would Have Thought It?* demonstrates, such imaginaries can be conservative and hegemonic rather than progressive and egalitarian.

Yet, despite Ruiz de Burton's conservative viewpoints, I ultimately argue that she offers glimpses of Latinx revolutionary horizons, no matter how unintended those glimpses may be. Much has been made of how the novel engages with the issue of race, particularly given the novel's startling premise: Dr. Norval returns to his New England home from an expedition in the Southwest with an orphan, María Dolores Medina (Lola for short). In addition to Lola, Dr. Norval met her mother, Doña Theresa Almenara de Medina, who explains that Apache Indians captured her in 1846 in Sonora and sold her to Mohave Indians in California.[27] During her time with the Mohave Indians, Doña Theresa asks them to extract precious gems for her, which she then stores. On her deathbed, she asks the doctor to take Lola with him, along with the jewels, securing Lola's wealth. She also dictates her testimonio to Dr. Norval's friend, Adrian Lebrun, who is charged with mailing the testimonio to Dr. Norval. Unfortunately, his letter is lost in the mail and ends up in the dead letter office, a point that will become important later in *Who Would Have Thought It?* As Doña Theresa explains, she gave birth to Lola five months after her capture. The Mohave Indians dyed the skin of both Doña Theresa and Lola black to prevent them from escaping and drawing attention, since presumably the black dye allowed them to pass as Native Americans. Upon first meeting Lola, Dr. Norval's family, including his wife, Jemima Norval, and neighbors speculate on whether Lola is Black or Native American and refuse to believe the doctor's claims regarding Lola's whiteness, underscoring what Natalie Molina calls "racial scripts," which "highlight the ways in which the lives of people of color are linked across time and space and thereby affect one another, even when they may not obviously appear to do so" (157).[28] Incapable of apprehending Lola's Mexican whiteness, the Norval family tries to fit her into the more familiar racial scripts of blackness and indigeneity.

As the dye fades from Lola's skin, she becomes spotted before eventually revealing skin whiter than even her New England counterparts. Ruiz de Burton uses Lola's skin color to make a case for Latin whiteness over Anglo-Saxon whiteness.[29] In making this argument, Ruiz de Burton must rely on an ethnic rather than a racial argument to fashion Mexicans as of Latin extraction and therefore white. Of course, to do so, she draws upon a different genealogy of whiteness than that offered by New England Anglo-Saxon models. Thus, Ruiz de Burton accidentally theorizes a non-white latinidad as, in admitting Mexicans are an ethnic, not a racial, identity, she opens up the possibility that Mexicans can be of different races. The role of the accidental is crucial here as, in imagining what an alternative to Anglo-Saxon whiteness might resemble, Ruiz de Burton offers an aperture to an even more liberatory latinidad not limited by the narrow confines of whiteness out of which such an opening appears. In other words, even though Ruiz de Burton is herself limited based on her investment in whiteness, if we extend her thinking in terms of what it means for Latinx racialization more broadly, a far more radical vision of race emerges that accounts for the multiplicity of Lola's own racial categories. After all, the Black and Indian Lola at the beginning of the novel testifies to this fact as Lola is still read in these terms despite—or because of—Dr. Norval's insistence that she's Mexican. While Marissa K. López argues that María Cristina Mena's work emerges during the time of the Mexican Revolution and reveals the moment when "Chicana/o literature incorporates the idea of its own race,"[30] I want to suggest that this happens even sooner, through Ruiz de Burton's meditation on the U.S.-Mexico War in *Who Would Have Thought It?*

Rather than focus solely on the racial implications of Lola's changing skin color and social status, I situate the discussions around Lola as well as her treatment in the Norval household as part of a larger argument the novel makes about governmentality. Although Ruiz de Burton's 1885 novel *The Squatter and the Don* is more often read in this light, given how it demonstrates the dispossession of Californio lands by U.S. Anglo-Saxon squatters, I suggest that in the slightly earlier period in which Ruiz de Burton published *Who Would Have Thought It?*, which followed both the U.S. Civil War and the Second French Intervention in Mexico, she was more focused on Anglo-Saxon versus Latin character in addition to Anglo-Saxon and Latin forms of governance. Indeed, Ruiz de Burton yokes her meditation on the consequences of the U.S.-Mexico War with the U.S. Civil War and regime change in Mexico. In so doing, she binds the two nations together, which is an especially savvy move, given the ways that the two wars mutually implicate one another.

As many scholars have noted, the absence of slavery in a novel ostensibly about the U.S. Civil War is conspicuous.[31] It's even more conspicuous since the novel drew upon well-known captivity narratives such as those of Mary Rowlandson and Olive Oatman. That said, I argue that it is exactly because of the issues of governance that preoccupy Ruiz de Burton that she leaves out the slavery question. The captivity narrative, with its anxieties about willing conversion to another belief system and way of life, illuminates Ruiz de Burton's anxieties about what it means to have Anglo-Saxon rulers in a formerly Latin territory.[32] By focusing on these aspects of the captivity narrative, I focus less on Lola's time as a captive of the Mohave Indians and more on scholars who read Lola as a captive of Mrs. Norval.[33] The ways that the latter holds Lola captive renders anxieties about conversion visible while highlighting Anglo-Saxon fears of an unassimilable Mexican population. In short, the captivity narrative offers us glimpses of Latinx revolutionary horizons, particularly through Ruiz de Burton's critique of the Anglo-Saxon U.S. We might even say that Ruiz de Burton is also held captive by the Anglo-Saxon genres in which she writes, from sentimental realism to the captivity narrative itself. Moreover, Ruiz de Burton is held captive to the very racial scripts that she seems to subvert—by insisting on Mexican whiteness, Ruiz de Burton still emphasizes a Black/white binary that refuses to acknowledge the history of racial mixture in Mexico. However much we may sympathize with her as a colonial subject, in avoiding the slavery question, Ruiz de Burton replicates the very oppression she is subject to, as she refuses to include African American and Afro Mexicans into her political framework, an exclusion that echoes Simón Bolívar's earlier exclusions and anticipates future exclusions of Afro Latinxs from Latinx revolutionary imaginaries.

At the beginning of *Who Would Have Thought It?* Lola travels from West to East, signaling a reverse Manifest Destiny trajectory that undoes the advancements that white Anglo-Saxon Americans have presumably made. As Amelia María de la Luz Montes argues, in *Who Would Have Thought It?* Ruiz de Burton "brings the West to New England. Rare are the nineteenth-century novels that formulate perspectives of eastern culture and thought from the vantage point of western sensibility—especially Mexican American sensibilities."[34] Such a sensibility is what allows Ruiz de Burton to critique the ostensibly advanced society of New England compared to the presumably savage West. Significantly, she does so through the foundational genre of early U.S. literature: the captivity narrative.

As Lola travels with Dr. Norval from West to East, her character trajectory follows the progressive, teleological arc of the typical Western hero.[35] Like the Western hero, Lola moves from a space of civility to a space of savagery (in the novel's terms), "calling into question the established relation of national margin to center."[36] This might seem like an odd statement to make, given that she is a Mohave captive and presumably aligned with savagery within the context of the novel; nevertheless, I do want to underscore that this is an instance of the kinds of inadvertent contradictions in the novel that offer a glimmer of what will later emerge as Latinx revolutionary horizons. After all, Ruiz de Burton is at pains to depict Lola as cultivated, fluent in both Spanish and English, and well-mannered, which suggests that perhaps she was not among "savages" after all.[37]

The circumstances of Lola's arrival in New England highlight the major role the captivity narrative plays in the novel. In terms of what we might consider the typical captivity narrative in which a white woman finds herself among Indigenous people, this part of the story largely takes place offstage and is certainly outside of the diegesis of the novel. In this way, Ruiz de Burton subverts the conventions of the captivity narrative and, as I will demonstrate, upends the form as part of her critique of New England society. According to Andrea Tinnemeyer, Ruiz de Burton specifically draws upon Olive Oatman's captivity narrative to inform Lola's background.[38] Olive's rescue in 1856 was widely published and sensationalized in numerous articles. Moreover, as Tinnemeyer points out, Olive was captured at the same place where Lola was rescued (170), and, like Lola, Olive was captured by Apache Indians and later sold to Mohave Indians (170).[39] Tinnemeyer also reads Lola's dyed skin as based on the markings the Mohave Indians placed on Olive's chin (171).

Ruiz de Burton's choice to use the captivity narrative in *Who Would Have Thought It?* is particularly striking, given the history of the form. As Christopher Castiglia notes, "Captivity narratives flourish in moments of racial 'crisis' in America: the colonial confrontation with Native Americans, the Civil War, [and] the civil rights movement,"[40] to which I would also add the U.S.-Mexico War. Additionally, the first American captivity narrative, *The Sovereignty and Goodness of God: Being a Narrative of the Captivity and Restoration of Mrs.*

Mary Rowlandson, published in 1682, was immediately popular and was reprinted numerous times, especially during the nineteenth century as the U.S. consolidated its national identity after the American Revolution.[41] As Greg Sieminski argues, Puritan captivity narratives "defin[ed] the American character by proclaiming the rejection of British culture."[42] As a uniquely American form, the Puritan captivity narrative was enlisted into the revolutionary cause as "the colonists began to see themselves as captives of a tyrant rather than as subjects of a king" (36). By depicting Lola as a captive in the Norval home, I argue that in much the same way that colonists in the U.S. used the captivity narrative as a metaphor for their predicament under British rule, Ruiz de Burton uses the captivity narrative as a metaphor for how the U.S. holds Mexicans and mexicanidades captive after the U.S.-Mexico War.

Mary Rowlandson's narrative set the initial terms by which the form was framed and understood; these are the very conventions that Ruiz de Burton destabilizes in *Who Would Have Thought It?* Mary Rowlandson's narrative was framed by a preacher's (likely Increase Mather's) prefatory material to ensure that her rescue would be read as an act of divine providence in line with Puritan thought.[43] From the beginning of the novel, Ruiz de Burton casts Protestant ministers in a negative light, as her characters the Reverends Hackwell and Hammerhard are immediately figured as lascivious men who use the church to further their own interests for personal gain. For example, both Hackwell and Hammerhard court Lavinia Sprig, Mrs. Norval's sister, only to marry other women. Hackwell, in particular, emerges as one of the major villains in the novel, along with Mrs. Norval, whom he later marries. His marriage, shockingly, does not stop him from preying on Lola inside the Norval household or hatching a plot to capture Lola for himself in which he enlists Hammerhard. As Anne Goldman notes, one of the revisions Ruiz de Burton makes to the captivity narrative is to show a "preacher who goes native and threatens the good name not of a Puritan blue-blood like Mary Rowlandson, but of an aristocratic 'Spanish' Mexican."[44] Goldman continues, "Ruiz de Burton's revision is less interested in foregrounding the relationship between Lola's ever-civil mother and her savage captors (although Native Americans are throughout Ruiz de Burton's writings demeaned as such) than in using it to critique the uncivil behavior of Major Hackwell, the ex-Presbyterian divine who in attempting to carry off Lola demonstrates a licentiousness in excess of Doña Theresa's Indian captors" (64).

As these descriptions make clear, *Who Would Have Thought It?* is written as a satire and takes particular care to critique the hypocrisy of New England society, especially in the figure of Mrs. Norval, the doctor's wife, who is a professed abolitionist yet despises Lola because of her black skin. Dr. Norval points out this contradiction explicitly by remarking, "My wife is a lady of the strictest Garrisonian school, a devout follower of Wendell Phillips's teachings, and a most enthusiastic admirer of Mr. Sumner. Compare these facts with the reception she gives this poor little orphan because her skin is dark" (18). Each of the three abolitionists Dr. Norval names—William Lloyd Garrison, Wendell Phillips, and Charles Sumner—were based in Boston, demonstrating how the abolitionist movement extended from a tradition rooted in the American Revolution, where several key events took place in Boston. In noting his wife's prejudice, Dr. Norval points to the difference between a stated politics of resistance and an embodied practice of resistance. Much like Faneuil Hall in Boston is the "Cradle of Liberty," illuminating how freedom in the U.S. is based on white freedom at the expense of Black enslavement, as it was also famously the site for auctions of enslaved people, Mrs. Norval calls herself an abolitionist at the same time that she mistreats Lola and attempts to steal her fortune.

Moreover, as Beth Fisher observes, once Dr. Norval flees the U.S. and presumably dies, Mrs. Norval effectively holds Lola captive within the Norval home.[45] As Lola transitions from blackness to whiteness, revealing her white status in the process, she also renders visible how, within the Anglo Saxon U.S., Mexican whiteness itself is also held captive. This happens at the level of plot, with Hackwell's attempt to capture Lola as well as with Mrs. Norval's attempts to keep Lola from her son Julian once she learns of their affection for each other. This also happens at the level of form, as even though the plot revolves around Lola, she speaks very little in the novel itself; most of what we know about her is through narrative description and what others say about her, demonstrating how despite being a key figure within the character-system of the novel, Lola is a minor character within the character-space of *Who Would Have Thought It?* As Alex Woloch theorizes, character-space is "that particular and charged encounter between an individual human personality and a determined space and position within the narrative as a whole,"[46] while the character-system is "the arrangement of multiple and differentiated character-spaces . . . into a unified narrative structure" (14). Extending Woloch's theory, Jennifer Harford Vargas examines how character-space speaks to larger issues of power and inequality.[47] Thus, despite the fact that Lola is the impetus for the narrative of *Who Would Have Thought It?*, she effectively remains a minor character in the novel, illuminating the subject position of Mexican whiteness within the Anglo-Saxon U.S.

Lola's fluctuating racial signifiers also indicate how the novel's racism is specifically grounded in anti-blackness and anti-Indigeneity as Ruiz de Burton makes a claim for Mexican equality based on shared whiteness at the expense of Lola's potential affiliations with both blackness and Indigeneity. The key figure for such Mexican whiteness is Lola, as, once the dye has completely disappeared, she is more white than the Norvals, revealing how, in Jesse Alemán's analysis, "within their geo-racial paradigms, the Northerners cannot conceptualize a dark-skinned body with claims to racial whiteness in the U.S., a historical problem Lola herself represents in the narrative as she introduces the New Englanders to the reality of *mestizaje* in the U.S. following the Mexican American War."[48] We get a sense of this confusion regarding skin color and race early in the novel when Mattie, looking at Lola's presumably black skin, says, "'I don't think she is so black. . . . See, the palm of her hand is as white as mine—and a prettier white; for it has such a pretty pink shade to it.'"[49] Lola's racial ambiguity points to another moment of formal captivity as the Norval women's attempts to classify her racially ultimately confine her to a more legible form of race that denies Mr. Norval's explanation of her racial heritage and Lola a voice altogether.

Only Mattie cares to understand Lola as Dr. Norval presents her, observing, once Lola's "true" skin color is revealed, "'Talk of Spanish women being dark! Can anything be whiter than Lola's neck and shoulders?,'" to which Ruth replies, "'Lola is not Spanish; she is Mexican,'" and Emma comments, "'I think Lola might teach us the secret of that Indian paint that kept her white skin under cover, making it whiter by bleaching it. I would bargain to wear spots for a while'" (232). Ruth's comment is especially important here, as Lola's whiteness is figured as Mexican, rather than Spanish. Emma's comments introduce the paradox of Mexican whiteness in the text—is Lola's skin white because it was "under cover" or because it was "bleached"? That is, does Lola's whiteness stem from merely being protected from the sun or from an artificial agent in the dye? In other words, is Lola's skin naturally white or altered to be white? Moreover, whereas before the dye was seen as another way of taxonomizing and caging Lola, in this moment, it is seen as a form of protection. Yet, by being "under cover," Lola's skin color reveals the ambiguity of racial identities, showing that the distance between whiteness and Indigeneity, as well as whiteness and blackness, is not so far after all. The ambiguity surrounding Lola's white skin, then, reveals yet another inadvertent moment in the text when the novel appears to contradict Ruiz de Burton's political project of aligning mexicanidad with whiteness by introducing the flexibility of racial categories.

The question of Lola's whiteness and, by extension, the privileging of Latin whiteness over Anglo Saxon whiteness leads us to the novel's odd discussion of Habsburg rule in Mexico in which Ruiz de Burton accidentally theorizes a non-white latinidad, as, in admitting that Mexicans are an ethnic, not a racial, identity, she opens up the possibility that Mexicans can be of different races.⁵⁰ The Habsburg moment occurs later in the novel; after Isaac (Mrs. Norval's brother) finds Doña Theresa's testimonio in the dead letter office, he travels to Mexico to find Doña Theresa's husband and father to share the contents of her letter with them. This means that roughly two-thirds of the way through the novel, we find ourselves in Mexico, where Ruiz de Burton relates a conversation between Don Felipe, Doña Theresa's father and Lola's grandfather, and Don Luis, Doña Theresa's husband and Lola's father. Before relaying the conversation, the narrator observes,

> When the allied troops of France, England, and Spain landed at Vera Cruz in 1862, Don Felipe de Almenara at once resolved to offer assistance to the government, in money, to drive off the invaders, he being too old to recommence the life of a soldier and take the field against them. But his son-in-law, Don Luis Medina, immediately joined the army and took an active part in checking Laurencez's progress, and in the obstinate and gallant defense of Puebla (196).

She continues, "Don Felipe and Don Luis, therefore, had been among the firmest and most prompt supporters of the republican government up to the winter of 1863" (196). In this way, Ruiz de Burton deftly shows Don Felipe's and Don Luis's commitment to defending the legacy of independence. In describing Don Felipe as "too old to recommence the life of a soldier," Ruiz de Burton references his participation in earlier wars to defend the republic. Don Luis continues this tradition by participating in the famous Battle of Puebla, where the French general, Charles de Lorencez (Laurencez), famously lost to Mexican forces, which is the Mexican victory that Cinco de Mayo celebrations commemorate. Yet, as Ruiz de Burton observes, Don Felipe and Don Luis's support for the Mexican republic, headed by Benito Juárez, the first Indigenous president of Mexico, waned by 1863.

This shift in loyalty is based on information the men receive that Archduke Maximilian would potentially assume the throne in Mexico (which he later does after landing in the country in May 1864). As their conversation shows, both men support a monarchy in Mexico, with Don Felipe making the following claim: "'Neither can any one dissuade me from the belief that the House of Hapsburgs has—if not an absolute and admitted right—at least a foundation for a claim, a valid justification, to entitle them to re-establish a sovereignty in Mexico. How do we know that Mexico would have declared her independence from Spain if she had been under a Hapsburg instead of a Bourbon dynasty? The Mexicans did not want a republic; they wanted a good and just prince" (197). Although this is only part of a lengthy speech, the crux of Don Felipe's argument is that Ferdinand II of Spain, a Bourbon, lost the majority of Spain's lands in the Americas after a series of independence movements in the early nineteenth century. He speculates that things may have played out differently if Spain had continued to be under Habsburg rule, a point that Gretchen Murphy underscores in her observation that "had the Habsburgs remained in power, Mexico might never have declared independence from Spain in 1824."[51] As Julie Ruiz points out, "resurrecting this genealogy means restoring the lands that the pro-Spanish Habsburgs were 'cheated' out of by France during the seventeenth century. This land includes Louisiana—that land stolen by France from Spain and then purchased by the United States in 1803."[52] Additionally, Don Felipe alludes to the earlier rule of Emperor Agustín de Iturbide, the first ruler of Mexico after independence. Significantly, Mexico was the only Latin American country that installed a monarchy after winning independence from Spain, which reinforces Don Felipe's claim—and that of other conservatives—that Mexico "did not want a republic." Such discussions about Mexico's future signal an alternate history according to Murphy, who further contends that "the conversations in the Almenara home are thus significant not primarily as a blueprint for monarchy in Mexico but as alternatives to the historic and geographic assumptions that grounded a U.S. foreign policy gaining ascendancy in the 1860s."[53] In imagining otherwise, Ruiz de Burton creates both a past and a future free of Mexican dispossession with whiteness at its center.

The novel makes an even more local argument in favor of a French monarchy via the Austrian Maximilian: Lola's father, Don Luis, is of Mexican descent, but was born in Austria, making him Austrian as well. Lola is metaphorically the offspring of a successful union between Austria and Mexico. As Sánchez and Pita observe, through this complicated political gambit, Ruiz de Burton attempts to make a case for a latinidad grounded in the bonds among the Latin peoples of France, Spain, and now, Mexico. More specifically, Sánchez and Pita point out "her steadfast defense of the Latin race and its need to stand up to Anglo-Saxon aggression."[54] They also point out that this contradicts Lola's marriage to an Anglo-Saxon as well as the "Anglo-Latin identity" that she advocates through the marriages in her texts, such as that between Lola and Julian in *Who Would Have Thought It?* (220).

Don Felipe's comments about Bourbon versus Habsburg Spain are also significant, given the myriad ways that the Habsburgs signify in the nineteenth century in the Spanish colonies, both during and after the wars of independence. As Raúl Coronado argues in his discussion of revolutionary documents in the early nineteenth century, such texts "seek instead a revolution, a full return to a centuries-old theory of sovereignty even as it was infused with new republican theories. It was premised on an unquestionable faith in a Catholic world, and a return to previous Habsburg principles of rule."[55] The desire for Habsburg governance in this instance signals a desire to return to Spanish colonial rule before the Bourbon Reforms, which limited the autonomy of the Spanish American colonies, thus turning them into colonies proper. In this way, the idea of a pan-Latin identity linking together Mexico and France was a theory that had advocates across the political spectrum over the course of the nineteenth century, from liberal to conservative advocates. As Edward Shawcross argues, while many scholars contend that pan-Latin formations gained traction in the 1850s, they were espoused as early as the 1830s.[56] By the time of the publication of *Who Would Have Thought It?* in 1872, however, both the idea of a pan-Latin Mexican identity and a Habsburg emperor no longer signaled revolution. That said, Don Felipe's and Don Luis's discussion of the Habsburgs reveal how Latinx revolutionary horizons emerge through textual disruptions: Ruiz de Burton publishes a conservative novel in 1872 that resurrects an earlier conservative imaginary, only to have that imaginary recall an earlier period when the signifiers of pan-Latinism and the Habsburgs signaled revolutionary, not conservative, ideals. Moreover, in contending with issues of governmentality and race in *Who Would Have Thought It?* Ruiz de Burton unintentionally offers revolutionary possibilities that, though unrealized in her lifetime, would inform later Chicanx revolutionary imaginaries.

The form of the captivity narrative serves as a repository of Ruiz de Burton's anxieties about the U.S. as well as the status of Mexico after the U.S.-Mexico War. Dr. Norval's insistence that Lola remain Catholic and observe her religion reveals one such anxiety—that incorporation into the U.S. will mean a loss of religion and culture. Additionally, Mrs. Norval's greed clearly articulates a concern that Americans will plunder Mexican wealth, which is what happened with the Californios. Consequently, it is no wonder that the novel ends with the union between Lola and Julian, as it demonstrates the successful integration of American and Mexican hegemonic class interests. As Aranda explains, "It is precisely because Spanish-Mexican colonialism had failed her that Ruiz de Burton ends her novel with a marriage between Lola Medina and Julian Norval that suggests a union between two colonial enterprises. Here Mexican colonialism and its material wealth are merged with U.S. colonialism and its promises of representative democracy."[57] Ruiz de Burton's imaginary of a unified nation allegorically represented by Lola and Julian speaks to her political desires for Mexican Americans in the U.S. as well as Mexicans in Mexico. As Beth Fisher points out, "Lola's eventual escape from the Norval home and return to her father's home in Mexico symbolically restore the ruptured integrity of the Medina family and the nation it represents."[58] She also notes that Lola's poor treatment at the hands of Mrs. Norval reinforces Ruiz de Burton's critique of New England civility and superiority as Mrs. Norval's home becomes the site of incivility and danger. Indeed, while *Who Would Have Thought It?* is rightly seen as a novel about the U.S. Civil War, Ruiz de Burton's anxieties speak equally to this tumultuous period in Mexico, which would eventually lead to the Mexican Revolution. Ultimately, in *Who Would Have Thought It?*, Ruiz de Burton herself prevents revolutionary imaginaries from taking hold, as she cannot imagine a Mexican American future without whiteness. In yoking Mexican American futurity to whiteness, Ruiz de Burton unintentionally depicts how she herself is captive to whiteness as it limits her own revolutionary horizons. In being held captive by whiteness, Ruiz de Burton in turn holds others—and thus latinidad—captive as well.

Captive Indigeneity

I have so far argued that even as *Who Would Have Thought It?* demonstrates a particular set of anxieties and concerns about race, the novel also offers glimmers of revolutionary possibility. I do want to point out that Ruiz de Burton also inaugurates a thread of Mexican American literature and thought to which we rarely pay attention that finds its contemporary manifestation in the work of Richard Rodriguez and the numbers of Latinxs who voted for Trump. On the other end of the spectrum, we have Cisneros, whose work is deeply tied to the political commitments articulated during the Chicano Movement.[39] To that end, I explore how *Caramelo* exemplifies what we typically mean when we refer to Chicanx literature (rather than the conservative thread we see with Ruiz de Burton). That said, I read Cisneros as exposing a conservative, exclusionary ideology that also informs the ideologies of the Mexican Revolution and the Chicano Movement. Cisneros does this by contending with both pre- and post-1910 Mexican revolutionary legacies; further, these legacies are an extension of the ways that Mexicans grappled with their national identity post-Independence, particularly in terms of 1848.

Whereas Ruiz de Burton marks the shift from Habsburg support as a marker of liberal ideology to a marker of a conservative one, ultimately what she's concerned with in *Who Would Have Thought It?* is Mexican national identity after 1848. If the novel tracks her case for a separate white identity grounded in an alternate latinidad, a latinidad that signals Latin whiteness over the Anglo-Saxon whiteness represented by the United States, then *Caramelo* illuminates how this white identity would be superseded by a romanticized Indigenous heritage after the Mexican Revolution, thanks to Vasconcelos.

Caramelo, as the novel's title suggests, is directly concerned with the complex role indigeneity (via skin color) plays in Mexican, Mexican American, and Chicanx thought, particularly in the ways that Indigenous futurity is held captive by the national imaginary of post-revolutionary Mexico and the cultural nationalist imaginary of the Chicano Movement. The novel contends with the superseded future of the Latin past and the legacy of Vasconcelos's imagined future for people of Mexican descent. Cisneros reveals that the ideals of this former future—namely, whiteness—continue to inform contemporary chicanidad at the expense of indigeneity. Crucially, the Habsburgs represent this alternative future while indigeneity is represented by the term "caramelo," which in the novel signifies both Lala's grandmother's candy-colored rebozo (shawl) and the skin color of Candelaria, one of the servants at the grandmother's house and Lala's half-sister.

Reading *Who Would Have Thought It?* alongside *Caramelo* makes clear not only the conservative legacy of a former revolutionary imaginary, but also how current revolutionary imaginaries rely on similarly exclusionary racial logics. Latinx revolutionary horizons must contend with such legacies to imagine a more liberatory future, which Cisneros does by staging the past Mexican imaginary represented by the Habsburgs alongside the Mexican Revolution to contend with the anti-Indigenous present. Much of this work happens in part two of *Caramelo*, where Lala tells the story of her family origins, before and after the Mexican Revolution.[60] The placement of Part Two is particularly significant, since it torpedoes the narrative trajectory up until that point in the novel, holding readers captive as they must read this section—and learn about the Mexican Revolution—before they can continue with the narrative begun in Part One. Part One ends on a bit of a cliffhanger, with Lala's parents arguing at the end of their trip to Acapulco, an argument that eventually leads to Lala's father having to choose between his mother (who Lala calls the Awful Grandmother) and his wife. Part One ends, somewhat ominously, "Then Father does something he's never done in his life. Not before, nor since" (86). However, as readers, we don't learn what her father does until Part Three (he chooses his wife over his mother). Instead, we are narratively diverted to the Mexican Revolution in Part Two, where we learn the story of the Awful Grandmother through a back-and-forth between Lala's storytelling and the Awful Grandmother, as a ghost, interrupting Lala's story to add detail, argue about Lala's departures from the truth, and generally scold her for an unkind portrait of the Awful Grandmother and her marriage, thus "fill[ing] in the gaps of official history."[61]

The first chapter of this section reveals how the rebozo is closely associated with Mexican national identity. As Lala explains, the Awful Grandmother's parents were famous rebozo makers, and her great-grandfather was especially good at dyeing shawls black. So famous were these shawls that the narrator says of Charlotte, Emperor Maximilian's wife, "When the crazed ex-empress Carlota was presented with one in her prison-castle in Belgium, she sniffed the cloth and joyously announced, — Today we leave for Mexico."[62] In referencing "the crazed ex-empress," Lala clarifies that Carlota makes this statement after her rule in Mexico. The rebozo is so closely connected with Mexico that as soon as Carlota sniffs it, she announces her desire to leave for the country.

More significantly, the mention of Carlota triggers a footnote that spans a full page at the end of the chapter, in which Lala explains, "The doomed empress Charlotte was the daughter of King Leopold of Belgium and wife to the well-meaning but foolish Austrian, the Archduke Maximilian of Hapsburg" (96). Far from making complicated arguments for Habsburg rule in Mexico, Lala frames this whole episode as a minor, "foolish" moment in Mexican history, demonstrating how dramatically Mexican politics have presumably shifted after the revolution, especially in terms of whiteness. *Caramelo* underscores how, in a novel rife with references to the Mexican Revolution, Latinx revolutionary horizons raise the specter of the Second French Intervention to mock it, illustrating a shift in political thought. Although Ruiz de Burton may have sincerely supported a return to pre-Independence Habsburg rule, by the time Cisneros publishes *Caramelo*, the whole affair appears to be nothing more than a historical oddity, a novelty. Regardless, as the anti-indigeneity of the characters in the novel renders visible, the ideals of whiteness the Habsburgs represented are far from a footnote in history. As Latinx revolutionary horizons make clear, such conservative imaginaries may be suppressed, but they cannot be contained or forgotten. In fact, the Carlota footnote further disrupts the disruption enacted by Part Two, demonstrating how Latinx revolutionary horizons do the work of carrying and remembering these earlier moments of uncanny resemblance. Moreover, it brings them to the surface in strange ways and unlikely places, exemplifying how contemporary Latinx authors contend with and revise both the revolutionary imaginaries and anxieties of the past.

In noting that Carlota was not only Maximilian's wife, but also the daughter of King Leopold of Belgium, Cisneros also marks another history, that of a larger imperial history that led to the further dispossession and genocide of Africans. The Berlin Conference of 1884–85 authorized King Leopold's claim to what is now the Democratic Republic of the Congo. King Leopold's rule was so violent that contemporary estimates suggest it led to the deaths of as many as ten million Africans.[63] His ostensible goal was to improve the lives of the Congolese people, but in reality his rule was marked by enslavement and atrocities as he made a fortune from the ivory, rubber, and minerals the Congolese people extracted through forced labor and coercion. While Lala offers a sympathetic portrait of the mad empress and her husband (who was killed by firing squad within two years of landing in Mexico during Carlota's trip to Europe), the comment about Carlota's father underscores the dangers that colonization posed globally well after the Wars of Independence.

The footnotes in *Caramelo*, which are marked by either an asterisk, a dagger, or a double-dagger symbol, also visually interrupt the text and redirect the reader. Accordingly, they signify the puncturing of the horizon that revolution generates. These notes are separated from the diegesis by a short line and italicized font. Although this might seem to be another form of captivity in which the narratives of the past are contained by the footnotes, the ruptures the footnotes create break through the text, as the reading experience they encourage asks the reader to turn to the footnotes for additional exegesis of the narrative, in effect "momentarily suspend[ing] the enunciation to point out the interpretation lines the reader has to follow before reentering the realm of fiction proper."[64] As Kristina S. Gibby observes, "Cisneros also confronts the official historical record by compiling a kind of history of her own within the thorough endnotes to many of the chapters."[65] Where Gibby argues that "Cisneros subverts the place of official history by placing it in the margins, so to speak, of her family history" (98), I contend that by interrupting the text, the footnotes actually draw more attention to Mexican history. In short, we cannot understand the story Lala tells us without understanding the historical framework she offers, both within the narrative and, especially, in the footnotes.

The Carlota footnote spans three-quarters of a page, but the Empress also maintains a presence within the diegesis proper. After Lala's family moves to Houston, for example, we learn, "—And where am *I* to sleep? the Grandmother asked the moment we got here, in a voice as regal as the empress Carlota's."[66] Then, later, when Lala explains her father's comments about how customers don't appreciate the fine upholstery work he does at his store and instead choose cheap, but ornate furniture, "The poor pretend they're kings. They don't like being poor, and if they can fool themselves a little with a bed that looks like the empress Carlota or Elvis slept there, all the better" (398). As we learn much earlier in the novel, from the Awful Grandmother, Elvis "is a national enemy" (27) for making anti-Mexican comments during filming in Acapulco. Even as Lala's narration of this scene seems to gently poke fun at her grandmother in later aligning Carlota with Elvis, Lala suggests that Carlota, too, is a national enemy. Finally, in the chronology at the end of the novel, Cisneros writes that in 1927 "in Belgium, the ex-empress Carlota dies.

Adiós, mi Carlota" (436). Conspicuously, the chronology makes no mention of the Second French Intervention that led to Carlota's presence in Mexico in the first place. What I want to suggest here is that after Carlota's initial textual disruption, the continued references to her signal this earlier interruption, causing tiny tears—and pointing to punctures in the horizon—in the narrative fabric even when, in Part Three, the narrative is presumably back on track.

If these Carlota allusions illuminate how the novel references the history of Mexican investment in whiteness, then the discussions of Candelaria's skin color reflect the conflicted relationship to indigeneity in Mexican communities. In fact, in Candelaria I see Cisneros's most important revision of Ruiz de Burton, particularly in terms of the politics of race. More specifically, I read Candelaria as a revision of Lola's captivity in *Who Would Have Thought It?* as another way that indigeneity is held captive in Chicanx literature and how "Lala is positioned to excavate Mexican indigeneity."[67] Importantly, the revelation of Candelaria's parentage (she is the daughter of Lala's father, Inocencio, and the laundress Amparo) is what precipitates the fight in Acapulco. Candelaria's proximity to indigeneity—and the proximity to indigeneity she forces the Reyes family to recall from their own family lines—is what prompts the textual disruptions found in the Carlota footnote and in Part Two as a whole. Or, to make my point even more clear: Candelaria's parentage reveals the failed project of the Mexican Revolution, which provokes a revisiting of this earlier Latinx revolutionary horizon to imagine one that recognizes and upholds Indigenous ancestry rather than sublimating it. The structure of the novel, then, suggests that to understand the present of *Caramelo*, we must revisit not only the Mexican Revolution, but the series of events that led to it, including the Second French Intervention, which directly led to an embrace of indigeneity as represented by Juárez's presidency.

When Lala meets Candelaria, she knows nothing of this history. She only knows that Candelaria is the young girl who helps Amparo do laundry at Lala's grandmother's house in Mexico City. Upon first seeing her, Lala observes, "The girl Candelaria has skin bright as a copper *veinte centavos* coin after you've sucked it. Not transparent as an ear like Aunty Light-Skin's. Not shark-belly pale like Father and the Grandmother. Not the red river-clay color of Mother and her family. Not the coffee-with-too-much-milk color like me, nor the fried-*tortilla* color of the washerwoman Amparo, her mother. Not like anybody. Smooth as peanut butter, deep as burnt-milk candy."[68] Embedded in this description is a critique of café-con-leche skin color, which has a particular pride of place among mestizxs. Lala critiques her own lightness at the same time she admires Candelaria's darkness; Candelaria has the skin of a caramelo, and Lala's taxonomy of color can't account for it. While elsewhere in the novel Lala comments on how light skin is valued and preferred, for her caramelo is the most beautiful color.

For Lala, seeing Candelaria results in a fundamental change in not only her worldview, but also her conception of herself and her people. As Lala remarks, "Until I meet Candelaria I think beautiful is Aunty Light-Skin, or the dolls with lavender hair I get at Christmas, or the women on the beauty contests we watch on television. Not this girl with too many teeth like white corn and black hair, black-black like rooster feathers that gleam green in the sun" (34–35). Lala's description of Candelaria's skin color echoes the descriptions of Lola's, but with a difference; rather than recoiling from Candelaria's complexion, Lala falls in love with it. Rather than insisting on whiteness as the valued skin color, Lala prizes Candelaria's caramelo coloring. In short, Lala revises Lola both in terms of Lala's role as a narrator through her descriptions of Candelaria and as the protagonist of *Caramelo* through her refusal to align beauty and value with whiteness.

Yet even as Lala reimagines Lola, Candelaria is still subject to the anti-Indigenous racism that continues to permeate Mexican, Mexican American, and Chicanx cultures. In much the same way that Ruth ridicules Lola, Lala's cousin Antonieta Araceli (the daughter of Aunty Light-Skin, no less), remarks, of Candelaria, "How can you let that Indian play with you? . . . If she comes near me, I'm leaving" (36). Antonieta's comments frame the narrative events that follow, from the discovery that Candelaria does not wear "real" underwear, but "a coarse pleat of cloth between her legs" (36) to Lala's mother ordering her to never play with Candelaria again after getting lice to the family's callous treatment of Candelaria during their Acapulco trip. In Lala's telling, Candelaria almost drowns in the ocean, which makes her incapable of helping with the children on the trip. Rather than "someone first taking care of her" (69), the family sends her back to Mexico City with nothing but a note to help her navigate her way back. As Lala tells us, Candelaria becomes "one of the countless unfortunates seen hiccupping terrible tears" (69) because the note is lost.

The family's poor treatment of Candelaria intersects with the presumed sexual availability of la muchacha, the house servant. In the following paragraph, we learn that the Little Grandfather sees Candelaria on the television and sends for her, which results in Amparo asking "permission to have her removed from her job at the Grandmother's because her daughter is already of an age, and a mother can't be too careful, can she?" (69). Here, Amparo signals the danger of rape from being left alone on a bus and subsequently getting lost, but also the dangers of the Reyes house itself in much the same way that Lola in *Who Would Have Thought It?* constantly experienced the dangers of sexual assault at the hands of Reverend Hackwell in the Norval household once Dr. Norval is presumed dead. As we learn in Part Two of *Caramelo*, when Narciso (the little Grandfather) returns from the United States after fleeing there during the revolution, he takes up with Soledad (the Awful Grandmother), who is his parents' servant. As Lala explains, "Soledad could not have known Narciso was not singling her out among all women, but simply enjoying her as his birthright. Was she not 'la muchacha,' after all, and was it not part of her job to serve the young man of the house?" (156). While Eleuterio, Narciso's father, forces his son to marry Soledad after she becomes pregnant, no one forces Inocencio, Lala's father, to marry Amparo, who also serves as la muchacha.

Candelaria's role in the house indicates a larger culture of sexual predation and signals the complicated relationship to indigeneity Mexicans have, as exemplified by the Reyes side of the family. Despite the fact that the male line is imagined as white from Seville (I say "imagined" because Cisneros also points to the racial mixture among the Spanish themselves), the women with whom they have sexual relationships are often not. We already know about Candelaria's Indigenous features, which she presumably acquires from her mother. Yet Soledad (the Awful Grandmother) herself has such features, as we learn from her mother-in-law, Regina: "It must be remembered that Soledad was a Reyes too, although of that backward, Indian variety that reminded Regina too much of her own humble roots,* a peasant Reyes from the country filled with witchcraft and superstition, still praying to the old gods along with the new, still stinking of *copal* and firewood" (113). I will discuss the note that the asterisk indicates shortly, but for now I will observe that here we learn that the Reyes family does not have a "pure" family line, even in Mexico. Although Regina is described as having "the same face you see in the Mayan glyphs" (113), a face that is "ancient, historic, eternal, so common it doesn't startle anyone but foreigners and artists" (113), signaling the enduring indigeneity of the Mexican population, this is an indigeneity that Lala consistently points to as a disavowed heritage that is often the result of rape, sexual coercion, or sexual exploitation. Yet, this heritage is presumably celebrated in the period following the Mexican Revolution (as exemplified by Soledad and Narciso's relationship) when scholars such as Vasconcelos had presumably contained the threat of indigeneity by incorporating it as a part of Mexico's past and an amalgamated future, but not of its present.

What remains unsaid in the novel, but is implied by Lala's fascination with Candelaria's features, is also the attraction that such features prompt.

The asterisk in the previous quote, after all, provides more details about Regina's romantic background. Of her eventual marriage to Eleuterio, we learn:

> *He was like a big grizzled vulture, but so pale and hazel-eyed, Mexicans considered him handsome because of his Spanish blood. She, on the other hand, thought herself homely because of her Indian features, but in reality she was like la India Bonita, that Indian girl, wife of the gardener, whose beauty brought Maximilian to his knees as if he was a gardener too and not the emperor of Mexico. In other words, Regina was like the papaya slices she sold with lemon and a dash of chile; you could not help but want to take a little taste (117)

We know from Lala that before she met Candelaria, she thought "beautiful is Aunty Light-Skin," but this footnote, which seems to be from the perspective of an older Lala, illustrates not only the arbitrariness of aligning whiteness with beauty, but also how, in the case of Eleuterio, his features actually belie this association. Instead, Lala returns again to Maximilian, though this time to describe the other woman in his life, la India Bonita, the beautiful Indian girl. Little is known about her, other than that her name may have been Concepción Sedano or Margarita Leguizamo Sedano, and she presumably had a child with Maximilian. The story of La India Bonita is thus where the Habsburg and Candelaria referents intersect, illuminating how, despite Lala's flippant comments about the Habsburgs, they signal an important moment in Mexican, Mexican American, and Chicanx identities vis-à-vis a "Latin" character constructed in opposition to the Anglo-Saxon north that the United States exemplifies. Candelaria signals yet another key moment: the rhetoric of indigeneity that was central for imagining Mexican identity after the Mexican Revolution. However, as Candelaria's example indicates, the rhetoric of inclusion and the embrace of an Indigenous past—and, significantly, not an Indigenous present—was a method of containment that failed to actually incorporate indigeneity into the nation while la muchacha became a figure of both indigeneity and captivity, as only dire circumstances led to someone like Amparo asking to be relieved of service, no doubt because of limited social mobility.

Lala ties the anti-indigeneity of her present with the Porfirian past when she asks the ghost of the Awful Grandmother to describe the centennial celebrations of Mexican Independence on September 16, 1910, right on the eve of revolution. According to Lala,

> Indians and beggars were routed from the downtown streets where you lived so as not to spoil the view. Thousands of pairs of machine-made

> trousers were handed out to the poor with instructions to wear these instead of those peasant cotton-whites. The parents of the shoeless were scolded into buying their children footwear or else face terrible fines, while the little girls of the well-to-do were recruited to toss rose petals in the Centennial parade before a phalanx of Indians dressed as "Indians." (125)

In this description, actual Indigenous people are made to play Indian to celebrate an Indigenous past even as the Indigenous present of poor Indians is covered up with machine-made clothes.

Such an attitude toward Indigenous peoples persists in Lala's description of her father's youth, during the reign of Lázaro Cardenas, who was president of Mexico from 1934 to 1940. As Lala tells us, "Assisted by the new government, the arts flourished, creating a new *mestizo* identity proud of its Indian heritage, though in reality Indians were still treated like Indians everywhere, like dirt" (206). Lala's description, "like dirt," is particularly striking, given the emphasis on dirt in her method of storytelling. As she tells us at the beginning of Part Two, "'When I was dirt' . . . is how we begin a story that was before our time. Before we were born. Once we were dust and to dust we shall return" (89). Yet, if Indigenous people are also dirt, then Lala seems to suggest that such an origin story, of being of dirt and dust, also implies being Indigenous. Indigeneity, then, is where the story begins and ends.

The arc of the novel carries out this logic as *Caramelo* ends with Candelaria, first in the last chapter of the novel proper, Chapter eighty-six, then in the short section that follows, "Pilón," named after the Mexican grocer's *"something extra tossed into your bag as a thank-you for your patronage just as you are leaving"* (433). In Chapter eighty-six, at her parents' anniversary party, Lala imagines "Candelaria dancing a *cumbia*, like a Mexican Venus arriving on sea foam" (425), an image echoed in the penultimate paragraph of the "Pilón" chapter, where Lala sees

> a girl with skin like *cajeta*, like goat-milk candy. The *caramelo* color of your skin after rising out of the Acapulco foam, salt water running down your hair and stinging your eyes, the raw ocean smell, and the ocean running out of your mouth and nose. My mother watering her dahlias with a hose and running a stream of water over her feet as well, Indian feet, thick and square, *como de barro*, like the red clay of Mexican pottery. (434)

Where Nassim Balestrini reads this scene as an indication of "Candelaria's role of affirming Celaya's mestizoness,"[69] I read this scene as one that affirms

Lala's *indigeneity* because it extends the project of affirming Indigenous beauty and critiquing anti-indigeneity in Mexican, Mexican American, and Chicanx communities and because of the non-sequitur to Lala's mother's feet. The girl at Caleta beach triggers a memory of Candelaria, which then triggers a memory of Lala's mother. Lala's mother herself is a figure of suppressed indigeneity as her family, the Reynas, "are all built like a mountain range. It's their Indian blood. Pure Yaqui,"[70] according to Lala's father. Lala observes that her mother "doesn't like to be called Yaqui in front of her mother-in-law" (241), which indicates not only the Awful Grandmother's ongoing anti-indigeneity, but also the suppressed history of Yaqui (Yoeme) resistance in the novel. Subject to genocide campaigns during the Porfiriato, the Yoeme battalions under General Álvaro Obregón during the Mexican Revolution were key to his success, particularly his eventual presidency from 1920 to 1924. At the same time that indigeneity emerges in the novel as a failed project of the revolution and an ongoing cultural crisis, it also signifies the revolutionary history of Mexico, where in holding indigeneity captive, Latinx revolutionary horizons retreat as one approaches, at least in the hands of mestizx authors.

Falling through the Cracks

The cover of *Caramelo* (see Figure 2) signifies the Mexican revolutionary history I have tracked as the Edward Weston photograph, "Rose, Mexico" (1926) also references the braided buns of the Mexican women who fought during the revolution.[71] Coupled with my discussion of Princess Leia's buns that opened this chapter, both "Princess Lupe" and the woman on the cover of *Caramelo* represent not only revolutionary women, but also indigeneity via the Hopi women who inspired the hairstyle. In other words, the buns create a rupture within Mexican revolutionary signification that allows a more expansive revolutionary horizon to emerge. While my reading of "Princess Lupe" underscores the importance of an imagined past to the project of creating a more liberated future, Ruiz de Burton reanimates the discourse around whiteness in her theorization of latinidad, and Cisneros critiques the logic of inclusion that structures mestizaje and erases indigeneity in the process; "Princess Lupe" contends with both of the histories traced by Ruiz de Burton and Cisneros such that a white past is acknowledged and rewritten and indigeneity becomes the focus for a liberatory Latinx revolution horizon.

The turn to the speculative that undergirds such a revolutionary horizon imagines a latinidad that is not yet here but for which we already have a rich set of models and possibilities. Indeed, the speculative is key for filling in the gap between the "Latin" and the "x" that comprise Latinx. The "x" invites

Figure 2. *Caramelo* Book Cover, featuring Edward Weston photograph, "Rose, Mexico" (1926)

such speculations and encourages us to engage in critical fabulations to address Latinx absence and erasure in much the same way Alcaraz does with "Princess Lupe." In embracing the "x" as marking an unknown future for latinidad, Latinx literature, and Latinx scholarship, Latinx revolutionary horizons inspire us to create a world that lives up to the "x." That is, rather than attempt to definitively name and delineate what counts as latinidad, Latinx revolutionary horizons welcome the possibilities such an unknown variable makes available because, even though such possibilities may not always be immediately visible or intelligible, they can be drawn out through encounters with aesthetic objects.

As *Who Would Have Thought It?* and *Caramelo* make clear, one ongoing hallmark of latinidad is the shifting signifiers of race, the ultimate unknown variable epitomized by the "x" in Latinx that marks not only the gaps, but the tensions that exist between "Latin" and "x." As Claudia Milian argues, the "x" "is falling through the Latin cracks—the spaces between the o's and the a's, the conventional understandings of what it means to be Latino or Latina."[72] The "x" exposes how Afro Latinxs and Indigenous Latinxs fall through these Latin cracks, uncovering the whiteness of latinidad that in nineteenth-century Mexico informed the "Latin" part of the equation. However, as both *Caramelo* and "Princess Lupe" underscore, Chicanx authors and artists grapple with this falling through the cracks to mark such histories and revise them. At the same time, falling through the cracks signifies fugitive latinidades as blackness and Indigeneity are no longer held captive by the "Latin" that informs latinidad. Reading *Who Would Have Thought It?* as an aperture allows us to read *Caramelo* otherwise such that the possibilities contained within Princess Lupe reorients discussions of the "x" toward Chicanx and Latinx indigeneity, away from the kind of latinidad Ruiz de Burton imagines and the kind of mestizaje that enamors and captivates Cisneros.

In Chapter 2, I will examine another population that has fallen through the Latin cracks: Filipinxs. While the Philippines shares a colonial and revolutionary history with Latin America, few scholars have considered the Philippines within the framework of latinidad—this despite the fact that the name of the archipelago derives from King Philip II of Spain, who was the reigning monarch at the time of the Philippines' so-called discovery. Turning to presumably unconventional frameworks for latinidad as I do in Chapters 2 and 5 illuminates the potential and the promise of a future latinidad. Further, building on the captivity narratives' anxieties about conversion to analyze guerrilla conversions underscores how the genres I discuss take part in conversations across centuries and even oceans.

PART II
Latinx Revolutionary Pedagogies

2
Romancing Revolution
The Queer Future of National Romance in Rizal, Rosca, and Hagedorn

Although critics have tended to read Jessica Hagedorn's *Dogeaters* (1990) and, to a lesser extent, Ninotchka Rosca's *State of War* (1988) as multicultural or Asian American novels, recent work by Filipinx and Filipinx American scholars examines Filipinx-specific traditions that do not necessarily align with Asian American experiences.[1] From Lucy Mae San Pablo Burns's notion of *puro arte*, which analyzes the epistemological implications of histrionics, to Vicente L. Rafael's theorization of white love, which interrogates the benevolent paternalism of the United States toward the Philippines, scholars are shifting away from a focus on the migration of peoples and literatures to the United States to reading authors like Hagedorn and Rosca back into their national literary traditions. Reading Hagedorn and Rosca in this way demonstrates how their formative involvement with historical events and genres elsewhere reshapes our understanding of transnational American literature such that we can productively read the Philippines through Latinx Studies.

My reading of Hagedorn and Rosca responds to Burns's call to investigate what has "fall[en] away" in such single-nation readings[2] by similarly viewing Hagedorn and Rosca transnationally through layers of colonial occupation in the Philippines, especially by Spain and the U.S. In so doing, I consider what it means to think of the Philippines through its ties to Latin America. As Kochi Hagimoto observes, Latin America "is too often reduced to the terms of apparent geographical boundaries."[3] As he notes more forcefully, "Even though the Philippines are *outside* of 'Latin America,' they are explicitly *inside* the Hispanic imperialist trajectory at least until the nineteenth century ... the juxtaposition of the Asian archipelago and the Caribbean island illuminates that they equally belong to the Hispanic imperial and postcolonial circle"

(18). Hagimoto's comments bring to mind Walter Mignolo's *The Idea of Latin America* (2005),[4] which traces how the concept of the Americas was itself an invention of the European mind, which then splintered the Americas into North and South and, I would add, created a continental model incapable of apprehending how the Spanish imperial project exceeded the continental form.[5]

Reading the Philippines through such a framework demonstrates how Hagedorn and Rosca radically revise an influential literary tradition—what I identify as the guerrilla conversion narrative—in the Philippines.[6] In this tradition, which we first see in José Rizal's novels, the nation is built not through the heterosexual romance but instead through chosen kinships. Further, this narrative is a flexible, historically specific genre that responds to the conflicts and concerns of its time. Situating Hagedorn and Rosca firmly within this Filipinx literary tradition reveals a previously unrecognized generic form that highlights the long history of colonial occupation and intervention in the Philippines. This history creates affinities between not only Latin America and the Philippines, but also among the Philippines, Puerto Rico, and Cuba more specifically, since the first two nations became unincorporated territories of the United States after the Spanish-American War (1898) and the latter was immediately occupied after presumably achieving independence following the war.

In what follows, I argue that we cannot appreciate Hagedorn's *Dogeaters* or Rosca's *State of War* without a clear understanding of how guerrilla conversion narratives operated at their inception. I first discuss Rizal (1861–96), the Filipino nationalist hero and professed father of Filipino literature, and argue that Rizal inaugurated the novelistic tradition of the guerrilla conversion narrative with his *Noli Me Tangere* (1887) and its sequel, *El Filibusterismo* (1891).[7] The homosocial mentorships found in *Noli* and *Fili* follow a similar pattern: within the context of a friendship between a young man and a revolutionary, the latter encourages the former's commitment to the revolution. At first, the young, reform-minded man resists and seeks a more moderate path; then a pivotal event occurs, at which point the mentee converts and becomes a revolutionary under the tutelage of his mentor. Because Rizal's novels hinge on friendship rather than romance as a decolonial model of relation, they offer homosocial relationships, rather than heterosexual romances, as the basis for Filipino nationalism. Reading the guerrilla conversion narrative as a genre predicated on the homosociality of chosen kinships based on revolutionary consciousness departs from and is indebted to Doris Sommer's *Foundational Fictions* (1991) in which she argues that the heterosexual romance is the paradigm for the nation in the nineteenth century.[8] In this way, my reading builds on Hagimoto's important work, particularly his reading of how both *Noli Me Tangere* and José Martí's *Lucía Jerez* (1885) use romance "not so much [as] a way to imagine national conciliation through sexual desire as to expose the crisis of such conciliation and to challenge the hegemony of Spanish colonialism."[9] For Hagimoto, such a use of romance offers an alternative model to that of Sommer's foundational fictions, one that emphasizes political resistance rather than national consolidation (29). Along similar lines, I suggest that Rizal imagines the nation otherwise, even though the nineteenth-century Philippines shared a similar colonial framework with nineteenth-century Latin America.

I then turn to *State of War* and *Dogeaters* to analyze how these texts, taken together, demonstrate a concern with similar sets of issues—namely, revolutionary kinships—regarding the 1986 People Power Revolution. The genesis for Rosca's *State of War* began in 1973, when Rosca was held as a political prisoner in Camp Crame, the infamous detention center that eventually became a point of contention during the revolution. Rosca and Hagedorn memorialize the time period of the Marcos regime (1965–86) as a historical moment ripe with revolutionary potentiality. By refusing to represent the People Power Revolution, Rosca and Hagedorn are able to forestall the revolution's inevitable failure while simultaneously attempting to rewrite this revolutionary outcome in the present. That is, both authors respond directly to the recent past of 1986 to galvanize structural change in the present. In this way, Rosca and Hagedorn are not able to think about revolutionary change without comparing their work to the historical People Power Revolution. Each author grounds her work within the specter of the revolution, as evidenced by the narrative climax in *Dogeaters* happening on Epifanio de los Santos Avenue, the same street where Camp Crame is located and on which the People Power protests occurred (which is why the revolution is often called EDSA). Further, Rosca revisits the time period during which Rizal lived because it was another historical moment when the Filipino people were inspired to rise up and fight against colonial rule.

By thinking outside of the framework of the national romance and looking back at Rizal's guerrilla conversion narratives, Rosca and Hagedorn reimagine models of relation through the paradigms of the heterosexual romance and the love triangle. Although the heterosexual romance in Sommer's formulation consolidates the nation, the love triangle, according to Eve Kosofsky Sedgwick, reveals homosocial desire. Rosca and Hagedorn extend the scope of Rizal's guerrilla conversion narrative by emphasizing the role of women in revolution and by transforming Rizal's implicitly queer relationships into an explicitly queer framework. This queer framework allows for the existence of multiple forms of kinship and resists the couple and nuclear family forms emblematic of the national romance. Chosen kinship networks in these novels are a way to resist the primal scene of colonial rape—a point Rosca renders visible by depicting the legacy of a single Capuchin monk and his rape of an unnamed Indigenous woman. Rehabilitating social and sexual relationships in both Rosca and Hagedorn becomes a way to reimagine romantic and platonic relationships while radically revising the influential literary tradition, based in the Philippines, of the guerrilla conversion narrative. In this tradition, the nation is built not through the heterosexual romance, but instead through chosen kinships. Additionally, this narrative is a flexible, historically specific genre that responds to the conflicts and concerns of its time. By situating both authors firmly within this Filipino literary tradition, I unearth a previously unrecognized generic form that richly engages with the long history of colonial occupation and intervention in the Philippines. Unlike Rizal, who privileges the homosocial, Rosca and Hagedorn explore the political possibilities of the heterosocial as the site for revolutionary potential.

Reading both authors in light of Rizal's work serves as an antidote to the problematic familial paradigms that frame Filipino politics because each author provides a sharp contrast to the Marcos regime's perverse conjugal rule, which began with Marcos's presidency in 1965 and ended with the People Power Revolution in 1986. In his description of conjugal rule, Rafael argues that the Marcoses performed their intimacy on the national stage, going so far as to commission portraits of themselves as Malakas and Maganda, the mythical first Filipino couple.[10] In so doing, Rafael suggests that the Marcoses effectively established themselves "as the father and mother of an extended Filipino family" (122). By foregrounding their own heterosexual romance, particularly along mythological lines, the Marcoses justified their extended rule and advocated benevolent paternalism predicated on familial paradigms that rely on a hierarchical relationship between those who rule and those who are ruled. Rosca and Hagedorn's novels, by privileging friendship over familial relationships, dispense with this hierarchical framework and offer lateral kinship networks among the guerrillas in its stead.

The Marcoses's conjugal rule was not the only political context for *State of War* and *Dogeaters*: at the same time that the Marcoses problematized intimate relationships, *cacique* (the term popularized in Latin America for prominent political bosses) rule further infected Filipino politics by constantly drawing power to only a few elite families. As Benedict Anderson explains in his description of cacique democracy, one outcome of colonization in the Philippines was the creation of an elite ruling class: "They might dislike one another, but they went to the same receptions, attended the same churches, lived in the same residential areas, shopped in the same fashionable streets, had affairs with each other's wives, and arranged marriages between each other's children. They were for the first time forming a self-conscious *ruling* class."[11] Even though prominent Filipino families might fight with one another—as the Marcoses and the Aquinos (who galvanized the people to revolt against the Marcos regime) famously did—they still operated within a dynastic framework that reaffirmed rather than unsettled forms of power and spectacle. Hagedorn's guerrilla conversion narrative thus acts as an antidote to corrupt Filipino politics. Where cacique democracy draws power inward by continually consolidating power among the elite, the guerrilla conversion narrative of *Dogeaters* spreads power outward to incorporate the Filipino people into the nation.

Given the historical specificity of conjugal rule and cacique democracy, I look at the Philippines within the context of Spanish colonization and U.S. occupation to argue that such readings further expand Latinx revolutionary horizons. By focusing on such shared histories of colonization and occupation, I explore how the Philippines is also a site of what Simón Ventura Trujillo calls "disappeared relations," as the U.S. occupation severed ties between the Philippines and the rest of Latin America, while the Asian American and Latinx studies models for the Philippines also disappear this relationship.[12] I follow critics such as Benedict Anderson, Adam Lifshey, John Blanco, and Koichi Hagimoto in considering how the Philippines can just as easily be viewed from a Latin American as from an Asian perspective.[13] Examining the Philippines in this context, then, means reading the chosen kinship framework Rizal ushers in with the guerrilla conversion narrative as restoring and revisibilizing the kinship ties between Latin America and the Philippines that were imposed by Spanish colonialism and U.S. neocolonialism and that are also revitalized through the forged alliances of revolution. In this way, Latinx revolutionary horizons also expand field imaginaries as well as the political and literary possibilities for thinking about the Philippines and Latin/x America alongside one another. After all, the construction of the Philippines as Asian is a fairly recent development, considering the three hundred years of Spanish rule that preceded the twentieth-century manifestation of an Asian racial identity. Because of this complex history, Filipinx and Filipinx American literature illustrates an intricate transnational framework that engages with the Philippines' multiple colonial histories. Therefore, I argue that we need to read Rosca and Hagedorn back into Philippine literature to examine how their work participates in literary traditions occluded by the periodization and nationalist frameworks that dominate literary studies. Strange as it may seem, doing so highlights the connections between Filipinx and Latinx Studies.

Rizal's Homosocial Nationalism

Although José Rizal gained notoriety as an alleged leader of the Katipunan organization that would plan the 1896 Philippine Revolution, he was already famous for anti-colonial critiques of Spanish rule. These critiques, though present in *Noli Me Tangere*, became significantly more palpable in *El Filibusterismo*. *Noli* was written during Rizal's first trip abroad, when he left the Philippines to pursue his medical studies and avoid the political tensions at home. His older brother Paciano precipitated these tensions because he was a student of Father Burgos, one of the three priests garroted for his involvement in the Cavite Mutiny of 1872. Paciano's relationship with Burgos was a dangerous association for the Rizal family, and the family's predicament would only worsen with the publication of *Noli* and Rizal's subsequent label as a subversive, or filibustero.[14] Tensions increased even more with the publication of *Fili*, which he dedicated to the three priests. Rizal was exiled to the city of Dapitan shortly after his return to Manila in 1892. Accused of leading the Katipunan revolt in 1896, Rizal was subsequently arrested, tried, and executed. Shortly thereafter, the Philippine Revolution broke out, followed by the Spanish-American War in 1898.

Even though he is a popular figure in the Philippines, Rizal's widespread familiarity in the United States' academy stems from Benedict Anderson's *Imagined Communities: Reflections on the Origin and Spread of Nationalism* (1983).[15] Anderson's key concepts are tied to his analysis of Rizal, but critics focus on his foundational ideas while forgetting the famous Filipino author and national hero who inspired them. The very definition of the imagined community—that it is imagined because one cannot actually know each person who comprises the nation (6) and that it is a community "conceived as a deep, horizontal comradeship" (7)—originates in the first paragraph of *Noli Me Tangere*, which describes the seemingly unremarkable event of a dinner party at Captain Tiago's house. As Anderson argues, the dinner party stages what it means to be connected as a nation, given that the dinner party is discussed by "hundreds of unnamed people, who do not know each other, in quite different parts of Manila, in a particular month of a particular decade" (27). Anderson's imagined community, then, already signals a model of national consolidation not founded on the heterosexual romance's biologically grounded conception of unity. Anderson points to one type of national imaginary in Rizal; I point to another through the guerrilla conversion narrative. Like the imagined community, the guerrilla conversion narrative is similarly based on "deep, horizontal comradeship" rather than biological, familial connections. However, the guerrilla conversion narrative also offers an explicit critique of the heterosexual romance by constructing a national imaginary based on homosociality and demonstrating the limits of romance for national allegory. As Anderson reminds us, "One could argue that every modern conception is based on a conception of 'meanwhile'" (25n34). Anderson's notion of "meanwhile" points to the simultaneity of revolutionary conversion and plotting in Rizal as well as the heterosexual romances that Sommer details. In other words, if we see heterosexual romance as a limit for revolutionary horizons, then the meanwhile of revolution is a way of crossing that limit, of puncturing the horizon.

Rizal's novels were incendiary because they imagined both resistance to colonial rule *and* a unified Filipino people. Under Spanish rule, "Filipino" signified a creole class distinction by naming people of Spanish descent who were born in the Philippines. Yet, in the late nineteenth century, Rizal shifted this meaning of "Filipino" to signify a national identity that crossed class and racial lines.[16] The configuration of the Filipino as Asian rather than as Spanish creole, then, owes much to Rizal's impact on the Filipino national imaginary. As Anderson tells us, Rizal is the "first Filipino" because he is the first to imagine Filipino as a national, rather than colonial, identity.[17] Rizal makes possible Asian American readings of Filipino American literature by making "Filipino" signify an "Asian" ethnic identity rather than a classed, "Spanish" one. This history of identification reveals the class politics that underpin the construction of Filipino ethnicity in the novels of Rizal, Rosca, and Hagedorn.

Crucial to Rizal's conception of Filipino ethnicity were the homosocial societies that informed his ilustrado homosociality and were central to the plot of the Philippine Revolution and his guerrilla conversion narratives in *Noli* and *Fili*. As Raquel A. G. Reyes reminds us, Rizal formed a number of homosocial societies before he organized Los Indios Bravos, a society inspired by a Wild West show he observed at the 1889 Paris Exposition.[18] In naming this organization, Rizal drew a structural connection between Native Americans in the United States and indios in the Philippines, a connection that Sharon Delmendo reads as a subversive undercutting of the racial slur, indio.[19] In this way, Rizal's conceptualization of a Filipino national identity grounded in Asianness as a rejection of Spanishness also relied on a sense of Filipino indigeneity. Los Indios Bravos played an important role in establishing Rizal's subsequent organization, La Liga Filipina. While these societies mark significant advances in the nascent conception of the Philippine national and ethnic identity, they were additionally solidified in the well-known Katipunan organization, which E. San Juan Jr. argues could only be conceptualized because of Rizal's Liga Filipina.[20]

Such all-male societies relied on male comradeship and the exclusion of women, a feature that defines Rizal's guerrilla conversion narrative. As Reyes observes, the ilustrados bonded over their conquest of European women, which is in sharp contrast to the entirely different standards to which they held Filipinas, who were supposed to be icons of virtue.[21] The sexual culture of these societies was predicated on the exclusion of Filipinas specifically, which is rendered visible by the excised chapter of *Noli*, "Elías and Salomé." Carol Hau argues that the missing chapter suggests that women are nothing more than distractions to the masculine calls for patriotism and revolution.[22] Because women in Rizal's novels emerge as nothing more than hindrances, it is no wonder that Rizal found homosocial societies necessary and emphasized the importance of male homosociality in *Noli* and *Fili*.

By reading these affirmative homosocial relationships in Rizal, we can recover Filipinx history from the problematic homosocial discourse that pervaded United States' rhetoric about the Philippines during the Philippine-American War (1899–1902). Rafael explains that the United States historically constructed Filipinos as "orphans of the Pacific"[23] and "little brown brothers," a term infamously coined by William Howard Taft, governor-general of the Philippines from 1900 to 1904. As Juliana Chang points out, this framework describes the colonial project as predicated on "homosocial, paternal-fraternal relationships in which the United States would provide tutelage and protections."[24] This paternalistic framework characterized the United States' political discourse at the time, as President William McKinley's justification confirms: "'There was nothing left to do but take them all, and educate the Filipinos, and uplift and civilize them.'"[25] Whereas the United States condescendingly used the language of homosociality and racial uplift to justify Philippine intervention, Rizal's representation of homosociality offers a vision of solidarity based on shared political goals. In this way, by revisiting Rizal, I argue that he crucially decolonizes homosociality and, in so doing, resists imperialist discourse.

In *Noli* and *Fili*, love for the nation or love for a woman are competing choices rather than allegories à la Sommers, a point rendered explicit by how love triangles depart from Sedgwick's influential reading of homosocial relationships. Sedgwick argues that the love triangle reveals homosocial bonds, rather than confirming heterosexual ones when two men compete for the love of a woman.[26] However, in *Noli* and *Fili*, a woman competes for the love of a man who is simultaneously wooed by a mentor to join the revolution. As a national allegory, the woman in each case represents the nation, illuminating how nationalism interrupts the queer possibility of the homosocial relationships that develop between men. What's more, as evidenced by Sommer's work, the project of nationalism requires that heterosexual romance replace the homosocial forms of relationality that marked the Latin American independence movements. While Rizal takes up such homosocial forms in a later independence period, the ways that Rosca and Hagedorn build on his work demonstrate how heterosexual romance need not be the model for revolution or the nation. Such an argument anticipates and extends Ileana Rodríguez's influential *Women, Guerrillas, and Love* (1996),[27] in which she argues that the exclusion of women from the revolutionary project leads them to stand in for all disenfranchised peoples, which she refers to as "people, masses, troops, bases" (xv) in contrast to the privileged revolutionary categories of "vanguard parties, political leaders, and engaged writers" (xv). Although Rizal's texts may line up with the latter, his work nevertheless forms the foundation for Rosca's and Hagedorn's incorporation of the former.

In *Noli*, the love triangle involves Ibarra, María Clara, and Elías; in *Fili*, the triangle shifts to Ibarra/Simoun (Ibarra is disguised as the foreigner Simoun for much of *Fili*), Basilio, and Julí. Despite the fact that the death of each woman motivates revolutionary zeal in the novels, the real work of the revolution can only be done once the women are offstage: we never see María Clara in *Fili* (she is locked away in a convent for the duration of the novel), and Julí dies roughly halfway through *Fili*. The women offer a normative cover for the mentor-mentee relationship between Ibarra and Elías and, later, Basilio and Simoun, such that the homosocial bonds between men are fostered and cemented in an implicitly queer framework. My use of "queer" here stems from the more expansive sense of the term Martin Joseph Ponce suggests, in which "queer" is "an unraveling of the normative lineup of biological sex, gender, and sexuality" such that "the term's critical force derives from its expulsion from and opposition to the normal."[28] The relationship between Ibarra and Elías as well as Simoun and Basilio hinges on this expansive notion of queerness because both sets of homosocial relationships oppose Spanish rule through resistance to the structurally normative. They resist heteronormativity by forming allegories for the nation that rely on the guerrilla conversion narrative rather than the heterosexual romance.

In this way, Rizal signals a decisive break from Spain by dispensing with Spanish class-based racial categories and the typical nationalist romance. In contrast to Sommer's argument that nineteenth-century Latin American novels aspired to consolidate the nation through the unification of heterogeneous couples via marriage, *Noli* looks outside heterosexual coupling to frame national consolidation and unification in the Philippines. In *Noli*, the relationship between Ibarra, the protagonist of the novel, and María

Clara, his love interest, would seem to be the key to this nationalist romance. However, the more compelling—and convincing—"romance" that occurs in the novel is that between Ibarra and the Indigenous revolutionary Elías. Because *Noli* pivots around the relationship between Ibarra and Elías, Rizal suggests that homosociality is central to nation-building. In this way, Rizal paves the way for a broadened understanding of kinship, one that underscores chosen networks rather than family ties or heterosexual coupling. Guerrilla conversion narratives, with their focus on political commitments and new national imaginaries, underpin these chosen kinships, which are another kind of "deep, horizontal comradeship" predicated on relationships between men.

Rizal's fascination with homosocial relationships crucially informs his work such that the relationship between Elías and Ibarra—the first iteration of Rizal's national imaginary—paradigmatically reveals the centrality of homosociality to the national project. Importantly, in Rizal the relationship to indigeneity is markedly different than in Sommer's model, as, rather than embracing indigeneity to consolidate power, such a choice stems from the thinking that underlies his organizations, Los Indios Bravos and La Liga Filipina, in which Filipinos turn toward indigeneity and away from their Spanish ties to form revolutionary organizations. Not only does the relationship between María Clara and Ibarra do little to forward the national project as conceived in Latin American countries, but Denise Cruz even goes so far as to argue that the heterosexual romance in *Noli* is satire.[29] Unlike the Latin American novels Sommer describes, which bridge the racial and class differences that Spanish imperialism created, the relationship between Ibarra and María Clara would merely act as a ballast, not a bridge, since both are from the same class and racial background. The relationship with the most potential for national consolidation is that between the creole Ibarra and the Indigenous Elías. This homosocial pairing cements the Filipino elites' relationship to the common people by crossing, rather than reinforcing, class and racial lines.

As Ibarra's relationship with María Clara declines throughout *Noli*, his relationship with Elías strengthens. At the end of the novel, Ibarra is on the run; he chooses to leave María Clara in favor of Elías. As Ibarra explains to his guerrilla mentor, "'you owe your misfortune to my family, twice you've saved my life, and I owe you not only my thanks but the restoration of your fortune. You advise me to live abroad, well, come with me and we can live as brothers. I am an outcast here, too.'"[30] In this miming of the marriage proposal, Ibarra imagines a homosocial future rather than a heterosexual one. By offering Elías brotherhood, Ibarra points to the kind of national consolidation Sommer suggests: Elías, a self-proclaimed indio, would be coupled with Ibarra, an upper-class creole.

Though *Noli* suggests the possibility of lateral, homosocial bonds as the vehicle for national consolidation, this relationship fails, as Elías ultimately refuses to escape with Ibarra because he does not agree with Ibarra's vision for the future, particularly on the role of violence in their political aims. The relationship cannot proceed, and Elías sacrifices himself; he dies by luring the Civil Guard away from Ibarra. That said, the possibility for future revolution is reignited by Ibarra's encounter at the end of the novel with Basilio. Rizal takes up this homosocial relationship more fully in *Fili*, when Basilio and Ibarra meet once again. If in *Noli*, Elías attempts to convert Ibarra to the revolution, in *Fili*, it is Ibarra as Simoun who attempts to mentor and convert Basilio. In other words, Simoun is the guerrilla convert who in turn must convert his own mentee. As Hagimoto notes, Rizal's naming of Simoun is telling as it recalls Simón Bolívar,[31] which "render[s] explicit Rizal's reference to the history of the Latin American revolutions."[32] Hagimoto illuminates how the figure of Simoun creates additional connections between the Philippines and Cuba, noting that Simoun "spends 13 years of exile in Cuba before his trip to the Philippines."[33] He also observes,

> The narrator recounts that Simoun "took part in the war in Cuba, helping one party and then another, but always winning" ("tomó parte en la guerra de Cuba, ayudando ya á un partido ya á otro, pero ganando siempre") (281). Therefore, it is possible to claim that his secret plot for an uprising is linked to Cuba. This reference suggests that the origin of the Filipino struggle against the colonial regime can be found not only in Europe and nearby Asia, but also in the United States and the Caribbean, which is where the reformist Ibarra is transformed into a more radical anticolonialist Simoun. In a way, the novel implies that Cuba could potentially offer a productive setting for Rizal's filibuster. (121, translation Hagimoto's)

In this way, Rizal explicitly references the Latin American independence movements and cements the ties between the parallel struggles for independence in Cuba and the Philippines.

Much like Ibarra's initial resistance to Elías in *Noli*, Basilio refuses Simoun's advances at first, but then joins the revolution after a pivotal event, Juli's death. By converting to the revolutionary cause, Basilio replaces his filial and fraternal bonds with a new filial relationship based on revolutionary genealogies and a new kind of fraternity based on homosocial bonds. He situates his chosen kinship within the framework of his biological one; as he tells Simoun, "'I've been a bad son and a bad brother. I forgot the murder of one and the torturing of the other and God has punished me. What remains is only the will to pay back evil for evil, crime for crime, and violence for violence.'"[34] Basilio has been a bad son because he has forgotten how his mother was driven to madness; he has been a bad brother because he has forgotten the murder of his brother Crispín at the hands of the sextons. Much like Ibarra at the end of *Noli*, Basilio has nothing left to lose. He commits to the violence of Simoun's revolutionary vision and becomes the newest convert to the cause.

Simoun plans to disguise a bomb inside a beautiful lamp, which he will leave at the wedding reception for Paulita Gómez and Juanito Peláez, a couple whose union consolidates power and wealth between two powerful families à la cacique democracy, rather than bridging the gap between the Indigenous and creole populations. The wedding guests, who are all from the elite classes—friars, government officials, and other prominent society members—represent the oppressive class who subjugate the people. By choosing the wedding reception as the location for the bombing, Simoun implicitly critiques the heterosexual romance, which retains power among the elite. However, the plot fails after Basilio explains the plan to his friend Isagani, who throws the lamp into the sea.

Isagani destroys the bomb because of his love for Paulita. His decision reverberates in both novels as heterosexual romances impede revolutionary plots. After all, Ibarra abandons the first revolutionary plot in *Fili* because of María Clara's death. Although love for women seemingly drives the plot of each novel—Simoun for María Clara, Basilio for Julí—by the end of *Noli*, but especially *Fili*, romantic love ultimately fails to demonstrate (or consolidate) love for the people, thus failing to meet the requirements of national allegory. As Father Florentino articulates to Simoun on his deathbed after the latter has poisoned himself to escape the authorities, "'Only love can bring about wondrous things. Only virtue is redemptive! No, if someday our country can be free, it will not be by vice and crime, not by corruption of our children, by cheating some, and buying others. No, redemption supposes virtue, sacrifice, and sacrifice, love!'" (324). In critiquing Ibarra's methods and motivations, Father Florentino reveals how Simoun's love is distorted because it comes at the expense of the people. Ibarra's plan to foment revolution in *Fili* relies on escalating the crisis in the Philippines by further oppressing the poor and disenfranchised; in so doing, Simoun forgets to love the people and, as a result, worsens their conditions.

Tellingly, at the end of *Fili*, Father Florentino invokes the youth who will rise up and fight for independence when he queries, "'Where are you, you children who must embody the vigor of life that had fled from our veins, the purity of ideas that has become stained in our minds and the fire of enthusiasm that has gone out in our hearts? We await you, Oh youth! Come, we await you!'" (326–27). As this call to arms indicates, the most important relationships in Rizal's work are lateral, chosen kinships in which ordinary citizens are converted into revolutionaries. We see this in *Noli*, when Elías educates Ibarra on revolution; we also see it in Simoun's education of Basilio in *Fili*. The national paradigm that emerges from Rizal's novels is based on homosocial bonds that suggest brotherhood and fraternal relationships will win independence and free the Philippines. Yet, each relationship and each revolutionary attempt ultimately fail in Rizal's novels, signaling a failed revolutionary horizon. In *State of War*, Rosca takes up this tradition, but features Anna Villaverde, a female mentee who becomes a guerrilla leader and suggests the possibility of a biological future because Anna has a son whom she intends to raise in a matriarchal tradition. In *Dogeaters*, Hagedorn reimagines a successful queer alternative to the heterosexual romance that also relies on chosen kinship networks. In her version of the guerrilla conversion narrative, as with Rosca, the key to the success of the revolution is the incorporation of the feminine. By taking up Father Florentino's call, Rosca and Hagedorn return to the superseded revolutionary horizon in Rizal to resurrect it. Hagedorn's Daisy and Rosca's Anna create the kind of revolution by propagation that Father Florentino advocates; they produce the youth on whom Father Florentino calls.

Colonial Legacies in *State of War*

In *State of War*, Rosca introduces a cyclical model of time that relies on patriarchal notions of power. Nevertheless, Anna transforms this cycle by offering a matrilineal tradition that commemorates revolutionary history and love in place of the colonial legacy perpetuated by the Marcos regime. Moreover, the love triangle among Anna, Adrian, and Eliza complicates Sedgwick's argument in *Between Men* by offering multiple, shifting objects of desire that open up the possibilities for love and kinship. Rosca fashions this cycle by covering roughly the same time period as *Noli* and *Fili* (the end of the nineteenth century) through the time frame described by *Dogeaters* (1965–83). As Rosca indicates in her comment to *The Monsoon Collection*, her 1983 book in which we first encounter Anna, Eliza, and Colonel Amor, her idea for the novel is deeply tied to her own experiences as a political prisoner in Camp Crame. Simultaneously, *State of War* is also an extended meditation on Philippine history and the events that led up to the Marcos regime. The issues in *State of War* demonstrate palimpsestic layering as Rosca builds upon earlier events to inform the cycle of revolution that occurs in the present of the diegesis. While the nostalgia that permeates such palimpsestic layering can, as Dolores de Manuel remarks, signify a desire to return to a "lost Eden," I extend Manuel's claim to suggest that the project of looking back indicates an attempt to mobilize the present through a fuller knowledge of the past, thus offering an aperture into a revolutionary horizon.[35] Part of this mobilization includes the need to revisit and reshape the most horrifying moments in Philippine history, such as systematic colonial rape committed by the friarocracy, the church officials who ruled the Philippines.

The cyclical notion of time in *State of War* contributes to the novel's peculiar temporality, which critics often remark upon to link this notion of time to postmodernist technique. The novel is broken up into three sections: the Book of Acts, the Book of Numbers, and the Book of Revelations. Importantly, the Book of Numbers section takes us out of the present of the novel and back in time to the late nineteenth century, on the eve of the Philippine Revolution, in much the same way that Sandra Cisneros's *Caramelo* (2002) returns readers to the past before allowing them to continue in the present of the novel. Meanwhile, the Book of Acts and the Book of Revelations sections concern the present of *State of War*, during a festival where revolutionaries intend to plant a bomb and kill the Commander (Ferdinand Marcos). This structure creates a nonlinear relationship to time and history that Myra Mendible reads as resistance to Western conventions and that I read as a puncture in the horizon.[36] As Mendible observes, Rosca "uses repetition and contiguity to establish links between past and present, self and other, contemporary state violence and colonial violation."[37] Rosca plays with cyclical notions of time by emphasizing repetition as well as beginning and ending *State of War* with the festival, the present of the diegesis, which comprises the first and last sections.

In the novel, the three protagonists—the wealthy Adrian Banyaga, the widowed Anna Villaverde, and the well-connected Eliza Hansen—do not know that they are all related to one another, suggesting a kinship network already in place. Critics often read the relationship between the historical elements of the novel and the characters' interrelatedness as symbolic; for instance, Rocio G. Davis argues that the novel revises "centuries of Philippine cultural and imaginative history through the metaphor of familial relations."[38] In this view, because the protagonists are related to one another, we can think of them as an extended family that allegorically represents the Philippines. Significantly, this kinship network stems from a single Capuchin monk who fathers multiple genealogies. Adrian is the great-great-grandson of the monk and an unnamed Indigenous woman, "a brown Venus rising from the waves" (154). Anna is the great-granddaughter of the same monk and Maya de Villaverde. Anna and Eliza share the same grandfather, Hans Zangroniz (who later changes his name to Chris Hansen). Hans was the lover of Mayang Batoyan, Carlos Lucas's wife. Carlos Lucas was the son of Maya and the monk and is the assumed grandfather of Anna, since no one knows about Mayang's affair.

The failure to know personal history contributes to the cyclical notion of time as characters repeat earlier events and dynamics. As the plot progresses, we learn that Anna's dead husband, Manolo Montreal, is actually alive and a traitor to the cause. However, as readers, we should be forewarned of this betrayal, since Manolo's father, Jake, betrayed Luis Carlos, Anna's father, years earlier. As Davis observes, *State of War* implies "that because most of the persons involved are not aware of their history or their bloodlines, they are condemned to repeat the errors of the past."[39] Yet, because the characters never learn of their complex relationships to each other, *State of War* suggests that what is at stake is not refusing to "repeat the errors of the past," but transforming the cycle from one based on the colonial legacy of rape and subjection to a new cycle that inaugurates a revolutionary horizon that celebrates revolutionary kinships.

Revolutionary kinships necessitate a rethinking of conventional forms, including that of the love triangle and, by extension, the guerrilla conversion narrative. More specifically, the relationships among Anna, Adrian, and Eliza upend both Rizal's binary formulation and the formulation of the love triangle Sedgwick describes. Sedgwick examines men who rival each other for the love of a woman; in a simple reversal of this model, we might expect two women fighting for the love of a man. Crucially, *State of War* offers neither; instead, we have a man and a woman who are both in love with the same woman and a man who is potentially in love with both women, multiplying the possibilities for romance. These possibilities are first introduced by Adrian, whose interest in both women demonstrates how his desire overlaps between them. Imagining himself as a prince consort, Adrian remarks upon Eliza and Anna's startling similarity: "Were it not for their color, the two women could have been twins. But where Eliza was of that rare fortuitous sienna skin, accidentally bred by a mingling of Caucasian and Malay blood, Anna was fair, of a golden tint that testified to an indefinable mixing of Chinese, Malay, and other strange bloods. A true child of the Philippine archipelago."[40] As readers, we do not know yet that

Eliza and Anna are related, though their remarkable similarity links them together. Significantly, Eliza's skin is "accidentally bred," as she is the product of Mayang's affair with Hans. Anna, meanwhile, is the "true child of the Philippine archipelago" because her fairness, while it fails to place her particular "mix," suggests a long history of conquest and cultural mixing. Torn between Eliza and Anna, Adrian thinks of them as "two fairy-tale women," "the laughing princess and the princess who could not laugh" (13). Inserting himself into the fairy-tale narrative, he speculates, "If anyone, anywhere in the world, had ever created a story for the two. Or for the three of them—for there was no doubting his own role as fairy-tale prince. Perhaps, the Festival would weave it for them, he told himself wryly" (13). Adrian creates a love triangle between him, Anna, and Eliza. Unlike the triangles described by Sedgwick, Adrian has no male rival; rather, he cannot decide between the two women. For their part, Anna and Eliza do not vie for Adrian's attention, further shifting the terms of the love triangle away from male desire.

Whereas the love triangle Sedgwick describes and the homosocial imaginaries Rizal envisions marginalize the female love object, in *State of War*, women are central. Adrian and Eliza's mutual love for Anna foregrounds the importance of Anna to the plot rather than relegating the female love object to the background, as in *Noli* and *Fili*. Moreover, because Eliza loves Anna, the novel highlights female sexuality as well as relationships between women, two concepts not found in Rizal. As the novel progresses, Anna increasingly becomes the primary revolutionary figure and, as such, the model for revolution and thus, the mentor, in the novel. While Eliza bridges the gap between the homosocial and the homosexual, Anna queers the heterosexual by exceeding the logic of the couple form. Although Anna and Adrian eventually pair off, their relationship is unconventional. They do not marry; in fact, by the end of the novel, they are not together. Adrian is crippled from the explosion that was meant to kill the Commander; Eliza is dead. Yet, Anna continues to be part of multiple couplings on a continuum of romance and friendship. She begins her revolutionary journey with her husband, Manolo Montreal, continues her revolutionary work with the guerrilla leader Ismael Guevarra, has a relationship with Adrian, and ends the novel by running to the mountains with Rafael, Guevarra's lieutenant. By the end of the novel, Anna is unmarried and pregnant. More importantly, she has the mobility to move to the mountains because of her revolutionary couplings—her friendship with Guevarra and her comradeship with Rafael, which demonstrates the importance of lateral kinship networks rather than hierarchical family ties to both revolutionary horizons and the guerrilla conversion narrative.

In the tradition of Elías, Anna becomes a guerrilla who lives in the utopian space of the mountains; additionally, she does what Elías could never do — biologically reproduce a revolutionary. Moreover, Anna decides to raise her son within a matrilineal tradition. Rosca inserts women into the Filipinx imaginary in two ways. First, rather than dispatching Anna to a convent, as Rizal does to María Clara, or have Anna commit suicide because of her disgraced virtue (similar to Julí, who kills herself rather than jeopardize her honor), Rosca creates a strong female character who becomes a guerrilla. Second, Rosca erases the patriarchal legacy of colonization by inaugurating a specifically Indigenous and matrilineal tradition for Anna's son. As Anna comments, her son "would be born here, with the *labuyo*—consort of mediums and priestesses—in attendance" and "that her son would be a great storyteller, in the tradition of the children of priestesses" (382). By situating her son within a tradition of mediums and priestesses, Anna suggests a female line of heritage, if not genealogy (though Ismael will have some of that, too, with Maya as his progenitor). In other words, guerrilla conversion in *State of War* also entails a spiritual conversion. Anna's son inaugurates a lineage that accounts for the strength of women, from his own ancestors to the mediums and priestesses to whom Anna refers.[41] Further, he is free to defy gender expectations and, by operating out of a matrilineal tradition, blend together multiple, gendered traditions. Anna's son begins a new line of men who operate out of a tradition separate from the patriarchal culture established historically by the friarocracy and culturally by Rizal. Anna's son offers the potential for a line of men who can incorporate femininity rather than violently act against it.

In this rare moment of biological reproduction, Rosca hints at a possible future that is represented by Anna's son, Ismael Villaverde Banyaga.[42] As his name suggests, he bridges the link between the two bloodlines founded by the Capuchin monk: the Villaverdes and the Banyagas. In so doing, he "marries" the brown Venus to Maya in an act that effectively cancels out the monk and recuperates the primal scene of the colonial encounter.[43] Importantly, Anna and Adrian's heterosexual romance produces a child who consolidates the family line. This relationship echoes the earlier relationship between Carlos Lucas and Juan Itak, half-brothers (Carlos Lucas is the offspring of Maya and the monk; Juan is the offspring of the brown Venus and the monk) who are unaware of their fraternal relationship and engage in a sexual relationship with one another. Anna transforms the cycle by mirroring an earlier event, with a difference. This difference—the consolidation of the family line—brings together the larger Filipinx family despite the legacy of colonization and rape that threatens the family form.

Through his naming, Ismael also suggests another coupling, that between his two family lines—the Villaverdes and the Banyagas—and the revolutionary after whom he is named, Ismael Guevarra. Anna's decision to join her familial line with Guevarra's suggests that Anna chooses to commemorate her chosen family and, thus, her own revolutionary conversion and history. Anna's naming of her son also participates in the greater proliferation of Ismael Guevarras—pages earlier, we learn, "A fledgling guerrilla group overran and destroyed a military base. The leader, a young man of few words, had named himself after a great man. He called himself Guevarra" (378). An Ismael here, a Guevarra there—what the revolutionaries are doing is keeping their own myth-making alive by reproducing, through naming, the next generation of revolutionaries. Anna's act of naming participates in this same reproductive urge, demonstrating how Anna participates both in biological reproduction and the nonbiological reproduction via mentorship first observed in Rizal.

Unbeknownst to Anna, choosing the name "Ismael" reinforces an earlier historical thread and contributes to the palimpsestic layering of people and events. As a child, the revolutionary Guevarra was saved by Anna's father, Luis Carlos. Before departing, "[Guevarra's] eyes focused on the name tag on Luis Carlos's uniform. He was committing it to memory: Villaverde'" (317). Guevarra owes a debt to the Villaverdes, which he repays by assisting Anna, though he never tells her how her father saved him. Thus, Anna participates in naming structures that link matrilineal with patrilineal lines; however, in addition to offering Ismael a biological genealogy, she also provides him with a revolutionary one. In this way, Ismael consolidates family lines and allows for the possibility of productive heterogeneity through revolutionary struggle rather than the destructive heterogeneity spawned by colonial rape. Although Anna may not know her own family history, she chooses to memorialize her chosen family through her son's naming and incorporates the revolutionary Ismael Guevarra into her family line.

Through this act of naming, Anna solidifies her relationship with Guevarra, reaching into the future while simultaneously relaying her past. At the end of the novel,

> She heard him speak of her father, not knowing who he was; the music and that act of kindness, never forgotten, in the midst of cruelty. They were, Anna thought, ordained to meet each other again and again, through time, reenacting stories of love, of abuse, of kindness, of betrayal. But of kindness above all, which enabled them to survive, which in turn allowed the archipelago to keep on dreaming its history. (380–81)

As her father helped Guevarra, so Guevarra helps and guides Anna. Their destinies intertwined, Anna both names and perpetuates their relationship through her son. Through these acts of kindness—and of mentorship and friendship—the Philippines survives. Moreover, by noting how she and Guevarra are "ordained to meet each other again and again," Anna offers a view of the future that transforms the historical cycle to a revolutionary horizon that relies on guerrilla conversion narrative's chosen kinship networks, networks that, as they persist, will keep the archipelago's dreams alive.

Guerrilla Integration in *Dogeaters*

In *Dogeaters*, Jessica Hagedorn replicates and invokes Rizal's mode of narration by moving among characters and cutting across class lines to demonstrate the interconnectedness of these different social strata, from country clubs to night clubs.[44] Nowhere is this clearer than in the transformation of the beauty queen, Daisy Avila, into a guerrilla queen. Although Daisy is enfolded into the revolutionary plot by her lover, Santos Tirador, *Dogeaters* quickly jettisons the romance plot in favor of a radical queer relationship with the gay hustling DJ, Joey Sands. The two meet coincidentally after a series of events revolving around the assassination of Daisy's father, Senator Domingo Avila, which is modeled on the real-life execution of Benigno "Ninoy" Aquino Jr. in 1983. Initially part of a different plot line, Joey seduces Rainer, a German film director in town for the Manila International Film Festival. At the end of Rainer's trip—and their liaison—Joey witnesses Avila's assassination. The fictional Marcoses, like the real Marcoses who ordered Aquino's death, are behind the murder. They leave the assassination in the hands of the fictional General Nicasio Ledesma, who in turn delegates the task to his protégé, Pepe Carreon. Following this turn of events, the General tortures and interrogates Daisy, who has already renounced her pageant title. She is eventually released and exiled from the Philippines, only to return in secret to live with the guerrillas in the mountains. There, she meets Joey Sands, who finds refuge among the guerrillas after witnessing Senator Avila's murder.

Whereas homosocial mentorship emerges as the generative site of revolutionary reproduction in Rizal, Hagedorn dispenses with the love triangle entirely. Both disenfranchised sexual minorities from radically different social strata, Joey, the queer sex worker, and Daisy, the wealthy single woman, come together not to unify themselves through romance, but to introduce ambiguity and friendship as the foundation for political futures and subsequently, revolutionary horizons. The role of friendship removes love as the ideal relation between men and women and, instead, emphasizes the political value of friendship across gender difference. Moreover, Hagedorn foregrounds the importance of women to the revolution by placing Daisy in the role of mentor rather than mentee. In so doing, Hagedorn locates women within political discourses of friendship, a discourse from which they are often excluded, particularly in Rizal's work.

Daisy's friendship with Joey simultaneously echoes and differentiates itself from the guerrilla conversion narrative found in Rizal. Whereas Rizal excludes the feminine from his mentorship model, Rosca foregrounds the importance of women. However, even in Rosca the mentorship models are led by men; each of Anna's mentors are male guerrillas, for example. Meanwhile, in *Dogeaters*, though Daisy's lover Santos initially mentors her, this mentoring happens offstage. Instead, we see how Daisy mentors Joey in an inversion of the mentorships found in Rosca, which is a completely different model than that offered by Rizal. Before joining the guerrillas, Daisy's role as pageant queen reinforces the "double exclusion" of the feminine from political discourses that Jacques Derrida articulates in *The Politics of Friendship*. Because, according to Derrida, homosocial relationships shape political discourses, the double exclusion of the feminine stems from "the exclusion of friendship between women [and] the exclusion of friendship between a man and a woman."[45] Rather than perpetuate this double exclusion, Hagedorn introduces the feminine and shows Daisy mentoring Joey, which revises Rizal's mentorship model and introduces heterosociality as a politically productive relationship. Although Rosca introduces and centralizes the figure of the revolutionary woman, Hagedorn radically excises romance from the equation entirely. None of the relationships in Hagedorn are successful; romantic failure in this context becomes a means to imagine women as political subjects who are capable of the kind of political friendships implied by notions of "fraternity" and "comradeship."

In Asian American criticism, the consensus is that Daisy and Joey's relationship reinforces heteronormative values. Rachel Lee observes that "once Joey becomes a nationalist hero, his homosexuality also goes 'underground,'"[46] while Stephen Sohn argues that a queer subjectivity is not available to Joey once he is among the guerrillas because of the way in which queerness is closely aligned with the corruption and decadence of the Marcos regime.[47] Because of this connection, Sohn suggestively argues that, as an orphan, Joey "cries out for a strong maternal figure" (330), which he finds in Daisy (332). Discussing the final reference to Joey in the novel—"They are together all the time. She teaches him how to use a gun"[48]—Sohn suggests that the moment "reveals the unique bond that develops between him and Daisy as they drink 'cane liquor' in an act of heterosocial bonding."[49] I extend Sohn's claim by reading Joey and Daisy's relationship as queer, not to suggest a sexual relationship between the two, but to foreground their opposition to the norm.

If we read Daisy and Joey's relationship as outside of the heterosexual couple form and unpack the political possibilities of their friendship, then we can see how the ambiguous relationship between Joey and Daisy allows the novel to step outside the framework of domination and subordination upon which the nationalist romance is predicated and, instead, offers intimacy and kinship horizontally rather than vertically. Further, in operating outside of the nationalist romance, Daisy and Joey illuminate how this model limits revolutionary horizons by focusing on heterosexual coupling. Such a reading departs from Viet Thanh Nguyen's insistence that the productive "perversion" of the nationalist romance allows for the introduction of queerness.[50] Instead, novels like *Noli Me Tangere*, *El Filibusterismo*, *State of War*, and *Dogeaters* reveal that the nationalist romance was perverted at its inception. That is, the couple and family forms already existed in perverse relation to one another because they were founded upon colonial rape and exploitation. Rather than reading queerness in *Dogeaters* as a necessary "perversion" of the nationalist romance that will lead to a sexual revolution, queerness instead offers the possibility of rehabilitating kinships *despite* the perversion of the couple and family forms.

In this context, it is worth recalling, as Sarita See reminds us, that Filipinxs "are structurally queer to the United States" because, like the Philippines, Filipinxs are unincorporated into the United States national imaginary.[51] Importantly, Daisy and Joey's relationship revises this structurally queer relation by offering a queer Filipinx national imaginary based on incorporation and inclusion. Moreover, given the neocolonial turn to sex work around United States' military bases (let us not forget that Joey is the product of one such union), heterosocial relationships are "queer" because they radically oppose the sexual subjugation that undergirds the heterosexual romance, from the sexual economy that dictates Joey's relationship with Rainer to Daisy's rape at the hands of General Nicasio's men. Instead of Joey's sexuality going "underground" once he is among the guerrillas, Joey refuses to participate in an exploitative sexual economy. Hagedorn's guerrilla conversion narrative amplifies the role of sexual subjugation by making it the pivotal event that turns first Daisy (through her rape), then Joey (through his witnessing of Senator Avila's assassination) into guerrillas. In this way, she creates a through-line between the sexual subjugation that undergirds *Noli* and *Fili*—Father Salví's lust for

María Clara and Julí's decision to take her own life rather than succumb to a priest's advances—and the neocolonial sexual exploitation that characterizes the Marcos regime.

The transition from pageant queen to guerrilla queen signals Daisy's transformation from object of romance to political subject. As Mendible cogently observes, Hagedorn frames the Daisy sections of *Dogeaters* around notions of sleep to emphasize the character's political awakening.[52] We are first introduced to Daisy in a chapter titled "Sleeping Beauty"; Daisy's subsequent desire to stay awake stems from "a dawning consciousness, a painful process of political awakening."[53] Daisy's political consciousness is underscored by the Rizal quotation that Hagedorn uses to open the second half of the novel, in which Senator Avila is killed and Daisy is tortured and raped: "The sleep had lasted for centuries, but one day the thunderbolt struck, and in striking, infused life."[54] By recalling Rizal in this context, Hagedorn suggests literature's potential to galvanize a people to action, much in the same way Rizal's novels precipitated the Philippine Revolution. Daisy, then, represents the dawning political consciousness of the Filipinx people.

Like the unnamed Indigenous woman in *State of War*, Daisy's rape exemplifies how the novel demonstrates the need to revisit and work through the violence that attends the legacy of colonization, which General Ledesma epitomizes. Under the fictionalized version of the Marcoses, the General oversees the detentions and interrogations that characterize the Philippines during martial law. The General, like the other orphans and "bastard sons" who populate *Dogeaters*, represents both a threat to the nuclear family and the stability of the nation. The description of Severo Alacran's illegitimate children is illustrative from the viewpoint of his legitimate daughter, Girlie: "Because her father threatens to acknowledge his bastard sons. Because he employs them in menial jobs. Because his bastard sons worship him, love him, plot against him" (19). Severo Alacran's bastard sons reveal the love/hate relationship between illegitimate sons and their powerful fathers: they love him, but they also want to plot against him. Such plots reveal the subversive potential of bastard sons. As described here, the sons are everyday workers—part of the people—but also leverage against an unruly wife. That said, the sons still have the power to overthrow their father, a threat rendered visible by General Ledesma, whose desire for legitimacy propels him to the top of the social ladder, where he assures his position by carrying out the regime's most unseemly acts. And yet, the desire for legitimacy still contains within it the potential for subversion, and it is this instability upon which Filipinx politics are placed.

Daisy's torture uncovers how the General's desire for legitimacy undermines the family and couple forms and attempts to foreclose revolutionary political futures. Significantly, the chapter that describes Daisy's interrogation is titled, "The Famine of Dreams," which suggests how torture threatens political awakening by numbing the mind and inducing a "famine" of dreams or, in the case of revolution, of utopian possibilities. Dreams here limit revolutionary horizons. By this time in the novel, Daisy has run off with the guerrilla leader Santos Tirador, in the process abruptly ending her short-lived marriage to Malcolm Webb, a British banker, without bothering to initiate a divorce. Additionally, Daisy's father, the well-known critic of the Marcos regime, Senator Domingo Avila, has been assassinated for his political views. Daisy's connection to both a guerrilla leader and a prominent critic, along with her own critique of the regime, makes her a prime target for interrogation. During Daisy's interrogation and torture, the *Love Letters* episode, "Diwa" plays in the background. Crucially, while the focus of the scene is actually on the torture, formally the torture resides in the background because it exists as a set of parentheticals to the main "stage" of the chapter, which is the *Love Letters* episode. As Rio, the protagonist of the novel, remarks in the first chapter of *Dogeaters*, "Without fail, someone dies on *Love Letters*. There's always a lesson to be learned, and it's always a painful one. Just like our Tagalog movies, the serial is heavy with pure love, blood debts, luscious revenge, the wisdom of mothers, and the enduring sorrow of Our Blessed Virgin Barbara Villanueva" (12). Given this description of the soap opera, the juxtaposition of "Diwa" with Daisy's interrogation foreshadows the "painful" lesson to come.

The rape reveals how the colonial encounter perverts the heterosexual romance by co-opting the language of chivalry and love. Additionally, because the novel juxtaposes the rape scene with *Love Letters*, *Dogeaters* suggests a perverse kind of moralism at the center of Daisy's torture and rape. If the heterosexual romance and the nuclear family of which it is a part allegorically represent the nation, then Daisy's refusal to subscribe to such national myths is therefore punished by perverting both the romance and family forms. The plot of "Diwa" compares the potentially subversive activities of a man named Ponciano with Daisy's rape. Despite the formal separation between the soap opera and Daisy's narrative, when the man comes for Ponciano, the men come for Daisy. Her rape disturbingly mimics the language of romance and intimacy as one of the men says, "'Lover boy talaga'" (216) as he waits for his turn, the "talaga" (really) heightening the sense that what happens to Daisy is not "really" love; the man is not her "lover boy." This act distorts sexual intimacy and painfully parodies the language of coupledom. With a "lover boy" like this, *Dogeaters* implies, there is no room for romance in the revolution.

Throughout the torture scene, the General emerges as a perverse father figure who distorts the family logic and structure through his torture techniques. He adopts a paternalistic tone by calling Daisy *"hija"* even as he shows her pictures of Santos's torture and references her father, implicitly reminding her that he is behind the assassination. The General's performed civility contributes to his depraved technique as his tone mimics that of a concerned father or uncle. Not only does he act like a father to Daisy in this scene, but he also exhibits fatherly pride in his soldiers, as indicated by his admiration for their ingenuity when it comes to inflicting pain. Further, his relationship to both Daisy and the soldiers demonstrates the twisted logic of the family that the General has created at the detention center. As an illegitimate son himself, the General perpetuates the degeneration of the family form by overseeing the rape of his "daughter" by his "sons." In the final scene of Daisy's torture, the General actively participates in her defiling. He calls her "hija" once more, and, as his men rape her, he

> leans over to whisper in Daisy's ear. He describes the special equipment set up in another room, a smaller room where the General plans to take her after his men are through. "We can finally be alone," the General says. He calls her hija once again, exclaims at her extraordinary beauty. He promises to make her dance. (216)

By speaking to Daisy as she is raped and making her "dance"—itself a perversion of a daughter's debut into society—the General completes Daisy's debasement.

General Ledesma's destruction of the family form additionally manifests in Daisy's miscarriage. Pregnant at the time of her torture, Daisy "is barely showing, and wonders if the General suspects her condition" (215). Santos Tirador is the father of Daisy's child, and she keeps this knowledge hidden even as she "imagines she is not pregnant with Santos's child, that somehow she will steal the General's pistol and open fire on all the men in the room" (215). Even as she pretends she is not pregnant, Daisy is reminded of the father of her child while the General forces her to recognize that he has stolen the possibility of a family from her. In fact, we later learn that Daisy's "unnamed baby girl was born premature and dead" (233), the result no doubt of Daisy's sustained torture and rape. Thus, General Ledesma is responsible for the total annihilation of Daisy's family, from her father to her lover and, finally, her child. If we read the General as an illegitimate son who seeks legitimacy on the national scale by doing the Marcos regime's bidding, then we can also understand how even this type of legitimacy is twisted. Even as his actions are sanctioned by the state, the General still contributes to the destruction of the nuclear family and demonstrates the impossibility of the family form after its perversion through colonial contact and discourse.

The General renders visible the perversion of the family form under the Marcos regime, but Daisy's decision to create a family among the guerrillas suggests a new family form via chosen kinship. This model of the family recalls the process of guerrilla conversion and political awakening seen earlier in Rizal's novels. Daisy, already converted into a revolutionary by her lover, in turn converts Joey Sands into a guerrilla fighter. In doing so, Daisy extends the nonbiological reproduction found in Rizal and Rosca. The utopian space of the jungle, where the guerrillas live, recuperates the primal scene of colonial rape, which, as we saw in *State of War*, is often described in pastoral, romanticized language (the Capuchin monk's desire for "a brown Venus rising from the waves," for example).[55] Daisy and Joey's friendship offers a new model for kinship based on friendship networks rather than the incestuous family networks that persist in cacique democracy.

Joey's ability to recognize Daisy as a mentor and friend pivots on his ability to empathize with the feminine through his mother. Sold to his "uncle"—a known hustler and pimp—for fifty pesos, Joey is the orphan offspring of a sex worker and an African American GI stationed in the Philippines. Growing up with Uncle, Joey first learns to hustle, then to turn tricks. Himself an orphan and a bastard son, Joey recognizes himself in his mother, since they are both "disgraced and abandoned."[56] Through this act of recognition, Joey emerges as a redemptive figure who discovers his absolution among the guerrillas but, more importantly, with Daisy.

Joey and Daisy's friendship links together generations of colonial occupation. Whereas the possible relationship between Elías and Ibarra would have brought together the (pre-colonial) indio and the (Spanish) creole, the friendship between Daisy and Joey links the Filipinx with the neocolonial Filipinx/African American mixed-race figure. Half African American, Joey is "Joey Taboo: my head of tight, kinky curls, my pretty hazel eyes, my sleek brown skin. 'Where's the little GI baby?' [Neil would] ask Andres, if I wasn't around" (72–73). This "little GI baby" is unassimilable into the Filipino national identity because he is linked inextricably with his U.S. parentage. Neil, one of Joey's johns, says, "'HEY, little pretty black boy . . . ain't seen nothing like you since I left Detroit . . .'" (72), which situates Joey within a specifically African American context. However, by incorporating Joey into the guerrilla conversion narrative, Hagedorn demonstrates a Filipinx national imaginary that is capable of absorbing new racial mixtures into the Filipinx identity.

Paradoxically, Joey's uneasy position within the Philippines makes him a synecdoche for the larger Filipino nation. Two paratexts render this relationship visible: the *Jungle Chronicle* quote that precedes the chapter about Joey's mother, "His Mother, the Whore," and the excerpt from McKinley's 1898 address that precedes another chapter on Joey, "Heroin." *Jungle Chronicle* excerpts a section from Jean Mallat's 1846 work *The Philippines*:

> The most inaccessible lairs of these wild mountains are inhabited by a great number of those small Negroes called "Negritoes" whom we spoke about earlier; sometimes they are chased out of their homes, taken prisoners, the youngest among them being chosen to be raised by inhabitants in their homes until the age of reason, in the meantime being used for diverse chores, after which they are set free. One of our friends owned one which he gave to us; he was called Panchote, was not lacking in intelligence and was most of all very mischievous. (41)

The treatment of the "Negritoes" parallels Joey's life with Uncle, as Hagedorn makes clear through the juxtaposition of Mallat's piece with the description of Joey's upbringing in the following chapter. Like the negritos, Uncle takes Joey in at a very young age, where he is forced to earn his keep. Yet, unlike the negritos, Uncle does not set Joey free after he has reached "the age of reason"; rather, Joey continues to be indebted to Uncle. Read in this light, Joey's escape at the end of the novel signifies his freedom and a metaphorical return home, back to the "wild mountains." Although Joey does not return home by tapping into his African American heritage, Joey's mountain hideout suggests that there was always already a place for a "Negrito" like him within Filipino culture and geography. Never able to make it to the United States (despite his repeated attempts to find a john who can take him there), Joey finally locates his blackness within a Filipino imaginary—the mountains—that is often coded as revolutionary and Black. In this way, Joey also demonstrates another site of revolutionary possibility, another horizon.

McKinley's description of the Filipino people echoes Mallat's description of the negritos. McKinley delivers his address to a group of Methodists and describes how, after praying on the Filipino question, he finally received guidance:

> And one night it came to me this way—I don't know how it was, but it came: one, that we could not give them back to Spain—that would be cowardly and dishonorable; two, that we could not turn them over to France or Germany—our commercial rivals in the Orient—that would be bad business and discreditable; three, that we could not

leave them to themselves—they were unfit for self-government—and they would soon have anarchy and misrule over there worse than Spain's was; and four, that there was nothing left for us to do but to take them all, and to educate the Filipinos, and uplift and civilize and Christianize them. (71)

Much like Panchote, the Filipino people are property; in McKinley's address he alone must decide what to do with them. He cannot "give," "turn them over," or "leave them," but must instead "take them all." By seeking to "educate," "uplift," and "Christianize" them, McKinley will help them reach "the age of reason," in Mallat's terms. McKinley's address shares thematic similarities with Mallat's observations. Additionally, both Mallat and McKinley's statements precede Joey's chapters in the novel, indicating how imperialist discourses converge on Joey's subjectivity as a Black Filipinx. Joey synecdochically stands in for the larger Filipinx people across multiple colonizations and occupations, illuminating the geography that brings together the U.S., the Philippines, Latin America, and Africa in a multiracial network of colonial and neocolonial exploitation.

More specifically, Joey's background positions him as a synecdoche for United States' neocolonialism. Even though his narrative shares a structural similarity to General Ledesma's own illegitimate heritage, Joey and the General take two markedly different paths. The General's desire for legitimacy compels him to carry out the regime's most unseemly acts in an attempt to please the "father" of the nation, Ferdinand Marcos. In contrast, Joey emerges as an antidote to the General by sympathizing with his mother, a move that sets him apart from the bastard sons who threaten national cohesion. Instead of working for a corrupt regime to gain legitimacy, Joey chooses to fight for the revolution and, in so doing, converts from an apolitical hustler to a guerrilla who ardently fights to save the Philippines from dictatorship. The nontraditional relationship between Daisy and Joey defines this newfound order; only alternative kinships can create familial connections under a dictatorship that has perverted those family relationships through conjugal rule. Once in the mountains, Daisy and Joey create a new home and, by extension, a new national imaginary that productively revises Rizal's guerrilla conversion narrative to include women and finally incorporate the orphans and bastard sons who were previously unassimilable into the nation.

In *Dogeaters*, rather than simply "speaking back" to Rizal, Hagedorn revises and reinvigorates Rizal's ideas to imagine revolutionary horizons otherwise. Most notably, instead of using women as devices to move the plot forward, she illuminates the effect of empire on women through figures like Zenaida, the dead sex worker abandoned by an American GI who is also Joey's mother, and Daisy, the wealthy woman who decides not only to join the revolution, but to lead it. Most importantly, Daisy and Zenaida reveal the threat and perversion of romance that undergirds the colonial enterprise. The offspring of such encounters, Joey Sands, stands in for the Filipino nation as a whole; no longer "orphan[s] of the Pacific," the guerrilla conversion narrative finally offers a model for incorporation and unity in which the Filipino nation becomes a Filipinx one.

Reading Rizal's novels means reading the guerrilla conversion narrative in media res. Writing on the eve of an imminent revolution, Rizal knew that relationships were already in flux as revolutionaries sought to overthrow the existing social order. And yet, in a sense, guerrilla conversion narratives fail in Rizal: at the end of *Noli*, Elías is dead; at the end of *Fili*, so is Ibarra. These failures happen because the specter of romance still haunts the mentor/mentee relationships found in both novels; generic conventions grip the heart of the guerrilla conversion narrative. Because of this specter, Hagedorn must dispense with romance completely to unite Daisy and Joey. Reading *Dogeaters* via Rizal allows us to imagine kinships beyond the binaristic framework offered by heterosexual romance. With Rizal as her mentor, Hagedorn rejuvenates anti-colonial critique for the neocolony.

Out of Empire

As I have explored throughout this chapter, the heterogeneity of Filipinx American studies provides a model for thinking through many different fractured and ambiguous kinds of relations, both historical and interpersonal. Reading Hagedorn alongside Rizal reveals a queer national imaginary that importantly resists cacique democracy by illustrating how the combination of class, ethnic, and gender differences informs this alternative national imaginary. In Rizal, the shift from Filipino as a class identity to an ethnic one strengthens the national project of unification Ibarra and Elías exemplify. Hagedorn, meanwhile, updates these issues of class and ethnicity by showing how the neocolonial mixed-race subject (and Elías's double), Joey, could be incorporated into the nation through a queer heterosocial framework.

Rizal, Rosca, and Hagedorn illuminate the revolutionary horizons that are made available when we read the Philippines through Latin America, as I have done here. Looking to the Philippines allows us to resurrect other revolutionary imaginaries that the national romance paradigm renders invisible. Reading the Philippines within Latin American and Latinx contexts sheds light on yet another Latinx revolutionary horizon, one that rethinks the terms of kinship outside of the hegemonic frameworks of conjugal rule and cacique democracy and thus other forms of futurity beyond the linear, progressive teleology offered by the national romance model. Latinx revolutionary horizons bring disavowed hemispheric connections, such as the Philippines, to the foreground, illuminating the archipelago as an important site of both revolutionary history and potentiality. Looking at Filipinx and Filipinx American literature allows for a more expansive notion of latinidad built not only on a shared culture, but on shared revolutionary histories and goals. More importantly, such a capacious view of latinidad offers yet another form of Anderson's "deep, horizontal comradeship" in which disappeared relations and chosen kinships inform the connections among Filipinx, Filipinx American, Latin American, and Latinx relationships.

Latinx revolutionary horizons also illuminate generic affinities, as the guerrilla conversion narrative is indebted to the captivity narratives discussed in Chapter 1. Meanwhile the alternative kinship structure Rizal, Hagedorn, and Rosca offer is akin to how Junot Díaz and Julia Alvarez contend with the Trujillo regime's own sexual politics and how these politics inform dictatorial rule through the form of the casa chica, or the second family and home of a Dominican man, installing adultery and promiscuity as the core of Trujillo's regime. Excavating these disappeared affinities as well as the previously unacknowledged tradition of the guerrilla conversion narrative contextualizes and invigorates Rosca's and Hagedorn's work by locating the source of their radical politics. In fact, reading Rizal through Rosca and Hagedorn illustrates modes of relation that are not held captive, as I discussed in Chapter 1. Rather, Rizal and Hagedorn modify the anxiety of conversion in the captivity narrative to a model of conversion as political consciousness. Such a project is constantly shifting; after all, Hagedorn and Rosca promote the social advances that Rizal could not yet imagine, which includes the incorporation of female and queer subjects into the national imaginary. However, the importance of this tradition extends beyond recovery, as Latinx revolutionary horizons show us.

Moreover, each of the novels discussed here—*Noli, Fili, State of War,* and *Dogeaters*—upend our expectations of novelistic endings and subsequently, of revolution. Despite the proliferation of romances in the novels, from Ibarra and María Clara to Anna and Adrian to Daisy and Santos, none of these novels ends with marriage. Each of them features marriage plots and revolutionary plots, but that is all they remain: plots. Although each novel includes a denouement, they imply that more events are forthcoming: Father Florentino calls on the youth of the future; Anna and Daisy fight offstage, in the mountains. We always end in media res with no conclusion in (clear) sight. These novels not only subvert our expectations, they also perform their own resistance to developmental models of progression. Rather, they leave the possibility for revolution within a state of suspension; as a result, they hold out hope for a revolution that is yet to come, a Latinx revolutionary horizon that is not yet here, and encourage the reader to recall what Anderson has elsewhere termed the "specter of comparisons," both between time periods and between novels that revisit similar events. To encourage such a revolution, the novels privilege the guerrilla conversion narrative as a model of nonbiological reproduction.

These guerrilla conversion narratives pivot on the friendship that develops between a revolutionary mentor and mentee. By focusing on these friendships, new political actors come into play as female and queer revolutionaries are incorporated into the revolutionary family. These chosen kinship networks then become a way to imagine a Filipinx nation for the people rather than a Filipinx nation for the elite. In this way, national consolidation still occurs; that said, it does so in a radically different form than that of the heterosexual romance. Although the guerrilla conversion narrative is a nonbiological mode of reproduction, *State of War* allows for the biological reproduction of revolutionaries once the colonial legacy of rape has been transformed into a new cycle that advocates matrilineal lines and the incorporation of femininity into the nation. Heteronormative revolutionary reproduction can only continue once reparations have been made; in other words, queer kinship models of chosen relation also entail the active acknowledgment of complicity and historical responsibility as well as the recognition of the feminine that isn't appropriative. Like Ismael, Joey in *Dogeaters* emerges as a paradigmatic figure who demonstrates how the colonial inheritance of orphans and bastard sons can be recuperated through the recognition rather than the refusal of the feminine. Given that friendship and choice rather than biology form the basis for the family model, Rizal, Rosca, and Hagedorn further suggest that chosen kinship networks offer a way of reclaiming the family form after its perversion by colonization in much the same way that Latinx revolutionary horizons allow us to reclaim the connections between the Philippines and Latin/x America.

I now turn to the Dominican Republic to explore another such literary tradition, the revolutionary bildungsroman. Like the guerrilla conversion narrative, the revolutionary bildungsroman offers another way to examine how forms from seemingly elsewhere engage with a longer history of the Americas and crucially influence U.S. literature. Chapter 3 analyzes yet another model of conversion, this time with an eye toward readers in the U.S. By focusing on narratives of political development, Junot Díaz and Julia Alvarez extend the idea of the guerrilla conversion narrative into a larger hemispheric project that aims to convert the U.S. reader to a broader hemispheric consciousness.

3
Teaching Revolution
The Latinx Bildungsroman in Alvarez and Díaz

In Junot Díaz's *The Brief Wondrous Life of Oscar Wao* (2007),[1] the narrator of the novel, Yunior, frequently admonishes readers for their lack of knowledge in terms of Dominican history. Addressing his readers directly, he offers historical context for those who missed their "mandatory two seconds of Dominican history" (2n1) and nudges the reader by making remarks such as, "Hatüey, in case you've forgotten . . ." (212n23). However, these rebukes are only true for the first reading of the text, as once the reader is familiar with the history detailed in the footnotes, Yunior's sarcastic "in case you've forgotten" becomes a process of remembering after the book is closed. You can't remember what you don't know, Yunior suggests. In acknowledging the historical amnesia that accompanies revolution and visually marking it through the use of explanatory footnotes, Yunior points to the revolutionary consciousness that subtends the novel.[2]

Julia Alvarez's *In the Name of Salomé* (2000) and *Oscar Wao* carefully switch from "schooling" their U.S. readers, as Yunior does here, to placing them in the subject position of Dominicans.[3] Both authors trace how a return to the homeland leads to the development of political consciousness, compelling readers to see how Dominican history is also U.S. history. Although the Dominican Republic is not a homeland for the U.S. reader, this search for origins reveals the U.S.'s entanglement with the so-called periphery. "Schooling" the U.S reader reveals the complicity between dictatorship in the Dominican Republic and U.S. intervention and, by extension, the complicity of U.S. readers.

To write their narratives of political consciousness, Alvarez and Díaz fashion the bildungsroman into a novel of political education that is a genre I have termed the "revolutionary bildungsroman."[4] In focusing on bildung—understood as "formation" or "education"—each author underlines the centrality of revolutionary education to political development. Such a revolutionary bildung traces how the diasporic subject confronts the dual history of colonization and dictatorship of the homeland. Significantly, in also writing for the Dominican diaspora, Alvarez and Díaz teach the forgotten history of their country, a history that Dominican diasporic subjects were never taught in the first place. Bildung emphasizes this process of learning and becoming rather than the "transcendental" model of revolutionary conversion outlined by María Josefina Saldaña-Portillo in revolutionary autobiographical writings, in which the "underdeveloped subject must make the ethical choice to enter development and thereby history, to leave behind a prodigal life in favor of a productive one, with this prodigal life most often thematized negatively as ethnos—as clan, caste, tribe, or extended family."[5] In *Salomé*, Camila, the protagonist of the novel who is the daughter of Salomé Ureña, the famous nineteenth-century Dominican poet whose patriotic poetry called the Dominican Republic's national identity into being, appears to hold a merely nostalgic view of revolution; that said, in revisiting her mother's history—and her mother's role in history—Camila also traces her own revolutionary heritage, which allows her to see herself as the heir to her mother's revolutionary legacy.[6] Given the dearth of material on her mother (very little of her work has been translated into English, and her work in Spanish is hard to come by), I triangulate the work of Alvarez and Díaz with Ureña and the nineteenth century to show how my transhistorical reading method can be applied to contemporary texts, particularly when there are absences in the archive.

Turning to *Oscar Wao*, I examine how the politically unaware subject returns to his origins to enter history, while simultaneously pointing to a recursive historical framework that returns to key events of Rafael Leónidas Trujillo Molina's regime—the Haitian genocide, the rise of the fourteenth of June movement, and the assassination of the Mirabal sisters, to name a few—to unearth the forgotten and invisible histories that underpin empire, modeling the importance of historical excavation to the project of political development for the reader. As these descriptions make clear, revolution and resistance in these novels form the backdrop rather than take center stage. In this way, Alvarez and Díaz ask us to consider how to make a revolutionary legacy not only usable, but also translatable across national borders.

Rather than reading "the curse of Diaspora" as simply another trauma of dictatorial regimes,[7] dispersal and exile necessitate this search for family history and, in the process, the development of political consciousness. That is, to learn their origin stories, the future generations must look to written history and, like Oscar, Yunior, and Camila, experience the process of return to render Latinx revolutionary horizons visible. Yunior's affiliation with Oscar, then Isis, and, potentially, future generations, along with Camila's imagined relationship with her mother, create links across time in a move that offers kinship without the underpinnings of the nation. Instead, the revolutionary bildung of the characters becomes the hemispheric project of Alvarez and Díaz.

In framing the bildungsroman within revolutionary terms, Alvarez and Díaz offer a vital corrective to the European bildungsroman, which Franco Moretti characterizes as a genre that "keep[s] history *at a safe distance*"[8] and features a "withdrawal from political life" (viii). For Moretti, these are both necessary qualities for a genre that, he suggests, attempts "to heal the rupture that had generated (or so it seemed) the French revolution and to imagine a continuity between the old and the new regime" (viii). *Salomé* and *Oscar Wao* collapse such distinctions between history and narrative, the political and the literary. More specifically, both novels refuse the bildungsroman's tendency to manage and contain its counterrevolutionary impulses and instead offer a bildungsroman that splits and synthesizes, thus formalizing the novels' commitment to a progressive future signified by the horizon.[9]

This hemispheric project emphasizes splitting as central to the political project of converting the reader into a revolutionary subject. The split between Camila and Salomé in Alvarez exemplifies the shift from a commitment to a revolution of particular people toward particular ends to a more generalized sense of revolutionary commitment in the Americas. Meanwhile, Díaz models the development of political consciousness through the way that Yunior takes up and completes Oscar's bildungsroman in *Oscar Wao*. Each pairing features the divide between those born in the Dominican Republic (Salomé, Yunior) and those who represent the figure of the Dominican immigrant to the U.S. (Camila, who is "American" in the sense of the Americas, not solely the United States, and Oscar), which emphasizes the hemispheric and diasporic projects of both Alvarez and Díaz.[10] Because these readerly proxies are Dominican-born (Camila, Yunior), and because both texts address themselves to U.S. readers, I suggest that the novels fuse together the two hemispheric perspectives of North and South.[11] In so doing, both authors expose and seam up the hemispheric divide to demonstrate the entangled political and personal histories between the United States and the Dominican Republic.

Both novels offer narratives of emergence through Camila's and Yunior's political development. For example, by focusing on the revolutionary power of education in the nineteenth-century Dominican Republic as well as the twentieth-century United States, Alvarez writes to a hemispheric readership that contextualizes the project of revolutionary education. If Rizal, Rosca, and Hagedorn offer guerrilla conversion novels as models for queer revolutionary kinship, then Alvarez and Díaz offer novels that are themselves guerrilla primers for readers to take the first steps into the political consciousness of latinidad. In Alvarez and Díaz, the revolutionary bildungsroman emerges as a pedagogical project as well as an oppositional one. Both authors shift their focus away from the conversion of characters to the larger project of converting the reader by instantiating proxies for the uninitiated reader within their respective texts. This is how readers are converted into historical agents aware of the web of colonial interconnection and postcolonial imperial culpability. These pedagogical projects reveal themselves through the focus on education in *Salomé* and the addresses to the reader peppered throughout the footnotes of *Oscar Wao*.

The focus on pedagogy in both texts participates in the longer arc of education and revolution in the Dominican Republic. In the nineteenth century, the Puerto Rican intellectual and independista Eugenio María de Hostos created the first normal school in the Dominican Republic. He worked closely with Salomé Ureña and her husband, Francisco Henríquez y Carvajal. Ureña participated closely in Hostos's educational project and established the Santo Domingo Institute for Young Women in 1881. As exemplified by the fact that Hostos Community College is part of the City University of New York (CUNY) education system, Hostos was a part of the late nineteenth-century independence fighters who often organized from New York, a revolutionary coterie that included José Martí and Arturo Schomburg.

An advocate for women's rights and the abolition of slavery, Hostos followed positivist thought.[12] As the work of April Mayes illuminates, even though Hostos's ideas in theory and, to a certain extent, in practice, were forward-thinking, his reliance on positivism limited his revolutionary vision.[13] Mayes explains that Hostosianismo as a political philosophy "gave dominant elites in the Dominican Republic a new identity—as the 'moral vanguard'—charged with protecting social order while pursuing economic development and political modernity. Hostos encapsulated his philosophy in the motto 'Civilisation or Death,' and his principle goal involved cultivating educated elites who would transform their 'backward' societies into modern, liberal, democracies" (350). As Lorgia García Peña reminds us, the focus on civility—often contrasted with barbarism, as in Domingo Sarmiento's novel, *Facundo: Civilization and Barbarism* (1845)—was "the very language of colonial dominance that was used to enslave Black people for nearly three centuries."[14] I discuss the notion of civilization versus barbarism at length in Chapter 5, but for now I would like to point out that Hostos's investment in civilization compromises his liberatory vision, as it is based on the superiority of the elite classes, which is often also a coded form of racial superiority, given that elites in the Dominican Republic were generally lighter.

In taking up the legacy of Salomé Ureña via her daughter Camila, Alvarez depicts the positivist foundation of pedagogical thought in the Dominican Republic as a form of revolutionary pedagogy that Camila exemplifies and that points us toward the kind of Latinx revolutionary horizon I have been tracking so far. More specifically, *Salomé* triangulates the Dominican Republic, Puerto Rico, and Cuba. According to David Vázquez, triangulation offers a useful metaphor for Latinx authors because the triangle "yields coordinates for the unknown position based on the distance from and angle of the other two."[15] While Hostosianismo connected the Dominican Republic and Puerto Rico in the nineteenth century, the angle from the Dominican Republic and Puerto Rico reveals the importance of Cuba in the twentieth century, particularly since Camila ultimately leaves the U.S. to join the Cuban Revolution (1953–59).

By focusing on the complicity of their readers along with their potential for conversion, Alvarez and Díaz show us how Latinx revolutionary horizons also point to the complicity of literature in upholding dictatorial regimes that, in Alvarez, illustrates how the revolutionary poetry of Salomé Ureña quickly became co-opted by the very authoritarian regimes her poetry was meant to write against and, in Díaz, undermines the counter-dictatorial imaginary that Jennifer Harford Vargas advocates, as I will discuss. Alvarez's depiction is particularly important, as, in the figure of Camila, she also writes against the figure of the charismatic leader who is embodied in the form of the dictator and may also be extended to key figures like Hostos. However, as Díaz's carefully crafted persona and his response to the allegations of sexual harassment against him exemplifies, the Latinx canon is often reliant on the charismatic leader model embodied by the author.[16] Where Chapter 2 argues that Latinx revolutionary horizons promote the idea of revolution as about relationality, not ideology per se, this chapter explores how charismatic leadership undermines such forms of revolutionary relationality and the liberatory horizons they make possible.

In what follows, I turn to *Salomé* to illustrate how, in the novel, both Salomé and Camila emerge as fully formed revolutionaries, only to become disenchanted with revolutions themselves, if not the project of revolution. For both Salomé and Camila, education emerges as the true revolution, which underscores how the novel of education transforms into the revolutionary bildungsroman. In *Salomé*, Alvarez privileges the behind-the-scenes work, often conducted by women, that forms the basis on which any revolution is founded.[17] From there, I investigate these tensions in *Oscar Wao* by examining Díaz's revolutionary bildungsroman as Yunior's narrative splits the novel of revolutionary education between himself and Oscar, thus modeling revolutionary conversion. In this way, Alvarez and Díaz track narratives of formation that establish revolutionary subjects whose conversion aligns with the scene of instruction, whether it's in the classroom or on one's own. These models of conversion not only offer paradigms for the reader's own political development, but also emphasize how the revolutionary bildungsroman refuses the predetermined narrative of the dictator novel to offer alternative futurities through an imagined readership. I demonstrate how the political role of the imagined relationships between Salomé and Camila as well as between Yunior and Oscar emphasizes the possibilities of felt kinship and the political awareness it instantiates. The guerrilla conversion narrative and the revolutionary bildungsroman become two sides of the same coin, with Rizal, Rosca, and Hagedorn focusing on political mentorship and Díaz and Alvarez emphasizing the mentee's experience of learning about revolution — and how to be revolutionary.

Revolutionary Legacies

Alvarez makes her suspicion of revolutionary texts the centerpiece of *Salomé*, which exemplifies how Alvarez contends with "the legacy of anticolonialism in order to thematize and think through the role of the contemporary writer in relation to politics."[18] As Dixa Ramírez observes, the choice of Ureña as "an icon of Dominican letters and education" is particularly striking, given that "the ideal patriot" was "a white man."[19] . That said, Ramírez also points out that "the reality of a mixed-race population" meant that "a nonwhite woman such as Ureña could only be considered 'the muse of the nation' among an elite that valued whiteness because Dominican territory had a history of black freedom and colonial neglect" (38). Therefore, even as the Dominican Republic looked to European models of whiteness as a paradigm for the nation and as a way to "explain Dominican difference from Haiti" (38), we can also look to the representation of Ureña within Latinx literature as instantiating a Latinx revolutionary horizon by raising the history of "free nonwhite subjects who comprised the real threat to the colonial order" (18) in the Dominican Republic, as exemplified by el monte, or the mountain, typically seen as the space of "black insurgency and freedom" (18), much like we saw in Chapter 2. As a character in Alvarez's novel, we can also see Salomé as a litmus test against which revolutionary imaginaries are evaluated, particularly as she grapples with how her poetry can be used by both revolutionaries and counterrevolutionaries to show support for very different visions of la patria, which Ramírez points out can mean "homeland, motherland, and fatherland" (49).

Salomé offers the poet's biography in chronological order and follows that of her daughter, Salomé Camila Henríquez Ureña (who goes by Camila), in reverse chronological order. The two stories are woven into alternating chapters, with each chapter bearing the name of one of Ureña's poems, with Salomé's chapter titles in Spanish, and Camila's in English.[20] As Ramírez notes, the order of the chapters follows the same pattern, even as the stories alternate, with the first Salomé chapter named "El ave y el nido" [Bird and Nest] and the final Camila chapter bearing the same name, but in English. Similarly, the first Camila chapter is titled "Light" and is also the name of Salomé's final chapter, but in Spanish.[21] Such a structure reveals how, while we witness Salomé's novel of education, her revolutionary bildungsroman does not reach its peak with revolutionary consciousness, but with education itself. Camila's narrative, on the other hand, begins by depicting her as a staid professor who seeks to join Castro's revolution in Cuba then moves back into the past to demonstrate not only Camila's earlier efforts with revolution, but also how she negotiates the illustrious background of her famous family. In the epilogue, though—and significantly the only place where Camila uses the first-person perspective—we see an older Camila after her thirteen years in revolutionary Cuba.[22] We also see how, though revolution and education were previously distinct eras in Camila's life, they come together at the novel's end.

According to Elena Machado Sáez, in *Salomé*, we have two different pedagogical models, one that focuses on *"how the characters teach"* and another that emphasizes how "the narrative structure employs a contrary mode of *teaching the reader* its comparative vision of history."[23] For Machado Sáez, the novel leans on Paulo Freire's notion of the "banking concept of education" in which students are passive recipients of the knowledge that teachers deposit. Such an approach, for Machado Sáez, means that "the novel assumes that the audience has little knowledge of historical contexts and imagines readers as empty vessels that must be filled with comparative analyses of history. In other words, the novel does not structurally engage the reader as 'coinvestigator' in the project of historical revisionism."[24]

In many ways I agree with Machado Sáez, but I argue that the banking model of education critique only obtains the first time a reader reads *Salomé* (and, as we will see, *Oscar Wao*). The student cannot emerge as a coinvestigator without a baseline of knowledge about the Dominican Republic, which the first reading of the novel offers. Then, in subsequent readings, as Dominican history becomes more of a remembering than a learning, readers become coinvestigators of the text and Dominican history more broadly.

Because we have in Salomé's narrative a sense of revolutionary exhaustion, of what happens when the dreamed-for revolution never arrives, it lends itself to additional readings as the novel reflects on revolutionary failure and the enduring potential of and hope for revolutionary change. While dictators appear in *Salomé*—Pedro Santana, Buenaventura Báez, and Ulises Heureaux, to name a few during her lifetime, and Trujillo and Fulgencio Batista after her death—their dictatorships seem fleeting when compared to the project of revolution and the dream of la patria toward which both Salomé and Camila work. Indeed, even as Camila mentions Trujillo, his role as a dictator is secondary to the U.S.'s role in Dominican politics, as evidenced by Camila's chapter five in the novel, "Love and Yearning," which details the summer of 1923 that her family spent in Washington, D.C., attempting to speak with President Harding regarding her father, Francisco Henríquez y Carvajal (affectionately called "Pancho" and "Papancho" in the novel) and his claim to the Dominican presidency despite the fact that Francisco stepped down after four months so that he would not be a puppet president for the U.S. once they began occupying the country in 1916.[25]

Salomé is about the meaning of la patria; defining la patria, as Alvarez demonstrates, is one way to form a politics because living in a country one does not recognize as one's own renders visible the ideologies that undergird such political imaginaries. The first Salomé chapter begins, "The story of my life starts with the story of my country, as I was born six years after independence, a sickly child, not expected to live. But by the time I was six, I was in better health than my country, for la patria had already suffered eleven changes of government."[26] In this way, Alvarez links the birth and vitality of the country to Salomé's life, which represents the disavowed racial mixture of the Dominican Republic, further underscoring Ramírez's point that despite the privileging of whiteness among elites, the celebration of Ureña as a Dominican icon points to at least a subconscious acknowledgment of the Dominican Republic's broader history on the island.

Part of what *Salomé* examines is what it means to define a nation for a particular class (and, by extension, race) of people over another as the specters of Haitian occupation and of blackness more broadly haunt the novel. For example, Haiti is presented as a threat so strong that it leads to the Dominican Republic once again becoming a Spanish colony, making it the only former Spanish colony to gain its independence and return to colonial status. Of this change, Salomé's father remarks, "'I'd rather be a colony than a cemetery' . . . 'I'd rather be Spanish than Haitian. We are not ready to be a patria yet'" (30). In aligning the cemetery with Haiti, Salomé's father suggests the specter of Haitian violence. Moreover, in claiming that the Dominican Republic is "not ready to be a patria yet," he echoes the U.S.'s framing of "places such as the Dominican Republic as wayward children in need of instruction and also feminiz[ing] them as helpless maidens in need of rescue."[27]

However, Salomé implicitly critiques such a position. Although she does not mention Haiti specifically, her association with independence and blackness suggest that for her the two struggles are intertwined:

> I think of Cuba and Puerto Rico about to fight for their independence, and of the United States just beginning to fight for the independence of its black people, and then I think of my own patria willingly giving up its independence to become a colony again, and I ask myself again, "What is la patria?" What is this notion of a country that will make so many people die for its freedom only to have a whole other set of its people put it back in a ball and chain again?[28]

Of course, this position is clearly narrated from a future perspective as, for example, Cuba would not officially begin their own Wars of Independence until 1868, with the Ten Years' War. That said, framing the United States's Civil War (1861–65) as a struggle "for the independence of its black people" is a generous reading that frames the United States as promoters of black freedom, as though the North weren't just as complicit in enslaving people as the South. By not referencing Haiti as a precursor for a country that successfully fought for both independence and abolition, Salomé's observations point to a telling absence in the text. Yet, at one point she suggests that the idea of the Dominican Republic as a nation has its origins in Haiti. As she relates, "Tía Ana has told me the story of our flag: how during the war of independence from Haiti one of the patriots tore up the Haitian flag and asked his aunt to sew up the scraps in a whole different pattern."[29] In this story, Salomé underscores a former revolutionary future that still informs a possible Latinx revolutionary horizon as, in her telling, the Dominican Republic emerges from the scraps of Haiti even as the Dominican Republic's own history of "black insurgency and freedom" ties the two countries together.[30]

Despite the Dominican Republic's position toward Haiti, it consistently emerges as a site of refuge for Dominican revolutionaries in the novel, pointing to the conflicted nationalisms that emerge in the text. As one of the characters in the novel, Don Eliseo, remarks, "'Soon there will be more Dominican politicians in Haiti than here.'"[31] Read in a certain light, Don Eliseo's remark seems to foretell how Dominicans will have a large diasporic presence, especially in the U.S.—how the formation of what it means to be Dominican will in part be defined by Dominicans abroad. Through his comment, Don Eliseo points to how the Dominican Republic will be theorized as a nation from both within (Salomé) and abroad (Camila), which also illuminates how the nation's own bildung is key in *Salomé*. At the same time, Don Eliseo's comments point to how anti-Haitianism isn't a strong enough ideology to define a nation—a nation has to be defined by what it stands for more than what it is against. If we read Haiti as representing the Dominican Republic's disavowed blackness, then we can also see how in turning to whiteness as a strategy to separate themselves from Haiti, Dominican nationalists point to an ongoing issue in both *Salomé* and *Oscar Wao*, which is the Dominican Republic as a fragmented nation that can never quite cohere into a unified one. Thus, the split bildungsroman textually signals this fracture across both texts, with *Salomé* emerging as the story of a nation in pieces.

Salomé posits a counter-dictatorial imaginary that focuses not on charismatic leadership, but on witnessing, of standing on the edges of history to pass on the story of what happened. For example, rather than a figure of charismatic leadership like Yunior in *Oscar Wao*, Camila has a "habit of erasing herself, of turning herself into the third person, a minor character, the best friend (or daughter!) of the dying first-person hero or heroine. Her mission in life—after the curtain falls—to tell the story of the great ones who have passed on" (8). Camila emerges as both the witness ("the third person, a minor character") and the compiler (who will "tell the story of the great ones who have passed on") of testimonio. I will discuss testimonio as a genre more fully in Chapter 4, but it's important to note the resonances across genres in *Latinx Revolutionary Horizons* as they often blend and bleed into each other.

We can observe the split bildung of the Dominican nation in Ureña's poems "A Mi Patria" ("To My Country") (1874) and "Sombras" ("Shadows") (1881), as well as in Alvarez's translations of these poems. For example, the first stanza of "A la Patria" reads:

> Desgarra, Patria mía, el manto que vilmente,
> sobre tus hombros puso la bárbara crueldad;
> levanta ya del polvo la ensangrentada frente.
> y entona el himno santo de unión y libertad.[32]

Ramírez translates this stanza as follows:

> Tear off, my homeland, the cloak that
> barbaric cruelty placed over your shoulders;
> lift your bloodied forehead from the dust,
> and sing the saintly hymn of union and liberty.[33]

Yet, in *Salomé*, Camila describes teaching "A la Patria" in one of her advanced Spanish classes and one of her students reading the first line, which is markedly different than Ramírez's translation: "Wake from your sleep, my Patria, throw off your shroud" (38).[34] Reading *Salomé* within the context of the nineteenth century uncovers connections that remain absent if we only read the novel alone. By reading Camila's scenes of instruction alongside the history of her mother's revolutionary history and pedagogy, Camila underscores the failed revolutionary pedagogical project promoted by Hostos and, ultimately, Ureña. In teaching her mother's poetry, Camila signals an awakening into political consciousness ("Wake from your sleep, my Patria") that is simultaneously a call to her students. Forced to make analogies of her to them—"Emily Dickinson is to the United States of America as Salomé Ureña is to the Dominican Republic"[35]—Camila attempts to approximate her mother's role in Dominican letters, but such comparisons occlude the revolutionary content of her mother's poetry. Rather, Camila's instruction and the novel as a whole, are an invitation to learn more about Ureña. By only reading the novel, readers miss out on a revolutionary poetry that had the ability to galvanize a people.

What's more, in only reading Alvarez's translations of Ureña's work, readers fail to understand the significance of her decisions as a translator. For example, in Alvarez's translation, "Patria" remains untranslated, suggesting that rather than use the possible translations Ramírez mentions—"homeland, motherland, and fatherland"[36]—Alvarez declines to translate "Patria," as in the original Spanish it contains each of these meanings with all their confusing possibilities—a homeland for a diasporic people, a feminized country in need of masculine leadership, a masculinized country in need of a muse. Moreover, in changing "Tear off" to "Wake from your sleep," Alvarez uses the metaphor of sleep for a lack of political consciousness, as we saw in Chapter 2, where the idea of waking is tied to the idea of becoming politically conscious. Even more telling, Alvarez replaces "cloak" with "shroud," which transforms this piece of clothing into a burial garment, suggesting that throwing off the shroud also means refusing to die and give up the dream of a homeland. Further, the shift from "cloak" to "shroud" emphasizes the secondary meaning of both terms, which is to obscure something. In Alvarez's translation, then, waking is also a way to cast off the scales from one's eyes and see clearly.

By foregrounding the obscuring effects of the shroud that covers the Patria, Alvarez also strengthens the connection between "A la Patria" and "Sombras." While the former is one of her early poems and indicative of the rousing patriotic poetry Ureña was famous for, in *Salomé*, Alvarez positions "Sombras" as a poem that indicates Salomé's disenchantment with la Patria and the ability of her poetry to effect change.[37] As Salomé explains, referring to the dictator Ulises Heureaux (Lilís) and Hostos,

> But I had lost heart in the ability of words to transform us into a patria of brothers and sisters. Hadn't I heard that Lilís himself liked to recite passages of my patriotic poems to his troops before battle? I found myself converted to Hostos's way of thinking. He was right. The last thing our country needed was more poems. We needed schools. We needed to bring up a generation of young people who could think in new ways and stop the cycle of suffering on our island. (187)

Within *Salomé*, "Sombras" marks Salomé's transformation from poet to mother and educator. Salomé's disenchantment with poetry also signals her disenchantment with the idea of the nation. Both are abstract concepts that can be used to serve diametrically different viewpoints. "A la Patria" can be recited by revolutionaries or dictators to rouse their troops. The function of "Sombras" in *Salomé* is to mark the shift in Salomé's politics as well as her belief that the only tangible way to help the nation grow is to educate. The novel therefore ends with her turn to education and away from poetry in the last years of her life. Ureña did continue to write poems, but her output was significantly diminished compared to this earlier period.

In "Mi Pedro" (1896), Ureña aligns her views on revolution with those of education; in fact, she suggests that education *is* the revolution. She imagines the following future for her then adolescent son:

> Mi Pedro no es soldado; no ambiciona
> de César ni Alejandro los laureles;
> si a sus sienes aguarda una corona,
> la hallará del studio en los vergeles.[38]

I translate this as

> My Pedro is not a soldier; he doesn't aspire
> for Cesar's or Alexander's laurels;
> if a crown awaits at his temples,
> you will find his study in the orchard.

Rather than imagining a future in which Pedro is also caught up in the wars and revolutions that plague the Dominican Republic, which is the barbaric cruelty that Ureña implies is its inheritance in "A la Patria," Ureña imagines Pedro's accomplishments as stemming from education. Pedro's study in the orchard suggests that his education is an empirical one that relies on the study of nature rather than the experience of war or even politics. In the next stanza, Ureña writes, "Nunca la Guerra le inspiró sus juegos:/la fuerze del progreso lo domina"[39] ("War never inspires his games:/the force of progress rules over him"). By juxtaposing war with progress, Ureña suggests that they are opposites; thus, the history of wars and revolutions in the Dominican Republic has continually set the country back. Movement forward therefore requires education; otherwise, the Dominican Republic will continue to regress.

By beginning Camila's story toward the end of her life, Alvarez demonstrates a life lived in the service of education. More importantly, she inserts two scenes that suggest Camila is Salomé's rightful heir, not Pedro. In one, Camila is present during the composition of "Mi Pedro" and asks her mother for a poem for her, to which Salomé replies, "'It *is* also for you, but I've already begun it and shown it to your brother, so I'll leave the title as is."[40] Unsatisfied with her mother's answer, ten years later, Camila returns to the poem and "with a pencil, line by line, she had changed all the pronouns and masculine endings—her first poetic endeavor!—so the poem was addressed to her, not Pedro" (120). In this radical act of revision, Camila also imagines herself as a world historical figure—not Cesar or Alexander, but a world historical figure nonetheless—who will also move her country toward the future. In editing Salomé's poem line by line, Camila dramatically changes the author's words such that a poem like "Mi Pedro" becomes a feminist one that imagines a future for Camila that, at the time of writing, was still foreclosed. In rewriting the poem, Camila foreshadows how she will become a critic of "the role of the heroic man of action as leader of the people,"[41] particularly "the anticolonial vision of the intellectual as spokesperson for the people, and the forms of hegemony that this move may reproduce" (151).

Pedro exemplifies such a man, yet when Camila thinks of him, she acknowledges "how high a price he has paid for being the one who received their mother's legacy."[42] That said, she also demonstrates how poor of a steward he has been for that legacy.[43] Pedro insists he is "'defending the last outpost,'" which is "'poetry.'"[44] That said, in terms of Salomé's more personal poetry, "in the posthumous edition of her mother's work, Pedro omitted many of these 'intimate verses.' But these are precisely the poems Camila has been poring over lately, relieved to know that her mother once felt what she is now feeling. *Put out my ardent fire with your kisses! Answer the wild longing in my heart!*" (161, emphasis Alvarez's). In this way, the Pedro of the novel as well as the historical figure continues his father's practice of distorting Salomé's legacy to align with their view of her as the muse of la patria, who is also a woman without a body, who is all voice. When Ureña's poems demonstrate otherwise, such as in her poem "Quejas" ("Complaints") (1879), written about her longing for Francisco, both her husband and Pedro excise these emotions from the historical record.[45]

Denying Salomé a body and, with it, embodied experience, contributes to the simultaneous denial of her blackness. In the novel, we learn that the images that circulate of Salomé are doctored; Camila tells one of her students that her father "'wanted my mother to look like the legend *he* was creating,'"[46] which means making her "'prettier, whiter'" (44) such that "in the posthumous portrait her father commissioned, Salomé is pale, pretty, with a black neck band and a full rosebud mouth, a beautifying and whitening of the Great Salomé, another one of her father's campaigns" (205). As Ramírez observes in her examination of the public images that circulate of Ureña, "the white elite approached Ureña with a kind of racial 'blindness' that prevented them from seeing her blackness, and, as such, allowed for their respect."[47] Pancho's whitening project in *Salomé* (and in real life) makes such blindness unnecessary, as the images ostensibly white Dominicans now see of Ureña present them with a white woman. In depicting Camila as the true heir of Salomé's legacy, Alvarez writes against this whitening.

The first line of *Salomé* describes Camila and emphasizes her blackness, thus demonstrating how the novel will center the embodied experiences of both women: "She stands by the door, a tall, elegant woman with a soft brown color to her skin (southern Italian? a Mediterranean Jew? a light-skinned negro who has been allowed to pass by virtue of her advanced degrees?)" (1).[48] The comments in the parentheticals point to how other people may view Camila and, more importantly, the various attempts they make to classify her from ethnic white categories such as "southern Italian" and "Mediterranean Jew" before considering the possibility that she might be a Black woman, which signals the difference in approaches to race in the U.S. and the Dominican Republic. Ramírez explains how in the latter "looking white meant being white,"[49] while in the U.S. "looking white did not preclude one's belonging within the African American community" (84). Ramírez also points to the Dominican practice of turning to Indigenous heritage to deny blackness: "Many Dominicans recognize that when they use the word *indio*—a practice instituted during the Trujillo regime—they are aware that they are not Indigenous in the same way as other subjects in the Americas and they are also aware that they have African ancestry" (107). In other words, one way that anti-blackness manifests in the Dominican Republic is through an identification with indigeneity. Yet paradoxically such an identification also signals a recognition of their blackness. Such a strategy allows us to reread the parentheticals in the description of Camila as ways that Americans recognize blackness through white ethnic categories, suggesting that the racial strategies in the U.S. and the Dominican Republic may not be as different as they seem.

I have so far focused on Salomé's and Camila's bodies as signifiers of the disavowal of their blackness and, in the case of Salomé, a simultaneous denial of her desires, and I turn now to a discussion of Salomé's voice to underscore its differences with that of the dictatorial voice we will see in *Oscar Wao*. Where Yunior's voice merges with that of the dictator's, Salomé's stands out as distinct through her love for la Patria and the critique of Dominican nationalism that Alvarez describes; more importantly, it especially stands out in relation to her erotic desires. Salomé quickly realizes that this later, more personal voice is one that cannot be co-opted by whatever regime is in power at the moment. As she describes, "With the last few poems, I had begun writing in a voice that came from deep inside me. It was not a public voice. It was my own voice expressing my secret desires."[50] After reading one of these more intimate poems, Pancho says that Salomé is "'singing in a minor key'" (177) and "'that tone of voice is not becoming'" (177). Pancho polices Salomé's sexuality and promotes the singular voice of la patria, a voice that Salomé increasingly writes against.

In the first part of the novel—and therefore the later stages of her life—Camila also focuses on her own desires, though this means articulating her revolutionary hopes, not the same-sex desires she has for her friend Marion.[51] Although her relationship with Marion persists throughout the Camila sections of the novel, we learn from the first Camila chapter that "Something has always been missing between them. She used to blame herself: she was not committed enough to Marion. Now she suspects she was not committed enough to living in this country."[52] Camila reflects on their relationship at the same time that she chooses to go to Cuba after the revolution (1953–59) to help with the post-revolutionary nation. Her lack of commitment to Marion exists alongside her commitment to revolution, as her rejection of Marion, and by extension the U.S., also means a confirmation of her allegiance to the revolutionary project of the Caribbean. When Marion asks her why she wants to go to Cuba, Camila reflects, "She has been afraid she will sound foolish if she explains how just once before her life is over, she would like to give herself completely to something—yes, like her mother" (7). Even though Camila invokes her mother's legacy here, her remarks also implicitly suggest that Marion is not the desire that she would like "to give herself completely to."

More specifically, in contemplating revolution and her relationship with Marion, Camila invokes the subjunctive tense, the tense that describes wishes and desires. The subjunctive is also the tense she emphasizes as her legacy for her students at Vassar College. In contemplating her students, "those young immortals" (2), Camila hopes to leave them with "the Spanish subjunctive filed away in their heads" (2). Camila singles out the Spanish subjunctive because it's a tense that's common in Spanish and rare in English. Within the larger context of revolution and Camila's rejection of the U.S., her embrace of the Spanish subjunctive suggests that her mother tongue is what makes the idea of revolution possible; we might even say that for Camila, a Latinx revolutionary horizon isn't thinkable in English because the language doesn't have the proper tense for articulating such wishes and desires. Thus, Camila's wish for her students—and therefore for the future through the nonbiological reproduction made possible through teaching and mentorship—is that their knowledge of Spanish will also open up the possibilities for futures that are unfathomable in English.

Such a teaching legacy is dramatically different than the one she witnesses during her return to Santo Domingo toward the end of her life. Camila visits Salomé's old neighborhoods, prompting her driver to inquire, "'Who is this Salomé Ureña?' . . . 'I read her name everywhere'" (340). The driver's comments reveal that, despite the various sites and streets named after Ureña, he has never actually learned about her. Moreover, despite seeing her name, he hasn't researched who she is, which foreshadows the subsequent scene in which the positivist method of guiding curiosity has been excised from Dominican pedagogy. The scene takes place at the Instituto de Señoritas, which Ureña opened in 1881, the same year she published "Sombras." As Camila walks the halls of the building, she hears the "din of scolding teachers and girls reciting their lessons" (341), which prompts her to wonder, "What had happened to the positivist method? . . . To young minds asking unsettling questions?" (341). In other words, Camila witnesses how the positivist method, which is grounded in questioning the world around us—Pedro's study in the orchard—has been replaced with the dictée, the scene of instruction that underscores rote learning.

The last scene of *Salomé* features Camila reinscribing her mother's pedagogical method as a way to continue the revolution. Camila visits the cemetery to examine her own grave plot and ensure that her nieces followed her instructions to change the inscription to include her first name—Salomé—on the tombstone. However, because of her cataracts, Camila cannot see where she needs to place her hands to trace the inscription. She meets a boy, José Duarte Gómez Romero, and asks him to help her, only to learn that he cannot read, a fact that she immediately compares to Cuba, where he would be able to read. After the boy guides her hands to the tombstone, she puts her "hand over his. 'Your turn,' I say to him. (My José Duarte in Los Millones!) Together we trace the grooves in the stone, he repeating the name of each letter after me. 'Very good,' I tell him when we have done this several times. 'Now you do it by yourself [sic]'" (353). Camila models how to read the letters for José, then uses guided practice so he can learn to trace and read the letters himself. Finally, she asks him to develop expertise by doing the exercise on his own, which he does, "again and again, until he gets it right" (353). The last act we see Camila perform in the month of her death is one in which she honors her mother's legacy by teaching José to read.

This final scene encapsulates Camila's philosophy of revolution, a philosophy that she shares with her niece Elsa. When Elsa brings up Cuba and states, "'But I don't think Castro is the answer'" (350), Camila replies, "'It was wrong to think that there was an answer in the first place, dear. There are no answers.' . . . 'It's continuing to struggle to create the country we dream of that makes a patria out of the land under our feet. That much I learned from my mother'" (350). Like Salomé's positivist pedagogy, Camila suggests that because there "are no answers," there are only questions, a constant interrogating of what it means to enact revolution. Echoing her earlier comment to her half-brother Rodolfo—"'We have to keep trying to create a patria out of the land where we were born. Even when the experiment fails, especially when the experiment fails'" (342)—Camila emphasizes that "revolution is not the final product . . . but the struggle to get there."[53] While Camila only refers to Fulgencio Batista (the Cuban president whom Castro overthrew) as a dictator and not Castro, her remarks toward Elsa underscore how her vision of revolution does not emerge from the figure of the dictator and his charismatic leadership; her revolutionary philosophy focuses on the people on the ground who work toward the revolutionary project, which for Camila is also a pedagogical project capable of apprehending Latinx revolutionary horizons.

The Revolutionary Bildungsroman

In *Oscar Wao*, Yunior's pedagogical project emerges through what Harford Vargas calls the Latinx dictator novel. Although it bears some resemblance to the Latin American dictator novel, it is also markedly different. For Harford Vargas, Latinx dictator novels create a "counter-dictatorial imaginary, which draws connections between authoritarianism, imperialism, white supremacy, heteropatriarchy, neoliberal capitalism, and border militarization in the Americas."[54] In exposing "a spectrum of authoritarian power in the United States and Latin America" (6), Latinx dictator novels illuminate how "the United States functions like a dictator abroad" (6) despite its "projected image of itself as the exemplary model for democracy in the hemisphere" (6). In this way, rather than viewing dictatorship as a parochial problem that only happens in presumably underdeveloped countries, Latinx dictator novels reveal the United States' complicity in authoritarian regimes and create a learning opportunity for U.S. readers.

As Roberto González Echevarría explains, Latin American dictator novels pivot on the dynamic between those who tell the story and those who write it down. In taking down the dictator's dicta, the scriptor (or secretary) replaces the orality of the dictator.[55] In this dynamic, the secretary becomes "the agent of the text" (77) who "prefigure[s] the real absence of dictator-authors, the coming of the TEXT" (77). For Echevarría, the dictator novel removes authority from the dictator; the scriptor "is the secretary of a voice no longer enthroned" (70) "who reigns, even if he is nothing but a Carnival king" (76–77). A harbinger of the death of the author, the secretary points to the centrality of the written word as in Latin American dictator novels: "The author dies, the dictator is killed, the secretary remains to tell the 'true' story" (71). Significantly, the dictation the secretary takes down is also called a dictée, which is both the act of writing down someone else's speech and a pedagogical exercise, one in which a teacher reads a passage out loud for students to write down. The dictée is also a scene of instruction and, more specifically, a scene of revolutionary instruction that pushes against the rote learning mandated by the dictée exercise. The dictator novel becomes a pedagogical event, not only because it tells a continental story of dictatorships and U.S. complicity, but also because it is an occasion for teaching queer kinship models that are a revolutionary subversion of such dictatorships.

In this section, I explore how *Oscar Wao* modifies the author/scriptor dynamic of the dictator novel by putting this genre in tension with the bildungsroman.[56] Crucially, to shift the bildungsroman away from its counterrevolutionary context in which the typical protagonist becomes assimilated into the middle class, these novels must imagine new forms of kinship rather than follow the romance paradigm. Instead, they create lines of filiation between characters and among readers. While Machado Sáez reads kinship as the queer relationship between Yunior and Oscar,[57] I add that these relationships, including that between Yunior and Oscar, do not occur contemporaneously but rather across time and across generations. The de León and Ureña family histories, after all, are fundamentally a generational view of time.

Díaz portrays the bildungsroman of a revolutionary subject whose process of emergence stands in sharp contrast to the subject of the dictator novel. Much like guerrilla conversion narratives, which spread power outward rather than consolidating it (as in cacique democracy in the Philippines), Díaz's oppositional dictator novel resists the totalizing narrative of dictatorship that emerged from the caudillo system with its emphasis on the cult of personalismo, or the elevation of a local, charismatic leader.[58] While *Oscar Wao* emphasizes the way that Trujillo oppressively haunts the Dominican revolutionary imagination (and the novel itself), it also depicts Trujillo as a minor character and a spectral presence rather than focusing on the dictator as the protagonist, like most dictator novels, as Harford Vargas reminds us. In choosing not to focus on the dictator as narrator or on his dicta, Díaz refuses to portray the dictator's perspective. In so doing, he attempts to evade the risk of sympathizing with the dictator and to maintain his critical distance from dictatorial regimes he has experienced and the ones he depicts in *Oscar Wao*. That said, this is a project that he ultimately fails at because he becomes the dictatorial voice of the novel, thus limiting the revolutionary horizon of *Oscar Wao*.[59]

Like the mentor/mentee relationships in Chapter 2, the author/scriptor relationship creates intimate relationships in which politically developed characters mentor those who are just beginning their own narratives of political consciousness. Díaz, like Alvarez, underscores the importance of education to political development by aligning the revolutionary subject with the act of reading and, more specifically, critical thinking, rather than installing the bourgeois subject into the middle class. The scene of reading becomes the primary scene of revolutionary instruction and alters the traditional association of author with dictator to critique the complicity of narrative with nation by featuring characters such as Yunior and Camila, who stand apart from the narrative and outside of national frameworks, to model the recursive project of political development. Both characters challenge the traditional author/scriptor dynamic described previously. For example, rather than taking down the dictator's dicta, Yunior collects stories from Oscar, his family, and other Dominicans.

Because dictator novels in general and those about Trujillo, specifically, question the absolute history the dictator legislates, critics often read novels such as *Oscar Wao* as texts that resist the totalizing logic of the dictator novel. Harford Vargas, for example, investigates the minorness of the dictator in *Oscar Wao* and explores the hierarchies present within the novel.[60] She argues that the entire book is about narratives of domination (the fukú) and narratives of resistance: the zafa, which Yunior defines as a counter spell and Harford Vargas reads as "dictating as recounting or writing back" (10).[61] In contrast, Machado Sáez draws upon a common preoccupation of dictator novels: the allegorical alignment between the dictator and the author him- or herself, which I will discuss later in this chapter. By examining Yunior's role as the narrator of Oscar's story, she argues against these liberatory readings of the text and instead contends that Yunior "enacts a narrative dictatorship"[62] and, more damningly, that he "charms and entices the reader, especially the academic reader, into becoming complicit with the heteronormative rationale used to police male diasporic identity" (523). We can see this, for example, in Yunior's attempts to make Oscar conform to Dominican ideals of masculinity when they are roommates at Rutgers.[63] These polarizing viewpoints on the novel point to the central tension of *Oscar Wao*: the competition between the bildungsroman and the dictator novel. While both Harford Vargas and Machado Sáez engage with the latter as a form, one to argue for speaking back, the other to point out the genre's tyrannical rule, both critics fail to recognize that the novel is also the story of *Oscar's* political emergence; moreover, Oscar's narrative becomes the foundation for the development of Yunior's political consciousness.

By emphasizing the literariness of his work (for example, the extensive use of footnotes in the novel), Díaz underscores the role of textuality in the formation of the revolutionary subject, thus emphasizing the revolutionary possibilities of the written word. Echevarría further argues that dictator novels remain complicit with a form of middle-class individualism that forecloses any form of collective political identity, even as the death of the author presumably democratically opens up the novel to the *text*, freeing readers from the constraints of intentionality.[64] However, I argue that the revolutionary bildungsroman revises the conservatism of the dictator novel Echevarría describes by imagining a collective political identity through the changing roles of author and scriptor. Moreover, this form of the bildungsroman also liberates the novel of education from a story of incorporation into the nation as a member of the bourgeoisie to a narrative that not only critiques such a trajectory, but also guides the uninitiated reader toward the political consciousness that the authorial figure lacks at the beginning of the narrative.[65]

Díaz's bildungsroman does so by revealing the inability to manage and contain the horrors of dictatorship. Rather than tending toward the unifying compulsion to marry outlined by the bildungsroman, *Oscar Wao* tends toward death as the central turning point that reconciles the competing genres of the novel by operating on a logic of dispersal and exile that pivots on the rupture that the tyrant's downfall creates. That is, even though the European bildungsroman assimilates the individual into the middle class and nation, another form of the bildungsroman that is specifically Latinx emerges as a response to the dictator novel. This novel works outside of the nation paradigm by focusing on diaspora and privileging dispersal rather than consolidation.

Oscar Wao illuminates such an emphasis on dispersal as the novel splits the narrative of education and maturation between Oscar and Yunior and, in so doing, fractures the totality of the dictator novel. Oscar's death signals the narrative divide and secures Yunior's felt sense of kinship and inspires his decision to take on the role of scriptor by investigating Oscar's family history. Oscar's political development begins with his acceptance as an outsider in the United States and ends with his search for his Dominican identity and his de León family history. This is the end point for Oscar's life, and it also becomes the occasion for Yunior to write his story, which is both the story of Oscar's life and the story of Yunior's own growing political consciousness. By excavating the de León family history, Yunior unearths the political history that accompanies it. Additionally, the novel performs its own model of education as Yunior's narrative indoctrinates the reader into the political history of the Dominican Republic and ties it inextricably to personal history. This leads Rune Graulund to suggest that "Díaz charges us, his readers, united across the board in a mutual and never-ending process of incomprehension, not only to become more perceptive but also more accountable; he forces us to take responsibility for our own readings rather than accepting a given version as authentic, official, or true."[66] By relying on the initial "incomprehension" of the reader, Díaz resists the totalizing narrative of the dictator and, according to Graulund, paradoxically *includes* the reader through seemingly exclusionary practices (32) by highlighting "just how specific (exclusive) a reader's expertise must be in order to achieve full cognition of his many esoteric registers."[67] In this model, then, *Oscar Wao* brings the reader into the knowledge of how much they do *not* know, though they are the western U.S. subject *presumed* to know. Further, in focusing on the processes of potential exclusion the novel instantiates, Díaz emphasizes how the process of revolutionary education never ends—there is always more to learn.

Similarly, Díaz opposes the romance as a narrative of inclusion by excising the bildungsroman's romance mandate, which allows the novel to create a narrative of political consciousness. Machado Sáez provocatively argues for reading the relationship between Yunior and Oscar as the suppressed relationship of the national romance that undergirds the novel and results in Yunior's extreme compulsory heterosexuality.[68] That said, I maintain that the supposed culminating romance in Oscar's life—that between him and Ybón—is not so much a strategy Yunior deploys to hide Oscar's queerness as a means to grapple with the novel's anxieties about miscegenation and citizenship following the fukú of diaspora, or what Yunior calls "Trujillo's payback to the pueblo that betrayed him."[69] That is, the heterosexual romance that Yunior narrates between Oscar and Ybón, according to Machado Sáez, allows Yunior to "authenticate" and "initiate" Oscar into "Yunior's community of compulsory heterosexuality," which plays the additional role of repressing Yunior's sexual desire for Oscar.[70] Therefore, while Yunior narrates "a romantic ending of consummated love" (538), I argue that the neat ending Yunior provides is also a way of papering over how the Trujillo regime affected both romantic and familial forms through the ways he coerced the men in his circle to offer up their daughters. Yunior's ending, then, uncovers the instability of romantic desire during the regime because the forced narrative of romantic love Machado Sáez outlines echoes Trujillo's own forced romances.

The family romance the Trujillato creates instantiates one form of this instability, but the two romances (between Beli and the Gangster, and between Oscar and Ybón) that find their denouement in the over-determined space of the cane fields highlights the persistent preoccupation with skin color that underlies the anxiety of romance in the Dominican Republic.[71] Or rather, skin color in *Oscar Wao* reveals the racial mixture that forms the core of Dominican identity, even as miscegenation is officially disavowed.[72] A Cabral, Beli comes from "one of the Cibao's finest families"[73] and "was born black. And not just any kind of black. But *black* black—kongoblack, shangoblack, kaliblack, zapoteblack, rekhablack—and no amount of fancy Dominican racial legerdemain was going to obscure the fact" (248). Beli's blackness exposes the truth of her family line, as the references to the Congo and especially to Shango, an orisha with ties to Santería in the Caribbean, make clear. Further, Beli, who after the death of her family initially lives with relatives until she is sold to a family who cage and pour hot oil on her, leaving a "scar on her back as vast and inconsolable as a sea" (51) recalls Sethe's back in *Beloved*, which heals into the pattern of a chokecherry tree after she is whipped at Sweet Home.[74] Beli's back, with its scars and "shangoblack" skin, renders visible, in material terms, the legacy of slavery in the Caribbean and the U.S. South; in short, the curse of diaspora.[75]

Beli's blackness, which marks her as foreign to the Dominican racial imaginary despite her lineage, extends to her children, Lola and Oscar, who similarly discover how their mixed race makes it difficult for anyone (including themselves) to place them in the racially coded factions of their neighborhood. Lola's straight hair, which makes her "look more Hindu than Dominican,"[76] becomes the object of neighborhood amusement once she transforms into a "punk chick": "The puertorican kids on the block couldn't stop laughing when they saw my hair, they called me Blacula, and the morenos, they didn't know what to say: they just called me devil-bitch. You, devil-bitch, yo, *yo!*" (54). The Puerto Ricans' name for her—Blacula—signifies her punk appearance and, more importantly, her blackness. Meanwhile, the morenos also do not know what to make of this supposed Black girl with her love for Siouxie and the Banshees (54). Signifying whiteness with her straight hair, green eyes, and punk music, but with skin like her mother's, Lola is an anomaly to everyone, including other Dominicans.

Oscar, similarly, fails to signify Dominicanness, a failure that will result in his death at the end of the novel. With a "Puerto Rican afro" (20) and skin that can easily make him "look Haitian" (32), Oscar, according to Yunior, "had none of the Higher Powers of your typical Dominican male, couldn't have pulled a girl if his life depended on it. Couldn't play sports for shit, or dominoes, was beyond uncoordinated, threw a ball like a girl. Had no knack for music or business or dance, no hustle, no rap, no G. And most damning of all: no looks" (19–20). Failing to mark himself as masculine in Dominican terms, Oscar identifies with the outcasts, "the fat, the ugly, the smart, the poor, the dark, the black, the unpopular, the African, the Indian, the Arab, the immigrant, the strange, the femenino, the gay" (264). Oscar's further identification with queerness occurs in his transformation from Oscar de León to Oscar Wao because of his resemblance to "that fat homo Oscar Wilde" (180), a nickname that Oscar eventually answers to, which Machado Sáez reads as his "quiet acceptance of a queer identity."[77] Oscar does not look Dominican but, more significantly, by not acting like a Dominican, he yields to this other identity that marks him as an outsider to his community.

Although Beli, Lola, and Oscar all reveal their mixed identities, Beli and Oscar's beatings in the cane field clearly reinscribe blackness into Dominican political history, though, importantly, at the expense of their Dominicanness. The cane fields signify the Haitian genocide, where Trujillo massacred "Haitians and Haitian-Dominicans and Haitian-looking Dominicans."[78] Beli and Oscar's skin and hair mark them as "Haitian-looking Dominicans," citizens who look foreign. This foreignness, along with the impetus for their beatings (Beli's relationship with the Gangster, Oscar's with Ybón) signals how, in the heterosexual romance, relationships are policed, approved, and condemned along racial lines. Beli's punishment ostensibly stems from the jealousy of the Gangster's wife, a Trujillo, but the real threat is Beli's pregnancy. As the Gangster's wife explains during her confrontation with Beli in the parque central, "It has reached my ears that you've been telling people that you're going to marry him *and* that you're having a child. Well, I'm here to inform you, mi monita, that you will be doing neither" (141). She then tells Beli that she will have an abortion. Such measures—refusing marriage, forcing Beli to abort the baby—run counter to the typical family framework in the Dominican Republic, which allows for both the official family and the casa chica for the second, unofficial family.[79] Yet, the wife insists on Beli's later beating in the cane fields, ensuring that Beli's baby will die.

This fear of mixed children and blackness stems from anxieties about citizenship and belonging. More specifically, Oscar's death in the cane field underscores the centrality of political consciousness to the novel by emphasizing the primacy of citizenship and Dominicanness to the narrative through Oscar's facility with Spanish. While the Trujillato created a unified citizenry based in large part on the homogenization of Dominican identity through its anti-Haitian framework, this question of citizenship arises, with a difference, during Oscar's death speech, which echoes the perejil test, yet another instance of the dictator's ability to exercise power through orality.[80] Taken to the cane field for his affair with Ybón, the capitán's girlfriend, Oscar tells Grod and Grundy (Yunior's names for the capitán's henchmen) "that what they were doing was wrong, that they were going to take a great love out of the world. Love was a rare thing, easily confused with a million other things, and if anybody knew this to be true it was him."[81] Oscar's proclamation of love, coupled with the consummation of his relationship with Ybón, would appear to install the romance plot in the novel. Oscar's relationship with Ybón would represent the union of diaspora as Oscar completes the cycle of exile and return and finds his home in the Dominican Republic.

This, however, is not Oscar's fate. Describing the scene of Oscar's death, Yunior remarks, "The words coming out like they belonged to someone else, his Spanish good for once" (321). Previously unable to speak Spanish well, Oscar fluently explains his commitment to love and, in so doing, linguistically passes as Dominican rather than American. Yet, once he is finished, the capitán's henchmen say, "Listen, we'll let you go if you tell us what *fuego* means in English" (322). Even though this request enacts the form of the perejil test, Oscar's response, "fire," makes this test about content rather than form. The noun "fuego" becomes the verb "fire" in English, which causes Oscar to seal his own fate by effectively dictating his own death.[82]

This is the moment that splits the bildungsroman. Oscar's response to his executioners is followed by Yunior's interjection, "Oscar—,"[83] which collapses the diegesis of Oscar's story with Yunior's extradiegetic narration. This rhetorical metaleptic moment is the only point in the novel where the two diegetic levels converge, signaling the termination of Oscar's search for identity and Yunior's inspiration for developing political consciousness. The em dash that follows Yunior's interjection demonstrates the speechlessness that accompanies the Trujillato as the traumas that became a regular part of the regime continue in the present. Neither Spanish nor English can capture the horror and the anguish of the regime, but Yunior's story, also titled, *The Brief Wondrous Life of Oscar Wao* (285), attempts to fill that silence, that void, with a narrative capable of filling in the space of the em dash.

Yunior's "Oscar—" is a synecdoche for the larger problem of ever knowing the whole story of a dictatorship. By referencing his research and his liberties with the truth, Yunior reveals the lie that undergirds the dictator novel: that the entire story can ever be told.[84] *Oscar Wao*, however, is a story not only about writing, but also about reading: how we read, what we read, and why we read, a point that "emphasizes the role of the reader as the ultimate interpreter of history."[85] Such a reader is the one imagined in the footnotes as, in mimicking the structure of an academic book,[86] the footnotes emphasize *Oscar Wao* as a text that must be read and annotated to be understood. As Harford Vargas reminds us, "The explosive and clandestine power of footnotes is heightened in a dictatorship novel since dictatorship is intent on repressing subversive agency" (54). In fact, it is primarily in the footnotes that the novel gives the historical background of the regime, from the Haitian genocide[87] to the Mirabal Sisters (83n7) and Johnny Abbes García (110n14), head of the secret police. The footnotes also detail a longer history of resistance by discussing Hatüey (212n23), the Taino leader during the Spaniard's "First Genocide in the Dominican Republic," (212n23) and Anacaona, "one of the Founding Mothers of the New World and the most beautiful Indian in the World" (244n29), who also resisted Spanish rule. In this way, revolutionary horizons interrupt the text, like we saw in *Caramelo*, making *Oscar Wao* a history book of sorts, a primer on the foundational resistance of Indigenous peoples as well as the Trujillato and its legacy.

As Yunior resolutely explains the political and historical context of Oscar's story, he also assumes an uninitiated reader who must be taken to task, as I discussed at the beginning of this chapter. The "you" that Yunior addresses is the uninformed reader, while the "mandatory two seconds of Dominican history" critiques the education system's neglect of the Dominican Republic, an admonishment echoed a few pages later when Yunior references the first American occupation from 1916 to 1924 and parenthetically comments, "(You didn't know we were occupied twice in the twentieth century? Don't worry, when you have kids they won't know the U.S. occupied Iraq either)" (19). By comparing the two occupations, Yunior points to a transnational network of forgotten wars and forgotten people. Describing Trujillo as "one of the twentieth century's most infamous dictators" allows Yunior to situate Trujillo among the well-known dictators during a century of endless dictatorship. Readers will no doubt know of Adolf Hitler, Joseph Stalin, Benito Mussolini, and, perhaps, Francisco Franco, but not knowing that Trujillo should be listed among such notorious leaders reveals the U.S. national amnesia that accompanies the so-called periphery. By framing Dominican history as a set of tutorials and reminders, Yunior fills the lacuna of Dominican-U.S. relations and chastises U.S. readers.

Although Yunior critiques readers who do not know their Dominican history, the playboy Yunior of the diegesis differs remarkably from the politically conscious extradiegetic narrator. The latter literally follows in Oscar's footsteps, but the former would rather spend his time womanizing. That said, in the chapter that describes Oscar's suicide attempt, Yunior begins to transition from the character in the diegesis to the narrator of the extradiegesis. Significantly, the chapter's title, "Sentimental Education" (168), alludes to Flaubert's 1869 bildungsroman of the same name, rendering visible the link between the events of this chapter and Yunior's narrative of emergence. In his description of the events that led up to Oscar's suicide attempt and its aftermath, Yunior recalls, "People asked me, Did you see the signs? Did you? Maybe I did and just didn't want to think about it" (188). Yunior, initially more concerned with forcing Oscar to conform to his notions of Dominican masculinity by implementing a workout regimen, becomes a more reflective character whose self-indictment forms the basis for his process of becoming, which culminates in Oscar's death.

Yunior's political consciousness stems from his relationship with Oscar even as Oscar develops his own awareness about the Dominican Republic's history and politics. However, Yunior only briefly remarks upon these scenes of Oscar's growing sense of his ethnic identity. Yunior tells us that Oscar looked for the "full story" but he's "not certain whether he found it either" (243); he mentions that Oscar wanted to read his grandfather's "grimoire" (245), and that Oscar visited his grandfather's grave toward the end (251) as part of his journey. Oscar's lost book is probably his own bildungsroman, his own narrative of his discoveries in the Dominican Republic, first as scriptor, then as author. As Oscar writes, the book "contains everything I've written on this journey. Everything I think you will need. You'll understand when you read my conclusions. (It's the cure to what ails us, he scribbled in the margins. The Cosmo DNA.)" (333). If the bildungsroman tracks the development from innocence to experience, then what Oscar's final letter gives us is the acknowledgment of development, the discovery of "the cure to what ails us" without the accompanying narrative of emergence.

Because of this gap in knowledge, the persistent references to páginas en blanco and the suggestive em dash encourage Yunior to enact Oscar's final journey. To piece together the story, Yunior speaks to "old-timers" (127), has Lola dictate her story (51), and records Beli's narrative (160), thus leaving it to the reader to fill in the gaps.[88] Unable to tell the full story, Yunior retraces Oscar's steps, which invites the reader to do the same, while creating a bildungsroman that describes his own process of becoming pays homage to Oscar's transformation. By telling these stories, Yunior not only uncovers the family history, but also demonstrates the close entanglement between the personal and the political. Oscar's story becomes part of Yunior's primer on the Dominican Republic. We cannot understand the dictatorship, Yunior implies, without examining its roots and ramifications. As Lola reminds us, "You can never run away. Not ever. The only way out is in" (209). To escape the totalizing narrative of the dictatorship and the hegemony of the dictator novel, Yunior must unearth the unofficial histories that undermine the regime and offer a new vision of a progressive future. In short, though the turn to textuality evidenced by Yunior's documentation of the de León's family history underscores the death of the author in Echevarría's terms, it also signals the rise of the reader, embodied in Lola's daughter, Isis.

In a novel full of dead children—Beli's sisters, Jackie and Astrid, Beli's first child, Lola's aborted fetus with Yunior—the narrative installs a nonbiological reproductive model of futurity instantiated by Oscar and Yunior's friendship: Oscar reproduces Yunior and Yunior reproduces Isis, but this model of reproduction pivots on revolutionary education rather than biological reproduction. Instead of relying solely on a reproductive future, *Oscar Wao* ends by imagining a future readership. When Yunior first describes Isis, he writes that she is "[a] little reader, too, if Lola is to be believed" (327), which reinforces her connection with both Oscar, the reader and fanboy, and Yunior, the Watcher.[89] Indeed, Isis represents the new generation of Watchers, as Yunior makes clear in his imagining of a future in which Isis also seeks out her family history. "When it starts getting late," Yunior envisions, "I'll take her down to my basement and open the four refrigerators where I store her tío's books, his games, his manuscript, his comic books, his papers—refrigerators the best proof against fire, against earthquake, against almost anything" (330). Isis, then, holds the promise of a past not forgotten, but preserved, of a paper trail that will eventually lead to the development of her own political consciousness à la Yunior and Oscar. If, as I have argued, *Oscar Wao* is a novel of instruction, then Isis stands in for its broader readership. In this way, the novel stages the classic scene of the bildungsroman—the scene of reading—by imagining the future reader, Isis, and the current reader of the book, the "you" addressed in the footnotes.

Figures of Instruction

In this chapter, my concern has been to show how Díaz and Alvarez revise the bildungsroman toward revolutionary ends by offering models of political development. Crucially, these models do not depend on heterosexual love as the foundation for kinship but, rather, underline the importance of fictive kinships that the author/scriptor dynamic of the dictator novel paradoxically makes possible. Whereas Yunior becomes seduced by the dictatorial voice despite his counter-dictatorial writing, I contend that Camila illustrates how divesting from the charismatic leadership model that guides both dictatorship and authorship is a way to counteract the dictator's seductive voice in favor of an embodied feminist voice that is also the voice of the teacher.

Salomé offers a unique take on the author/scriptor dynamic within the revolutionary bildungsroman because, while we witness Salomé's novel of education, her revolutionary bildungsroman does not reach its peak with revolutionary consciousness, but with education itself. In editing "Mi Pedro" line by line, Camila shows how the scriptor can dramatically change the author's words and inscribe a feminist revolutionary horizon for herself and those who will follow in her footsteps. At the end of the novel, Camila witnesses how the positivist method, which is grounded in questioning the world around us, has been replaced with the dictée, the scene of instruction that aligns pedagogy with the practice of writing down the dictator's dicta.

The multiple endings of *Oscar Wao* reveal how, despite the seeming authority granted him by the dictator's voice, Yunior is incapable of finishing the story. As Ramón Saldívar remarks, *Oscar Wao* contains no less than three distinct endings,[90] which points to the failure of Oscar's relationship with Ybón to offer narrative closure through "the classical plot of the love story" (13). Although Saldívar rightly points to Oscar's failure to be "redeemed by romance" (14), he neglects to fully account for the full potentiality of "utopian desire" (14) in the text, which *does* follow "the heroic story of deferred success" (13), only such success is achieved beyond the text, through the reader's revolutionary instruction. Similarly, Alvarez reveals her own utopian desires as she imagines a future readership as exemplified by Camila's last act of teaching José to read.

As these scenes demonstrate, both authors focus on their imagined readership. Yunior's fantasy of a grown-up Isis who learns her family history through Yunior's story and Oscar's archive models the behavior of the reader of *Oscar Wao* who similarly learns the de León family history. Meanwhile, in *Salomé*, Alvarez begins the novel by instructing her readers how it should be read. As Camila explains to Marion at the end of the prologue, to tell her story she has "'to start with [her] mother, which means at the birth of la patria, since they were both born about the same time.'"[91] When we turn the page and read the first Salomé chapter, Alvarez suggests that Camila has begun her story and is thus the writer of the text we are reading. After making her comment to Marion, Camila notices that "her voice sounds strangely her own and not her own" (8), implying that this moment is her first experience of speaking as a collective for and with her mother.

Although both authors focus on the U.S. reader as the subject of conversion, we must also remember the centrality of the figures that model such narratives of political development as they complicate conventional narratives of hemispheric relations, where one character allegorically represents the North (within the hegemonic sense of the U.S. as representative of "America") and another, the South. Alvarez and Díaz encourage their readers to assume a Dominican perspective, subverting conceptions of development more broadly as U.S readers face their own underdevelopment regarding hemispheric ties. Simultaneously, they are tasked with assuming the southern perspective of already politically developed subjects, such as Yunior, Salomé, and Camila, thus revealing the limited revolutionary horizons of U.S. readers.

Offering scenes of political instruction foregrounds how both authors resist the Global North's tendency to infantilize the Global South by demonstrating the development of characters' political awareness through homegrown literary traditions rather than those offered by the Global North. Further, they do so by refusing the teleological, developmentalist paradigm of the Global North by instantiating a recursive revolutionary bildung that focuses on repetition and return. And yet, while these novels revise, retell, and reread, they do so by creating within the diegesis the goal of the hemispheric project more broadly: to read these stories back into the Dominican Republic and, by extension, into their literary traditions.

In taking on the colonized subject's perspective, U.S. readers gain access to a globalized worldview from which they are typically protected, as they fail to see their direct connection to wars abroad. In his foreword to Franz Fanon's *The Wretched of the Earth*, Homi Bhabha points to the incongruity between a decolonization that aspires to liberation and a globalization governed by the free-market, and asks, "In what way, then, can the once colonized woman or man become figures of instruction for our global century?"[92] Learning more about Ureña, as Camila shows in her Spanish classes, is one way to see such a figure of instruction for our global century, as Ureña saw periods of upheaval in the Dominican Republic even as her revolutionary family became the leaders and historians of a legacy counter to what she envisioned.

Additionally, Alvarez and Díaz suggest that, despite the caution with which hemispheric studies should be approached, the colonized figures in their texts demonstrate how the U.S. reader can ethically and judiciously engage with the Americas more broadly, in large part by recognizing their complicity in U.S. occupations and interventions abroad. In so doing, such a reader can better understand how U.S. globalization depends upon imperialism to maintain the illusion of free markets and democracy. Understanding how their support for U.S. endeavors contributes to oppression elsewhere, U.S readers must at least recognize that not only are they a part of the shared history of war, genocide, and dictatorships in the Americas, but also that if they continue to feign ignorance and not act (because after reading these novels, ignorance is a choice), then they will further implicate themselves with the U.S. policies that lead to the continued instability of governments south of the border.

The importance of instructing a U.S. audience about wars and dictatorships abroad informs *Latinx Revolutionary Horizons* as a whole, as scenes of instruction and mentorship permeate the texts discussed in this project, from the scenes between Joey and Daisy in Chapter 2 to the "seclusions" we see in *Blake; or, the Huts of America*, in Chapter 5. The emphasis on instruction in such works demonstrates how in these texts, revolution emerges as a form of relationality. Readers, mentees, and converts can become historical individuals through resistance, albeit minus the deification implicit in Hegel's notion of "world-historical individuals," because, as Alvarez reminds us in another one of her revolutionary texts, *In the Time of the Butterflies* (1994), such idealized figures portray "the challenge of [the Mirabal sisters'] courage as impossible for us, ordinary men and women."[93]

Yet, while the authors mentioned in the previous two chapters make their revolutionary inheritances explicit, in Chapter 4 we will see how Cristina García's *Monkey Hunting* (2003) relies on a submerged revolutionary genealogy. I suggest that the only cue to this genealogy is through form — *Monkey Hunting* combines both testimonio and neo-slave narrative, which foregrounds how García uses solidarity on the level of form to imagine solidarities among people. Discussions of latinidad all too often pivot on notions of race and ethnicity; however, García illuminates a latinidad based on genealogies of revolutionary history that have the potential to inform the not yet here of Latinx revolutionary horizons.

PART III
Latinx Revolutionary Imaginaries

4
Retconning Revolution
The Solidarity of Form in García, Barnet, and Avellaneda

Cristina García's *Monkey Hunting* (2003) traces the story and legacy of Chen Pan, a Chinese indentured servant who travels from China to Cuba during the nineteenth century.[1] To fill in the biographical and historical details of Chen Pan's life in Cuba, García draws upon Esteban Montejo's testimonio as related in Miguel Barnet's *Biography of a Runaway Slave* (1966).[2] In Barnet's text, Montejo describes hitting an overseer, a move that precipitates his escape: "That's when I picked up a rock and threw it at his head. I know it hit him because he shouted for someone to grab me. But he never saw me again because that day I made it into the woods" (44–45). A similar scene in *Monkey Hunting* occurs when Chen Pan "picked up a sharp stone, aimed carefully, then hurled it at the overseer's temple—the very spot, Chen Pan knew, that if hit correctly would instantly kill a man."[3] In drawing such parallels between Chen Pan and Esteban Montejo, García revises Cuba's revolutionary project. A former enslaved person who fought for Cuban independence in the Spanish-American War (1898), Montejo became a symbol of a more racially inclusive nation after the Cuban Revolution ended in 1959. By tying together a famous escaped slave and a fictional Chinese indentured servant who also escapes, García expands the concept of marronage and imagines a more diverse revolution that acknowledges the contributions of Chinese Cubans in the fight for independence.[4] In fact, according to Manuel Martínez, in so doing García "explod[es] the idea of a binary mestizo Cuban identity, which privileges the white component."[5]

Montejo's narrative was central to that of the Cuban Revolution, which Fidel Castro saw as a 100 Years' War that began with the birth of José Martí in 1853 and continued with Castro's July 1953 attack on the Moncada Barracks in Santiago, culminating in the ousting of dictator Fulgencio Batista in December 1958.[6] In tracking 100 years of Cuban rebellion, Castro linked together the Ten Years' War (1868–78), the Guerra Chiquita (1879–80), and the Cuban War of Independence (1895–98), as well as resistance to U.S. intervention that began with the first U.S. occupation (1898–1902) and was preserved in the Platt Amendment, which among other things retained the U.S.'s right to intervene in Cuban politics as it saw fit. While the Platt Amendment was repealed in 1934, the rise of the U.S.-backed president Fulgencio Batista in 1940 illuminates how, in Castro's view, the Cuban Revolution was an ongoing war of independence from first Spain, then the United States. As Michael J. Bustamante observes, "In many ways, Cuba's history resembled a saga of unfinished business dating to the nineteenth century, a running series of 'what ifs.'" (6).[7] In other words, cubanidad reflects this history of a contested, unresolved relationship with Afro cubanidad exacerbated in the U.S. context by what Antonio López calls "Cuban America's normate whiteness."[8]

Such a normate whiteness stems from the notion that a raceless society would erase the very real differences between Black and white Cubans. During the fight for independence, a rhetoric of racelessness emerged as a way to counter Spanish colonization. As Ada Ferrer observes, "Since the end of the eighteenth century, advocates of colonial rule in Cuba had argued that the preponderance of people of color and the social and economic importance of slavery meant that Cuba could not be a nation."[9] Thus, "by declaring that there were no races and by asserting that racism was an infraction against the nation as a whole, nationalist rhetoric helped defeat Spanish claims about the impossibility of Cuban nationhood" (9). However, as Danielle Pilar Cleland reminds us, such a rhetoric of racelessness had powerful consequences: "What this notion of progressive racelessness truly represents is racism below the surface: the desire to allow racism to live untouched alongside the unequal status quo."[10] In short, although nineteenth-century Cuba advocated a postracial, raceless society that gave way to the ideology of mestizaje,[11] both forms of nationalism were ways of "providing room for Afro Cuban mobility [that] often failed to alter the nation's de facto white privilege" (7). In much the same way that mestizaje holds Indigeneity captive, as we saw in Chapter 1, the concept of racelessness holds blackness captive and, by extension, makes Cuban Asianness unthinkable.

In contrast to such normate whiteness, in *Monkey Hunting*, García critiques the Cuban Revolution, particularly in terms of its claims to inclusivity. She does this by reevaluating the revolution through Montejo via Chen Pan in addition to her depiction of China. Through the figure of Chen Pan, García evaluates Castro's revolutionary history by revealing the lie of racelessness in the nineteenth-century liberation wars (promoted by leaders such as Martí) and exposing the ongoing racial erasures perpetuated by the narratives of the Cuban Revolution, such as the absence of Chinese Cubans from Castro's revolutionary history.[12] Additionally, rather than merely "complicat[ing] the conventional black-white Cuban racial dyad by adding to it her protagonist's Asianness,"[13] through Chen Pan's marriage to the enslaved woman he buys but marries consensually after her liberation, Lucrecia, García "renarrates Cuba's social history as a direct function of the emergence of its nonwhite communities into both political and economic freedom if not full enfranchisement" (221). This allows García to portray the challenges these communities face in asserting their own "agency and self-determination" (221). Central to such assertations are the critiques of communism in *Monkey Hunting*, both through García's discussion of communism in Cuba and her depiction of communist China. In making these revisions to the official Cuban revolutionary history espoused by Castro, I argue that contemporary Latinx authors like García illuminate how such revisions centrally inform Latinx revolutionary horizons, which emerge out of a desire to intentionally revise earlier revolutionary imaginaries to project a more liberatory future.

More specifically, I contend that these revisions engage in retroactive continuity (retconning), which Joshua Clover defines as "an annealing of logical fissures in a given backstory after they have cracked open into system-threatening incoherence in the present and, further, threaten the ongoing or futural narrative."[14] For Clover, retconning "rescue[s] the present, which can now be rerendered with a continuous surface" (14).[15] I build on Clover's definition to contend that retconning is a reading methodology we can use as a way to render explicit the formation of history as ideology while tracking how historical events could have been otherwise. At stake in reading *Monkey Hunting* as a form of retconning specifically is an examination of the futures that her revisions to Castro's revolutionary history make available, particularly since a central concern of retconning is the effect of the present on the past. Earlier theories of retconning conceptualized it as "'history flow[ing] fundamentally from the future into the past, [such] that the future is not basically a product of the past.'"[16] Such a conceptualization of temporality has important implications for thinking about how revolutionaries themselves exercise forms of retconning, such as when Castro co-opts the nineteenth-century wars of independence in Cuba to trace an uninterrupted freedom struggle. Nevertheless, Latinx revolutionary horizons ask us to look for the alternative narratives of struggle that authors such as García trace in their work. Even more importantly, García directs us to the continuity errors that necessitate retconning in the first place, rather than relying on the ways that Cuba "conjures the specter of coherence and even coterminousness among national, cultural, and historical registers of whatever one wants to qualify as 'Cuban.'"[17] Rather than engaging in the kind of retconning that solely seeks to seam up continuity errors and offer coherence, García underscores how continuity errors are central to understanding not only how history is constructed and narrativized, but also how such errors direct us toward Latinx revolutionary horizons that were previously obscured by official state narratives of revolution.[18]

Significantly, to do so, García joins together two anti-colonial genres, the slave narrative and testimonio.[19] As Charles T. Davis and Henry Louis Gates Jr. suggest, the two genres are closely intertwined, given that their definition for slave narratives (or the slave's narrative, to use their term) is "the written and dictated testimonies of the enslavement of black human beings," which they have periodized as "those *written* works published before 1865."[20] Davis and Gates justify their decision by arguing that "once slavery was formally abolished, no need existed for the slave to *write* himself into the human community through the action of first-person narration" (xiii). Meanwhile, according to John Beverley, testimonio is a printed form "told in the first person by a narrator who is also the real protagonist or witness of events he or she recounts."[21] Curiously, for Beverley, as I discuss later, slave narratives do not count as testimonios—even when a prominent testimonio like Montejo's is also a slave narrative—though critics such as Rosemary Feal have pointed to the connections between the two genres.[22] Like slave narratives in which the formerly enslaved person does not write their own account, testimonios are often told to a compiler (in the case of slave narratives, an amanuensis), who transcribes and often organizes and edits the narrative.

García blurs the somewhat arbitrary distinction between slave narrative and testimonio in *Monkey Hunting* by using Montejo's testimonio as the basis for her neo-slave narrative, illuminating how distinctly American genres like these can map the racial crossings that have shaped latinidad since Spanish colonialism. By using the form of the neo-slave narrative, "those novels that literally assume the voice of the fugitive slave and employ while deviating from the formal conventions of the antebellum slave narrative,"[23] García reorients this genre as an African diasporic one to a form central to the Americas more broadly by drawing together the literary conventions of testimonio and slave narrative. Looking at these forms together illuminates their similarities, such as how the two genres share political goals in addition to formal features: for example, their role in bearing witness to atrocities, the authorizing hand of compilers and editors, and the ultimate goal of liberation. García connects these two genres through the figure of Chen Pan, who occupies a space outside of what might typically be seen as distinctive Black and Latin American (read: mestizx) experiences. In this way, García expands Latinx revolutionary horizons by resurrecting the forgotten histories and lineages of Cuban revolutions and by being attuned to Asian Cuban histories.

In drawing upon Montejo as a source for her work, García underscores forms of solidarity across literary traditions to demonstrate the interconnected literary and political histories that draw people together. While Chinese indentured servants were meant to alleviate the fear of revolution, García's deployment of Barnet's *Biography* sheds light on the revolutionary potential of this population.[24] Using scenes and moments in Montejo's narrative to write Chen Pan's life story allows García to highlight how *Biography* is a literary ancestor for *Monkey Hunting*. We can even read Montejo as an ancestor of sorts for Chen Pan, as he is the predecessor who sets the stage for Chen Pan's narrative. In this way, García expands the limits of cubanidad and offers a model for latinidad that we see in what Norma Alarcón calls identity-in-difference, which José Estaban Muñoz usefully glosses as "the structuring role of difference as the underlying concept in a group's mapping of collective identity."[25] In retconning Montejo's narrative, García underscores how multiple forms of difference infuse the collective identity of latinidad. In examining testimonio and slave narrative, then, I also analyze the forms such differences take in the hope of illustrating how they mutually inflect one another outside of a dialectical relationship that must necessarily operate based on opposition.

Following my discussion of *Monkey Hunting*, I turn to Gertrudis Gómez de Avellaneda's *Sab* (1841) to examine how the idea of retconning can inform and influence our understanding of nineteenth-century texts.[26] Rather than following a genealogical model in which Avellaneda initiates an innovation in genre that García then takes up, I suggest that we read García as initiating such an innovation, which then allows us to read Avellaneda as participating in a narrative strategy that was more progressive than she herself could have intended or imagined. While a figure like María Amparo Ruiz de Burton accidentally theorizes a revolutionary imaginary by pointing to the expansiveness of Latinx racial identities—which is a revolutionary imaginary we can only apprehend retroactively—Avellaneda also accidentally participates in creating revolutionary possibilities, albeit ones that only emerge within the longer legacy of abolition and revolution in Cuba. The role of the accidental is central here, as it illuminates how, in imagining a more liberatory world for Cuban women with *Sab* as a proxy for their plight, Avellaneda unconsciously suggests that the fates of both Cuban women and enslaved people on the island are tied together such that the liberation of one group cannot be thought without the other.

Even though Avellaneda's use of testimonio and slave narrative initially seems to lack liberatory potential, García allows us to retroactively see a Latinx revolutionary horizon in *Sab*. Although *Sab* is typically read as a novel in which Avellaneda seemingly testifies to her experience as a woman through the figure of an enslaved man, Sab, I contend that Avellaneda instead bears witness to the plight of the enslaved and uses her own autobiographical details to render Sab legible to her audience, which retroactively illuminates her radical vision of liberation. Much like Chen Pan revises Montejo's biography toward more liberatory ends, Sab revises Avellaneda's autobiography.

By analyzing the relationship between Avellaneda and Sab, I consider how the novel acts as Avellaneda's testimonio as a woman and colonial subject recast through the figure of the slave via the slave narrative. In so doing, I consider the political stakes of reading Sab's slave narrative as Avellaneda's testimonio, particularly in light of Cuba's colonial relationship with Spain at the time. By examining Sab and testimonio within a Latinx literary tradition that extends into García's work, I demonstrate how the novel can incorporate testimonio as an affirming, rather than hegemonic, act within a broader hemispheric context.

I demonstrate how such fictionalized testimonios can powerfully bear witness to injustices and atrocities in the present, especially for marginalized groups who are either absent or sidelined from both realist treatments and what Emma Pérez calls "normative historiographies." Focusing on fiction also allows me to take up Jennifer Harford Vargas's useful correction to Beverley. In Harford Vargas's formulation, rather than seeking to demarcate the boundaries of testimonio, we should keep in mind the ideological function of the genre, which is to examine systems of power and domination. With this idea in mind, we can focus on "how other narrative modes (such as fiction), other forms of witnessing (such as second- or third-hand hearsay), and other sites (such as the body) produce testimony."[27] Acts of retconning contribute to a theory of the "x" in "Latinx" as an invitation to create our own histories and genealogies rather than rely on normative historiographies or on nonfictional modes to produce testimonio. Ultimately, I argue that the Latinx revolutionary horizons that emerge through such retcons allow contemporary Latinx literature to testify to the controversial aspects of the past that continue to haunt the present and that current regimes would prefer to gloss over.

Textual Solidarities

Barnet opens the Spanish introduction to *Biografía* by outlining how he met Esteban Montejo: in 1963, he came across a newspaper article that highlighted people older than 100 years old and contained an interview with Montejo, who talked about living through slavery, the War of Independence, and his life as a runaway slave, or un cimarrón.[28] In both the Spanish and English introductions to Montejo's testimonio, Barnet outlines his own interest in Montejo's life story. Yet, in examining the differences between the two, William Luis highlights the role that Montejo's testimonio is made to serve both in the historiography around the Cuban Revolution and, subsequently, in the revolution's narrative of Cuban history. Both Luis and Michael Zeuske, for example, have focused on Barnet's decision to end *Biography* in 1905, with the death of General Máximo Gómez, rather than explore Montejo's life during the republic's rocky start, Fulgencio Batista's dictatorship (1952–59), and the Cuban Revolution. Luis goes so far as to suggest that "the allusion to Cuban politics, in the Spanish introduction, may be a personal statement reflecting, not Montejo's but, Barnet's standing within the Revolution,"[29] arguing that Barnet, "like Montejo, was also reflecting a certain political reality imposed upon him by the Cuban Revolution" (483). Luis gives the impression that, given Barnet's previous ties to North America (484) and his affiliation with the disgraced El Puente group (485), he "seized upon the story of Montejo as an opportunity to resume a public literary life" (485). In his examination of the fusing of Barnet and Montejo, Luis wonders whether the Montejo of *Biography* who talks of being silenced after the War of Independence is also "Barnet, hiding behind Montejo's voice, who really wants to come out and tell the whole story, but knows that it will not be possible to do so after experiencing censorship during the early years of the Revolution? Does Barnet's writing point to a form of self censorship in Revolutionary Cuba?" (490).

In addition to the ways that Luis seeks to read the political conditions under which *Biography* was published and Barnet established his reputation, of crucial importance for both Luis and Zeuske is the virtual absence of any mention of the Race War of 1912, in which Afro Cuban veterans of the Spanish-American War led a revolt to protest their continued disenfranchisement and were subsequently massacred by the thousands. Reflecting on possible reasons that *Biography* ends in 1905 and makes no mention of the Race War of 1912, in *Literary Bondage: Slavery in Cuban Narrative* (1990), Luis suggests that doing so is incompatible with the revolutionary project of the Cuban Revolution. Whereas the Ten Years' War and the Spanish-American War dealt with foreign powers (Spain and the United States), Luis points out that the Race War of 1912 "was a campaign of Cubans against other Cubans sufficient to discourage any black movement for many decades" (215). In refusing to include the Race War of 1912, Luis asserts that "Barnet leaves us with the impression that, at least from Montejo's point of view, Cuban problems were foreign-related" (215). In discussing the Ten Years' War in his English introduction to *Biography*, Barnet, according to Luis, illustrates how the Cuban "Revolution accomplished what the Ten Years' War and Spanish-Cuban-American War set out to do, that is, to liberate Cuba from Western domination"[30]; discussing the Race War of 1912 is at odds with this narrative of liberation.[31]

I detail this background to highlight the centrality of Montejo's testimonio to Cuban revolutionary history. Abraham Acosta, speaking of testimonio more broadly, even goes so far as to say that "the Cuban Revolution needs testimonio in order to justify itself; it needs to bring back the image or specter of subalternity in order to assert that subalternity no longer exists."[32] In his examination of Barnet's writing on testimonio specifically, Acosta argues that "what testimonio does is consolidate the de-subalternized, emancipated subject within a nationalist form" (138), which means that "testimonio ultimately has more at stake in constituting hegemonic national culture and identity than as a subaltern (antiliterary) narratology" (138). In retconning Montejo's testimonio into Chen Pan's, I suggest that García evacuates testimonio of its potential complicity with nationalism, particularly since the novel is ambivalent about any form of nationalism. As Marta Caminero-Santangelo argues, "In García's telling, *any* form of nationalist consolidation—whether formulated around whiteness, antiforeignness, or hybridity—is the potential foundation of violence."[33]

Acosta and Caminero-Santangelo point to the stakes of García's retconning of Montejo's testimonio in *Monkey Hunting*, particularly given the pride of place *Biografía* has in the history of the Cuban Revolution. While retconning as a project is typically understood as creating continuity out of discontinuity, I argue that García's retconning illuminates the discontinuities that underlie the Cuban revolutionary project under Castro. Although Black and Indigenous Latinxs often bear the burden of representing a more inclusive latinidad, Chen Pan's position in the text exemplifies the limits of the logic of inclusion by pushing against the boundaries that restrict Latinx revolutionary horizons and, in doing so, expands them. To do this work, García often turns to speculative modes such as the supernatural as a way of using the future to flow into a past that stands in marked contrast to that offered by Castro's revolutionary history. In this way, García's retconning epitomizes her commitment to a racially expansive vision of the Latinx in Latinx revolutionary horizons, where the "x" marks the speculative potential of latinidad.

Monkey Hunting is a multi-generational novel that centers on Chen Pan and his family. Once in Cuba and purchased by an enslaver, Chen Pan realizes that he was tricked and that he is actually an enslaved person, as his enslaver has no intention of releasing him after his eight-year term. Because he works on the La Amada Plantation (translation: the beloved plantation) we can hear an echo of Toni Morrison's *Beloved* and imagine an affinity between the two texts, with their shared interest in slavery and the ghosts that haunt the present.[34] Chen Pan cuts sugarcane for three years before he escapes. After marrying Lucrecia, he has three children with her. The novel focuses on the family line through their second son, Lorenzo, whose progeny traverse a range of locations, including China, New York, and Vietnam.

Focusing on a Chinese indentured worker and his family is a significant change to Montejo's testimonio, as in so doing García revises the anti-Chinese sentiment found mostly in the translation of *Biography*. For example, in a section of the original, the text reads, speaking of a game everyone played, "menos los chinos, que eran muy *separatistas* [except for the Chinese, who were very separatist]."[35] The English translation replaces "separatist" with "standoffish,"[36] which, while it may make sense within the context of that section where Montejo describes a couple social events in which the Chinese workers didn't participate, Montejo's later comments in the Spanish original that "no creían en nadie los chinos. Eran rebeldes de nacimiento [the Chinese didn't trust anyone. They were rebels from birth]" suggests that the word "separatista," which is italicized and thus emphasized in the original, could very well speak to a political position rather than a social one.[37]

Along similar lines, in a section where the original describes Montejo's experiences going to a Chinese theater, the paragraph ends, "Lo más fino que había en Cuba eran los chinos. Ellos lo hacían todo con reverencias y en silencio. Y eran muy organizados [The finest thing in Cuba were the Chinese. They did everything respectfully and in silence. And they were very organized]" (72). The English translation ends with "They did everything silent and bowing,"[38] which gives a sense that the Chinese are obedient; moreover, in excluding the sentence about how they were very organized, the English translation misses the segue to the following paragraph, which in both versions describes Chinese social clubs. In these clubs, we learn that it was a place where the Chinese "se reunían y conversaban en sus idiomas y leían los periódicos de China en alta voz. A lo major lo hacían para joder, pero como nadie los entendía, ellos seguían en sus lecturas como si nada [met and talked in their language and read Chinese newspapers aloud. Maybe they did it to fuck with us, but since no one understood them, they continued their reading as if nothing had happened]."[39] Instead of fucking with the non-Chinese people around them, the English translation reads, "They probably did it to be annoying,"[40] which takes away the playful element that joder—to fuck with—also implies.

These moments speak to the stakes of retconning Montejo's testimonio, especially the version that circulates for English-speaking audiences, as they are left with a text that is much more anti-Chinese than the original, a tension that García seeks to resolve in *Monkey Hunting*. That said, there are also several moments in which García has Chen Pan signify on specific scenes in Montejo's narrative, moments that aren't imbued with the anti-Chinese sentiment found in the previous examples. For instance, Montejo comments that the Chinese play "a game they called the button" (89), which is a moment that arises when we learn that Chen Pan was able to open his shop, the Lucky Find, "with the count's support and the money [he] won playing *botón*."[41] Such offhand references to Chinese Cubans, no matter how small, allow García to take up and revise Montejo's testimonio to carve out a space for a latinidad that can speak to a range of identities, a space that Latinx revolutionary horizons make visible through such retcons and resonances.

In one of García's revisions that's similar to the same moment in *Biography*, she takes up Montejo's superstitions about Chinese people, in which Montejo says, "I know the Chinese hypnotized their audiences. They've always had that ability. It's the foundation of the Chinese religion."[42] Echoing this scene, in the final section of *Monkey Hunting*, Chen Pan walks through Chinatown, where "he overheard one criollo commenting on the Oriental's hypnotizing skills. *It's part of their religion, more dangerous than the Haitians' voodoo. If you look them straight in the eyes, you're doomed.*"[43] Here, García places Montejo's claims into the mouth of a criollo, or a white Cuban. The term "Oriental" may be here for historical accuracy, but more importantly, it signals the Orientalizing discourse of white Cubans and their anxieties about both "Chinese religion" and Haitian voodoo, demonstrating that although Montejo may think nothing of hypnosis given his own supernatural beliefs, for white Cubans, both belief systems are a potential threat to the very systems that place them at the top of the racial hierarchy.

In this way, *Monkey Hunting* allows us to imagine a more liberatory future that depends on a past that emphasizes shared methods of resistance rather than unbridgeable differences. These connections also illuminate another form of affinity between Chinese Cubans and the broader Black diaspora in the Caribbean to emphasize their shared struggles. As Yu-Fang Cho argues,

"García's ambitious undertaking probes how the histories of 'Chino Latinos' and their ambiguous, shifting multi-racial identities problematize artificial racial categories—presumed to be intrinsically attached to particular geographical locations and nations—that Euro-American colonial knowledge produces and naturalizes."[44] By underscoring the artificiality of such racial categories, García also shows how Castro's revolutionary state co-opts Montejo's narrative while seemingly promoting anti-racism. Moreover, in signaling the discontinuity of Chinese Cubans in Castro's revolutionary history, she also emphasizes how centering the experiences of Chinese Cubans within this revolutionary history causes a rupture through which Latinx revolutionary horizons emerge.

García's own genealogical retconning reveals itself through the additional ways that she uses details from Montejo's escape to imbue Chen Pan's marronage, specifically within the context of African beliefs.[45] In addition to the scene with the overseer and the rock, she echoes Montejo's experience living in a cave covered with bat dung for a year and a half after his escape from the plantation. Yet, though Montejo finds in the cave a refuge, Chen Pan initially perceives the cave as a coffin: "So Chen Pan arranged a bed of cobwebs and silvery leaves on the bat guano that cushioned the floor of a limestone cave, smeared pollen on his face and hands. He would die there, leave his bones to crumble. He would die there in that nowhere cave, and then his ghost would fly home to China."[46] In flying home after death, Chen Pan's plan recalls the myth of the flying African, which Michelle Commander describes as outlined in folktales that "chronicle a group of Africans who, upon setting foot in the West, took a look around at the landscape and their imprisoned selves, and ascended into flight, 'stealing away' across the Atlantic back to their homelands."[47] In imagining flying back to China, Chen Pan parallels the passage across the Atlantic, demonstrating a form of solidarity based on shared experiences, yes, but also shared fates.

García also uses the tropes of the slave narrative to consider overlooked political contexts—such as the importation of Chinese workers and slavery in the Caribbean more broadly—for the genre's formation. For example, *Monkey Hunting* explicitly invokes the slave narrative to chart Chen Pan's journey to Cuba, which recalls the Middle Passage:

> The ship passed through the Straits of Sunda without incident, then followed the verdant curve of Africa before veering west across the Atlantic. In St. Helena they stopped for fresh water, continuing on to Ascension, Cayenne, the Barbadian coast, and Trinidad. Chen Pan heard the crew announcing each port of call, but the longer he

remained on board, the farther away Cuba seemed. Could his eight years of servitude have elapsed already?[48]

With the ghosts of suicides haunting the ship and the descriptions of claustrophobic spaces below deck, García draws upon the slave narrative to describe the horrors of Chen Pan's journey, which, once it begins to follow the African coast, replicates the Middle Passage. In so doing, she demonstrates how the horrors of the journey to Cuba exceed realist description and require alternate generic modes to capture Chen Pan's experience. In aligning his journey with the Middle Passage, García emphasizes how Chen Pan's embodied experiences allow him to bear witness to both Chinese and Afro Cuban experiences, especially since once he is on the plantation, he is the only enslaved Chinese person to befriend an African (Cabeza de Piña). He is also the only one among the Chinese who receives special treatment, albeit because he kills the overseer.

Monkey Hunting's depiction of Chen Pan's life on the plantation expands the Latinx revolutionary horizons García's revision of Montejo makes possible, as Chen Pan also bears witness to the gendered dynamics of the plantation, especially the multiple forms of violence that slavery produces:

> It became clear to the new overseer that Rita was of no more use in the fields. Within a few weeks, she was sold to a coffee plantation in the mountains of Oriente. Everyone said to pick coffee in the rain would finish off a slave in half the time of sugarcane. La Gorda, the Bantu witch, threw her divining cowries and predicted that Rita would not work in the fields again: *She will die upon reaching her destination, choking the boy-ghost in her womb*. (35–36)

Rita's pregnancy is the result of her rape at the hands of Don Urbano, the enslaver who owns the plantation. He switches her lover, Narciso, to a night shift at the mill and orders Rita sent to his bed. The next day, the overseer shoots Narciso and feeds him to the bloodhounds. Rita falls into a deep depression and is sent to the coffee plantation as punishment. Like the casual references to hypnotism and Haitian voodoo, the allusion to the Bantu witch's divining cowries highlights how commonplace magic and the supernatural are in the Chen Pan sections, illuminating how García's retconning uses the speculative elements often found in the quintessential form of the retcon, comics, to frame Chen Pan's testimonio and show how Latinx revolutionary horizons are most visible in speculative invocations. The use of the speculative here also frames Chen Pan's understanding of Rita's plight—he only knows of her future because of the witch—and illuminates how his testimonio is not only about his own experiences, but those of other enslaved people on the plantation. In other words, the speculative here operates as both something fantastical and something forecasted.

This is where I see García revising the slave narrative into a neo-slave narrative form that draws upon the conventions of testimonio. For me, the instances of Chen Pan bearing witness—as I described earlier—are a way of imagining the slave narrative as a form of collective witnessing in which Chen Pan's descriptions are of the community rather than a singular form of self-expression. For Beverley, testimonio is "the voice of the subaltern. But it is not the intention of this voice simply to display its subalternity. It speaks to us as an 'I' that nevertheless stands for a multitude."[49] This quality of the "I" that speaks for the multitude is what, for Beverley, distinguishes testimonio from slave narrative, which he argues is an individual form based on individual self-expression rather than a form of expression that can stand in for the community as a whole (40–41). While Beverley's theorization of "an 'I' that nevertheless stands for a multitude" is useful, his commitment to restricting the form of testimonio speaks more to his own desires as a critic, as Elzbieta Sklodowska has shown, than the features of testimonio.[50] Yet, as Chen Pan's example underscores, slave narrative also represents the community as a whole, especially since in many ways as a Chinese Cuban, Chen Pan receives better treatment than Afro Cubans; thus, his own slave narrative must necessarily testify to this unequal treatment.

Montejo's transformation into Chen Pan as witness is even more crucial toward the end of the novel, as Chen Pan's acts of bearing witness allow him to attest to notable absences in Barnet's *Biography* and testify to events that are incompatible with the political project of Barnet's text and, by extension, the Cuban revolution. In this way, García surfaces another history as she focuses on the forced coherence of Castro's revolution and the atrocities it glosses over, such as the Race War of 1912. Although García only briefly touches on the Ten Years' War, when Chen Pan leaves to deliver machetes to Commander Sebastián Sian, she pays careful attention to the Race War of 1912 in Chen Pan's witnessing of the results of Black resistance during the uprising. On the train to Havana with his son, Lorenzo, and grandson, Meng, Chen Pan sees two Black men dead on the side of the road, shot in the head: "Chen Pan wanted to comfort his grandson, to smooth his hair and make the dead men go away. But another part of him wanted to force Meng to look at them again and learn that evil existed in every hour. Lorenzo rocked his son as the train picked up speed. Over their shoulders, three hanged men swung from the limbs of a coral tree."[51] Here, Chen Pan wants to force Meng to bear witness to the Cuban Army's massacre of Afro Cubans to quell the uprising, highlighting how independence doesn't mean equality and how Chen Pan is uniquely able to point to the limits of the revolutionary imaginaries during this time period. By making this observation, Chen Pan demonstrates the historical reach of the changes he has seen in Cuba regarding the treatment of Afro Cubans on the island, from the plantation to the uprising. His embodied experiences working on the plantation inform his sympathy for Afro Cubans post-abolition. Moreover, in having Chen Pan make these remarks, García revises *Biography* to do the work that Barnet and Montejo could not—critique anti-blackness as a national, rather than a foreign, problem.[52]

Historically there was racial tension between Chinese and Afro Cubans, as Channette Romero points out, given that "slave masters also frequently used Africans as overseers on Cuban plantations, and urged them to be especially violent with the Chinese workers,"[53] which she notes is a common pattern in the *Cuba Commission Report*.[54] However, Romero argues that "*Monkey Hunting* chooses to downplay these racial tensions in an effort to rethink how we approach history"[55] to offer "an interracial account of its origins that works to inspire contemporary racial inclusivity (76). Rather than simply offering a vision of racial inclusivity and harmony, I suggest that embedded in *Monkey Hunting* is a critique of the ideology of racelessness that undergirded the wars of liberation in the nineteenth century. As the Race War of 1912 makes clear, promoting such an ideology does not lead to a raceless society; it leads to a society that cannot account for its racial divisions. Rather than reading García as downplaying racial tensions between Chinese and Afro Cubans—she makes it quite clear, for example, that, aside from Chen Pan, there is little mingling between them—she focuses more on the structural barriers that foster racial divides; one such barrier is how revolution is narrated and witnessed in Cuba.

Focusing on rampant anti-blackness such as the scene on the train allows García to point to a revealing absence in discussions of testimonio, which is that its connections to slave narratives are largely unremarked upon other than to define what testimonio is and what it is not (specifically, for Beverley, it's not a slave narrative). This is curious, given that Barnet's *Biography* is one of the first texts to be classified as testimonio. Another is that while Beverley cites *Biography* as an example of the genre, none of his work engages deeply with this text.[56] Significantly, then, García joins together testimonio and slave narrative in *Monkey Hunting* by building on such already existing connections in *Biography*. Further, in the figure of Chen Fang, Chen Pan's granddaughter in China, García cements the relationship to testimonio by having Chen Fang inhabit what Beverley calls the "testimonial 'voice'" in contemporary fiction.[57]

García modulates between Chen Pan's mode of witnessing and the traditional form of testimonio through Chen Fang. She is the only person in the novel who offers a first-person point of view. The chapters dedicated to her focus on significant events in her life, with the last chapter narrating her imprisonment under Chairman Mao. We can read this final Chen Fang section as turning to the form of the prison memoir, which, as Ricardo Ortiz explains, was a key genre of Cuban literature, especially in the 1990s.[58] Read in this way, Chen Fang's imprisonment recalls the Isle of Pines, the famous location where Castro held political prisoners. Such resonances illuminate how the China of *Monkey Hunting* does not describe an actual country but articulates a political position and set of ideological concerns that are deeply tied to the contentious relationship between Cubans and communism. I would even go so far as to suggest that the China of *Monkey Hunting* is simply another name for Cuba. Imagining China as a stand-in for Cuba allows for García to make a more strident critique of communist Cuba than we find in her other work.[59]

The last Chen Fang chapter highlights the immediacy and urgency of the testimonial "I" that Beverly describes. This chapter opens with, "The guards are beating the prisoner again. The same woman who tried to commit suicide last summer by sharpening her toothbrush against the cement floor and plunging it into her wrist. The poor thing wails half the day, fraying everyone's nerves. Other times she laughs so hard the guards beat her senseless."[60] The phrase "The guards are beating the prisoner again" uses the present progressive to indicate that the action is going on *now*; moreover, because it's a progressive tense, it also signals how the beatings are ongoing, unfinished actions that presumably will only end with the prisoner's death.

While Chen Fang's last chapter ends ambiguously, as she hopes to survive imprisonment and return to her family, I'm interested in the possibilities that open up if we read her as the compiler of the novel *Monkey Hunting*, particularly as she inhabits the narrative "I" of the testimonial voice. Inspired by the way that García encourages us to speculate on other revolutionary genealogies and imaginaries, I engage in a form of speculative criticism invested in what imaginaries specific interpretations make available to us rather than strictly adjudicating which characters participate in such imaginaries. After all, although Domingo, Lorenzo's grandson, might seem a better candidate as the compiler of *Monkey Hunting*, given the accuracy of his family knowledge compared to Chen Fang's understanding, the retrospective, diary-like quality of Chen Fang's sections suggests a narrator telling a story from a future perspective. Additionally, Domingo does not need to research his family history; he already knows it. Most tellingly of all, Domingo abandons the sex worker he impregnates, showing how, in the logic of the retcon, Domingo's abandonment of the future, represented by his child, signals an abandonment of the past.

As the compiler, Chen Fang would have had to research her family history, potentially interviewing community members and remaining family to put together her narrative. Of course, Chen Pan would be dead well before Chen Fang is freed. That said, she is familiar with a version of Chen Pan's story (90–91). Regardless, the multigenerational narrative with its multiple perspectives gives a sense of a polyphonic, communal voice that speaks *as* the multitude rather than a singular voice that *represents* the multitude, as we see in famous testimonios like *I, Rigoberta Menchú*. García weaves together the genres of slave narrative and testimonio to examine how to bear witness to events and perspectives that are largely absent from the historical record, and are cast in a new light through the discontinuities that her retconning renders visible.

While in prison, Chen Fang learns that the son she was forced to abandon, Lu Chih-mo, is a leader in communist China. Reflecting on the reputation he has built, Chen Fang reflects, "a reputation, no doubt, built on corpses" (230). In this act of witnessing, she echoes an earlier comment that Chen Pan makes after witnessing the hanged Afro Cuban men on the train. Looking at the sugarcane fields through the train window, Chen Pan thinks, "Who could fathom the mountain of corpses that had made these fields possible?" (190). García links together the brutality of enslavement through the image of the sugarcane fields to the brutality of regime change in communist China (and Cuba).

These final reflections of Chen Fang's testimonio occur in the last part of the novel, titled "Last Rites," and are followed by the last chapter, which depicts the last day of Chen Pan's life, in 1917. By arranging the chapters in this way, García offers a method to formally read Chen Fang's and Chen Pan's narratives as another form of the split, revolutionary bildungsroman. Even though the last Chen Fang chapter may also represent her death—her last rites—I suggest that both the Chen Fang and Chen Pan final chapters are elegies for a lost Cuba. Chen Fang mourns a Cuba that "is experimenting with a similar madness" (232) as communist China, while Chen Pan's comments on President Menocal's policy during World War I of "allowing more Chinese immigrants into the country for the duration of the war and for two years beyond it" (246) speak to his bitterness about the prevalence of sugar, as "the war meant the price of sugar was soaring. In times of misery, there were always profits to be made" (246).[61] The reference to President Menocal also recalls the "liberal rebellion [that] erupted in 1917 in the wake of electoral fraud perpetrated" to keep Menocal in power,[62] though Chen Pan would be dead by the time these events transpired.[63]

Despite the fact that Domingo might seem to be a better fit for the role of compiler, I argue that it's significant that they both know slightly different versions of their family's history. Differing versions point to the discontinuities that exist within García's retcon, discontinuities that create avenues outside of repeating cycles. It may seem like comparing the two characters to on- and off-island Cubans would seem like an uneasy fit, given that Chen Fang remains in China where she has always lived, but if we see the China as represented in *Monkey Hunting* as another way for García to critique communism in Cuba, then Chen Fang can be read as representing Cubans who remain on the island, whose version of events are censored and contingent on the ability to gain outside access to information. Yet, as a character who is not actually in Cuba, we can see Cheng Fang as an exilic figure as well, which underscores her ability to speak for both groups as she combines them into a single character.[64] Rather than creating a single cohesive version of events, Chen Fang symbolizes how different versions of events can exist—in this case her family history—and how as these varied histories come forward (as in, for example, Chen Pan's history of the wars of liberation and the fight for a democratic republic after), they illuminate the futility of imposing continuity in the first place; the minority report can never be fully suppressed. As Latinx revolutionary horizons demonstrate, revolutionary horizons reveal themselves in such discontinuities and ruptures, in moments when seeming cycles are proven to have been otherwise.

Retconning Abolition

Within the U.S., slave narratives and fictional representations of slavery in contemporary literature indicate distinct traditions. However, in Cuba, there was a rich antislavery narrative tradition that maintained a fictional quality from the beginning. As scholars such as Luis have demonstrated, the texts that comprise this corpus of material are part of a continuous tradition that extends from the nineteenth century to now. Cuba and Latin America more broadly did not have a tradition of slave narratives or efforts like the Works Progress Administration (WPA) recovery project like the U.S. In fact, Juan Francisco Manzano wrote the only slave narrative in Latin America in 1835. The antislavery narrative tradition as it developed in Cuba necessarily relied on imagined forms of slavery and liberation, as it did not have a corpus of material to build on and thus had to create a fictionalized notion of slavery. To that end, in a similar move as García's in *Monkey Hunting*, authors such as Anselmo Suárez y Romero built upon Manzano's slave narrative for his novel *Francisco* (published in 1880 in New York and in Cuba in 1947). In the

1830s, the liberal Domingo Del Monte sponsored the authorship of slave autobiographies and fictions "to found an Indigenous literary tradition."[65] That said, while Avellaneda wrote one of the most famous fictionalized versions of slavery in Cuba, she was not part of Del Monte's circle; she lived the majority of her life in Spain and published *Sab* there. In fact, the novel was not published in Cuba until 1883, when it finally appeared in serial form in *El Museo*; it was eventually published as a book in Cuba in 1914.

Nevertheless, I examine Avellaneda within this tradition exactly because she was outside of Del Monte's influence, and her work speaks to the boundaries that limn and limit revolutionary imaginaries in Cuban antislavery narratives.[66] For example, while Del Monte would seem to be an advocate for the abolition of slavery, he sought to reveal the horrors of slavery despite maintaining the status quo. In fact, he did not imagine a Cuban republic in which Afro Cubans would be part of the nation.[67] Although critics are divided on *Sab* as an abolitionist text, in many ways Avellaneda is able to imagine abolition in a way that Del Monte could not, exactly because she was not only outside of his circle of influence, but also because as an exile in Spain, she had the opportunity to further reflect on slavery as a metaphor for Cuban dependence on Spain.[68] Moreover, while questions about *Sab* as an abolitionist text continue to preoccupy critics, the fact remains that the novel was censored in Cuba, as it "contained doctrines opposed to the system of slavery in vogue in the Island."[69] Additionally, as Latin Americanist scholars point out, it shares similarities with Harriet Beecher Stowe's *Uncle Tom's Cabin*, published eleven years later in 1852; indeed, Judie Newman goes so far as to say that *Uncle Tom's Cabin* not only reveals "Stowe's unacknowledged debt to Cuban literature" but also the "wholesale adoption of features" from *Sab* (22),[70] thus establishing Avellaneda as a central figure in women's abolitionist writing.[71]

Through the metaphorical usage of slavery, Avellaneda retcons her personal history, splitting it, like the revolutionary bildungsroman, between Carlota, the protagonist of the novel, and Sab, an enslaved man who is the son of an enslaved African princess and a white enslaver, Don Luis, Carlota's uncle. Both of Sab's parents are dead at the beginning of the novel, and the plot revolves around Sab's love for Carlota, who is his cousin, and her love for Enrique Otway, an Englishman whom she eventually marries. In splitting her personal history across these two characters, Avellaneda attempts to create continuity in the struggles for women's rights, abolition, and independence. In this reading of the novel, Otway stands in for foreign intervention, as Carlota represents "'the simultaneous occupation of a colonial landscape and of a young woman's body,"⁷² the twin concerns of the novel that yoke slavery and women's right to the question of independence. Anna Brickhouse even reads the Otways as raising "the looming possibility of US annexation,"⁷³ given that Enrique Otway's father spent a significant amount of time in the United States (174), learning, it seems, to be a good capitalist.

The narrative of revolutionary possibility Avellaneda proposes relies on her feminist approach and stands in marked contrast to the wars of independence that would follow, in which women's rights were not part of the revolutionary struggle and abolition continued to be a point of contention, as exemplified by the Pact of Zanjón, which formally ended the Ten Years' War. The pact did not recognize Cuban independence and, more damningly, failed to immediately abolish slavery. Because of these concessions, the famous Black general Antonio Maceo initially refused to lay down arms, though he eventually surrendered and continued to lead the subsequent wars of independence until his death on the battlefield in 1896.

Avellaneda's act of retconning points to a revolutionary horizon more expansive than that of the liberators' imaginaries. That said, in equating women's struggles with those of enslaved people and the Cuban nation more broadly, Avellaneda enacts her own continuity error through the logic of inclusion, a continuity error that would be repeated through the rhetoric of racelessness in the wars of liberation. Here, the logic of inclusion is ultimately a conservative claim that, in insisting upon coherence, refuses the diversity of the Cuban population and, in so doing, refuses to see the inequality that persists among Afro Cubans, including during the Castro regime. To illuminate Avellaneda's retconning strategy and its promises as well as its pitfalls, I focus primarily on Sab's letter at the end of the novel as it most closely resembles Avellaneda's *Autobiography* (1839), which is written as a series of letters to the object of her unrequited love, Ignacio de Cepeda. I focus on how the sense of urgency that comes across in Avellaneda's *Autobiography* is transformed into the testimonial voice in Sab's letter, as well as how Sab's letter is Avellaneda's testimonio as a woman and a colonial subject.

In making the claim that Sab's letter is Avellaneda's testimonio, I rely on Doris Sommer's pivotal discussion of the resemblances between Sab and Avellaneda. Sommer carefully traces how this similarity is not an autobiographical likeness, but one predicated on literary production and the tactics both use to "destabilize the rhetorical system that constrains them."⁷⁴ While Sommer does nod briefly to the autobiographical similarity between the two as Sab turns to the epistolary form that Avellaneda's autobiography takes, she notes that the strongest resemblance between them lies in Sab's agency as an author and producer of the narrative *Sab*. As Sommer observes, "In other words, the end discovers Sab as the agent and the authority of the very story that portrayed him as a defenseless object of history" (116). In reclaiming Sab as an agent, not object, of history, Sommer implies that Avellaneda similarly carves out a space for her own writing, a point underscored by Stacey Schlau, who, in discussing Avellaneda's "alienated position" notes that she, "like the black slave she pities, . . . is thereby able to observe history, and perceive its distortions,"[75] making Sab the authorized figure for Avellaneda's own writing.

Sommer usefully refers to the associations between Sab and Avellaneda as "liberating linguistic disencounters,"[76] which I read most fruitfully as relating to the "new or American persona" (114) in the hemispheric sense that Sab represents. By extension, I argue that Avellaneda creates such a persona for herself via Sab. Sommer notes that "Sab is a new incarnation of an extinct aboriginal 'Cuban,' one who exceeds or violates the strict racial categories that have made slavery work" (118). Sab's connections to a specifically Cuban amalgamation of racial identities are further underscored by the fact that he "is spiritually related to the aboriginal masters through his adoptive mother Martina, an old slave who insists she is Indian royalty" (118). While the novel casts Martina's claims to indigeneity into doubt, I would add that the triangulation of Spanish, African, and Indigenous heritage contributes to the imagined future that Avellaneda makes possible via retconning, one that is not predicated on strict racial divisions, but on liberating linguistic disencounters that also provide liberating imaginative disencounters.

Avellaneda's *Autobiography* demonstrates one such linguistic discounter, specifically in terms of the sense of urgency, a hallmark of the epistolary form she creates in this text vis-à-vis *Sab*. Her first letter to Cepeda begins with, "I must attend to you; I offered to do so, and since I cannot sleep tonight, I want to write; I am attending to you while writing about myself, as I would only consent to do this for you."[77] Avellaneda's present moment of writing merges with the immediate future scene of writing as, in noting that she cannot sleep, Avellaneda decides to tell Cepeda about herself. The effect is of a continuous present that links her offer to write with the future scene of writing such that her own narrative of her childhood becomes part of the ongoing present of the moment of writing. Similarly, at the end of her first letter, Avellaneda writes, "I am tired and this pen is dreadful; what will you do now? Sleep, perhaps!" (3). In asking Cepeda what he "will" do "now," Avellaneda pulls the imagined future of Cepeda's actions into the present. As part of creating such a continuous present, Avellaneda intersperses her childhood anecdotes with markers of time that reflect the scene of writing: "the twenty-fifth, in the morning" (3), "the twenty-fifth, in the afternoon" (6), "at one at night" (6), and "at night" (15).

Sab deploys similar strategies in his letter to Teresa, Carlota's cousin. He begins the letter by writing, "My hour of rest approaches: my mission on earth is about to end" (139). Much like Avellaneda's opening lines in her *Autobiography*, Sab anticipates the immediate future; however, in his case he is faced with approaching death. Rather than his narrative in the letter merging with the present of its writing, Sab's letter hurtles toward the future, lending it a greater sense of urgency than that found within Avellaneda's letters. His voice recalls the "I" of testimonio rather than autobiography. This distinction is important because rather than installing the "free modern subject" (50) that Lisa Lowe sees in autobiographies such as the *Interesting Narrative of the Life of Olaudah Equiano, or Gustavas Vassa, the African, Written by Himself* (1789), Avellaneda turns her own autobiography into Sab's testimonial voice to speak to the ongoing oppression of slavery and subjugation under the colonial state.[78] In speaking for a multitude à la Beverley, Sab's testimonio reveals how he "is not so much concerned with the life of a 'problematic hero'—the term Lukács used to describe the nature of the hero of the bourgeois novel—as with a problematic collective social situation that the narrator lives with or alongside others."[79] Avellaneda's retconning of her own autobiography emphasizes a turn to the political that is also a turn to a *collective* engagement with politics.

Avellaneda illuminates the collective social situation Sab faces in the famous scene where he likens the plight of women to that of enslaved people. In this moment of identification between Avellaneda and Sab, *Sab* reveals itself as a retcon in which Avellaneda uses Sab's letter to speak to her own predicament as a woman. The passage reads:

> Oh, women! Poor, blind victims! Like slaves, they patiently drag their chains and bow their heads under the yoke of human laws. With no other guide than an untutored and trusting heart, they choose a master for life. The slave can at least change masters, can even hope to buy his freedom some day if he can save enough money, but a woman, when she lifts her careworn hands and mistreated brow to beg for release, hears the monstrous, deathly voice which cries out to her: "In the grave."[80]

If we look to the *Autobiography*, we can see how this quote echoes an earlier comment Avellaneda makes to Cepeda: "Where is the man who can fulfill the desires of this sensitive nature which is as fiery as it is delicate? For nine years I have searched in vain! In vain! I have found men! Men who are alike, to none of whom I could submit with respect and declare ardently: You are my God on this earth, and the absolute master of this passionate soul" (6). The *Autobiography* attests to Avellaneda's attempts to find a suitable companion, as her remarks to Cepeda demonstrate Avellaneda's view that finding a suitable husband means finding a suitable master. Moreover, by figuring the tension within the novel as one between Sab and his unrequited feelings for Carlota, who loves an Englishman, Avellaneda frames the tension as one in which a Cuban woman has sought a foreign "master" who proves to be unworthy of her affections. Avellaneda thus figures marriage metaphorically as referring to the colonizer/colonized dynamic.[81]

This dynamic is rendered more clearly toward the end of the novel when Carlota transforms into the questionably Indigenous woman Martina, an act of retconning that emphasizes how Avellaneda transforms her personal history into a representation of a broader collective. After reading Sab's letter, Carlota lives in Cubitas for three months.[82] During her stay, "news of a miraculous event began to circulate rapidly, which reported that the old Indian woman, after having been buried for half a year, returned nightly for her habitual walk and could be seen kneeling by the wooden cross which marked Sab's grave" (147). Although *Sab* acknowledges doubts about Martina's Indigenous heritage, for the community, Martina still signifies an extinct Indigenous past, which Avellaneda draws upon when she has Carlota mistaken for Martina. As Jenna Leving Jacobson compellingly argues, Martina acts "as a force of interruption"[83] with "a voice dissonant to what has become a dominant hermeneutic model applied to the novel" (174), which is that of Sommer's national romance. In Martina, then, we have a figure who enacts a proto-Latinx revolutionary horizon by telling the story of "the violence of the Conquest and the continuity of its brutality under the system of slavery" (174), thus "reveal[ing] the failure of the desire for national harmonization" (174).

In making this connection between Martina and Carlota, Avellaneda emphasizes the egregiousness of Carlota's bad match to a foreigner, which underscores how Avellaneda turns to gente de color to make her argument for independence and against foreign influence and incursion. As we learn before this quote, Carlota stays in Cubitas for so long because her husband was "indifferent" to her.[84] The novel ends by referring to Carlota as a "daughter of the tropics" (147); central to this designation is the novel's casting of her as an imagined—indeed phantom—Indigenous woman. As Reina Barreto points out, "Carlota's utopian vision of a past in which Cuba's native population lived happily and in harmony with nature carries over into her life when she appropriates Indigenous identity as her own."[85] The fact that indigeneity can only signal a lost past while conferring on Carlota a native claim to Cuba underscores how Cuban independence fundamentally relies on settler colonial imaginaries.[86]

This transformation is central to *Sab*, I argue, as the novel fundamentally ruminates on how the plight of enslaved people is a national problem. By having Sab testify to the predicament of women at the end of his letter, Avellaneda points to a failed moment of solidarity on Carlota's side. Whereas Sab's act suggests that enslaved people and women could potentially join their struggles, Carlota is unable to imagine how her struggle resonates with slavery, thus revealing how the continuity error of the novel stems from this failed act of solidarity, which points to the limits of the logic of inclusion. Although Sab writes the letter as he dies, Carlota does not read the letter until much later, as it was written to Teresa, who hands it to Carlota on Teresa's deathbed in a convent five years later. When Sab died, Carlota "had just been separated from her father, her brother was most likely dying at that very moment, and in comparison with these calamities the loss of the mulatto was very minor."[87] Thus, while Sab sympathizes with the difficulties women face because of marriage, the novel demonstrates that Carlota does not extend the same sympathy toward Sab. By highlighting Carlota's lack of sympathy, Avellaneda points to anti-blackness as a national, rather than foreign, problem.

Avellaneda is complicit in the national and racial scripts of her time. Although Sommer observes, "In *Sab* the violence is directed above all against the rhetorical system that organized races into a rigid hierarchy of color, from lightest to darkest,"[88] Carlota's failure of solidarity emphasizes how, ultimately, the violence is directed toward the enslaved, regardless of color, as Sab's light skin does not prevent him from dying at the end of the novel. Where Sommer sees *Sab* as about the difference between "'legitimate' Cuban protagonists, both black and white, and 'illegitimate' foreigners, the Otways" (133), Avellaneda reveals that for her, the legitimate Cuban protagonists are white women and that this legitimacy comes at the expense of Black characters and Indigenous erasure.

Nevertheless, it is striking that Sommer claims, "Sab is already a projection of national consolidation" (132). We can see how as a figure of national consolidation, Sab links to an alternative future while figures of foreignness like the Otways are tied to Cuba's problematic past, bound as they are with "the first Spaniards who left traces of blood in the caves of Cubitas" (133) intent on "exploit[ing] its wealth" (133). Sab is fundamentally a character who refuses to cohere in Avellaneda's text, as he represents the tension between her own failures of solidarity as well as her implied support for abolition. As Susan Kirkpatrick observes in her analysis of Sab's comments about his enslavement, *Sab* is fundamentally "a narrative divided against itself as it attempts both to justify and to contain Sab's anger."[89] Along similar lines, Julia C. Paulk argues that *Sab* exhibits "fragmentation and fluctuation rather than a unified message system,"[90] which leads to an incoherence that results in "a racist message that is antithetical to the novel's own progressive position" (229). Such fragmentation points to the discontinuities that Avellaneda's retcon render visible as, rather than insisting on coherence, her novel exposes a variety of political positions, including those in the text that seem to be at odds with Avellaneda's own views.

If we think of Sab as the figure of national consolidation par excellence, then it is particularly striking that he says, "I have no homeland to defend, because slaves have no country."[91] In making this comment, Sab points to the statelessness of those who are enslaved; however, placed within the context of Avellaneda's identification with Sab and Carlota's transformation into Martina, the emphasis here is not only on enslaved people not having a country, but also not having a homeland to defend. What Sommer's comment about national consolidation points to, and Carlota's transformation suggests, is that at the same time Cuba was a Spanish colony, it was beginning to form its own national identity separate from Spain. Thus, the issue of having a homeland is one in which enslaved people serve multiple masters—Cuban, but ultimately Spanish—rendering visible the untenability of maintaining multiple allegiances, particularly when a Cuban national identity begins to manifest.

Although Avellaneda's class and racial privileges ultimately limit her initially expansive revolutionary imaginary, reading her alongside García foregrounds how both women writers offer revolutionary horizons that exceed the official revolutionary imaginaries of the nineteenth and twentieth centuries. Moreover, seeing García's retconning at work in *Monkey Hunting* underscores how contemporary Latinx authors influence our understanding of past imaginaries, expanding Latinx revolutionary horizons from the present into the past.

Revolutionary Speculations

So far I have emphasized the resonances between neo-slave narrative and testimonio as well as how retconning can be a form of disruption rather than continuity. I have also demonstrated how both García and Avellaneda imagine new solidarities in light of historical erasures. For García, focusing on the figure of Chen Pan allows her to inscribe Chinese Cubans into Cuban revolutionary history while bearing witness to Cuban anti-blackness. Avellaneda, meanwhile, uses her background to make *Sab* into a sympathetic figure legible to her Cuban and Spanish audiences, with all the limitations that such a framework entails. Both authors also imagine new collectivities as García creates a collective voice in *Monkey Hunting* and Avellaneda imagines a Cuba that can account for a Cuban national identity of which both Afro and Indigenous Cubans are a part.

Whereas Chapter 2 focused on extending Latinx imaginaries to places outside of the hemisphere, like the Philippines, this chapter has focused on showing how such Asian and Latinx configurations also operate within the hemisphere. In thinking about retconning as a methodology, we can see how my reading of *Monkey Hunting* allows me to retcon Latinx literary criticism to account for productive moments of intersection that have mostly remained absent in the scholarship. In my reading of *Monkey Hunting*, I briefly alluded to the concept of speculative criticism, which is a form of criticism distinct from critical fabulation (which seeks to fill in the gaps in the archive) in that it seeks to answer the question, "What if?" Much like Bustamante's argument that "Cuba's history resembled a saga of unfinished business dating to the nineteenth century, a running series of 'what ifs,'"[92] I contend that revolutions themselves encourage us to think of the "what if." Revolutions pivot on bringing another world into existence, and retconning allows us to see visions of former futures, of how events could have unfolded otherwise. Speculative criticism, then, returns us to the "what if?" and asks us to see how reading speculatively—by imagining a Chen Fang who survives, for example—makes other readings and other worlds (we might even say horizons) possible.

Reading transhistorically, as I have done here, also highlights what revolutionary possibilities are made available by reading across periods and disciplines. Transhistorical reading also aids the project of speculative criticism through its focus on juxtaposition. While it's possible that Sandra Cisneros read Ruiz de Burton and intentionally revised Lola into Lala, for example, the fact of that reading remains irrelevant because of the startling similarities we see between the two by reading into the past. To apprehend liberatory futures, we must look to the past because, as David Scott reminds us, "the problem about postcolonial futures . . . cannot be recast without recasting the problem about colonial pasts."[93] Latinx revolutionary horizons recast colonial pasts by revealing the narrative cracks that let in other histories. Meanwhile, my reading of García and Avellaneda is the reverse of that in Cisneros and Ruiz de Burton: rather than imagining García as taking inspiration from Avellaneda, I suggest that *Monkey Hunting* allows us to read Avellaneda as, paradoxically (and speculatively), reliant on García. In short, recasting the colonial past here means rendering it into the present.

I extend the concept of speculative criticism into Chapter 5, where I examine how authors who typically don't identify as Latinx contend with Latinx revolutionary imaginaries. Through the work of Martin R. Delany and Leslie Marmon Silko, we will see how non-Latinxs productively use Latinx revolutionary history to imagine their own forms of rebellion. In the case of Silko, we will even see how her work anticipates an actual revolution in the form of the Zapatista uprising. Looking at authors like Delany and Silko, I argue, shows how they also contribute to theorizations of what latinidad can be—and how it has been theorized—outside of its typical constituencies in ways that underscore the alternatives that a nonnational framework like latinidad makes possible.

5
Speculative Revolutions
Otrxs Latinidades in Delany and Silko

Martin R. Delany's *Blake; or, the Huts of America: A Tale of the Mississippi Valley, the Southern United States, and Cuba* (1859)[1] and Leslie Marmon Silko's *Almanac of the Dead* (1991)[2] offer us two visions of revolution that depend on speculative imaginaries. While in the previous chapters I have focused on specific genres—from captivity and conversion narratives to Latinx dictator novels and testimonios—in this chapter, I examine how Delany and Silko turn to the speculative more broadly. Although speculative fiction often serves as an umbrella term that encapsulates a range of genres from horror to science fiction to fantasy, in this chapter I explore how the use of speculative modes and devices, such as resurrecting a Cuban historical figure, offer us revolutionary imaginaries. In this way, the speculative materializes not only as a mode, but also as a way to think through past revolutionary failures and imagine successful alternatives. The textual phenomenon of Latinx revolutionary horizons come into view in moments of rupture where glimmers appear that suggest another world is possible; speculative imaginaries offer us a way to stay with these glimmers and envision what such a world and such a future would look like, could look like.

In Delany, speculative imaginaries rely on the Caribbean and, more specifically, the infamous slave rebellion in Cuba called la Conspiración de La Escalera (the Ladder Conspiracy). The conspiracy was so named because of the method of interrogating alleged participants by tying them to a ladder and torturing them to elicit confessions. As readers, we are attuned to this connection given that Plácido (Gabriel de la Concepción Valdés), the famous Afro Cuban poet and martyr who was executed in 1844 by firing squad for his alleged role in leading the rebellion, is a character in the novel.[3] Given Plácido's historical importance, it's no wonder that, as Ifeoma Kiddoe Nwankwo observes, Plácido would come to figure in a range of nineteenth-century fictions such that "the battle over the humanity of people of African descent was fought, therefore, through dueling representations of Plácido as a savage leader of an inhuman population or a noble hero of an embattled collective."[4] In terms of the latter representation, Katy Chiles argues, "Plácido must be always already martyred so that his appearance in *Blake* can signify strong revolutionary leadership within the black community."[5] Plácido's role in the novel is especially surprising, given that it takes place between 1852 and 1853 (and therefore after his death), which Jennifer Brittan reads as "the kind of alternative history we associate with speculative fiction."[6] In short, Delany resurrects a famous Afro Cuban rebel to imagine a successful revolution among both the enslaved and free populations in Cuba. Significantly, in raising Plácido from the dead, Delany also makes La Escalera seemingly coterminous with events that happened several years later, such as the Fugitive Slave Law of 1850 and the Dred Scott decision of 1857. As Eric J. Sundquist notes, this leads to a sense of compressed time in the novel as events are "telescoped into the much shorter time frame of the novel,"[7] thus "creat[ing] a fictive world in which Cuban and American slavery are yoked together in historical simultaneity" (184). In so doing, Delany thickens the historical density of the novel by pointing to the shared experience of anti-blackness in the U.S. and the Caribbean, particularly, according to Sundquist, "the relationship between United States expansionism and Cuban revolution" (185), which leads to a sense of compressed space within the hemisphere.[8]

Almanac, meanwhile, offers a vision of coalitional politics as disparate groups are brought together toward a shared purpose. Unlike Delany, whose vision of liberation would remain unacknowledged in subsequent struggles, *Almanac* has been directly linked with the Zapatista uprising of January 1, 1994, in the Lacandón Jungle.[9] The summer before the uprising, Zapatistas reportedly read *Almanac* and were inspired by its vision of a hemispheric revolution.[10] In anticipating an uprising in Chiapas, *Almanac* reads like a profound act of divination. Even Silko's description of her writing process supports this view, as she explains to Ellen L. Arnold in her 1998 interview: "But of course, the spirits are writing *Almanac*, not me."[11] Silko also explains how the length of the book and its material were not decisions for her to make, but the spirits': "I completely was taken over, and everything about it [*Almanac*] was meant to be. The spirits just wanted it out there" (169). Commenting on Subcomandante Marcos, one of the leaders of the Zapatista uprising, Silko observes that Marcos "went to the mountains in 1980, and that's when I started to have transmissions. I started to have to spontaneously write down things from the

Almanac" (169). In Silko's telling, even as she was unaware of the Zapatistas and their movement, the spirits were guiding both the writing of *Almanac* and the Indigenous uprising. Silko has also stated that part of her process was attending to the news and collecting newspaper clippings, suggesting that the future she projects in *Almanac* is a speculative act in which she imagines how seemingly disparate struggles—from alleged eco-terrorists to the proto-Zapatistas—could merge into a single movement geared toward a form of liberation grounded in the return of all tribal lands (65). While the speculative aspects of *Almanac* would seem to reside in the ancestor spirits that speak to the living and the angry gods of the Americas, the speculative feat of *Almanac* lies in Silko's ability to proleptically envision a future revolution that actually occurs.

We can read Delany as frustrated with the accommodationist stance depicted by the likes of Harriet Beecher Stowe[12] and even Delany's own emigration plans, which quickly fell apart after his Niger Valley trip in 1859; we can also read Silko as frustrated with the radical movements of her time. As Chanette Romero explains, in *Almanac*, Silko "attempts to overcome the limitations of the American Indian Movement by presenting readers with the model of 'tribal internationalists,' individuals who work with international alliances to reclaim their Indigenous land."[13] For Silko, tribal internationalism was a way to overcome "secular politics based on ethnicity or race alone" (623) characterized by their "divisiveness and limitations" (623) and instead harness "the expansiveness of coalition politics that connects . . . living readers to the spirits of dead ancestors and the spirits of the earth and natural world" (623).[14]

In contrast to Delany's attempts to elevate those with "pure" African ancestry, Silko's vision of revolutionary change focuses on racial mixtures, thus writing against not only notions of blood quantum as signaling tribal belonging and kinship, but also the idea of sangre pura or sangre limpia (the latter literally means "clean blood"; both terms signify pure blood). Where blood quantum is a conception of dilution that leads to extinction, *Almanac* reconsiders how coalitional politics can restore the "disappeared relations" of colonization between both Indigenous people and Mexicans of Indigenous descent (both known and unknown).[15] Although Romero refers to these relationships as "forgotten past alliances"[16] and Simón Ventura Trujillo uses this term specifically to refer to the relationship between Latinxs and indigeneity, I extend Trujillo's term as part of Silko's tribal internationalism. This also allows me to emphasize the importance of Silko's thought for latinidad, which suggests that our pan-ethnic connections are not the result of an agreement, as alliance implies, but of long-standing familial bonds that have been disappeared through colonization. In accordance with this thinking, Silko's conception of coalitional politics is one in which racial groups, such as African Americans, are also disappeared kin whose relationship with Indigenous people is also restored. Connecting people to "the spirits of dead ancestors" renders visible how these kinships will be reanimated. Silko's focus on the African gods who came to the Americas via the Middle Passage (and the absence of the Christian god) is yet another way for her to signal and strengthen these bonds among the people of the Americas.

Turning to two authors who do not primarily identify as Latinx (though Silko is of Mexican descent, she primarily identifies as Laguna Pueblo), but nevertheless turn to Latin/x revolutionary imaginaries, expands our understanding of latinidad, as well as the scope and contours of Latinx archives and canons, as I also show within the context of the Philippines in Chapter 2 as well as the discussion of Chinese indentured servants in Chapter 4. In terms of latinidad, focusing on authors such as Delany and Silko illuminates how the hegemonic white latinidad that emerged after the Wars of Independence was not and is not the only genealogy and endpoint of latinidad. Examining *Blake* illustrates how the hemispheric heritage of latinidad is one in which Latin/x revolutionary imaginaries such as La Escalera also inform African American revolutionary imaginaries. In denying Delany's influence on conceptions of latinidad in the nineteenth-century U.S., we miss an opportunity to see a version of latinidad that was always Black, always insurgent, and always hemispheric in orientation. Silko, meanwhile, attunes us to how the U.S.-Mexico border, despite cleaving Mexico in half, hasn't necessarily divided a people, as she renders visible relations that colonization has tried to disappear. As Silko reminds us, Indigenous peoples in the U.S. and Mexico continue to participate in shared struggles even as anti-indigeneity manifests differently in both countries.

Despite the fact that introducing authors such as Delany and Silko to our canons and archives might seem to indicate the ever-widening gyre of latinidad and its incomprehensibility, my contention in this chapter is that turning to such revolutionary imaginaries strengthens the ability of latinidad to be a politics rather than solely a form of identification. Doing so recognizes that to expand our own imaginaries of what latinidad can be, we must turn to how non-Latinxs have also theorized latinidad. To put it another way, while the latinidad that must be cancelled stems from the Wars of Independence, a more revolutionary latinidad resides in the Black and Indigenous thinkers who have taken up the idea of revolution and turned to Latin/x America for inspiration. Delany's turn to Plácido rather than Simón Bolívar reflects such a shift and the possibilities it opens up for a liberatory latinidad that is not yet here.

Further, as Delany and Silko show us—and the chapters in this book also demonstrate—one of the primary challenges of latinidad is contending with the history of choosing whiteness as a way to access rights. Although there is much to be said about Delany's elitism and his emphasis on "pure" African heritage, the revolutionary vision we arrive at toward the end of the novel enlists Black people with a range of racial mixtures, emphasizing how, for the white-passing Black person, choosing blackness is a powerful solution to a world in which it may seem more useful to benefit from proximity to whiteness. Therefore, *Blake* is a useful text for examining how Black revolutionary imaginaries can expand Latinx revolutionary horizons, as well as how Latinx revolutionary imaginaries, broadly conceived, can become the basis for coalitional politics. In my discussion of Delany, I engage with his works calling for the elevation of Black people, which for him is a civilizing mission. That said, I argue that the vision of revolution Delany offers in *Blake* features a coalitional politics at odds with his comments about an elevated people. Yet Delany's line of thought persists into our contemporary moment through the discourse of the Talented Tenth during the fin de siècle and its transformation into respectability politics.

Silko contends with a similar intellectual heritage as she engages with the civilization or barbarism formulation inaugurated by Domingo Sarmiento in *Facundo: Civilization and Barbarism* (1845).[17] Joni Adamson reminds us that Silko also "expand[s] the definitions of 'indigeneity' into a different kind of collective label"[18] such that the coalition the novel envisions is one in which one "need only 'to walk with the people and let go of all the greed and the selfishness in one's heart'" (6). In short, as *Latinx Revolutionary Horizons* shows, the race thinking that emerged in the nineteenth century extends into the present, suggesting that for there to be a future for latinidad, we must confront the intersecting racial histories that inform it. In this way, latinidad emerges not only as a politics, but as a form of political consciousness in which we remember these histories and actively engage with this complicated inheritance.

Coalitional Conspiracies

Toward the end of *Blake*, a possible slave insurrection on board a ship, the *Vulture*, is averted: "Late in the afternoon a rainbow appeared above the horizon, telling in distant and silent eloquence as a harbinger of gladness, of a brighter prospect to all, as if conscious of the terror which pervaded the enslavers, and the future that awaited the enslaved."[19] In a novel about organizing revolution, this "harbinger of gladness" would seem to be out of place, since the insurrectionary plot is foiled by the passing of the storm that had mirrored the turmoil on the ship. Yet, the promising future "that awaited the enslaved" recalls the revolutionary motto of the book, which is to "stand still and see the salvation" (39), a reference to Exodus.[20] For Blake, successful revolutions rely on restraint, on waiting for the right moment to appear. The revolution is a future orientation that directs the enslaved people toward the rainbow that appears above the horizon. That the horizon appears at this point is instructive, particularly as it relates to the Latinx revolutionary horizons I have traced throughout this book. As I will discuss in what follows, the horizon here is ephemeral and abstract, as *Blake* shows, and arriving at the horizon can only happen by organizing: the novel joins together African American and Afro Cuban revolutionary imaginaries to show how this coalitional work—while it seems to emerge out of a racial alliance—arises out of a shared politics.[21] Yet such a politics is often difficult to apprehend in *Blake*, as the two characters who espouse Delany's political positions—Blake and Placido—also act in ways that run counter to his stated views. In situating the novel's publication within a brief overview of Delany's key political writings, I outline the complex politics with which *Blake* contends, as well as how the novel offers us a viable revolutionary imaginary.

Originally published in the *Anglo-African Magazine* in 1859, the first version of *Blake* was comprised of chapters 1–23 and 28–30.[22] After *Anglo-African Magazine* folded in March of 1860, the publisher, Thomas Hamilton, began another publication, the *Weekly Anglo-African*, which published seventy-four chapters of *Blake* from 1861 to 1862. As Robert S. Levine observes, given that Hamilton refers to the novel as consisting of eighty chapters in *Anglo-African Magazine*[23] and that the issues after April 26, 1862, are missing,[24] "critics have assumed that the final six chapters appeared in the May 1862 issues of the paper, which have yet to be found, if they in fact exist."[25] In casting doubt on the ostensibly missing final chapters, Levine argues, "Given the novel's multiple and conflicting sources, purposes, and audiences, and also its truncated ending, we need to be wary of efforts to develop a 'coherent' formalist reading of it" (179). That said, as Sundquist observes, formalist elements, such as the dividing of the novel into two halves, one that largely takes place in the U.S. South and the other in Cuba, "may be seen less as a mechanical device than a means to accentuate the fact that the Cuban situation was a kind of twin, a shadow play, of the American South for masters and slaves alike."[26] I would also add that Delany's own shifting viewpoints inform our reading of the novel as we follow Blake as he foments revolution; the precise nature of this revolution, however, is unclear, though reading Cuba as a twin for the U.S. South is telling.

I suggest that the lack of clarity stems from how the revolutionary organizing that actually takes shape in the novel is at odds with the revolutionary ideology Delany advocates in his political writings (and that are rehearsed to a certain extent in *Blake*).²⁷ One of Delany's most controversial claims (and one that is also espoused by Placido in *Blake*) focuses on the primacy of pure African blood. For example, in *The Condition, Elevation, Emigration and Destiny of the Colored People of the United States* (1852), Delany argues that "the elevation of the colored man can only be completed by the elevation of the pure descendants of Africa."²⁸ As Madame Cordora, one of the Cuban revolutionaries in *Blake* argues, such a position suggests that "'the mixed bloods are inferior to the pure blooded descendants of Africa.'"²⁹ Placido explains how this is not the case by repeating the claims Delany makes in *The Condition*; Placido argues that "'the instant that an equality of the blacks with the whites is admitted, we being the descendants of the two, must be acknowledged the equals of both.'"³⁰ In other words, to elevate Black people, one must first argue for the equality of "those of pure and unmixed African blood" (194), as doing so will mean that those of mixed heritage are also rendered equal, since they would then be descended from two equal races. Levine observes that Delany committed to this argument so that "white racists could not say about that person, as they could, for example, about Douglass or William Wells Brown, that the achievements could be 'explained' by the 'white' blood in the person's body."³¹ In choosing to make an argument based on what white racists think, Delany subscribes to the same notions of racial superiority—and supremacy—as white racists and compromises his own political vision.

We can see this compromised vision in Delany's incendiary remarks at the end of his *Official Report of the Niger Valley Exploring Party* (1861), which would seem at odds with his privileging of those with pure African blood. Although this shift in thinking no doubt stems from Delany's own changing political views, including his decision to focus his emigration efforts on Africa rather than the Caribbean or Central America, his recommendation of "*Africa for the African race, and black men to rule them. By black men I mean, men of African descent who claim an identity with the race*,"³² speaks to Delany's own imperialism as he advocates African Americans colonizing Africans. This stems, of course, from his viewpoint that African Americans are more elevated than the African people. This perspective once again cements Delany's position that white people are superior, since the difference between African Americans and Africans is the influence of Anglo-Saxons.

Shocking as these comments are, my examination of *Blake* largely focuses on the actual organizing tactics deployed in the novel.³³ For example, the argument may be made that Delany makes Blake an Afro Cuban to assert Blake's right to lead the revolution in Cuba, given the previous comments; it is nevertheless striking that rather than suggesting an African American rule the Afro Cubans, Delany depicts a partnership with the latter.³⁴ In much the same way that María Amparo Ruiz de Burton and Gertrudis Gómez de Avellaneda seem to accidentally stumble upon revolutionary imaginaries, Delany also ends up imagining a more liberatory revolution than his stated political positions suggest. Examining the differences between such positions and the revolution in *Blake*, then, affords us the opportunity to see how Delany imagines a successful revolution actually unfolding.

To apprehend what such a revolution would look like, the revolutionary imaginaries that inform *Blake* are particularly telling: primarily the American Revolution and La Escalera, though Haiti also has a spectral presence in the novel, given that during this time period the fear of a Black revolution was deeply tied to the memory of the Haitian Revolution. As Nwankwo reminds us, the fear of the Haitian Revolution was specifically a fear of "a transnational idea of Black community,"[35] which carried with it the broader threat "of people of African descent from and in a variety of locations connecting with each other and fomenting a massive revolution that might overturn the whole Atlantic slave system" (7). Blake embodies these different revolutionary imaginaries, especially its transnational community component, as, though we meet him as an enslaved man in the U.S., we also learn that he was originally born free in the West Indies and that his name is actually Carolus Henricus Blacus. However, like Chen Pan, Blake is tricked into slavery once he boards a ship and learns that not only is it a ship used for transporting enslaved people, but that he is also now part of the cargo. In this way, Blake brings together the revolutionary imaginaries of the West Indies with those of the U.S.'s own history of rebellions against slavery.

Moreover, the details of the plot conspire to bring Blake back to Cuba: purchased by Colonel Stephen Franks, a northerner, Blake frames his enslavement as a decision on his part as he continues in this role after falling in love with an enslaved woman, Maggie, whom he later marries. After Franks sells Maggie, Blake declares himself free and escapes with a mission to find Maggie in Cuba. The first part of the novel focuses on Blake's travels south as well as his work freeing the enslaved people owned by Franks and his neighbors, including his son, and the second part of the novel focuses on Blake's time in Cuba. These coordinates are crucial for the novel's depiction of a transnational revolution, as, while Blake is in the North, Delany depicts the hypocrisy of northerners. Meanwhile, Blake's travels in the South emphasize the connections that draw the Southern U.S. with Cuba through both the Ostend Manifesto of 1854 and the annexationist movement in Cuba.[36] Acquiring Cuba had been a goal for U.S. Southern enslavers, but the Ostend Manifesto took this position further by arguing that "Cuba belonged 'naturally to that great family of States of which the Union is the providential nursery' and that

SPECULATIVE REVOLUTIONS

the United States would be justified 'in wresting it from Spain.'"[37] Cuban enslavers welcomed annexation by the U.S. as a way to preserve the institution of slavery, which was a political position that Aisha Finch argues was a particularly powerful movement leading up to La Escalera.[38]

The idea of the American Revolution as an unfinished revolution because "the true revolution, for universal liberty, remains unfinished"[39] emerges in the Dismal Swamp scenes in the novel, which Andy Doolen argues positions "African Americans as the real heirs to the universal right of revolution" (158).[40] The Dismal Swamp, which was the site of a famous maroon community, also epitomizes the limits of resistance in the U.S. and explains Blake's turn to Cuba as the site of his revolutionary imaginary. Once in the Dismal Swamp, Blake is met with "a number of the old confederates of the noted Nat Turner,"[41] including the conjurors Gamby Gholar, a comrade of Nat Turner, and Maudy Ghamus, a comrade of Gabriel Prosser, who also led an unsuccessful rebellion. In the swamp, Blake learns that Maudy fought in the American Revolution (1775–83); however, Maudy also says that Prosser fought in the American Revolution as well, which is impossible, since Prosser was born in 1775, suggesting yet another speculative tactic Delany uses to fashion his revolutionary imaginary. A newly invigorated hemispheric revolutionary history is needed, Delany suggests, because, according to Ghamus, Black revolution in the U.S. has become increasingly futile. Ghamus observes, of the revolutionaries in the Swamp,

> that the Swamp contained them in sufficient number to take the whole United States; the only difficulty in the way being that the slaves in the different states could not be convinced of their strength. He had himself for years been an emissary; also, Gamby Gholar, who had gone out among them with sufficient charms to accomplish all they desired, but could not induce the slaves to a general rising." (114–15)

In Blake, Ghamus and Gholar see another figure akin to Nat Turner, who is capable of encouraging the enslaved people to rebel. To that end, the conjurors initiate Blake in their craft, going so far as to make "him conjuror of the highest degree known to their art" (116).

So anointed, Blake continues to travel across the South spreading his revolutionary plan from plantation to plantation. Unfortunately, that plan never comes to fruition, as this section ends with Blake boarding a ship to Cuba in search of Maggie. That said, once Blake arrives in Cuba, Delany quickly jettisons the Maggie subplot, suggesting that, similar to Rizal's novels, women are ancillary not only to revolution, but the texts themselves. Reunited with Placido, Blake continues to use the same tactics he deployed to foment revolution in the south. Doolen argues that Cuba becomes the site of revolutionary potential give the reality of "the U.S. national model as barren ground for a black revolution in the western hemisphere."[42] In Cuba, the conditions are substantially different and ripe for revolution—there are more Black people on the island than white,[43] there's a larger free population in part because buying one's freedom is an easier task on the island, and the specter of Haiti hangs over Cuba both in the novel and during this historical moment.[44] The other telling difference between the U.S. and Cuba that Blake does not mention is that in Cuba the question of abolition was often tied to the question of Cuban independence; thus, to a certain extent Afro Cubans had some white support. Even though Chiles suggests that Delany deemphasizes Haiti—the first country to achieve both abolition and independence—in *Blake*,[45] Grégory Pierrot carefully argues that, given the Haitian Revolution's "notoriety,"[46] "Delany hoped to replace the Haitian tale of collective black heroism with a new, fictional one rooted in historical and current fact. With *Blake*, Delany meant to write over Haiti."[47] I agree that Delany revises the Haitian Revolution; that said, I contend that the rebellion that haunts the novel even more is La Escalera, particularly because of how it allows Delany to imagine a hemispheric revolution.[48] In fact, such a reading is not necessarily at odds with Pierrot, since he argues that "Delany set out to break the paralyzing status of the Haitian Revolution as the absolute referent of black revolt and autonomy" (177).

Although scholars still debate whether La Escalera was an actual rebellion or one created by the colonial government to "dismantle a burgeoning—and notably multiracial—anticolonial struggle, targeting upwardly mobile free people of color,"[49] Finch convincingly shows how from 1843 to 1844 there were a series of revolutionary plots that, combined, can be referred to as La Escalera. Further, Finch writes against narratives that focus on Plácido's role as a key leader in the movement, arguing that La Escalera was "a series of smaller mobilizations at the level of the individual plantations" (7). As Finch's descriptions of La Escalera show, she also reads it as more than a series of slave rebellions; she explores how La Escalera was fundamentally an anticolonial movement. In fact, while the Cuban Wars of Independence are conventionally understood as beginning with the Ten Years' War (1868–78), Finch explains how "the leaders of Cuba's first black political party, the Partido Independiente de Color, continued to invoke the events of 1844 for their constituents" (220), going so far as to refer to "their own struggles with state violence [as] 'the epilogue of the trial of La Escalera'" (220). In this way, Finch demonstrates how the repercussions of the movement meant that it was a couple decades before another rebellion broke out with revolutionaries in the Ten Years' War, clearly articulating that their work was part of the same struggle.

By exploring how La Escalera unfolded on rural plantations, Finch underscores the affinities between Blake's revolutionary plan and the Ladder Conspiracy. For example, Finch describes how both enslaved and free people "frequently made their way to the homes of the legally free" (73), which highlights how Creoles "were unable to fully demarcate the boundaries of the world in which enslaved people moved, particularly at night" (74). Moreover, she describes what Blake calls seclusions, as Black people met at private gatherings; in fact, "throughout the early months of 1844 dozens and dozens of witnesses spoke of outside organizers coming to meet with resident captains on their estates" (66), suggesting that not only was there frequent communication among the plantations, but that this communication was often the result of organizers bringing together people to foment revolution. This decentralized structure was such that even though presumed leaders of the movement, including Plácido and David Turnbull, were suspected of doing most of the organizing, the planning was so widespread that "the majority of slaves in the plantation countryside never seem to have heard of any of these people" (169).

As Finch's research demonstrates, the structure of the conspiracy was diffuse and decentralized, much like the revolution Blake works to manifest. Although critics have remarked on the vagueness of the plan and how Delany chooses not to share the "secret" with his readership, Blake does offer a number of compelling descriptions of his strategy, descriptions that resonate with the tactics used to plan La Escalera. In his most explicit description of the secret, Blake tells his two friends, Andy and Charles, "to find one good man or woman—I don't care which, so that they prove to be the right person—on a single plantation, and hold a seclusion and impart the secret to them, and make them the organizers for their own plantation, and they in like manner impart it to some other next to them, and so on. In this way, it will spread like smallpox among them.'"[50] Blake advocates for enslaved people to band together in a decentralized revolution whose success depends on coordinating a number of leaders in much the same way Finch describes. Moreover, he frames the secret using the language of contagion, alluding to how Europeans such as Jeffrey Amherst intentionally infected Indigenous populations with smallpox. Like smallpox, Blake suggests, revolution is also contagious, but this disease will be used against the oppressors.

Many critics have pointed to Delany's comments about the need for an "elevated" Black populace, but others have noted the need for a sense of a Black political consciousness.[51] I argue that the notion of revolution Delany puts forward is one that relies on the development of a specifically Black political consciousness, one that imagines all Black people as part of the same community and that community as one that is united and organized to pursue the rights and interests of their people. Blake seems to share Delany's viewpoints about an elevated Black populace, especially given the disparaging comment he makes to Andy and Charles about conjuring, which he says "'makes the more ignorant slaves have greater confidence in, and more respect for their headmen and leaders.'"[52] He goes on to remark, "'we must take the slaves, not as we wish them to be, but as we really find them to be.'"[53] Although Blake may seem to be dismissive of the superstitions among enslaved people, he actually espouses a useful organizing tactic.

This tactic is central to Blake's revolutionary plotting, in which he claims that "'just here, for once, the slave-holding preacher's advice to the black man is appropriate—"Stand still and see the salvation."'"[54] Standing still allows for enough time to pass so that the secret can be transmitted from plantation to plantation such that when the call for revolution comes, the enslaved people will be prepared for "a continent-wide uprising."[55] The secret depends on the development of a Black political consciousness and community formed through the gatherings at the various seclusions. As Blake also describes, the secret "'is so simple that the most stupid among the slaves will understand it as well as if he had been instructed for a year'"[56] and "'so simple is it that the trees of the forest or an orchard illustrate it'" (40). Even though Blake once again uses disparaging language to describe his enslaved brethren, in remarking that the trees exemplify the plan, I maintain that he's describing not only strength in numbers, but also a united front as the enslaved people are brought together to work toward a shared purpose.

Much like La Escalera, where the "most visible agitators were largely African-born men,"[57] Blake's Cuban rebellion incorporates newly arrived enslaved African people. Not only does this group reinforce the revolutionary army, but they also exemplify yet another revolutionary tactic. As mentioned previously, in part two, Blake takes up the position of sailing master of a slave ship with the plan of staging a revolt on the way back from Africa with fresh reinforcements. Pierrot notes that Blake carefully selects the enslaved people who will board the ship for his mutiny.[58] However, as I've also described, this revolt is stymied. That said, Blake quickly develops an alternate plan: he tells Placido about the mutinous Africans, and Placido quickly spreads word through informal channels like gossip and more formal avenues such as newspapers. The knowledge that the enslaved Africans are seditious

> reduced the captives to a minimum price, which placed them in the reach of small capitalists, for whom they were purchased by agents, who pretended themselves to be spectators. These agents were among the fairest of the quadroons, high in the esteem and confidence of

their people, the entire cargo of captives through them going directly into black families or their friends.[59]

Whereas in both *Blake* and in his political writings Delany emphasizes the need for pure African blood, here we see "the fairest of the quadroons" working toward the emancipation of those whom Delany views as the true liberators.[60] Yet a couple paragraphs before outlining this plan, we learn that "were Cubans classified according to their complexion or race, three out of five of the inhabitants called white, would decidedly be claimed by the colored people, though there is a larger number much fairer than those classified and known in the register as colored."[61] Delany's implication here is that the majority of white Cubans are actually Afro Cubans. The juxtaposition of this quote followed by the "fairest" of the people of color suggests that there is potentially an even larger base from which to find recruits to Blake's cause. We might also read this comment on white-passing Cubans as referring to Afro Cubans who have chosen whiteness over solidarity, but the example of the agents who buy the enslaved Africans underscores how one can always choose otherwise.

In this scene, then, we have an example from African American literature that illuminates a Latinx revolutionary horizon that challenges positivist divisions among races and, like the horizon described on the slave ship, points to an unknown, but hopeful future built on solidarity rather than a possessive investment in whiteness. The defining feature of the Black populations Blake organizes is that they come together around a shared politics and a shared purpose. So powerful is the goal of liberation and equality that those who benefit from proximity to whiteness work to help those of their people who are enslaved. In her examination of Plácido's figuration in *Blake*, Nwankwo reflects on Plácido's significantly lighter skin, arguing that "Delany chooses to make him politically, if not phenotypically, Black,"[62] underscoring the diversity of positions within blackness and the need for blackness to become a political choice rather than an identity marker to be useful. The specific political circumstances of Cuba are key: an alignment between white/white-passing Cubans and Afro Cubans emerges out of the shared condition of colonization.

As I mentioned in the Introduction, the Latin American independence movements, unlike the U.S., grappled with what it meant to fight for liberation while enslaving a significant portion of the population. José Martí's solution to this paradox was to advocate for a raceless society in which white and Afro Cubans could unite over their shared Cubanness. Ada Ferrer argues that these nationalist aims created the conditions for an uneasy alliance and that by the end of the Spanish-American War (1898) the inequality among the two Cuban populations reasserted itself so that white Cubans who belatedly sided with the fight for independence were made officers and recognized for their contributions at the same time that Afro Cubans who actually fought in the war—including its previous iterations, such as the Ten Years' War—were demoted and entered a political landscape in which their interests were not considered.[63] As we saw in Chapter 4, the struggle between white and Afro Cubans continued into the twentieth century, a point made painfully clear by the Race War of 1912.

Blake's plan to free the enslaved Africans points to the inspiring possibilities that are available to revolutionaries if they act in concert with one another, but, as the historical record confirms, these solidarities can be precarious. Although we do not see examples of white collaborators in *Blake*, the novel does offer an example of grounds for a potential alliance with white Cubans: namely, the fear of U.S. annexation. Indeed, we learn of two key instances in which the Americans in Cuba clearly try to sow discord among white and Afro Cubans to prevent them from successfully fighting off the U.S. should they invade.[64] We learn that the Americans on the island are "a restless, dissatisfied class, ever plotting schemes to keep up excitement in the island."[65] So insidious is the U.S. presence in Cuba that when Count Alcora, the Captain General, hears complaints "that the creoles had not the right of franchise, being ineligible to positions of honor" (298), he dismisses them, noting that these "statements originated in the principal commercial cities in the United States, by such speculators as frequent the exchanges in Dock, Wall and State streets, backed by the brokerages of Baltimore, Richmond, Charleston and New Orleans. They had openly declared that Cuba and Porto Rico must cease to be Spanish Colonies, and become territories of the United States" (299).[66] In other words, the Americans represent the U.S.'s financial, as well as colonial, interests in Cuba. After all, it was in the best interest of both U.S. and Cuban plantation owners to maintain slavery on the island to extract maximum profits from the plantations.

In addition to encouraging creole complaints, the Americans also actively tried to drive a wedge between white and Afro Cubans. In fact, American attempts to give the impression of an imminent Black rebellion simultaneously thwart Blake's plans by forcing him and his comrades to continue to wait for the right moment and desensitize the Captain General to such plots, thus paradoxically offering the opportunity for a rebellion to take place. The fictional plot at the Hotel de Americana Nord exemplifies one of the Americans' efforts to redirect "the attention of the authorities to the negroes."[67] As one of the American conspirators observes, the Black population on the island is "'the only formidable enemy in the event of a patriot movement we should have to contend against, must be got out of the way. That can only be done successfully by getting the government down on them. This once effected, we are safe, as they will never again place confidence in those who once go against or deceive them'" (304). Ironically, in plotting against the Afro Cubans, the Americans admit that the Black population is the most patriotic of Cubans; likewise, the Americans acknowledge that independence and abolition are twin projects. Most tellingly, the Americans point to the number and organizing capacity of the Afro Cubans, indicating that Cuban independence can only be won with their aid.

Remarkably, the issue of Cuban independence only arises once in the novel, when Madame Montego née Cordora asks Placido about potential allies on the other Caribbean islands. While Placido says that they cannot expect help from the British colonies or even Haiti, he has this to say about Cuban independence: "'Should we under such circumstances strike for liberty, it must also be for independent self government, because we have the prejudices of the mother-country and the white colonists alike to contend against. Whereas were we as we should be, enfranchised by Spain, we would then only have the opposition of Cuba and Porto Rico, and should be loyal to Spain'" (289). Here, Placido implies that were Spain to grant freedom to the enslaved people, there would be no occasion to rebel. However, since that is not the case, to fight for freedom means fighting against both slavery and colonization. That said, I argue that the issue of independence only briefly arises in the novel because of Delany's own imperialism. As we learned in Delany's *Official Report of the Niger Valley Exploring Party*, in his advocacy for Black emigration, Delany suggests that in Africa, African Americans would colonize Africans. Delany's previous emigration plans, when he looked at the Caribbean and Central America, are no different as he imagines that African Americans will migrate en masse to these locations and permanently settle, without accounting for the populations who already live in these areas.

In *Blake* Delany rehearses the arguments he has made about black emigration elsewhere and does so on the level of narration. Jerome McGann argues that the providential design that will lead toward liberation in the novel operates on what he calls "levels of representation."[68] According to McGann, the levels are "first, in the plot of the action, the career that Blake undertakes; and second, even more, in Delany's construction of that career as a prophecy of black liberation. In the first case, the design comes about as a fictional representation; in the second, as a conscious effort by Delany, often speaking in his own voice, to promote and participate in the achievement of that design" (xx). In this way, Delany aligns his goals as author and narrator with those of his protagonist, underscoring how *Blake* is just as much—if not more—a political argument as a fictional novel. To that end, Delany-as-narrator makes the following argument for Black priority in the Americas:

> Their justification of the issue made was on the fundamental basis of original priority, claiming that the western world had been originally peopled and possessed by the Indians—a colored race—and a part of the continent in Central America by a pure black race. This they urged gave them an indisputable right with every admixture of blood, to an equal, if not superior claim to an inheritance of the Western Hemisphere.[69]

Significantly—and once again in contrast with his arguments about pure Black blood—here Delany aligns Indigenous Americans with Black people in the hemisphere by referring to the Indigenous people as "a colored race." There are certainly arguments to be made about a cynical use of indigeneity to justify Black imperialism; however, I suggest that when Delany-as-narrator refers to Indigenous people as "a colored race," he is nevertheless pointing to a coalitional politics between the two groups.[70]

Shortly after making the claim to original priority, Delany's narration gives way to the first level of representation, that of the plot of the novel. Blake picks up the narrative thread that Delany-as-narrator initiates, arguing that in Cuba, "'we are the many and the oppressors few; consequently, they have no moral right to hold rule over us, whilst we have the moral right and physical power to prevent them.'" (288). For Blake, the oppressed have the numerical advantage. More importantly for Blake, the white people have no "moral right," particularly given the notion of original priority that extends to Indigenous people and, by extension, Black people, given the shared condition of being "colored races" (288). Further, as Delany argues, such races "were by nature adapted to the tropical regions of this part of the world as to all other similar climates, it being a scientific fact that they increased and progressed whilst the white decreased and continually retrograded, their offspring becoming enervated and imbecile" (288), indicating that the fact of Black survivance and white death proves that Black people are equal, if not superior to, white people and therefore have an equal and even a superior claim to the land.

In *Blake* we have the contours of a revolutionary imaginary useful for conjuring a Latinx revolutionary horizon that centers Black people of the Americas in a coalitional politics geared toward the shared purpose of liberation, one that for Afro Cubans means not only the abolition of slavery, but also independence from Spain. That said, given that the version of *Blake* available to us is presumed to be incomplete, *Blake* leaves us with a revolutionary imaginary, but not an actual revolution. That said, numerous critics have speculated on what such a revolution would look like, offering additional revolutionary imaginaries that allow us to envision additional Latinx revolutionary horizons.[71] McGann observes in his introduction to the novel that La Escalera is the key for understanding the revolutionary possibilities of Blake's organizing; he writes,

> When Delany replays La Escalera, however, he executes a countermove against that entire dreadful inheritance. Placido and La Escalera are precisely *not* replayed in *Blake* as sacred talismans that can be recovered and then used to inspire "insurrection." Slave rebellions, free black rebellions, even white-led risings like John Brown's—all would have seemed like recycled, traumatized history for Delany when he conceived and published *Blake*. When white history is recovered through a deep black perspective it reemerges as a history of alienation.[72]

In other words, given that the history of revolution in Delany's home country of the U.S. is tied to white revolutionary imaginaries, Delany must turn to revolutionary histories from elsewhere to conceptualize a successful revolution. For McGann, "in *Blake*, the very word 'insurrection' becomes slowly glossed as a white word drawn out of white history. Delany argues that when blacks look at the past, white culture and history encourage them to see it in a white perspective. Translated into a black perspective, this history emerges as a series of either martyrdoms or weak accommodations" (xxiv–xxv). Based on this claim, McGann argues that Delany's revolutionary imaginary "lies beyond either insurrection or accommodation" (xxv) and is instead based on "a story that reimagines the past. Black emigration from America, from white American Memory, is the only way to freedom for both blacks and whites because it is the only sure way to see history from multiple perspectives" (xxv).

Although Delany was certainly a proponent of Black emigration (to Central America or the Caribbean, then Africa), I contend that the document we have in *Blake* does not support this argument. In fact, as we saw in Delany's revision of the American Revolution as an unfinished revolution, I would argue that it is not because of Black emigration but Black transnationalism that Delany can imagine a successful revolution; he could apprehend Black histories because he knew about revolutionary movements such as La Escalera. Delany's work underscores the importance of transnational and hemispheric literary history, as such frameworks enable us to more accurately read texts that are provincially siloed into national histories. To situate *Blake* properly, then, requires putting the novel into conversation with Latinx and Latin American Studies as well as histories of liberation more broadly.

While I agree with McGann's observations that La Escalera was not replayed in *Blake*, particularly given that its very name is tied to the brutal suppression of the conspiracy, I suggest that Delany finds the model of organizing that led to La Escalera a useful paradigm, as exemplified by the fact that he promotes some of the same organizational strategies in *Blake*. The difference between revolution in *Blake* and La Escalera extends from particular organizing tactics to broader conceptualizations of the meaning of revolution. One key tactic Blake uses that does not seem to be part of La Escalera is driving down the price of the enslaved Africans, pooling resources, and using white-passing Afro Cubans to then buy and free Africans.[73] Notably, what's most revolutionary about *Blake* is not only the coalitional politics Delany depicts, but also—and more importantly—how organizing around a specific issue such as the abolition of slavery allows for disparate groups (Africans, Afro Cubans across a spectrum of statuses, from those marked by color to those marked as enslaved or free) to imagine what it means to be a people.

As Pierrot points out, ultimately "Blake's plan is to federate around blackness as a political choice."[74] In imagining a people out of a politics, *Blake* revises the terms of the imagined community. If for Benedict Anderson print culture made it possible for the formation of an imagined community, for Delany the seclusions and the willingness to work toward the freedom of people one does not know makes it possible for the formation of not only an imagined community, but an imagined revolution.[75] As Rebecca Skidmore Biggio notes in her discussion of "the community of conspiracy,"[76] "The coherence of Blake's militant movement is less dependent on the actual realization of the violence than on a community *capable* of realizing the violence they portend, on a community both able and willing to kill their enemies" (448).[77] In this way, the novel's seeming incompleteness perfectly exemplifies the imagined community of conspiracy—and, by extension, revolution—as it leaves the fact of revolution up to revolutionaries, but offers a compelling imaginary in which, "black futurity [emerges] as a practice rather than a promise."[78] As Brittan suggests, "Finding value in fiction *as fiction* (speculating *about* rather than *in*), Delany links black futurity to the worldmaking capacity of the subjunctive imagination" (96). The subjunctive tense speaks to desires and wishes and returns us to both Camila's subjunctive imaginaries in Chapter 3 and Ricardo Ortiz's discussion of latinidad "as desire, as wish, and as *project*."[79] Latinidad itself is a worldmaking project, and turning to Delany's conceptualization of Black futurity through revolution offers us a way to imagine a Latinx future that centers Black imaginaries.

Delany offers a prescient and additional way to view the Cuban Wars of Independence outside of the narrative of "white-led risings." Conventional understandings of the Ten Years' War (1868–78), which would subsequently lead to thirty years of fighting for independence, began on October 10, 1868 (six years after the last installment of *Blake*), with the Grito de Yara, when Carlos Manuel de Céspedes freed the people he had enslaved. Ferrer relays, "'You are free,' he told them, 'as I am.' Then addressing them as 'citizens,' he invited them to help 'conquer liberty and independence' for Cuba. Thus began the first war for Cuban independence."[80] She also observes, "The timing of their efforts was surprising" (1) and, while it was "led initially by a handful of prosperous white men, the revolution placed free men of color in local positions of authority. It also freed slaves, made them soldiers, and called them citizens" (3). Although she includes brief references to La Escalera and another rebel plot in El Cobre in 1864, Ferrer adheres to this version of the Wars of Independence, despite the fact that in her telling, fighting for independence is directly tied to abolition. Reading *Blake* in light of this framing allows us to see how he proleptically envisioned the centrality of Afro Cubans in the fight for hemispheric liberation as, though the Grito de Yara was seemingly a surprise, Delany reveals the extent of Afro Cuban organizing, which suggests that such a movement shouldn't have been a surprise at all. That is, in imagining the fight for independence as distinct from the abolition of slavery, histories like those offered by Ferrer seem to forget how often abolition and independence were twinned in what seems like a continuous struggle, from the Aponte Rebellion in 1812 to "the Soles y Rayos de Bolívar conspiracy in 1823 and the Gran Legión del Águila Negra conspiracy in 1829"[81] to La Escalera and El Cobre and the Wars of Independence.

Destroyer Futures

In much the same way as I began my discussion of *Blake* with a vision of revolution on the horizon, here I open with one offered by Silko, as seen by the character Menardo on the television. Menardo is a Mexican man who disavows his Indigenous heritage and owns Universal Insurance, which "insured against all losses, no matter the cause, including acts of God, mutinies, war, and revolution."[82] As Menardo tells his customers, "The 'new world' could belong to them just as the old one had" (261); in other words, Menardo's job is to secure the future for the elite and in the process procure a modern-day form of gracias al sacar, the Spanish colonial practice of buying whiteness.[83] Haunted by visions of his own death, increasing civil unrest means that "For years Menardo had not had to worry about the 'civil strife, strike, or insurrection' clause of his insurance policies" (481). However,

> one night Menardo had awakened to a loud buzzing sound. The screen of his television had been filled with what appeared to be larvae or insects swarming. When Menardo had raised the volume and looked closely, he saw the swarms were mobs of angry brown people swarming like bees from horizon to horizon. At first Menardo had thought he was seeing a rerun of videotapes taken at the Mexico City riots years before; then, looking more closely, he had seen the city was Miami, and the mobs, American. (481–82)

From Menardo's perspective, the riots he sees in Miami are a brown revolution that extends from horizon to horizon. Yet, rather than view these riots as a good thing—a way for people to protest for their rights, to mobilize en masse against their own oppression—the television scene causes Menardo to worry more about his bottom line, about the financial losses he will incur to insure his clients. The most famous of "the Mexico City riots years before" would be the Tlatelolco massacre, which was the culmination of months of protesting the 1968 Olympics to be held in Mexico City. That Menardo cannot tell the difference between Miami and Mexico City points to the browning of revolution in the U.S. and the shared sense of disenfranchisement and unrest.

Within this context of a brown revolution and a whitened Menardo, his disavowal of Indigenous ancestry is significant. Importantly, the description of Menardo's relationship to his indigeneity occurs in the first chapter of part two of the book, titled "Mestizo" (257). Initially, Menardo had a strong relationship with his Indigenous grandfather, who told him stories of their ancestors; that said, once Menardo makes the "horrible discovery" (259) that "the people the old man called 'our ancestors,' 'our family,' were in fact Indians" (259), he refuses to visit his grandfather again, and his grandfather dies shortly afterward. Convinced that "without the family nose, Menardo might have passed for one of *sangre limpia*" (259), Menardo is relieved when his grandfather is buried because his nose is "the evidence the flat nose was inherited" (259).[84] Menardo invents a story that his nose was smashed in a boxing match (260), which, to his mind, allows him to enter the more elite circles in Tuxtla Gutiérrez, the capital of Chiapas.

Returning to the title of the chapter—"Mestizo"—Silko seems to suggest that to be mestizo is to deny one's indigeneity to move up the social ranks. Silko's perspective is an important one, as she is of Laguna, Mexican, and white ancestry and grew up on Laguna Pueblo. Primarily known as a Native American writer, in some ways Silko is the reverse of Menardo as an

Indigenous and Mexican person who embraces her indigeneity. *Almanac* shows that to embrace one's indigeneity does not mean refusing one's Mexicanness, but to refuse the culture in which gracias al sacar and sangre limpia are goals to achieve, which is a Latinx revolution horizon that often seems like an insurmountable barrier.[85] Trujillo elegantly argues, "*Almanac* deposes Native American indigeneity, Latinidad, and Blackness from identity politics by abandoning revolutionary modalities premised on state recognition or capture."[86] Put another way, not seeking state recognition of how one identifies is a way to bypass the legal structures that enforce such identifications. Extending Trujillo's argument, I would add that settler law weaponizes blood quantum and identification as methods for isolating these communities from each other rather than recognizing their "disappeared relations" (44).

Within this context of brownness, revolution, and sangre limpia, I turn my attention to the David, Beaufrey, and Serlo narrative, particularly since there is a curious absence in the *Almanac* scholarship in terms of this plotline in general, but in regard to how it intersects with revolution in the novel specifically.[87] Although we are first introduced to David and Beaufrey early in *Almanac* as part of Seese's narrative—she's convinced that David kidnapped their son, Monte, and works for Lecha, a psychic who can find the dead— we eventually see their stories unfold from their perspectives.[88] This happens once David and Beaufrey flee first to Cartagena, then to Serlo's finca after kidnapping Monte and after the gallery show in which David exhibits the graphic photographs he took of his former lover Eric's body after Eric took his own life. At first it seems that David is at the center of the erotic dynamics in the group—he's Beaufrey's lover, but also takes on Eric as a lover before turning to Seese—but, as the later chapters emphasize, David is merely a pawn in a much more sinister dynamic between Beaufrey and Serlo. In fact, Eric was originally Beaufrey's lover until Beaufrey met David. To the extent that critics have considered this narrative vis-à-vis revolution, it's to mention, briefly, that this plotline is an example of the Destroyers, the name Silko gives to people "who fed off energy released by destruction" (336) and "who delighted in blood" (336).

Silko additionally explains that while the Destroyers play a key role in the brutal colonization of the Americas, there were also Destroyers (called Gunadeeyahs) in Mexico and "Montezuma had been the biggest sorcerer of all" (760). In Silko's telling, "The appearance of Europeans had been no accident; the Gunadeeyahs had called for their white brethren to join them. Sure enough the Spaniards had arrived in Mexico fresh from the Church Inquisition with appetites whetted for disembowelment and blood. No wonder Cortés and Montezuma had hit it off together when they met; both had been members of the same secret clan" (760). In this way, Silko links atrocities committed by the Spanish on their own continent to the atrocities they commit in the Americas.[89]

The absence of the David, Beaufrey, and Serlo plot from the existing scholarship makes sense, especially given that this particular narrative features some of the most violent and brutal actions in the novel, an excess of violence that seems unnecessary in a text where most of the stories converge around revolution. I insist that this plotline is central to our understanding of the novel, as, in my reading, this narrative, especially the events that take place on Serlo's finca in Colombia, revise the eugenicist thought that's persisted in Latin America since the Wars of Independence.[90] More specifically, I speculate that Silko revises the famous Argentine Domingo Sarmiento's thesis in *Facundo* in which he argues that people of color, especially Indigenous people, are barbarous, and the Creole population is civilized.[91] Sarmiento privileged European ideas and promoted European immigration to Argentina; as Katherine Gordy observes, "Sarmiento believed not only in the superiority of European ideas, but also in the possibility that they could and should be imported to Argentina (and Latin America) unchanged."[92] According to Juliet Hooker, Sarmiento was a foundational thinker for José Vasconcelos,[93] who also promoted eugenicist thought in his theorization of la raza cósmica, where Vasconcelos made troubling statements (that echoed Sarmiento) such as "Latin America owes what it is to the white European, and is not going to deny him"[94] and, in terms of the mixing of races, "the lower types of the species will be absorbed by the superior type" (32). Although the method for improving the race for both Sarmiento and Vasconcelos seems to be mostly a natural process (accelerated in the case of Sarmiento by European immigration), their logic informs the David, Beaufrey, and Serlo plotline, especially in light of Serlo's own eugenicist research, which I will discuss shortly.

We can see this distinction between civilization and barbarism further reinforced by the Ariel/Caliban binary as theorized by the Uruguayan intellectual José Enrique Rodó's *Ariel* (1900) and Roberto Fernández Retamar's "Caliban: Notes Toward a Discussion of Culture in Our America" (1971).[95] For Rodó, "Shakespeare's ethereal Ariel symbolizes the noble, soaring aspect of the human spirit. He represents the superiority of reason and feeling over the base impulses of irrationality";[96] moreover, "Ariel is the ideal toward which human selection ascends, the force that wields life's eternal chisel, effacing from aspiring mankind the clinging vestiges of Caliban, the play's symbol of brutal sensuality" (31). As these descriptions make clear, Ariel represents the heights of civilization, particularly a civilization that has reached those heights from "human selection." Speaking of evolution, Rodó notes that it "has assured that the most beautiful within a species survive over those less fortunately endowed" (55). Yet the most pernicious of Rodó's observations is his view of democracy, in which he manifests his fear of popular rule, arguing that if left up to the masses, "democracy will gradually extinguish any superiority that does not translate into sharper and more ruthless skills in the struggles of self-interest, the self-interest that then becomes the most ignoble and brutal form of strength" (59). Shockingly, Rodó views popular rule as one in which the refinements of civilized culture are stripped away, leading him to argue that "rationally conceived, democracy always includes an indispensable element of aristocracy, a means of establishing the superiority of the finest, achieved through free consent" (67). Thus, in Rodó's democracy we find a monarchy that ensures that the ethereal Ariels of Latin America remain in the higher realms while the base and debased Caliban toils on the ground.

Yet, as Retamar observes, the Ariel/Caliban distinction is a false binary because "both are slaves in the hands of Prospero" (16).[97] In Rodó's formulation, Ariel seems to be an inspiration for "those who labor and those who struggle, until the fulfillment of the unknown plan permits him . . . to break his material bonds and return forever to the center of his divine fire."[98] This demonstrates how, despite his noble efforts, Ariel remains in bondage. Retamar offers a corrective to Rodó's theorization by claiming Caliban for Latin America as the masculine revolutionary of the Americas.[99] In doing so, as Ortiz argues, "the most consistent pattern to be detected in Retamar's treatment of those figures he rejects is, for better or worse, the feminization or hysterization of these otherwise male writers."[100] Ortiz insightfully parses out that Retamar's strategy for countering opposing views is "through the rhetorical use of the sexual innuendo" (97) such that Retamar does "the cultural police work required by his project" (98). In revising Rodó's formulation but keeping the same terms, Retamar exemplifies the limits of his revolutionary imaginary—and horizon—as, "rather than subvert this binary construction, however, he replicates it by simply inverting the hierarchy of its terms," according to María Josefina Saldaña-Portillo.[101]

Even though it is unclear if Silko was familiar with Sarmiento's thought as well as its later manifestations in Rodó and Retamar, what is clear is that these binary forms of thinking continue to inform theories of race, particularly indigeneity, in the Americas. After all, as Retamar argues, the Caliban/Ariel binary stems from the conquistadors' experiences with the Carib and Arauaco people in the Caribbean, figuring the former as violent and the latter as peaceful.[102] In my reading, to realize the revolutionary project of *Almanac*, Silko must also grapple with those harmful ontological and epistemological framings that led to the present-day oppression of Indigenous people and people of color more broadly. Though scholars often point to Silko's message in *Almanac* that we must remember our histories and our ancestors, little attention has been paid to the intellectual histories that inform the historical conditions of the Americas.[103] Indeed, Marxist, and to a certain extent, Freudian, thought have been examined in the novel, but not the Latin American intellectual traditions that inform the Destroyers' thinking, a tradition that Silko subverts in the scenes that take place on the finca.[104] In offering a brief overview of this intellectual history and comparing it with the eugenicist project at the finca, I explore how Silko offers us a Latinx revolutionary horizon that reaches into the past rather than the future, since for Silko there is no future without a thorough interrogation of the past.

The chapters on David, Beaufrey, and Serlo point us to Destroyer futures and the horrific events that take place on Serlo's finca, where Indigenous and mestizx people are forced to endure brutal labor conditions. Beaufrey and Serlo both come from elite families who believe that those with blue blood or "*sangre pura* were entirely different beings, on a far higher plane, unconceivable to commoners."[105] While for Rodó Caliban typifies primitivism, crudeness, and utilitarianism, and for Retamar Caliban is a figure of resistance who signifies revolutionary potential in the Caribbean, Silko revises the Caliban/cannibal figure in her depiction of Beaufrey. The first chapter on Beaufrey introduces him as a child who had an early fascination with Albert Fish, the infamous serial killer and cannibal whose victims were children. For Beaufrey, it's crucial that the "Fish family had been blue bloods directly off the *Mayflower*" (534). Despite the fact that there do not seem to be any sources that verify this information, Beaufrey nevertheless feels that "Albert Fish and he were kindred spirits" (534).

Disturbingly, "as Beaufrey had read European history in college, he had realized there had always been a connection between human cannibals and the aristocracy. Members of European aristocracy were simply more inclined to hunger and crave human flesh and blood because centuries of *le droit du seigneur* had corrupted them absolutely" (534–35). Although we do not know Beaufrey's specific ancestry—he seems to be descended from European aristocracy but was able to compete for Argentina in equestrian competitions—what we do know is that unlike Rodó's Caliban, Beaufrey is presumably the height of civilization and good breeding. In contrast to Retamar's Caliban, Beaufrey is far from a revolutionary: he preys on those he views as beneath him, including David. In figuring Beaufrey as a type of cannibal, but not a Caliban, Silko illuminates how capitalism serves the elites by offering them an endless supply of consumable goods and, especially, people. David is one such person, as he serves as a form of entertainment for Beaufrey, who plays a game in which he "permit[s] gorgeous young men such as David to misunderstand their importance in the world" (537), then "destroy" (537) them as he did with Eric and subsequently does with David—in Cartagena, Beaufrey stages Monte's kidnapping. He then has Monte killed and has graphic photographs taken of the baby's autopsy and organ harvesting (563).

Central to Beaufrey's line of thinking—which he shares with Serlo—is the droit du seigneur (the lord's right) mentioned previously, which is the presumably medieval practice of feudal lords raping the women who work for them, in much the same way that we saw in Chapter 1 with the discussion of "la muchacha." Yet, for Beaufrey the droit du seigneur is an informal practice, but for Serlo it is a eugenicist project and a technology. We learn that Serlo "believed the human race would die out without a proper genetic balance. All along the *droit du seigneur* had been aimed at constant infusion of superior aristocratic blood into the peasant stock" (541), which is exemplified by Serlo's memories of his uncles raping young Indigenous women "because they believed it was their God-given duty to 'upgrade' mestizo and Indian bloodstock" (541). Serlo's views of improving the "mestizo and Indian bloodstock" is a continuation of Sarmiento's belief in European immigration to Argentina to whiten the population. This line of thinking has been an established practice in Latin America, from Nazi immigration to countries such as Brazil, Chile, and Argentina, to the Dominican Republic taking in Jewish refugees with similar hopes of whitening the population.[106]

Serlo takes these ideas even further by theorizing "that even the most perfect genetic specimen could be ruined, absolutely destroyed, by the defects of the child's mother" (541–42), the implication of which, given his previous ideas, is that mestizx and Indigenous women are the cause of this "ruin." One of the aims of Serlo's eugenicist project is to excise women from the equation such that "a child's 'parents' were both male" (542). To that end, Serlo takes up the practice instituted by his grandfather of "masturbate[ing] into steel cylinders where his semen was frozen for future use" (547). Serlo similarly stores his semen to enact the future his grandfather envisioned, one where "the masses of Europe might someday be upgraded through the use of artificial insemination" (547). Moreover, Serlo supports research "to develop an artificial uterus because women were often not reliable or responsible enough to give the 'superfetuses' their best chance at developing into superbabies" (547). In short, Serlo exemplifies how the height of Western civilization is barbarism. Not only has the European influence not "upgraded" the Indigenous populations of Latin America through blood or education, but Serlo's research underscores how the European influence in the Americas has been a continuation of the horrific practices begun during colonization.

Serlo's plan for the creation of "alternative earth units" exemplifies the aristocracy's fear of the masses, which is another through line in Latin American thought from the likes of Sarmiento to Rodó. This might seem odd, given the Wars of Independence, but I suggest that the independence movements are the root of this particular fear, since the Creole population could not defeat Spain without the help of people of African and Indigenous descent. After all, if the masses of people of color could rise up in Haiti and fuel the independence movements continent-wide, surely they can do so again. Serlo's finca is supposed "to become the stronghold for those of *sangre pura* as unrest and revolutions continued to sweep through" (541). Meanwhile, the alternative earth units are "modules that would orbit together in colonies, and the select few would continue as they always had, gliding in luxury and ease across polished decks of steel and glass islands where they looked down on earth" (542) to protect the elite from "the upheaval and violence [that] threatened those of superior lineage" (543). If there's anything hopeful to be found in *Almanac*, it's that the novel imagines an imminent future in which the masses *do* rise up—ideally before the alternative earth units can be created. In fact, just before Serlo describes the finca as a stronghold, we learn, presumably, of Serlo's family, who "years before they had all the mestizos and Indians relocated to work on their ranching operations in Argentina" (541), suggesting that the stronghold has already been infiltrated.

Significantly, the chapter that precedes the David, Beaufrey, and Serlo chapters on the finca are the ones dedicated to the trial of Bartolomeo, the Cuban revolutionary who runs a freedom school in Mexico and organizes supplies from his contacts in Cuba to the Indigenous revolutionaries in Mexico. Such a juxtaposition suggests that the revolution is happening at a much faster pace than Serlo's own efforts; after all, no sooner is Bartolomeo tried than the revolutionaries begin their march north. Angelita La Escapía, a colonel in the Army of Justice and Redistribution (the name chosen by the Indigenous revolutionary organization), flies ahead to attend the International Holistic Healers Convention, while the heroic twin leaders of the movement, El Feo and Wacah, follow on foot, leading the people.[107]

However, before any of this happens, Angelita heads up the trial proceedings and finds Bartolomeo "'guilty of crimes against history!'" (531), which is part of what she terms his broader denial of "'the holocaust of Indigenous Americans! Seventy-two million people in 1500 reduced to ten million people by 1600!'" (531). To support her claims, Angelita's verdict is preceded by a lengthy list of Indigenous uprisings, which "had been far more extensive than any Europeans wanted to admit, not even the Marxists, who were jealous of African and Native American slave workers who had risen up successfully against colonial masters without the leadership of the white man" (527). In this description, Africans are figured as Indigenous—indeed, in the map that precedes the novel, Haitians are referred to as "The First Black Indians" (15). Additionally, in referring to the resistance movements conducted by both African and Native Americans, Silko, in a move similar to Delany, aligns the two groups based on their shared political achievements.

Bartolomeo fails to apprehend the gravity of his circumstances: "What right did they, ignorant Indians, have to put educated Cuban citizens on trial?" (526). Unlike the Afro Cuban revolution we witnessed in *Blake*, which valued each of the revolutionaries equally, Bartolomeo's own anti-Indigenous prejudices emerge through the trial proceedings. In much the same way that Michel-Rolph Trouillot argues that the French could not recognize the Haitian revolution *as* a revolution because they couldn't conceptualize a world in which Haitians were able to mount an uprising, Bartolomeo fails to recognize that not only is he on trial, but he is on trial for his life.[108] Bartolomeo's misrecognition on the scale of the trial is indicative of his broader inability to conceive of a wide-scale Indigenous-led uprising. Bartolomeo's "crimes against history" are therefore also a failure to realize how, as Angelita remarks, "'each day since the arrival of the Europeans, somewhere in the vastness of the Americas the sun rises on Native American resistance and revolution'" (527). Angelita's version of the history of the Americas, then, is one of continuous, ongoing revolution. Moreover, these revolutionary imaginaries precede the Ariel/Caliban binary and Marxist thought, which demonstrates the limits of these imaginaries for apprehending both the history and future of Indigenous resistance. Bartolomeo fails to recognize this history and is subsequently hanged. Reflecting on what Bartolomeo's execution means for the revolution, Angelita thinks, "Change was on the horizon all over the world. The dispossessed people of the earth would rise up and take back lands that had been their birthright, and these lands would never again be held as private property, but as lands belonging to the people forever to protect" (532).

The movement led by Angelita, El Feo, and Wacah is the very uprising that Serlo and his class fear. Angelita displays a formidable knowledge of Marxist thought. Central to her understanding of Marxism is that Marx is one of the few white people who "understood what tribal people had always known" (520), from the way "the maker of a thing pressed part of herself or himself into each object made" (520) to the power of stories, which "are alive with the energy the words generate" (520). That said, as Angelita also observes, there are limitations to Marxist thought, since "'Marxists don't want to give Indian land back'" (519) and "Marx did not understand the power of the stories belonged to the spirits of the dead" (521). In other words, Marxists still endorse a European view of property, with Marx himself displaying his own "crimes against history" by not recognizing that our histories come from our ancestors, from our dead. While Saldaña-Portillo has elegantly demonstrated the disturbing similarity between the presumably underdeveloped subject of the Second and Third Worlds and the fully developed political consciousness of the revolutionary subject, Silko's Angelita seemingly resolves these contradictions by illustrating, through her reading of Marx, how Third World subjects already have a fully developed theory of revolution. Marx does not foster the development of revolutionary thought among the Indigenous people; rather, he represents the first European to know what Indigenous people already knew.

Along similar lines, Clinton, one of the leaders in the Army of the Homeless, a revolutionary organization comprised of unhoused veterans in the Tucson area, contends that "African and other tribal people had shared food and wealth in common for thousands of years before the white man Marx came along and stole their ideas for his 'communes' and collective farms" (408). Through the characters Angelita and Clinton, Silko highlights how people of color have created their own theories of relation and governance well before any form of European influence.[109] In this way, Silko clarifies how some European thought can be useful for revolutionary organizing in creating alliances—Angelita outlines the limits of Marxism and Clinton uses it to historicize the history and traditions of his people. Meanwhile, in the David, Beaufrey, and Serlo plotline, Silko underscores the European-influenced thought that must be resisted even as it pervades Latin American cultures and intellectual histories.

Almanac famously doesn't end with a revolution (though, unlike *Blake*, this is intentional on Silko's part).[110] Rather, *Almanac* ends with the potential for revolution, though its nature is unclear. Though the revolution seems to be led by Angelita, El Feo, and Wacah, Angelita and Wacah represent two ends of the revolutionary continuum with El Feo in the middle. In many ways, Angelita's viewpoints seem to stem from a lack of faith in the spirits—or at least a lack of faith in how the U.S. would react to being overcome by a massive throng of pilgrims from the south. Because, unlike El Feo and Wacah, she thinks that "the U.S. government would bomb its own border just to stop unarmed religious pilgrims" (711) or that "any spiritual change could [not] take place overnight, especially not in the United States where the people of whatever color had become desperate in the collapse of the economy" (712), Angelita attends the Holistic Healers Convention "to make contacts with certain people, the people with the weapons she needed to protect the followers of the spirit macaws from air attacks" (712). More specifically, Angelita tries out "shoulder-mounted missiles" (712), convincing herself that they "were purely defensive measures, of course, against government helicopters and Wacah and El Feo need never know" (712). We learn that "Angelita heard from spirits too—only her spirits were furious and they told her to defend the people from attack" (712). Thus, in Angelita we have a more typical form of revolution, one led by violence.[111] Although she listens to the twins to the extent that she doesn't plan on using offensive strategies, in working behind their back, she undermines their movement. As Silko remarks in her 1993 interview with Laura Coltelli, "The rain will follow the Twin Brothers with the sacred macaws and the thousands of people walking North. Rain will not follow if La Escapía is forced to use her hand-held rockets to protect the Twin Brothers and the people from attacks by the U.S."[112] In subscribing to the masculinist form of revolution represented by figures such as Che Guevara, Angelita has the potential to destroy the revolution.

In contrast to this masculinist mode of revolution, El Feo and Wacah insist that "if the people kept walking, if the people carried no weapons, then the homeless would have land; the tribes of the Americas would retake the continents from pole to pole" (711). In El Feo and Wacah's revolution, the tactics of nonviolence prevail. Of course, this doesn't mean that the pilgrims walking north won't be subject to violence—El Feo thinks that "the unarmed people would most likely be shot down before they even reached the border" (711)—but their revolution's success is contingent on the fact that "they must not shed blood or the destruction would continue to accompany them" (712). The twins know that the revolution will not be easy and "it might require five or ten years of great violence and conflict" (711–12), but the years of violence seem to be curtailed by the revolution's practice of nonviolence. In seeking to defend her people, Angelita violates the terms of the twins' revolution, which will no doubt extend the period of violence. In short, Angelita is the destruction that accompanies the twins on their pilgrimage north.

Almanac features multiple endings, but the ending I want to turn to now is actually from the beginning of the novel in the map that precedes the narrative proper. While the majority of the map tracks the various plotlines of the novel, with all roads leading to Tucson, the map also contains a prediction: "Ancient prophecies foretold the arrival of Europeans in the Americas. The ancient prophecies also foretell the disappearance of all things European" (14). In divining the disappearance of all things European, the prophecy tells us that the twins' revolution will be successful, even if the specifics of that revolution remain murky. The predictive quality of almanacs themselves also signals yet another form of speculation at work in the novel. By formalizing revolution through the structure of the almanac and the chronicle of revolutions foretold in the map, Silko guides her readers through revolutionary thought and speculation, encouraging guerrilla conversions of her own as she retcons the history of the Americas.

Browning Revolutions

The models of revolution we have—and that *Latinx Revolutionary Horizons* tracks—are ones that are led by violence. From the deeply factionalized Mexican Revolution that led to the assassination of many Mexican presidents during the revolution to the almost immediate betrayal of the Cuban Revolution as exemplified by the televised executions of former Cuban revolutionaries, the masculinist mode of revolution reveals one that, rather than offering a revolution in thought and in governance, is actually carceral logic applied to the state. The desire to discipline and punish becomes the prevailing ethos, which is why we can see how so many Latin American revolutions result in dictatorships.

Yet in both *Blake* and *Almanac*, we have alternatives to the revolutions typically depicted, particularly in terms of gender. For example, Nwankwo observes how Blake is the prototypical masculine revolutionary; however, the juxtaposition of Blake and Placido undermines this claim, as she also notes.[113] Both characters are seen as extensions of Delany's thought and are treated as equals in the text. That said, as Nwankwo outlines, their physiques are remarkably different,[114] with Blake representing the figure of Black masculine virility and Placido representing a softer, feminine blackness: "a person of slender form, lean and sinewy, rather morbid, orange-peel complexion, black hair hanging lively quite to the shoulders, heavy deep brow and full mustache, with great expressive black piercing eyes."[115] The incongruous descriptions "morbid" and "orange-peel complexion" point to Delany's own biases toward those with lighter skin. Moreover, as is typical of Delany in *Blake*, he describes Placido's "orange-peel complexion" as "morbid," but the significant power Placido holds in the revolutionary organizing suggests that not only does Placido's "morbid" complexion not exclude him from revolutionary participation, it also emphasizes the egalitarian nature of the revolution as those of all hues can rise to the highest positions.

Figuring Blake as masculine and Placido as feminine would seem to suggest a masculine/feminine binary for these two revolutionaries; nevertheless, both characters counteract the stereotypes associated with their gendered representations. For instance, even though Blake is portrayed as hyper-masculine, he's also "strangely passive" (238) in moments of heightened insurrectionary potential, such as on the *Vulture* when the captives nearly stage a mutiny on board. Meanwhile, toward the latter half of the second part of the novel, Placido takes center stage as the ostensible revolutionary leader.[116] Yet, rather than take charge of a violent revolution, Placido takes on the role of mentor and teacher as he guides recruits like Madame Cordora toward a vision of Black community based on shared politics.

Significantly, Delany's version of Placido also leads us toward a brown revolution via his "orange-peel complexion," which Nwankwo also reads as a way to uplift the mixed population "despite his own professed views of the abnormality and inferiority of mixed race people."[117] Such a description directly counters the Brown Society that Delany mocks in the first part of *Blake*, which he characterizes as "the bane and dread of the blacks in the state, an organization formed through the instrumentality of the whites to keep the blacks and mulattos at variance."[118] In his figuration of Placido, Delany offers a model of brownness in which brownness isn't a way to disavow blackness, where a brown revolution isn't anti-Black. Silko does similar work in her description on the map that opens the book, where she describes Haitians as the first Black Indians. Notably, Silko does not offer this distinction to other Caribbean islands with significant Black populations.

Because the Haitian Revolution hailed Haiti as a national identity into being, I contend that in calling Haitians the first Black Indians, Silko suggests that the "Indian" quality of Haitianness is that of revolution and resistance. This connection is further underscored by the fact that both Clinton and Angelita are the characters who offer histories of resistance and these histories illustrate the connections between Black and Indigenous uprisings, with Angelita including the Haitian Revolution on her list[119] and Clinton recounting the multiple rebellions led by enslaved people with the help of Native Americans (743–46). Indeed, though "the Christian God was absent" (417) in the Americas, "Africans in the Americas had always been 'home' because 'home' is where the ancestor spirits are. From the gentle giants, Damballah and Quetzalcoatl, to the Maiz Mother, and the Twin Brothers and old Woman Spider, Africa and the Americas had been possessed" (742). Clinton's description emphasizes the connections between Black and Indigenous people in the Americas, as the ancestor spirits of both communities root them there, while those who follow the Christian God will never find a home in the Americas, as their ancestor spirits did not follow them. Moreover, Clinton leaves for Haiti at the end of the novel (742), suggesting that African American resistance in the U.S. can learn from Haiti's revolutionary legacy and that Haiti is the connection that joins together African American and Indigenous struggles. In this way, Silko also "browns" the revolution.

The browning of revolution in *Blake* and *Almanac* offers a way to reach for a Latinx revolutionary horizon not limited by the anti-blackness and anti-Indigeneity that currently informs understandings of latinidad, one where caramelo doesn't signify disavowed indigeneity or diluted blackness, but recalls Placido's orange-peel complexion and Silko's Black Indians, all committed to a revolutionary movement dedicated to resisting Destroyer pasts and Destroyer futures. The brown revolution Delany and Silko point us toward recall José Esteban Muñoz's brown commons, "a commons that is of *and* for the multitude."[120] As Muñoz argues, such a commons moves "beyond the singular subjectivity and the individualized subjectivities" (2), which we can see most clearly in Delany's imagined community of conspiracy and the broad-based coalition that forms at the International Holistic Healers Convention in *Almanac*. For Muñoz, brownness is a more capacious alternative to latinidad. While I think that brownness can also be a more limiting term, as exemplified by the Brown Society in *Blake*, Delany's and Silko's work does illustrate how brownness expands the revolutionary horizon of latinidad precisely by building on the coalitional possibilities to which Muñoz alludes. Such coalitional work depends on the speculative imaginaries both authors invoke for their visions of revolution. Because latinidad is not yet here and the horizon points us to the deferred site of the arrival of latinidad, authors like Delany and Silko and theorists like Muñoz offer speculative imaginaries for what such a world could look like.

For Delany and Silko, brownness arises from histories of resistance as exemplified by Delany's resurrection of Plácido and La Escalera and Angelita and Clinton's lists of acts of rebellion. We also see this resistance playing out on the field of ideology and knowledge production, both through Delany's own incriminating writings about "elevating" his people and Serlo's eugenicist research. Muñoz reminds us that this revolution of the mind is also central to the project of brownness; he argues "that the potential and force of brownness are intimately linked to the production of knowledge is not something that escapes the notice of the enemies of brown life" (4). Although enemies of brown life such as Serlo are clearly marked in *Almanac*, Delany's example points to the need to reckon with one's own counterrevolutionary ideas even for those who have written revolutionary works. This is the task for Latinx studies as a field and for all of us who seek revolutionary change. As we have seen throughout this book, actual violent revolutions failed across the board, as, for example, when the Mexican Revolution failed to lead to the actual uplifting of Indigenous people. Such examples demonstrate that despite these revolutions, the actual revolutionary terrain is in thought, in ideology, and in practice.

Coda
Is the X a Commons?

A consistent theme throughout this book has been a suspicion of masculinist forms of revolution and the need (and desire) to see how contemporary Latinx literature engages with the revolutionary past to theorize alternate models of revolution and liberation. We see this in Sandra Cisneros's critique of the Chicano Movement and the idea of la raza cósmica that preceded it. We see it in Cristina García's treatment of not only the Cuban Revolution, but also the longer history of Cuban revolutionary politics. We see it, also, in how Ninotchka Rosca and Jessica Hagedorn revise José Rizal's homosociality to offer a revolutionary vision in which women are crucial for change, an idea taken up by Julia Alvarez in her recovery of Salomé Ureña's revolutionary legacy. Finally, we see it in Martin R. Delany's use of La Escalera and Silko's critique of the Ariel/Caliban binary (particularly the limits of Caliban as a revolutionary figure) in addition to her framing of Indigenous revolutionary theory as preceding Karl Marx. In short, *Latinx Revolutionary Horizons* has been preoccupied with the legacies of revolutionary thought in and through literature and how the authors in this project have built upon, critiqued, and extended these ideas.

What has emerged in such a study of revolution is the horizon as method, which is a practice—and here, a reading practice—that asks us to think the future and imagine it otherwise. In juxtaposing nineteenth-century texts with contemporary ones, I have illuminated how the seemingly former futures of the nineteenth century are alive and well in our contemporary moment. Moreover, in reading for a latinidad that is not yet here, I have shown how a text like *Who Would Have Thought It?* reveals the political project of *Caramelo*, while a text like *Monkey Hunting* allows us to read *Sab* differently. By reading outside of conventional periodizations, across ethnic and area studies and the category of Latinx revolutionary imaginaries and the latinidades that attend them expansively, I have shown how the limits of such frameworks curtail our methods and limit our ideas of what's possible.

Turning to the horizon as a method and a reading practice demonstrates how we can imagine, finally, a brown commons. In Lázaro Lima's helpful gloss of José Esteban Muñoz's theory of a brown commons, Lima emphasizes the importance of Muñoz's call to think otherwise as it focuses on the exclusions that frame how we think and how we exist in the world. As Lima writes,

> What types of knowing and being are excluded from analytical engagement and meaningful world making? What ways of being in the world are erased when we presume certain forms of knowledge to be unworthy of philosophical interrogation and investigation? Muñoz called this process of unlearning philosophical universalism "thinking otherwise," and phenomenology provided an entry point for understanding the "Brown democratic commons" as a space for participation unhampered by normative forms of legal and epistemic violence that delimit and demean "other" ways of being in the world.[1]

The horizon, I suggest, is one such method for thinking otherwise. The stakes of such a method reside in how we think of ourselves, our communities, and our kin. The horizon encourages us to think of latinidad as one of disappeared kin, one where we do the work of finding each other and tracking disappeared relationships such that we recognize that the presumed whiteness of latinidad is based on our disappeared relationships staying disappeared.[2]

In what follows, I explore the commons as both affect and genre as well as the queering of the Latinx commons. To do so, I briefly examine two genres that I have not covered in *Latinx Revolutionary Horizons*, the manifesto and poetry, but that have been foundational to Latinx revolutionary thought before examining another iteration of what novels have to offer for a theory of the brown commons. I begin with Karla Cornejo Villavicencio's *The Undocumented Americans* (2020), before turning to the republication of Juan Felipe Herrera's *Akrílica* (2022), and end with Joseph Cassara's *The House of Impossible Beauties* (2018)[3] to sketch out the challenges to and potential of a brown commons.

Brown Affects

The jacket copy of *The Undocumented Americans* declares the book as an act of bravery—in writing it, Cornejo Villavicencio publicly reveals her undocumented status—yet she expresses her motivations quite differently. Specifically framing *The Undocumented Americans* as a consequence of the 2016 election, Cornejo Villavicencio takes a hostile stance that emphasizes the role of affect and feeling in creating a brown commons according to Muñoz. As Cornejo Villavicencio reminds us in her polemical introduction, "To write a book about undocumented immigrants, in America, the story, the full story, you have to be a little bit crazy. And you certainly can't be enamored by America, not still. That disqualifies you."⁴ Disenchanted with the U.S., Cornejo Villavicencio explicitly warns her readers, "Maybe you won't like it. I didn't write it for you to *like* it. And I did not set out to write anything inspirational, which is why there are no stories of DREAMers" (xvi). Her issue is not with the DREAMers themselves, but how "they occupy outsize attention in our politics" (xvi). In focusing on "our politics," Cornejo Villavicencio foregrounds the political in her discussion of undocumented immigration and shapes her intervention *as* a politics.

The first three pages of the book after the title page illustrate Cornejo Villavicencio's affective intervention. These pages form a triptych: a dedication page that says "Chinga la Migra" (Fuck ICE/the Border Patrol), an epigraph featuring a quote from Joan Didion's *The White Album*, and a memorial page. In the first instance, "Chinga la Migra" takes the place of a dedication—rather than a dedication *to* someone, Villavicencio offers a proclamation, a war cry that situates her anti-ICE, pro-immigrant stance. Her Didion quote establishes her political position: "A place belongs forever to whoever claims it hardest, remembers it most obsessively, wrenches it from itself, shapes it, renders it, loves it so radically that he remakes it in his image." The relationship between a person and a place in this quote is nothing short of a god power ("he remakes it in his image"). And it's a violent one, at that, as the person wrenches and renders. The final piece of the triptych says, simply, "In memory of Claudia Goméz Gonzáles." Goméz Gonzáles was a twenty-year-old Guatemalan woman who was shot by Border Patrol as she crossed the U.S.-Mexico border into Texas. The memorial acts as the raison d'être for the proclamation with which the book's paratexts open. The essays that follow, which are a mixture of reporting on undocumented communities and personal history, take place in the second piece of the triptych, the space of place-making.

Suspended between the affective registers of "fucking" with ICE and memorializing immigrants who have not survived crossing, *The Undocumented Americans* carves out a space for immigrant anger. In the book, Cornejo Villavicencio displays an excess of affects, illuminating how the narrative "I" of the immigrant bildungsroman is at odds with the "I" of immigrant nonfiction. Rather than a narrative of uplift, of family reunification after separation, Cornejo Villavicencio demonstrates the toll immigration takes, such that reunification is never possible, the border fence symbolizing an irreparable divide within families. Specifically framing *The Undocumented Americans* as unfolding out of the 2016 election, Cornejo Villavicencio shows the continuity between the Obama and Trump administrations through Trump's extension of Obama-era policies and deportation infrastructures. In a world in which neither political party offers safety, Cornejo Villavicencio dedicates herself to "fucking" with the system that oppresses her.

She also explicitly takes issue with genre. Addressing the book agents who wanted her to write a memoir, she counters, "A *memoir*? I was twenty-one. I wasn't fucking Barbara Streisand" (xiv). To counter what she feels is her own lack of experience, Cornejo Villavicencio uses her experiences to frame her community's. She ultimately categorizes her work as "creative nonfiction, rooted in careful reporting, translated as poetry, shared by chosen family, and sometimes hard to read" (xvi). Refusing to name the novel form, she also resists taxonomizing her work as testimonio; instead, she accentuates its poetic effects. Moreover, in tying the book's genre to community, she suggests that it will only reveal itself if "shared by chosen family."

Cornejo's Villavicencio's genre trouble underscores the broader issues of belonging in *The Undocumented Americans*. There is yet to be a theory of latinidad that centers the role of citizenship, which is perhaps the biggest divide among Latinx communities, more so than issues of language or country of origin. Given that Cornejo Villavicencio is writing in the post-Trump era, I read her book as demonstrating how a shift in political terrain also necessitates a shift in generic terrain as Latinx literature apprehends how to address our dystopian present. Poetry and the manifesto are foundational genres that are largely concerned with issues of the present, and Cornejo Villavicencio illustrates why we need to return to such insurgent forms when our communities are under attack. In *The Undocumented Americans*, we can see how Cornejo Villavicencio returns us to the U.S. as a site of struggle, a place that needs to be fucked with to enact change. Turning now to *Akrílica*, I analyze how the speculative project of its republication attempts to create a past to imagine a future for Latinx poetics.

Latinx Commoning

Issues of form and community come together in *Akrílica*. In the introduction, Farid Matuk describes the collection, first published in 1989, as an act of "retrieval" rather than "recovery."[5] "We steal *Akrílica* away from literary institutions, away from the discipline of literature, and away from traditions of experimental poetics that should hope to claim it," Matuk continues.

"Akrílica belongs somewhere else; it belongs in the hands of those finding one another in a gathering that has yet to take place" (9). Yet, Matuk seemingly introduces a paradox in the paragraph that follows these lines as he observes that Herrera's "work as a whole has been excluded from genealogies of experimental or avant-garde U.S. poetry" (10), which means that the collective who came together to publish *Akrílica* (Carmen Giménez Smith, J. Michael Martinez, Rosa Alcalá, Suzi F. García, hanta t. samsa, and Anthony Cody, along with Matuk), had to contend with how their "own writing practices suffered for passing through sites . . . without having encountered *Akrílica* or a book like it on the reading lists that were handed to [them]" (10). Therefore, it would seem that part of the project of publishing *Akrílica* isn't stealing it away from anything, but an act of installation: *into* the institution, the discipline of literature, and traditions of experimental poetics.

Rather than reading Matuk's statements as antithetical to one another, I focus on how he points to "a gathering that has yet to take place" and suggest that this both means in the past—an encounter with *Akrílica* that never happened and the Latinx poets who suffered because of it—and a future created by *Akrílica*. That said, moving into the institution, the discipline, and the tradition of experimental poetics does not mean that *Akrílica* is institutionalized or disciplined. Instead, in pointing to a future gathering, Matuk also suggests a future in which *Akrílica* circulates not only on reading lists, but also "in the hands of those finding one another." The aesthetics of such a communal exchange informs the collection, which features photos and abstract art in black and white, giving the collection a zine-like feel, which makes it easier to photocopy, staple, and pass around.

Each section of the collection enacts the kind of gathering that Matuk points to. For example, in the Gallery section, J. Michael Martinez creates what he calls an "infected text" (153). Responding to how "Covid-19 continues to disproportionately impact Latinx and other communities of color," Martinez translated the poems in this section "by distributing DNA codons to represent each word in each poem; after, each poem had its own unique dictionary of 64 DNA codons, each codon representing a potential (set of) word(s)" (153). Codons, which, according to Google, are "a sequence of three nucleotides which together form a unit of genetic code in a DNA or RNA molecule," thus speak to the way that Martinez's translation of Herrera's poetry creates a genetic code for future Latinx poetry. Moreover, within the context of Covid-19, Martinez's project materializes how writing this genetic code is another way to establish Latinx survivance in the face of Latinx mass death.

As Martinez's genetic code makes clear, the collective translated Herrera's poetry not from Spanish to English or vice versa (though both the 1989 and

2022 editions contain the original Spanish text with its English translation), but riff on the English language poems based on "an impression of the work, an approach that speaks to how the translators see *Akrílica*" (153). Although such translations can be seen in the grayed-out Martinez poems that appear alongside Herrera's work, they can also be viewed through the typographical experimentation employed by Anthony Cody in the América section. For example, in "Exile Boulevard," Cody takes the word "float" (87) and has it float in a circular, clockwise pattern, turning upside-down before ending with "fall" (87), underscoring how the typography mimics the content of the poem.

Another layer of translation exists in the language of the poems themselves. For example, there is a consistent effort across the poems to make the female characters in them more agentic. In "Eclipse/Watercolor 41 x 80/San Francisco," where the 1989 poem reads, "what woman is being pulled/out of the tombs?" (9), the 2022 version says, "which woman tears herself from the tombs?" (45). Similarly, such changes occur in relation to feminized labor: "Concerning the Anti-Theater of Quentino's Diary" (the 2022 version replaces "concerning" with "about"), "secretaries" is changed to "assistants"; in "Poetic Report on Maids: Toward a Model for Urban Hispaniks in the USA," the title changes to "Poetic Report on Domestic Workers: Towards a Model of Being Urban Hispanik in the US," with all former mentions of "maids" in the poem subsequently changed to "domestic workers."

Such translations also extend to how the text engages with race. "Arab's grocery store" becomes "The Arab grocery" in one poem; all references to enslavement are changed to captive (for example, "enslaved salt" in "Quentino" becomes "captive salt"); "plantation" becomes an "estate" in "Minerals in Our Legs." Yet not all changes have the same ramifications—though making female figures more agentic and not referring to a person as "Arab" makes sense, changing "plantation" to "estate" erases an entire history. The full quote in the 1989 version reads, "biting the plantation of the centuries' corpse," which becomes "that bites the ancient cadaver's estate" in the 2022 version. Given the 1989 poem's dedication, "for Isabel Alegría and El Salvador," I can only assume that the plantation referenced in the poem is a coffee plantation. Notably, the 2022 version of the poem dispenses with the dedication, which suggests that the shift from "plantation" to "estate" then means an additional erasure of Salvadoran people and history. The 2022 version also changes the title to "Minerals in the Legs," which suggests an even bigger shift from the communal "our" to the clinically specific article "the."

By focusing on the issues that plague latinidad, such as anti-blackness, which Matuk discusses in his introduction, the translators subsequently erase what the 1989 version of *Akrílica* did so well, which was express solidarity with

Central American struggles, particularly in Nicaragua and El Salvador. As Ana Patricia Rodriguez has shown solidarity fictions by Chicana writers have tended to privilege the experiences of Chicana protagonists;[6] however, in his poetry, Herrera creates an experimental poetics of solidarity that foregrounds Central American history over Chicanx experiences. Moreover, while the list of translators notes the sections they translated (for example, "Galería/Gallery and Terciopelo/Velvet"), none of the translators actually worked with the original Spanish-language version of *Akrílica*. J. Michael Martinez's beautiful genetic code does not exist in the "Gallería" section; Anthony Cody's typography does not adorn and amplify the "América" section.

Most tellingly, women continue to not be agents in the Spanish version, as the line "¿cuál mujer se arranca de las tumbas?" remains the same. Salt is still enslaved; secretaries remain secretaries. But the plantation? It remains "la finca" in Spanish. A finca can never be an estate; it recalls exploited Indigenous labor at the hands of ladinos.[7] The only English word that comes closest to approximating this meaning is—you guessed it—the plantation. In changing "plantation" to "estate" in the 2022 version of the poem, the translators enact a double erasure: of the Indigenous populations on the finca and of the history of enslavement on the plantation in the U.S. Where the plantation reference could have acted as a moment of solidarity bringing together Indigenous and Black Latinxs, the translator's use of "estate" erases this possibility and, in doing so, participates in the anti-blackness they hoped to avoid. Additionally, the dedication in the Spanish-language version of the poem remains intact, suggesting that this act of solidarity can only exist alongside the finca and the plantation.

In *Latinx Revolutionary Horizons*, I have focused on a latinidad that is not yet here, and in Matuk's introduction, I find him calling for that future latinidad and calling on Herrera to help us realize that liberatory future. That said, by privileging Latinx experiences that are bounded by the English language and not experimenting with the Spanish language poems, the translators missed the opportunity to install the kind of hemispheric latinidad Herrera points to through his solidarity with Central American countries like El Salvador in the 1989 edition. In other words, in many ways *Akrílica* was already performing the work of the brown commons, and the reissue erased the work of commoning. Despite the fact that I am drawn to Matuk's distinction between "recovery" and "retrieval," we must remember that the two words are synonyms of each other, a kind of slant rhyme that encodes the work of retrieval in recovery and vice versa. To imagine "a gathering that has yet to take place," we must also retrieve the Spanish-language poems, for a brown commons also means a multivocal commons. I turn now to *The House of Impossible Beauties* to consider one of the major lacunae of Latinx revolutions—how they can be homosocial or homoerotic, but not explicitly queer.

Queering Revolution

The House of Impossible Beauties focuses on the House of Xtravaganza in the ballroom scene from 1976 to 1993. Early in the novel, Hector, who would go on to found the House of Xtravaganza, goes to a tattoo parlor with his lover, Tyler. Hector "wanted to get a /, and Tyler would get a \. Together, their / \ would equal an X. If overlapped. Apart, the slashes would symbolize a separation of two halves."[8] Hector's vision of the X here is one of intimacy and connectedness. Heartbreakingly, when Tyler dies, Hector is left with only a /, a permanently separated half. Hector's missing \, suggests that the "X" in Xtravaganza fills in his missing half; a queer family replaces his lover.[9] Largely based on Jennie Livingston's famous documentary *Paris Is Burning* (1990),[10] the novel focuses on the house structure that ties together Hector, Angel, Venus, Daniel, and Juanito Xtravaganza. Abandoned by the state during the HIV/AIDS crisis, one of the ways that the queer of color community handles the crisis is through ballroom and the chosen family structure on which it operates, as signified by the X.

Founded as the first "Latin" house of ballroom, many of the members were Puerto Rican. And yet, unlike recent books by Puerto Rican authors like Jaquira Díaz's *Ordinary Girls* (2019) and Xochitl Gonzalez's (who is also half Mexican) *Olga Dies Dreaming* (2021), in which the Puerto Rican fight for independence looms large, *The House of Impossible Beauties* rarely mentions Puerto Rico, much less the ongoing struggle for independence of the island. While Hector nostalgically reflects on growing up in Puerto Rico, we learn later that the one trip Juanito Xtravaganza took to the island to visit his father led to his father's discovery of his queerness. The rest of the summer, Juanito's father rapes him. Puerto Rico, in this rendering, is like the homes the Xtravaganzas grow up in—then run away from—where they are rejected by their biological families.

There are of course vibrant queer communities in Puerto Rico, but I'm interested in how *The House of Impossible Beauties* depicts Puerto Ricans who are divested from the revolutionary struggles of their people. I read this absence as indicating the separation of / and \, where the forward slash represents Latinx queerness and the backward slash represents revolution and liberation. Thus far, *Latinx Revolutionary Horizons* has traced the implications of reading the "X" as a marker of race and a space of speculative possibility, but here I turn to the more typical representation of the "X" as speaking to gender inclusivity and, by extension, sexual inclusivity, to illuminate the need to center queerness in our revolutionary horizons. With the exception of Chapter 2 on the Philippines, after all, queerness in the texts I have discussed exists largely on the margins or is deeply repressed, as we saw in Junot Díaz's *The Brief Wondrous Life of Oscar Wao* (2007).

Indeed, I'm interested in the ways that Latinx literature separates queerness from revolution. For example, in an incisive reading of *The Lady Matador's Hotel* (2010), Ricardo Ortiz points to how Cristina García, much like she did with Chen Pan, bases a character on a real person's testimonio. In this case, she uses details from Reinaldo Arenas's testimonio *Before Night Falls* (1994) to inform Ricardo Morán's storyline. Yet, in making this revision, García eliminates Arenas's queerness in the figure of Morán. Even though we know that the latter was also imprisoned in Fidel Castro's Cuba, we don't know why; of course, Arenas was imprisoned for his homosexuality. Morán is hardly a revolutionary figure in the novel; he's a critic of the Cuban revolution, but not a revolutionary himself. Moreover, not only does García remove Arenas's homosexuality from Morán's backstory, but she also installs him into the nuclear family by making his storyline about buying a child in an unnamed Central American country (which is clearly Guatemala) with his wife. Morán ultimately leaves his wife and takes the baby with him, but his life is still one that adheres to reproductive futurity, whereas Arenas's story is one where futurity is ultimately foreclosed.

The absence of revolutionary references in *The House of Impossible Beauties*, then, demonstrates how liberation must also happen within the home. Gloria Anzaldúa's *Borderlands / La Frontera: The New Mestiza* (1987), reminds us that the struggle for liberation cannot be separated from gender and sexual liberation. She elaborates on the violent space of the home by recounting how one of her lesbian students "thought homophobia meant fear of going home."[11] For Anzaldúa this remark renders visible the homophobic space of the Catholic household alongside the fear of erasure and the fear of sexual violence. "So, yes, though 'home' permeates every sinew and cartilage in my body," she writes, "I too am afraid of going home" (43). Anzaldúa's comment reveals the home as the primal scene of colonial violence and perhaps the most painful site of struggle for liberation, particularly for queer Latinxs.

Taken together, *The Undocumented Americans*, *Akrílica*, and *The House of Impossible Beauties* show us the work that has yet to be done to call a brown commons into existence. They underscore the areas where solidarity fails, where our liberatory imaginaries are still held captive by conservative thought, whether that be in terms of citizenship or sexuality or any number of differences that are deemed unbridgeable in Latinx communities. And yet, the horizon as method points us toward other futures and other worlds where we can summon a politics to conjure a people. The texts I have discussed here point us to yet other Latinx revolutionary horizons that aren't necessarily capital "R" revolutions, but are the revolutions in thought, in language, in community that need to take place to imagine a latinidad that is not yet here in a gathering that has yet to take place.

Acknowledgments

In many ways, this is a book about mentorship, a book about the forms of relation that make revolution thinkable. Thus, it is fitting that I begin by naming the mentors who made this project possible. My deepest thanks go to Yogita Goyal, Rafael Pérez-Torres, Marissa K. López, Shelley Streeby, and Ricardo Ortiz. Yogita, you are my model for everything—for scholarship, for mentorship, for teaching. I still can't believe all the time you've spent talking with me about this book. Thank you for encouraging me to write the book I wanted to write even when—especially when—other paths seemed so much easier. Rafa, I'm so glad we've stayed in touch, and I appreciate your kindness and seemingly never-ending well of optimism. Marissa, thank you for letting me come to Latinx literary studies on my own and for being there to guide me in the field once I was ready. Shelley, thank you for your steadfast support and for being there when I struggled with the realities of my first job. Ricardo, I still can't believe that I stumbled into a friendship with you. You've been a fantastic interlocutor, and I hope to be as generous a scholar and mentor to others as you have been to me.

At UCLA, I was lucky enough to be part of the Revolutionary Women Writing Group, where I was surrounded by incredible women of color. Thank you so much for giving me the community I needed as I reached the finish line: Juliann Anesi, Carolina Beltrán, Isabel Gómez, Kimberly Mack, Erica Onugha, Sandra Ruiz, Erin Suzuki, Ester Trujillo, Brandi Underwood, and Joyce Pualani Warren. I'm so glad that our paths have continued to crisscross and that we've managed to stay in touch through the years. I'd also like to thank Abraham Encinas, Guadalupe Escobar, Tara Fickle, Doran George, Georgina Guzmán, Sal Herrera, Elyan Hill, Efren Lopez, Andy Martinez,

Eric Newman, Val Popp, and Mathew Sandoval. Doran, I miss you every day and will always remember you saying, "Darling, they don't like laughing!"

During my UCSD Chancellor's Postdoctoral Fellowship, I was lucky to be in community with Juliann Anesi, Tina Beyene, and Melanie Masterton Sherazi. Katie Walkiewicz, I'm so glad I met you while I was in San Diego, and thanks for introducing me to cool comics and always making sure I celebrated my achievements (it's still hard, but you make it easier). At the University of Massachusetts, Boston, I would like to thank my incredible colleagues who helped get me through a difficult time in my life: Neal Bruss, Lillian-Yvonne Bertram, Sari Edelstein, Sarah Hamblin, Holly Jackson, Scott Maisano, Jill McDonough (and Josey Packard), Alex Mueller, Hugh O'Connell, Dan Remein (and Megan Manas), Emilio Sauri, Susan Tan, and Susan Tomlinson. I'd also like to thank my students: Shanarah Bargan, Eduardo Chaves, Derek Diaco, Maria Gonzalez, Taj Madison, Bridget McColgan, Adam Mooney, Tanairi Sorrentini, and Ariel Tirado.

To put it lightly, Boston and I were not a match. That said, I found a wonderful community there; without them, my life would have been much more difficult. Thanks so much to Cassie Alexopoulos, Ayendy Bonifacio, andré carrington, Bridget Colvin, Doug Ishii, Maria John, Roanne Kantor, Joey Kim, Irene Mata, Takeo Rivera, and Petra Rivera-Rideau. Ayendy and Joey, I'm so glad we've stayed in touch, and I love the beautiful life you're creating together. Bridget, thank you for continuing to chat with me about speculative fiction—I look forward to our catch-up sessions and always want to know what you're reading. Doug, I'm so glad we met and that, after conspiring together to leave Boston, we've continued to be academic accomplices. Brilliant Roanne, I've loved being in conversation with you, and I'm glad that we've kept it up since we both came back to California. Thanks so much, my friend, for always checking in on me.

I participated in the First Book Institute shortly after we went on lockdown during the pandemic. While this meant we couldn't meet in person, I'm deeply grateful for the space that Sean Goudie and Priscilla Wald created for us. It was a difficult time when the last thing on my mind was my book, but Faith Barter, Justin Mann, and Ana Schwartz gave me the sense of community I needed as I also transitioned to another job. Our group thread gives me life.

At Chapman, I would like to thank the friends and colleagues who have sustained me and made this a place I can call home: Julia Ainley, Ian Barnard, Jessica Bocinski, Amy Buono, Allison Devries, Samantha Dressel, Sarah Gordon, Natalie Figueroa, Talisa Flores, Mateo Jarquín, Jennifer Keene, Laura Loustau, Rafael Luévano, C. K. Magliola, Nora Rivera, Nancy Rios-Contreras, Stephanie Takaragawa, and Tammy Yi. My students at Chapman are incredible, and I'm delighted to be in conversation with Sinclair Adams, Su Chen, Jubilee Finnegan, Catherine Gallegos, Cassandra Garate, Marissa La Mantia, Eliana Nava, Tegan Rosso, Justin Soto, and Constance Von Igel de Mello. You have all helped me with my own learning and thinking, and I can't wait to see what your future holds.

After my first semester at Chapman, I began a year-long Institute for Citizens and Scholars (formerly the Woodrow Wilson) Career Enhancement Fellowship. My deepest thanks go to Kaysha Corinealdi for shepherding me through the application process. I'm grateful for the writing group that emerged from the fellowship and thank Kwami T. Coleman, Crystal Donkor, María Regina Firmino-Castillo, Aria Halliday, Amaka Okechukwu, and Ester Trujillo for being in community with me.

I would also like to thank my co-conspirators in the field of Latinx Studies: Tommy Connors, Maia Gil'Adí, Joe Miranda, Bill Orchard, Ricardo Ortiz, Israel Reyes, John Ribó, and Marion Rohrleitner. I've loved being on numerous panels with you over the years, and I look forward to many more in the years to come. Maia, thank you for consistently corralling us to do great things. Our friendship holds a special place in my heart, and I know I'm a better thinker, writer, and reader because of you (even if we disagree on pretty much everything!).

Latinx Studies is a beautiful community, and I consider myself lucky to be in conversation with Jesse Alemán, Leticia Alvarado, John Alba Cutler, Lorgia García Peña, Marcos Gonsalez, Teresa Gonzales, Kirsten Silva Gruesz, Joshua Javier Guzmán, Jennifer Harford Vargas, Jeanelle Horcasitas, Ylce Irizarry, Carmen Lamas, Elena Machado Sáez, Emily Maguire, Curtis Marez, Regina Mills, Randy Ontiveros, Yolanda Padilla, Roy Pérez, Christofer Rodelo, Valentina Román, María Josefina Saldaña-Portillo, Kristie Soares, Kristy L. Ulibarri, Gabriela Valenzuela, Alberto Varón, David Vázquez, and Ariana Vigil. I'm inspired by all of you.

Special thanks go to Kirsten Silva Gruesz, Jennifer Harford Vargas, Ricardo Ortiz, María Josefina Saldaña-Portillo, and David Vázquez for reading my manuscript and supporting me through the final stages of the revision process. My book is much better because of you, and I can't thank you enough for helping me write a book that's even better than I could have imagined.

My thanks go to the friends who were part of the writing, reading, and accountability groups that got me through the pandemic: Juliann Anesi, Bridget Colvin, María R. Estorino, Tara Fickle, Maia Gil'Adí, Doug Ishii, Kimberly Mack, Melanie Masterton Sherazi, Ariana Vigil, and Katie Walkiewicz.

My deepest thanks go to Richard Morrison and everyone at Fordham University Press for the thought and care they put into my book. I'm especially grateful to Nao Bustamante for letting me use her work as the cover image for my book; I couldn't be more thrilled. My family came to the U.S. over a hundred years ago as my ancestors fled the Mexican Revolution, and seeing your beautiful Kevlar dresses reminds me of the long line of strong women I come from. Here's hoping to a world where we don't need to be bulletproof.

I'd also like to thank the Faculty of Color Writing Group, housed at the University of Connecticut, for hosting symposia that have lifted my spirits as a woman of color in academia. Thank you to *MFS: Modern Fiction Studies* for allowing me to publish a revised version of my article "Guerrilla Conversions in Jessica Hagedorn and José Rizal: The Queer Future of National Romance," copyright 2016 Purdue University. This article first appeared in *MFS: Modern Fiction Studies* 62, no. 2 (Summer 2016): 330–49. Thanks, also, to the *Los Angeles Review of Books* for allowing me to publish a revised version of my book review "Juan Felipe Herrera's *Akrílica* and the Not Yet of Latinidad."

Finally, I would like to thank my family: my dad, for teaching me about genre and the importance of details in the stories we read and the stories we tell, and my mom, for being the fiercest person I know and giving me her strength. I love you.

Notes

Introduction: Forming Revolutions

1. Tatiana Flores, "Latinidad Is Cancelled: Confronting an Anti-Black Construct," *Latin American and Latinx Visual Culture* 3, no. 3 (July 2021): 58–79.
2. Quoted in Flores, "Latinidad Is Cancelled," 63.
3. Flores, "Latinidad Is Cancelled," 60.
4. Angel Rama, *The Lettered City* (Durham, N.C.: Duke University Press, 1996).
5. José Martí, "Our America" (1891), in *Selected Writings*, ed., trans. Esther Allen (New York: Penguin Books, 2002), 288–96.
6. Rodolfo Gonzalez, "I Am Joaquín" (1967), in *Literatura Chicana, 1965–1995: An Anthology in Spanish, English, and Caló*, ed. Manuel de Jesús Hernández-Gutiérrez and David William Foster (New York and London: Garland, 1997), 207–22.
7. Anonymous, "El Plan Espiritual de Aztlán," in *Aztlán: Essays on the Chicano Homeland*, ed. Rudolfo A. Anaya and Francisco A. Lomelí (Albuquerque: University of New Mexico Press, 1989), 1–5.
8. I thank Lorgia García Peña for this insightful observation.
9. Mark C. Jerng, *Racial Worldmaking: The Power of Popular Fiction* (New York: Fordham University Press, 2017).
10. Flores, "Latinidad Is Cancelled," 64.
11. For a useful overview of state-centered approaches, see Jeff Goodwin, "State-Centered Approaches to Social Revolutions: Strengths and Limitations of a Theoretical Tradition," in *Theorizing Revolutions*, ed. John Foran (London and New York: Routledge, 1997), 9–35. For a foundational text in this area, see Theda Skocpol, *States and Social Revolutions*, 2nd ed. (Cambridge: Cambridge University Press, 2015). For an overview of structural theories of revolutions, see Timothy P. Wickham-Crowley, "Structural Theories of Revolution," in *Theorizing Revolutions*, ed. John Foran (London and New York: Routledge, 1997), 36–70. See

James DeFronzo, *Revolutions and Revolutionary Movements*, 5th ed. (Boulder: Westview Press, 2015), for an alternate method of organization as he distinguishes among factors that lead to revolution rather than methods for examining revolutions. Other key theorists include Charles Tilly (*From Mobilization to Revolution* [Reading, Mass.: Addison-Wesley, 1978]), John Foran (*Taking Power: On the Origins of Third World Revolutions* [Cambridge: Cambridge University Press, 2005]), and Jack A. Goldstone (*Revolutions: Theoretical, Comparative, and Historical Studies*, 3rd ed. [Independence, Ky.: Cengage Learning, 2002], and "Theories of Revolution: The Third Generation," *World Politics* 32, no. 3 [1980]: 425–53).

12. DeFronzo, *Revolutions and Revolutionary Movements*, 10.

13. Jacques Derrida and Elisabeth Roudinesco, *For What Tomorrow . . . : A Dialogue*, trans. Jeff Fort (Stanford, Calif.: Stanford University Press, 2004), 83.

14. Ricardo Ortiz, "Burning X's: Critical Futurities within Latinx Studies' Disidentifying Present," *Latinx Temporality as a Time of Crisis*, dossier of *Aztlán: A Journal of Chicano Studies* 45, no. 2 (Fall 2020): 203.

15. Rodolphe Gasché ("Piercing the Horizon," *Journal of French Philosophy* 17, no. 2 [2007]: 6) neatly combines Derrida's writing on the horizon across Derrida's corpus of material. While I rely on his synthesis of Derrida's work on the horizon and revolution, I cite from Derrida's own works when the Derrida quotes do not necessitate Gasché's framing.

16. Derrida and Roudinesco, *For What Tomorrow*, 83.

17. Gashé, "Piercing the Horizon," 9.

18. Derrida and Roudinesco, *For What Tomorrow*, 83.

19. Emily García, "On the Borders of Independence: Manuel Torres and Spanish American Independence in Filadelphia," in *The Latino Nineteenth Century*, ed. Rodrigo Lazo and Jesse Alemán (New York: NYU Press, 2016), 74.

20. As García also demonstrates, such narratives neglect any understanding of how cities in the U.S. like Philadelphia were actually "sites of Latin American independence" (76, 79).

21. María Josefina Saldaña-Portillo, *The Revolutionary Imagination in the Americas and the Age of Development* (Durham, N.C.: Duke University Press, 2003), 7.

22. For a contrasting view of how resistance operates in the field of Latinx Studies, see B. V. Olguín's *Violentolgies: Violence, Identity, and Ideology in Latina/o Literature* (Oxford: Oxford University Press, 2021), in which he provocatively argues that the resistant subject of Latinx Studies is markedly different from actually existing Latinxs. The Latinxs who emerge out of Olguín's archive illustrate how an "inchoate subaltern agency could involve tactical calculations that comprise a negotiated *hegemonic*, rather than oppositional, subject position" (11). Olguín goes so far as to suggest that key theories of the field, such as Chela Sandoval's notion of differential consciousness or scholars who have taken up Homi Bhabha's notion of third-space theory, can actually be used toward hegemonic ends, which leads him to suggest that Latinx agency *"may even be more hegemonic than*

oppositional" (20, italics his) and point out that ultimately his archive "reveal[s] *Latina/o history as violence*" (20, emphasis his).

23. Catherine S. Ramírez, "Deus ex Machina: Tradition, Technology, and the Chicanafuturist Art of Marion C. Martinez," *Aztlán* 29, no. 2 (Fall 2004): 78.

24. Catherine S. Ramírez, "Afrofuturism/Chicanafuturism: Fictive Kin," *Aztlán* 33, no. 1 (Spring 2008): 188.

25. José Esteban Muñoz, *Cruising Utopia: The Then and There of Queer Futurity* (New York: NYU Press, 2009).

26. Simón Ventura Trujillo, *Land Uprising: Native Story Power and the Insurgent Horizons of Latinx Indigeneity* (Tucson: University of Arizona Press, 2020), 37.

27. Helmut Kuhn, "The Phenomenological Concept of 'Horizon,'" in *Philosophical Essays in Memory of Edmund Husserl*, ed. Marvin Farber, 3rd ed. (Cambridge, Mass.: Harvard University Press, 2014), 113.

28. Andrea Davis, *Horizon, Sea, Sound: Caribbean and African Women's Cultural Critiques of Nation* (Evanston, Ill.: Northwestern University Press, 2022), 41.

29. Didier Maleuvre, *The Horizon: A History of Our Infinite Longing* (Berkeley: University of California Press, 2011), xiv.

30. Davis, *Horizon, Sea, Sound*, 22.

31. Jacques Derrida, *Edmund Husserl's Origin of Geometry: An Introduction* (Lincoln: University of Nebraska Press, 1989), 117.

32. Ricardo Ortiz, *Latinx Literature Now: Between Evanescence and Event* (Cham, Switzerland: Palgrave Macmillan, 2019), xviii.

33. See Leticia Alvarado, *Abject Performances: Aesthetic Strategies in Latino Cultural Productions* (Durham, N.C.: Duke University Press, 2018), 6, and Cristina Beltrán, *The Trouble with Unity: Latino Politics and the Creation of Identity* (Oxford: Oxford University Press, 2010), 19 and 157.

34. María Josefina Saldaña-Portillo, "Indians Have Always Been Modern: Roma, the Settler Colonial Paradigm, and Latinx Temporality," *Latinx Temporality as a Time of Crisis*, dossier of *Aztlán: A Journal of Chicano Studies* 45, no. 2 (Fall 2020): 225.

35. Miriam Jiménez Román and Juan Flores, eds., *The Afro-Latin@ Reader: History and Culture in the United States* (Durham, N.C.: Duke University Press, 2010).

36. Maylei Blackwell, Floridalma Boj Lopez, and Luis Urrieta Jr., eds., *Critical Latinx Indigeneities*, Special Issue of *Latino Studies* 15 (2017).

37. María Josefina Saldaña-Portillo, *Indian Given: Racial Geographies across Mexico and the United States* (Durham, N.C.: Duke University Press, 2016), 40.

38. Benedict Anderson, *Imagined Communities: Reflections on the Origin and Spread of Nationalism* (London and New York: Verso, 1983), 50.

39. John Lynch, *The Spanish American Revolutions: 1808–1826*, 2nd ed. (New York: W. W. Norton, 1986).

40. Indeed, despite receiving aid from the Haitian president Alexandre Pétion in 1815 to continue waging his war of independence, Bolívar would go on to

exclude Haiti from his Congress of Panama in 1826 in which he hoped to "create a permanent structure of Hispanic American collaboration"; David Bushnell, "Introduction," in *El Libertador: Writings of Simón Bolívar*, trans. Frederick H. Fornoff (Oxford: Oxford University Press, 2003), xliv.

41. Lynch, *Spanish American Revolutions*, 224.

42. Doris Sommer, *Foundational Fictions: The National Romances of Latin America* (Berkeley: University of California Press, 1991).

43. Lorgia García Peña, *Translating Blackness: Latinx Colonialities in Global Perspective* (Durham, N.C.: Duke University Press, 2022), 39.

44. Carmen Lamas, *The Latino Continuum and the Nineteenth-Century Americas: Literature, Translation, and Historiography* (Oxford: Oxford University Press, 2021), 21.

45. Morúa is infamously known for Morúa's Law, "which made illegal the organization of any party based on race"; Lamas, *Latino Continuum*, 203. As Lamas observes, Morúa had no idea that the law would lead to the Race War of 1912 in Cuba and the subsequent massacre of thousands of Afro Cubans. In many ways, Lamas's work on Morúa is a work of recovery that seeks to situate his revolutionary thought within his broader experiences and archives rather than reducing him to this one law. As Lamas points out, Morúa "directly alludes to his own experience living in the post-Reconstruction US in the 1880s and witnessing the continuing racist legislation in the US employed to disenfranchise African Americans, especially in education. This experience had taught him about the pernicious intent behind the separation of races" (204), which, in turn, led to his proposal of what became known as Morúa's Law.

46. Enrique Dussel, *The Invention of the Americas: Eclipse of the Other and the Myth of Modernity*, trans. Michael D. Barber (New York: Continuum, 1995).

47. Edmundo O'Gorman, *The Invention of America: An Inquiry into the Historical Nature of the New World and the Meaning of Its History* (Bloomington: Indiana University Press, 1961).

48. Ignacio López-Calvo, ed., *Alternative Orientalisms in Latin America and Beyond* (Newcastle upon Tyne: Cambridge Scholars, 2007).

49. That said, there are an increasing number of scholars who are working to draw connections between Asian, Latinx, and Asian Latinx populations. As the compelling title of Anthony Ocampo's *The Latinos of Asia: How Filipino Americans Break the Rules of Race* (Stanford, Calif.: Stanford University Press, 2016), attests, there's something to be said for the Latinization of Filipinxs. More specifically, he interrogates "those times when Filipinos have felt a sense of collective identity with either Latinos or other Asians. That Filipinos share historical and cultural connections with both Latinos and Asians makes this an even more interesting puzzle to investigate" (4). Meanwhile, other scholars examine the slightly more indirect connections that link together these two populations. For example, Long Le-Khac's *Giving Form to an Asian and Latinx America* (Stanford, Calif.: Stanford University Press, 2020) analyzes how specific forms of oppression, such as that which

accompanies immigration, is a site of potential solidarity for Asian Americans and Latinxs. In this way, Le-Khac "counters the image of separation to reveal the linked stories of contemporary Latinxs and Asian Americans" (5). Jayson Gonzales Sae-Saue, meanwhile, in *Southwest Asia: The Transpacific Geographies of Chicana/o Literature* (New Brunswick, N.J.: Rutgers University Press, 2016), considers "how the oppositional values of Chicana/o texts committed to expressing local social dilemmas regularly emerge from an interest in exploring and imagining the racial dynamics of Pacific Rim politics" (4).

50. Ortiz, "Burning X's," 203.

51. Note that I use "genre" to describe historically legible forms while I use "form" more broadly because, as Yogita Goyal points out, "form is often a proxy for a host of other terms (including style, genre, aesthetics, coherence, autonomy, and pleasure)"; Goyal, *Runaway Genres: The Global Afterlives of Slavery* (New York: NYU Press, 2019), 31.

52. In thinking about the idea of a repository, I am indebted to Ylce Irizarry's contention that narrative repositories are "for communities finding things out about themselves both through and outside the rhetoric of US neocolonialism"; Irizarry, *Chicana/o and Latina/o Fiction: The New Memory of Latinidad* (Urbana: University of Illinois Press, 2016), 9.

53. Kirsten Silva Gruesz, "The Once and Future Latino: Notes Toward a Literary History *todavía para llegar*," in *Contemporary U.S. Latino/a Literary Criticism*, ed. Lyn Di Iorio Sandín and Richard Perez (New York: Palgrave Macmillan, 2007), 117.

54. I am grateful to María Josefina Saldaña-Portillo for pointing out this connection between latinidad and Marx's distinction of class in *The Eighteenth Brumaire of Napoleon Bonaparte* (1852).

55. Marta Caminero-Santangelo, *On Latinidad: U.S. Latino Literature and the Construction of Ethnicity* (Gainesville: University Press of Florida, 2009); Raphael Dalleo and Elena Machado Sáez, *The Latino/a Canon and the Emergence of Post-Sixties Literature* (New York: Palgrave Macmillan, 2007); Irizarry, *Chicana/o and Latina/o Fiction*; and David Vázquez, *Triangulations: Narrative Strategies for Navigating Latino Identity* (Minneapolis: University of Minnesota Press, 2011).

56. Caminero-Santangelo, *On Latinidad*, 218.

57. Ortiz, "Latinx Literature Now," xvIII.

58. To that end, scholars such as Michel-Rolph Trouillot have made compelling cases for thinking about Haiti within the larger context of the Caribbean and the event of Christopher Columbus's "'stumbl[ing] on the Bahamas'" (Trouillot, *Silencing the Past: Power and the Production of History* [Boston: Beacon, 1995], 115), even as he remarks on the silence around the Haitian Revolution in Latin American textbooks at the time (99), which imply a refusal to think about Haiti within both Latin American and Latinx Studies. However, scholars such as Lorgia García Peña and Ortiz have made discussions of Haiti central to Latinx Studies. As a field, we cannot continue to forget Haiti's revolutionary example and the assistance it provided to Simón Bolívar during his own fight for independence.

59. Robert McKee Irwin, "Almost-Latino Literature: Approaching Truncated Latinidades," in *The Latino Nineteenth Century*, ed. Rodrigo Lazo and Jesse Alemán (New York: NYU Press, 2016), 113.

60. Elda María Román, "The Future of Demographobia, Latinxs, and the Realist-Speculative Convergence," *Latinx Temporality as a Time of Crisis*, dossier of *Aztlán: A Journal of Chicano Studies* 45, no. 2 (Fall 2020): 185–99.

61. Gruesz, "Once and Future Latino," 120.

62. For Viego, for example, the future anterior ties together both the threat and the promise of latinidad as it acknowledges a Latinx past and a potential future in which Latinxs are in positions of power, thus redefining what the United States signifies (Antonio Viego, *Dead Subjects: Toward a Politics of Loss in Latino Studies* [Durham, N.C.: Duke University Press, 2007], 122). For Ortiz, Latinx literary studies is still a field in the process of becoming; therefore, his use of the future perfect allows for imagining Latinx studies from the perspective of the future; Ortiz, "Burning X's." Aligned with Ortiz and Viego, but putting pressure on how literary history shapes the future of latinidad, Gruesz playfully puns on the legend of King Arthur to contemplate how writing a Latinx literary history shapes the future of latinidad; Gruesz, "Once and Future Latino."

63. Ortiz, "Burning X's," 203.

64. Raúl Coronado, *A World Not to Come: A History of Latino Writing and Print Culture* (Cambridge, Mass.: Harvard University Press, 2016).

65. For a detailed discussion of the other white strategy, see Martha Menchaca, *Recovering History, Constructing Race: The Indian, Black, and White Roots of Mexican Americans* (Austin: University of Texas Press, 2002), 583–603, and Laura E. Gómez, *Manifest Destinies: The Making of the Mexican American Race*, 2nd ed. (New York: NYU Press, 2018), 306.

66. Esmeralda Santiago, *Conquistadora* (New York: Vintage, 2012). Although I do not discuss Puerto Rico in this monograph because I focus on countries that are independent and thus not under explicit colonial rule, I mention it here to observe how a contemporary text that reimagines the nineteenth century takes up the issues that preoccupy conceptions of latinidad while pointing to the work that still needs to be done to imagine a liberatory latinidad.

67. Ileana M. Rodríguez-Silva, *Silencing Race: Disentangling Blackness, Colonialism, and National Identities in Puerto Rico* (New York: Palgrave Macmillan, 2012), 3.

68. See Flores, "Latinidad Is Cancelled," 58–79.

69. Santiago, *Conquistadora*, 172.

70. Lynch, *Spanish American Revolutions*, 197.

71. See Lynch, *Spanish American Revolutions*, 197–98.

72. Jeffrey Brown, "Conversation: Esmeralda Santiago, Author of 'Conquistadora,'" *PBS News Hour*, August 12, 2011, September 15, 2021, https://www.pbs.org/newshour/arts/conversation-esmeralda-santiago-author-of-conquistadora.

73. Ibid. https://www.pbs.org/newshour/arts/conversation-esmeralda-santiago-author-of-conquistadorahttps://www.pbs.org/newshour/arts/conversation-esmeralda-santiago-author-of-conquistadora.
74. Santiago, *Conquistadora*, 216.
75. Domingo Faustino Sarmiento, *Facundo: Or, Civilization and Barbarism* (1845), trans. Kathleen Ross (Berkeley: University of California Press, 2004).
76. Goyal, *Runaway Genres*, 65.
77. Miguel Barnet, *Biography of a Runaway Slave* (1966), trans. W. Nick Hill (Evanston, Ill: Curbstone, 1994).
78. Rigoberta Menchú, *I, Rigoberta Menchú* (London and New York: Verso, 2010).
79. John Beverley, "The Margin at the Center: On *Testimonio* (Testimonial Narrative)," *MFS: Modern Fiction Studies* 35, no. 1 (Spring 1989): 11.
80. Edward W. Said, *Culture and Imperialism* (New York: Vintage, 1993), 71.
81. Goyal, *Runaway Genres*, 30.
82. Jerng, *Racial Worldmaking* (9, emphasis mine).
83. Colleen Lye, "Racial Form," *Representations* 104, no. 1 (Fall 2008): 96.
84. Of course, Lye here is thinking within a specifically Asian American Studies context; however, her comments, drawing on Lisa Lowe ("Heterogeneity, Hybridity, Multiplicity: Marking Asian American Differences," *Diaspora: A Journal of Transnational Studies* 1, no. 1 (Spring 1991): 24-44), about the heterogeneity of Asian American communities, resonate within a Latinx context as well and can be productively extended into Latinx Studies.
85. Ralph E. Rodriguez, *Latinx Literature Unbound: Undoing Ethnic Expectation* (New York: Fordham University Press, 2018).
86. Jennifer Harford Vargas, *Forms of Dictatorship: Power, Narrative, and Authoritarianism in the Latina/o Novel* (Oxford: Oxford University Press, 2017).
87. Rodriguez, *Latinx Literature Unbound*, 3.
88. Vázquez, *Triangulations*, 4.
89. Cristina García, *Monkey Hunting* (New York: Ballantine, 2003).
90. Cristina García, *The Lady Matador's Hotel* (New York: Scribner, 2010).
91. The work on hemispheric Latinx Studies is rich and wide-ranging. For a discussion of the hemispheric nineteenth century, see Kirsten Silva Gruesz's *Ambassadors of Culture: The Transamerican Origins of Latino Writing* (Princeton, N.J.: Princeton University Press, 2001); Carmen Lamas's *The Latino Continuum and the Nineteenth-Century Americas*; and Rodrigo Lazo's *Writing to Cuba: Filibustering and Cuban Exiles in the United States* (Chapel Hill: University of North Carolina Press, 2005), as well as *The Latino Nineteenth Century*, edited by Rodrigo Lazo and Jesse Alemán (New York: NYU Press, 2016). For work that discusses nineteenth-century texts alongside contemporary ones, albeit with a focus on Chicanx literature, see Marissa K. López's *Chicano Nations: The Hemispheric Origins of Mexican American Literature* (New York: NYU Press, 2011). For scholarship on contemporary hemispheric Latinx literature, see Harford Vargas's *Forms of Dictatorship*; Claudia

Milian's *Latining America: Black-Brown Passages and the Coloring of Latino/a Studies* (Athens: University of Georgia Press, 2013); John D. "Rio" Riofrio's *Continental Shifts: Migration, Representation, and the Struggle for Justice in Latin(o) America* (Austin: University of Texas Press, 2015); Ana Patricia Rodríguez's *Dividing the Isthmus: Central American Transnational Histories, Literatures, and Cultures* (Austin: University of Texas Press, 2009); José David Saldívar's *Trans-Americanity: Subaltern Modernities, Global Coloniality, and the Cultures of Greater Mexico* (Durham, N.C.: Duke University Press, 2012); and Ariana Vigil's *War Echoes: Gender and Militarization in U.S. Latina/o Cultural Production* (New Brunswick, N.J.: Rutgers University Press, 2014).

92. Caminero-Santangelo, *On Latinidad*, 9.

93. See Elena Machado Sáez, *Market Aesthetics: The Purchase of the Past in Caribbean Diasporic Fiction* (Charlottesville: University of Virginia Press, 2015).

94. For more on how Rizal and Martí are read together, see John D. Blanco, "Bastards of the Unfinished Revolution: Bolívar's Ismael and Rizal's Martí at the End of the Nineteenth Century," in *Imagining Our Americas: Toward a Transnational Frame*, ed. Sandhya Shukla and Heidi Tinsman (Durham, N.C.: Duke University Press, 2007), and Koichi Hagimoto, *Between Empires: Martí, Rizal, and the Intercolonial Alliance* (New York: Palgrave Macmillan, 2013).

95. Caminero-Santangelo, *On Latinidad*, 9.

96. This is not to say that authors of different backgrounds aren't haunted by revolutions elsewhere—after all, Cormac McCarthy's Border Trilogy, specifically *All the Pretty Horses* (1992), and Thomas Pynchon's *Against the Day* (2006) are haunted by the Mexican Revolution. However, as *All the Pretty Horses* shows us, the concern is less with how to revive a lost revolutionary future and more about how the protagonist of the novel, John Grady Cole, romanticizes Mexico and views it as a tabula rasa upon which he can map his own desires. The Mexican Revolution serves as a corrective to his viewpoint, as his inability to apprehend Mexico as a place with its own history foils his plans for his life there.

97. Interestingly, to better capture the transnationalism of nationalist movements, a text like Benedict Anderson's *Under Three Flags: Anarchism and the Anti-Colonial Imagination* (London and New York: Verso, 2006) focuses on three key figures of revolution in the Philippines: José Rizal, Isabelo de los Reyes, and Mariano Ponce. Focusing on specific people offers one way to see how revolutionary ideas circulate; we get a sense of this in my chapter on the Dominican Republic, with my discussion of Camila Ureña, who was the daughter of the famous Dominican poet Salomé Ureña. Alan Eladio Gómez, in *The Revolutionary Imaginations of Greater Mexico: Chicana/o Radicalism, Solidarity Politics, and Latin American Social Movements* (Austin: University of Texas Press, 2016), meanwhile, turns to festivals and strikes, among other events, as another way of apprehending the revolutionary exchanges that happen across borders.

98. Vázquez, *Triangulations*, 171.

99. María Amparo Ruiz de Burton, *Who Would Have Thought It?* (1872) (Houston: Arte Público, 1995).

100. Sandra Cisneros, *Caramelo* (New York: Vintage, 2002).

101. Sommer, *Foundational Fictions*.

102. José Rizal, *Noli Me Tangere* (1887) (New York: Penguin, 2006).

103. José Rizal, *El Filibusterismo* (1891) (New York: Penguin, 2011).

104. Jessica Hagedorn, *Dogeaters* (New York: Penguin, 1990); Ninotchka Rosca, *State of War* (New York: W. W. Norton, 1988).

105. Julia Alvarez, *In the Name of Salomé* (Chapel Hill, N.C.: Algonquin Books of Chapel Hill, 2000), and Junot Díaz, *The Brief Wondrous Life of Oscar Wao* (New York: Riverhead, 2007).

106. Gertrudis Gómez de Avellaneda. *Sab and Autobiography* (1841) (Austin: University of Texas Press, 1993).

107. Martin Delany, *Blake; or, the Huts of America* (1859) (Cambridge, Mass.: Harvard University Press, 2017); Leslie Marmon Silko, *Almanac of the Dead* (New York: Penguin, 1991).

1. Captive Revolutions: Revolutionary Consciousness as Racial Consciousness in Ruiz de Burton and Cisneros

1. The date of the piece is unknown, since, although Alcaraz posted pictures of the painting's progress to Twitter on April 9, 2016, and April 28, 2016, he also tweeted a link to purchase the print on December 12, 2015.

2. In this way, Alcaraz's print also participates in the ongoing revolutionary legacy of the Virgin of Guadalupe, as she is often a figure of resistance, from the protest posters during the United Farm Worker's strikes and pilgrimages to the work of Alma López and Yolanda López, who make the Virgin a centerpiece of their Chicana feminist iconography. In other words, the form that the Virgin of Guadalupe takes—the sunburst mandorla that frames the image, the woman in the center with a star-covered mantle—allows us to recognize not only the image, but also the revolutionary histories to which the image contributes.

3. Antonio Viego, *Dead Subjects: Toward a Politics of Loss in Latino Studies* (Durham, N.C.: Duke University Press, 2007), 108.

4. Yara Simón, "Princess Leia's Iconic Buns Were Inspired by These Revolutionary-Era Revolutionary Women," *Remezcla*, December 28, 2016, July 30, 2021, https://remezcla.com/culture/princess-leia-hair-buns/.

5. While the Facebook post no longer exists, the *Remezcla* article in the previous note describes it in their reporting of the finding.

6. This then led to Aura Bogado's critique, also found in the *Remezcla* piece, that George Lucas's story and Eric Tang's post erased Indigenous women from the narrative, as Clara de la Rocha is of European descent and Tang's post focused on her rather than the Hopi women who also inspired the iconic hair style.

7. Within this context, a vulnerability refers to a security flaw within a computer system that can then be exploited to bypass security protocols.

8. See Curtis Marez, *Farm Worker Futurism: Speculative Technologies of Resistance* (Minneapolis: University of Minnesota Press, 2016), 138.

9. Shelley Streeby, *American Sensations: Class, Empire, and the Production of Popular Culture* (Berkeley: University of California Press, 2002), 6.

10. María Amparo Ruiz de Burton, *Who Would Have Thought It?* (1872) (Houston: Arte Público, 1995); Sandra Cisneros, *Caramelo* (New York: Vintage, 2002).

11. As Julie Ruiz argues, "Because she views the Civil War as a struggle between Franco-Latin and Euro-American races, Ruiz de Burton considers the South an extension of Latinidad and thus, for her, a 'white' nation is designed to prevent the immersion of South America by North America"; Ruiz, "Captive Identities: The Gendered Conquest of Mexico in *Who Would Have Thought It?*," in *María Amparo Ruiz de Burton: Critical and Pedagogical Perspectives*, ed. Amelia María de la Luz Montes and Anne Elizabeth Goldman (Lincoln: University of Nebraska Press, 2004), 117.

12. Rosaura Sánchez and Beatrice Pita, *Conflicts of Interest: The Letters of María Amparo Ruiz de Burton* (Houston: Arte Público, 2001), 193–94.

13. Walter Mignolo, *The Idea of Latin America* (Malden, Mass., and Oxford: Blackwell, 2005).

14. Juliet Hooker reads Vasconcelos more sympathetically by theorizing his conceptualization of "mestizaje as an anticolonial ideology"; Hooker, *Theorizing Race in the Americas: Douglass, Sarmiento, Du Bois, and Vasconcelos* (Oxford: Oxford University Press, 2019), 21.

15. My deepest thanks to María Regina Firmino-Castillo for pointing out the specific erasures of indigeneity in the national imaginaries of the Mexican Revolution and the Chicano Movement.

16. B. V. Olguín, "Raza," in *Keywords for Latina/o Studies*, ed. Deborah R. Vargas, Nancy Raquel Mirabal, and Lawrence La Fountain-Stokes (New York: NYU Press, 2017), 190.

17. José Enrique Rodó, *Ariel* (1900), trans. Margaret Sayers Peden (Austin: University of Texas Press, 1988).

18. Roberto Fernández Retamar, *Caliban and Other Essays*, trans. Edward Baker (1974) (Minneapolis: University of Minnesota Press, 1989).

19. Gloria Anzaldúa's *Borderlands / La Frontera: The New Mestiza*, 3rd ed. (San Francisco: Aunt Lute, 1987) revises much of the Chicano Movement's mythology, but her use of Vasconcelos as the basis for theorizing the New Mestiza illustrates the continued appeal of his ideas as well as the continued constraints on Latinx revolutionary thought, as the seemingly broad implications of a term like la raza are confined to Chicanxs—that is, the term only applies to those Mexican Americans who identify with a particular politics that centers around a mythic Indigenous past. For more on Anzaldúa's revisions of the Chicano Movement

mythology, see Sonia Saldívar-Hull, "Introduction to the Second Edition," in *Borderlands / La Frontera*, 1–15.

20. See María Josefina Saldaña-Portillo, "Who's the Indian in Aztlán?: Re-Writing Mestizaje, Indianism, and Chicanismo from the Lacandón," in *The Latin American Subaltern Studies Reader*, ed. Ileana Rodríguez (Durham, N.C.: Duke University Press, 2001).

21. In *Mestizaje: Critical Uses of Race in Chicano Culture* (Minneapolis: University of Minnesota Press, 2006), Rafael Pérez-Torres argues for a critical mestizaje that is more liberatory than the lineage I have traced previously. He writes, "Moreover, mestizaje signals the embodiedness of history. As such, it opens a world of possibilities in terms of forging new relational identities" (3). While I am sympathetic toward such a view, I read Cisneros's invocation of mestizaje as one in which she highlights how it has limited the forging of new relational identities that Pérez-Torres describes.

22. While in this context I am pointing to the important political work that Cisneros does in *Caramelo* to address anti-indigeneity in Mexican and Chicanx communities, I want to underscore, as I did in the introduction, that Cisneros herself is a problematic figure whose performance of chicanidad signals the limits of the horizon for a broader theory of latinidad. For example, by fashioning herself after Frida Kahlo, Cisneros plays into stereotypes that homogenize Mexican, Mexican American, and Chicanx identities. Cisneros also limits the horizon of latinidad by acting as a gatekeeper in the publishing industry, going so far as to promote books that promote harmful views of immigrants, like Jeanine Cummins's *American Dirt* (2020), while demonizing authors critical of this decision, thus attacking Latinx authors who expand the horizons of latinidad in favor of an author who forecloses it. To read more about Cisneros's insistence on supporting Cummins, see Yxta Maya Murray's *New Yorker* piece "Sandra Cisneros May Put You in a Poem," *The New Yorker*, September 21, 2022, https://www.newyorker.com/culture/the-new-yorker-interview/sandra-cisneros-may-put-you-in-a-poem.

23. "Recovering the U.S. Hispanic Literary Heritage," July 30, 2021, https://artepublicopress.com/recovery-program/.

24. María Amparo Ruiz de Burton, *The Squatter and the Don* (1885) (1992; repr. Houston: Arte Público, 1997). Rather than reading Ruiz de Burton as signaling a break with Chicanx literary history as typically understood, John M. González examines how the recovery project and the Chicano Movement's cultural nationalism go hand in hand, noting that "the recovery of texts (p/re) figures the recovery of land; the desire for the Aztlán nation finds its romance of reunion in recovery projects. The romance between subjectivity and land (or the promise of its recovery) underscores the nationalist framework and the creation of community along those contours"; González, "Romancing Hegemony: Constructing Racialized Citizenship in María Amparo Ruiz de Burton's *The Squatter and the Don*," in *Recovering the U.S. Hispanic Literary Heritage*, ed. Erlinda Gonzales-Berry and Chuck Tatum (Houston: Arte Público, 1996), 25.

25. José Aranda, "When Archives Collide: Recovering Modernity in Early Mexican American Literature," in *The Latino Nineteenth Century*, ed. Rodrigo Lazo and Jesse Alemán (New York: NYU Press, 2016), 147.

26. For a foundational discussion of Ruiz de Burton's place in the archive of Mexican American literature, see José Aranda, "'Contradictory Impulses': María Amparo Ruiz de Burton, Resistance Theory, and the Politics of Chicano/a Studies," *American Literature* 70, no. 3 (1998): 551–79.

27. In his discussion of why Doña Theresa is carried off in the first place, Jesse Alemán argues that "not just any Mexican citizens were targeted. The Indians carry Doña Theresa off her Sonoran hacienda, emphasizing the intersecting colonial conflicts that make up the 'secret' of Lola's Indian paint: the U.S.'s expansion into Mexico displaced Mexican landowners and made them vulnerable to Native American attacks, but Indigenous groups attacked landholders such as Doña Theresa in the first place precisely because they dispossessed Native Americans of their land and natural resources"; Alemán, "Citizenship Rights and Colonial Whites: The Cultural Work of María Amparo Ruiz de Burton's Novels," in *Complicating Constructions: Race, Ethnicity, and Hybridity in American Texts*, ed. David S. Goldstein and Audrey B. Thacker (Seattle: University of Washington Press, 2015), 11.

28. For a discussion of Lola's passing, see María Carla Sánchez, "Whiteness Invisible: Early Mexican American Writing and the Color of Literary History," in *Passing: Identity and Interpretation in Sexuality, Race, and Religion*, ed. María Carla Sánchez and Linda Schlossberg (New York: NYU Press, 2001), 64–91, and Pascha A. Stevenson, "Reader Expectation and Ethnic Rhetorics: The Problem of the Passing Subaltern in Who Would Have Thought It?," *Ethnic Studies Review* 28, no. 2 (January 2005): 61–74.

29. As Jesse Alemán argues, "Whiteness comes into a crisis in Ruiz de Burton's narratives as they imagine Hispano racial whiteness but also emphasize the cultural difference between Hispanos and Anglos, especially in the context of Spanish and Anglo American colonialism"; "Citizenship Rights," 5.

30. Marissa K. López, *Chicano Nations: The Hemispheric Origins of Mexican American Literature* (New York: NYU Press, 2011), 17.

31. See Margaret D. Jacobs, "Mixed-Bloods, Mestizas, and Pintos: Race, Gender, and Claims to Whiteness in Helen Hunt Jackson's 'Ramona' and María Amparo Ruiz de Burton's 'Who Would Have Thought It?,'" *Western American Literature* 36, no. 3 (2001): 223; Jesse Alemán, "'Thank God, Lolita Is Away from Those Horrid Savages': The Politics of Whiteness in Who Would Have Thought It?," in Montes and Goldman, *María Amparo Ruiz de Burton*; and John-Michael Rivera, *The Emergence of Mexican America: Recovering Stories of Mexican Peoplehood in U.S. Culture* (New York: NYU Press, 2006), 82–109.

32. As Beth Fisher points out, the "opposition between Spanish-Mexican civility and Indian savagery aligns the story of Doña Theresa with captivity stories contributed by Californios to the Hubert Howe Bancroft historiographical project during the 1870s" ("The Captive Mexicana and the Desiring Bourgeois Woman:

Domesticity and Expansionism in Ruiz de Burton's *Who Would Have Thought It?*," *Legacy* 16, no. 1 [1999]: 61), and "for Ruiz de Burton as for many of her contemporaries, the captivity narrative thus provides a means of representing the circumstances that led to the Californios' recent loss of political power" (61).

33. In her reading of the relationship between Lola and Mrs. Norval, Fisher argues that "Ruiz de Burton uses a contest between competing discourses of womanhood to represent, and to intervene in, the historical conflict between elite Mexicans and middle-class Yankees. In this contest, Lola Medina's endangered purity represents the political vulnerability of an elite, culturally superior Mexican civilization as it is incorporated into the greed-driven economy of the United States"; ibid., 60.

34. Amelia María de la Luz Montes, "María Amparo Ruiz de Burton Negotiates American Literary Politics and Culture," in *Challenging Boundaries: Gender and Periodization*, ed. Joyce W. Warren and Margaret Dickie (Athens: University of Georgia Press, 2000), 208.

35. Indeed, Kate McCullough reads Lola as representative "of both the 'West' and 'Mexico,'" that "disrupts a Civil War regional model of America as North/South and simultaneously locates that particular sectional divide in relation to the American geopolitics of imperial expansion"; McCullough, *Regions of Identity: The Construction of America in Women's Fiction, 1885–1914* (Stanford, Calif.: Stanford University Press, 1999), 136.

36. McCullough, *Regions of Identity*, 140.

37. Jesse Alemán reads Lola's alignment with civility against savagery as "collaps[ing] the imaginary distance between the North and South, showing that, despite the Mason-Dixon line, the North's racism is not far removed from Southern slavery"; Alemán, "Politics of Whiteness," 100.

38. Andrea Tinnemeyer, "Rescuing the Past: The Case of Olive Oatman and Lola Medina," in Montes and Goldman, *María Amparo Ruiz de Burton: Critical and Pedagogical Perspectives*, 169.

39. Tinnemeyer remarks that Oatman refers to Apache Indians in her lecture notes (ibid., 170), but scholars generally think that she was wrong about who attacked her and her family. Kathryn Zabelle Derounian-Stodola notes that her family was in fact attacked by Yavapais; Derounian-Stodola, "The Indian Captivity Narratives of Mary Rowlandson and Olive Oatman: Case Studies in the Continuity, Evolution, and Exploitation of Literary Discourse," *Studies in the Literary Imagination* 27, no. 1 (1994): 34.

40. Christopher Castiglia, *Bound and Determined: Captivity, Culture-Crossing, and White Womanhood from Mary Rowlandson to Patty Hearst* (Chicago: University of Chicago Press, 1996), 14.

41. According to Derounian-Stodola regarding Rowlandson's narrative, "Only with the sixth edition in 1770 do we see a regular pattern of reprinting established for the next century"; Kathryn Zabelle Derounian, "The Publication, Promotion, and Distribution of Mary Rowlandson's Indian Captivity Narrative in the Seventeenth Century," *Early American Literature*, 23, no. 3 (1988): 248.

42. Greg Sieminski, "The Puritan Captivity Narrative and the Politics of the American Revolution," *American Quarterly* 42, no. 1 (1990): 36.

43. See Derounian-Stodola, "Indian Captivity Narratives," 240–42.

44. Anne E. Goldman, "'Who Ever Heard of a Blue-Eyed Mexican?': Satire and Sentimentality in María Amparo Ruiz de Burton's *Who Would Have Thought It?*," in *Recovering the U.S. Hispanic Literary Heritage*, ed. Erlinda Gonzales-Berry and Charles Tatum (Houston: Arte Público, 1995), 64.

45. Fisher, "Captive Mexicana," 61.

46. Alex Woloch, *The One vs. the Many: Minor Characters and the Space of the Protagonist in the Novel* (Princeton, N.J.: Princeton University Press, 2003), 14.

47. Jennifer Harford Vargas, *Forms of Dictatorship: Power, Narrative, and Authoritarianism in the Latina/o Novel* (Oxford: Oxford University Press), 2017, 39–41.

48. Alemán, "Citizenship Rights," 9.

49. Ruiz de Burton, *Who Would Have Thought It?*, 17.

50. Please note that while Ruiz de Burton uses the "Hapsburg" spelling, I use the more contemporary "Habsburg" spelling.

51. Gretchen Murphy, "A Europeanized New World: Colonialism and Cosmopolitanism in *Who Would Have Thought It?*," in Montes and Goldman, *María Amparo Ruiz de Burton: Critical and Pedagogical Perspectives*, 136. Significantly, José Aranda argues that the Bourbon connection also creates an ethnic connection, as in his reading of this scene he argues that "electoral politics has left Mexico weak, its sovereignty in debt to foreign nations, and defenseless against armed invasion. Maximiliano's aristocratic pedigree at least assures a claim on behalf of the Spanish Bourbons, an ethnic tie that is commensurate with these men as the minimum requirement for recognition of Mexico as a prior extension of Spain and therefore European"; Aranda, "Contradictory Impulses," 567.

52. Ruiz, "Captive Identities," 130–31.

53. Murphy, "Europeanized New World," 141.

54. Sánchez and Pita, *Conflicts of Interest*, 220.

55. Raúl Coronado, *A World Not to Come: A History of Latino Writing and Print Culture* (Cambridge, Mass.: Harvard University Press, 2016), 248.

56. Edward Shawcross, *France, Mexico and Informal Empire in Latin America, 1820–1867: Equilibrium in the New World* (Cham, Switzerland: Palgrave Macmillan, 2018), 21.

57. Aranda, "Contradictory Impulses," 569.

58. Fisher, "Captive Mexicana," 64.

59. As David Vázquez reminds us, Cisneros is one author who is "not ready to jettison the nation" and instead "maintain[s] a focus on the nation as one strategy for social and political empowerment"; Vázquez, *Triangulations: Narrative Strategies for Navigating Latino Identity* (Minneapolis: University of Minnesota Press, 2011), 189. For a useful discussion of *Caramelo* and its commitments to the Chicano

Movement, see Randy J. Ontiveros, *In the Spirit of a New People: The Cultural Politics of the Chicano Movement* (New York: NYU Press, 2013), 170–96.

60. Sandra Cisneros, *Caramelo* (New York: Vintage, 2002). In addition to the fact that Lala's grandfather was in the Mexican Army during the Revolution—and subsequently fled to Chicago until the war was over—*Caramelo* is peppered with references to the revolution. For example, early in *Caramelo*, Lala relays the story of how her grandmother had all of Lala's hair cut off in Querétaro, the same city where Maximilian was executed by firing squad.

61. Kristina S. Gibby, "Ghostly Narrators in Zoé Valdés's *Te di la vida entera* and Sandra Cisneros's *Caramelo: or Puro Cuento*," *Chiricú Journal* 2, no. 1 (2018): 97.

62 Cisneros, *Caramelo*, 92.

63. Georgina Rannard and Eve Webster, "Leopold II: Belgium 'Wakes Up' to Its Bloody Colonial Past," *BBC News*, June 13, 2020, July 30, 2021, https://www.bbc.com/news/world-europe-53017188.

64. María Laura Spoturno, "Thresholds of Writing: Text and Paratext in Sandra Cisneros' *Caramelo or Puro Cuento*," in *The Landscapes of Writing in Chicano Literature*, ed. Imelda Marín-Junquera (New York: Palgrave Macmillan, 2013), 51.

65. Gibby, "Ghostly Narrators," 98.

66. Cisneros, *Caramelo*, 314.

67. Tereza M. Szeghi, "Weaving Transnational Cultural Identity through Travel and Diaspora in Sandra Cisneros's *Caramelo*," *Gender, Transnationalism, and Ethnic American Identity*, Special issue, *MELUS* 39, no. 4 (Winter 2014): 178.

68. Cisneros, *Caramelo*, 34.

69. Nassim Balestrini, "Transnational and Transethnic Textures; or, 'Intricate Interdependencies' in Sandra Cisneros's *Caramelo*," *Amerikastudien/American Studies* 57, no. 1 (2012): 74.

70. Cisneros, *Caramelo*, 241.

71. Ellen McCracken offers an opposite reading of the *Caramelo* cover, arguing that it indicates "female docility to some, and an unthreatening safe image of Mexicanicity to others"; McCracken, "Postmodern Ethnicity in Sandra Cisneros' *Caramelo*: Hybridity, Spectacle, and Memory in the Nomadic Text," *Journal of American Studies in Turkey* 12 (2000): 8.

72. Claudia Milian, *LatinX* (Minneapolis: University of Minnesota Press, 2019), 2.

2. Romancing Revolution: The Queer Future of National Romance in Rizal, Rosca, and Hagedorn

1. See Jessica Hagedorn, *Dogeaters* (New York: Penguin, 1990), and Ninotchka Rosca, *State of War* (New York: W. W. Norton, 1988). When discussing Filipinxs and Filipinx Studies more broadly, I use the "x" to signal the horizons of possibility included in the "x." However, I use "Filipino" and "Filipina" for historically specific contexts in which the distinction makes a difference. For example, José Rizal's

revolutionary imaginary solely relies on men as revolutionary figures; referring to his revolutionary imaginary as Filipinx would thus make it seem more liberatory than it actually was.

2. Lucy Mae San Pablo Burns, *Puro Arte: Filipinos on the Stages of Empire* (New York: NYU Press, 2012), 5.

3. Koichi Hagimoto, *Between Empires: Martí, Rizal, and the Intercolonial Alliance* (New York: Palgrave Macmillan, 2013), 18.

4. Walter D. Mignolo, *The Idea of Latin America* (Malden, Mass., and Oxford: Blackwell, 2005).

5. In conceptualizing the Philippines within a Latinx context, I take inspiration from Ricardo Ortiz's "Edwidge Danticat's *Latinidad: The Farming of Bones* and the Cultivation (of Fields) of Knowledge," in *Aftermaths: Exile, Migration, and Diaspora Reconsidered*, ed. Marcus Bullock and Peter Y. Paik (New Brunswick, N.J.: Rutgers University Press, 2009). In this essay, Ortiz "dislodge[s], if not expel[s], a certain construction of U.S./Latino/Latina identity, not through *diminution but through augmentation and complication*" (152, emphasis his). In so doing, Ortiz underscores the importance "of a historical perspective and practice that reconfigure[s] such identitarian terms as 'Latino' and 'American'" (162–63).

6. The guerrilla conversion narrative I discuss in this chapter differs markedly from the nonfictional guerrilla conversion narratives that emerged in Latin America in the twentieth century. As María Josefina Saldaña-Portillo observes of Che Guevara's *Guerrilla Warfare*, the "guerrilla subject bears a compelling tropological resemblance to the hero of development discourse: he is resolute, destructive *and* productive, a risk taker, an advantage seeker, flexible and highly mobile; he is loving, strong, frugal, and self-determining"; Saldaña-Portillo, *The Revolutionary Imagination in the Americas and the Age of Development* (Durham, N.C.: Duke University Press, 2003), 67. Moreover, guerrilla subjects, in converting to the revolution, become "shadows or ghosts of their former selves because they have made an epochal choice in choosing to become guerrillas, and thus their former identities are figuratively eviscerated as a consequence of it" (68). Where the guerrilla conversion narrative I trace is one based on mentorship and collectivity, the Latin American conversion narratives are individualistic and necessitate an erasure of the self to be part of the revolution.

7. José Rizal, *Noli Me Tangere* (1887) (New York: Penguin, 2006), and *El Filibusterismo* (1891) (New York: Penguin, 2011).

8. Doris Sommer, *Foundational Fictions: The National Romances of Latin America* (Berkeley: University of California Press, 1991), 6.

9. Hagimoto, *Between Empires*, 23.

10. Vicente L. Rafael, "White Love: Surveillance and National Resistance in the U.S. Colonization of the Philippines," in *Cultures of United States Imperialism*, ed. Amy Kaplan and Donald E. Pease (Durham, N.C.: Duke University Press, 1991), 124.

11. Benedict Anderson, "Cacique Democracy in the Philippines: Origins and Dreams," in *Discrepant Histories: Translocal Essays on Filipino Cultures*, ed. Vicente L. Rafael (Philadelphia: Temple University Press, 1995), 11.

12. Simón Ventura Trujillo, *Land Uprising: Native Story Power and the Insurgent Horizons of Latinx Indigeneity* (Tucson: University of Arizona Press, 2020), 44. While Trujillo discusses "disappeared relations" between Indigenous and Mexican people, such a framework is not much different than that between the Philippines and Latin America and even the United States. After all, during the colonial period, the Philippines was administered from Mexico, and during the U.S. occupation they were administered by the Bureau of Indian Affairs. See Anthony Ocampo, *The Latinos of Asia: How Filipino Americans Break the Rules of Race* (Stanford, Calif.: Stanford University Press, 2016), for a robust reading of how Filipinxs trouble the distinctions between Asian Americans and Latinxs.

13. Benedict Anderson discusses the "historical vertigo" of the Philippines and argues that we can track multiple historical trajectories based on whether the Philippines is viewed from Asia or Latin America; Anderson, *The Specter of Comparisons: Nationalism, Southeast Asia and the World* (New York: Verso, 1998), 227. Adam Lifshey remarks upon the curious fact that the Philippines is "virtually unacknowledged by Spanish departments despite over three centuries of Spanish colonialism; by English departments despite being, according to some measurements, the third or fourth largest Anglophone country in the world; and by Asian departments despite geography, because of all the Western presences in the islands"; Lifshey, "The Literary Alterities of Philippine Nationalism in José Rizal's *El Filibusterismo*," *PMLA* 123, no. 5 (2008): 1435.

14. For a detailed discussion of what a filibustero is for Rizal, see Filomeno V. Aguilar Jr., "Filibustero, Rizal, and the Manilamen of the Nineteenth Century," *Philippine Studies* 59, no. 4 (2011): 429–69, especially 430–33, in which he explains how the filibustero was a revolutionary figure rather than a pirate (though Aguilar Jr. notes that piracy can never be completely removed from the concept). Rodrigo Lazo offers a similar definition in his work on the Cuban newspaper *El Filibustero*, which was first published in New York in 1853; see "Los Filibusteros: Cuban Writers in the United States and Deterritorialized Print Culture," *American Literary History* 15, no. 1 (Spring 2003): 87–106, and *Writing to Cuba: Filibustering and Cuban Exiles in the United States* (Chapel Hill: University of North Carolina Press, 2005). In noting the resonances between the Philippines and Cuba, I point to the revolutionary connections that bind the two islands together. Indeed, Aguilar Jr. observes that "by associating Simoun [the protagonist of *El Filibusterismo*] with Cuba . . . Rizal uncannily called upon the imagery of American filibusters, from Narciso López to José Martí and the Cuban exiles who longed for the island's independence" (460). For more on filibusteros in the Philippines, see Hagimoto, *Between Empires*, 115–24.

15. Benedict Anderson, *Imagined Communities: Reflections on the Origin and Spread of Nationalism* (London and New York: Verso, 1983).

16. Lifshey explains that during the late nineteenth century, Filipinos were considered creoles, people who were of Spanish descent but born in the Philippines. Read in this way, "Filipino" designates this grouping apart from two other racial (and class) groupings: indios (Indigenous people) and peninsulares (people who were actually born in Spain); Lifshey, "Literary Alterities," 1436.

17. Anderson explains this idea of the "First Filipino" as follows: "The Spain from which so many of the characters have at one time or another arrived is always offstage. This restriction made it clear to Rizal's first readers that 'The Philippines' was a society in itself, even though those who lived in it had as yet no common name. That he was the first to imagine this social whole explains why he is remembered today as the First Filipino"; Anderson, *Specter of Comparisons*, 230.

18. Raquel A. G. Reyes, *Love, Passion and Patriotism: Sexuality and the Philippine Propaganda Movement, 1882–1892* (Singapore: NUS Press, 2008).

19. Sharon Delmendo, *The Star-Entangled Banner: One Hundred Years of America in the Philippines* (New Brunswick, N.J.: Rutgers University Press, 2004), 27.

20. E. San Juan Jr., *Rizal in Our Time: Essays in Interpretation* (Manila: Anvil, 2011), 9–10.

21. Reyes, *Love, Passion and Patriotism*, xxix.

22. Caroline S. Hau, *On the Subject of the Nation: Filipino Writings from the Margins, 1981–2004* (Quezon City: Ateneo de Manila University Press, 2004), 165.

23. Rafael, "White Love," 185.

24. Juliana Chang, "Masquerade, Hysteria, and Neocolonial Femininity in Jessica Hagedorn's *Dogeaters*," *Contemporary Literature* 44, no. 4 (2003): 639.

25. H. W. Brands, *Bound to Empire: The United States and the Philippines* (Oxford: Oxford University Press, 1992), 25.

26. Eve Kosofsky Sedgwick, *Between Men: English Literature and Male Homosocial Desire* (New York: Columbia University Press, 1985), 21.

27. Ileana Rodríguez, *Women, Guerrillas, and Love: Understanding War in Central America* (Minneapolis: University of Minnesota Press, 1996).

28. Martin J. Ponce, *Beyond the Nation: Diasporic Filipino Literature and Queer Reading* (New York: NYU Press, 2012), 26. This usage marks a larger shift in queer theory reflected in the work of scholars David L. Eng, José Esteban Muñoz, Jack Halberstam, and Jasbir K. Puar, who view queerness as invested in critiques of the normative. These queer scholars imagine queerness as not solely tied to sexuality and sex acts, but as "a political metaphor without a fixed referent"; Eng, Halberstam, and Muñoz, "What's Queer About Queer Studies Now?" *Social Text* 23, nos.3–4 (2005): 1.

29. Denise Cruz, *Transpacific Femininities: The Making of the Modern Filipina* (Durham, N.C.: Duke University Press, 2012), 82.

30. Rizal, *Noli Me Tangere*, 399.

31. Hagimoto, *Between Empires*, 122.

32. John D. Blanco, "Bastards of the Unfinished Revolution: Bolívar's Ismael and Rizal's Martí at the End of the Nineteenth Century," in *Imagining Our Americas:*

Toward a Transnational Frame, ed. Sandhya Shukla and Heidi Tinsman (Durham, N.C.: Duke University Press, 2007), 71.

33. Hagimoto, *Between Empires*, 121.

34. Rizal, *El Filibusterismo*, 280.

35. For Dolores de Manuel, women writers like Rosca "aim at a recovery of the Filipina and the Filipino American woman as a colonial and neocolonial subject"; Manuel, "Decolonizing Bodies, Reinscribing Souls in the Fiction of Ninotchka Rosca and Lynda Ty-Casper," *MELUS* 29, no. 1 (2004): 99.

36. Myra Mendible, "The Politics and Poetics of Philippine Festival in Ninotchka Rosca's *State of War*," *International Fiction Review* 29, no. 1 (2002), https://journals.lib.unb.ca/index.php/IFR/article/view/7714, accessed November 11, 2021.

37. Ibid.

38. Rocio G. Davis, "Postcolonial Visions and Immigrant Longings: Ninotchka Rosca's Versions of the Philippines," *World Literature Today* 73, no. 1 (1999): 66.

39. Davis, "Postcolonial Visions," 68.

40. Rosca, *State of War*, 12.

41. Although critics like Leonard Casper critique Rosca's decision to have Anna give birth to a son, rather than a daughter, I read this decision differently. Rather than view gender as following a set binary, Rosca—and, later, Hagedorn—offers a spectrum for gender identification; see Casper, "Minoring in History: Rosca as Ninotchka," *Amerasia* 16, no. 2 (1990): 201–10.

42. Ismael's name also recalls Jose Martí's 1882 collection of poems, *Ismaelillo*, a reference that further strengthens the connections between Martí and Rizal, Cuba and the Philippines; José Marti, *Ismaelillo* (1882), trans. Tyler Fisher (Chicago: Wings Press, 2007).

43. However, it is important to note that this connection happens in name only. Because of Mayang's affair with Hans, Anna is not a Villaverde by blood.

44. Jessica Hagedorn, *Dogeaters* (New York: Penguin, 1990). Eugenio Matibag notes the proto-postmodernism elements in Rizal by remarking upon self-referentiality in *Noli* and the way in which *Fili* is a "metafictional rereading" of *Noli*); see Matibag, "'El Verbo del Filibusterismo': Narrative Ruses in the Novels of José Rizal," *Revista Hispánica Moderna* 48, no. 2 (1995): 258–59.

45. Jacques Derrida, *The Politics of Friendship* (London and New York: Verso, 1997), 279.

46. Rachel Lee, *The Americas of Asian American Literature: Gendered Fictions of Nation and Transnation* (Princeton, N.J.: Princeton University Press, 1999), 101.

47. Stephen Hong Sohn, "From Discos to Jungles: Circuitous Queer Patronage and Sex Tourism in Jessica Hagedorn's *Dogeaters*," *MFS: Modern Fiction Studies* 56, no. 2 (2010): 337.

48. Hagedorn, *Dogeaters*, 233.

49. Sohn, "From Discos to Jungles," 331. While many critics focus on Joey as a gay man, still others, like Mendible, point to his sexual fluidity: "[Joey's]

sexual identity is determined, not by inclination or preference, but by income potential. Like his hybrid ancestry, Joey's bisexuality is simply another commodity that broadens his appeal and increases his marketability (and thus viability)"; Mendible, "Dictators, Movie Stars, and Martyrs: The Politics of Spectacle in Jessica Hagedorn's *Dogeaters*," *Genders* 36, no. 3 (2002), https://www.colorado.edu/gendersarchive1998-2013/2002/12/01/dictators-movie-stars-and-martyrs-politics-spectacle-jessica-hagedorns-dogeaters, accessed November 11, 2021. Removed from the consumer market of underground Manila, it is not that Joey's sexuality goes underground, but that he is no longer forced to sell his body for profit. Rahul K. Gairola similarly points to the fluidity of Joey's sexuality and goes so far as to argue that "[Rachel] Lee's reading essentializes gender difference and undermines what is otherwise an important feminist reading of the novel . . . this interpretation risks defaulting on a binary that female must oppose male when tallying the stakes of gender equity"; Gairola, "Deterritorialisations of Desire: 'Transgressive' Sexuality as Filipino Anti-Imperialist Resistance in Jessica Hagedorn's *Dogeaters*," *Philament* 7 (2005): 37. Joey's sexuality continues to be a contested issue in *Dogeaters* criticism; see Victor Mendoza, "A Queer Nomadology of Jessica Hagedorn's *Dogeaters*," *American Literature* 77, no. 4 (2005): 818, and Viet Thanh Nguyen, *Race and Resistance: Literature and Politics in Asian America* (Oxford: Oxford University Press, 2002), 138.

50. Nguyen, *Race and Resistance*, 138.
51. Sarita E. See, *The Decolonized Eye: Filipino American Art and Performance* (Minneapolis: University of Minnesota Press, 2009), 117.
52. Mendible, "Dictators, Movie Stars, and Martyrs."
53. Ibid.
54. Hagedorn, *Dogeaters*, 119.
55. Rosca, *State of War*.
56. Hagedorn, *Dogeaters*, 42. Juliana Chang offers a suggestive reading of Joey's mother: "Hagedorn's figure of illicit native female labor puts pressure on the fantasy of the U.S.-Philippine neocolonial romance as legitimate homosocial family romance. Both the younger brother and the prostitute as metaphors for the neocolonial nation are figures of dependence, but the metaphor of the prostitute calls into question the fictions of legitimacy, benevolence, and autonomous subjecthood that underpin the fantasy of neocolonialism as fraternity"; Chang, "Masquerade, Hysteria, and Neocolonial Femininity," 640–41. In this way, Joey participates in the precedent set by his mother, one in which the fantasy of a homosocial relationship between colonizer and colonized is revealed as exactly that, a fantasy.

3. Teaching Revolution: The Latinx Bildungsroman in Alvarez and Díaz

1. Junot Díaz, *The Brief Wondrous Life of Oscar Wao* (New York: Riverhead, 2007).
2. Crucially, as Jennifer Harford Vargas remarks, "The footnotes are also

important to an analysis of domination and narrative form because they play out power relations structurally within the novel"; Harford Vargas, *Forms of Dictatorship: Power, Narrative, and Authoritarianism in the Latina/o Novel* (Oxford: Oxford University Press, 2017), 53.

3. Julia Alvarez, *In the Name of Salomé* (Chapel Hill, N.C.: Algonquin Books of Chapel Hill, 2000), and Díaz, *Brief Wondrous Life of Oscar Wao*. While I read Alvarez generously here, it's important to note that she's typically read as privileging elite, light-skinned Dominicans. I have chosen *Salomé* because it offers an extended meditation on blackness in the Dominican Republic that I find different from her other work. That said, part of her ability to sympathize with Ureña no doubt stems from their shared elite status. Although Dominican authors such as Elizabeth Acevedo center Dominican blackness, I find Alvarez useful because her work often participates in the presumed whiteness of latinidad, which makes her engagement with blackness in *Salomé* all the more striking. In other words, I am interested in thinking about how authors like Alvarez who seem to point toward the horizon as limit actually guide us past it.

4. For an incisive reading of another type of bildungsroman at work in *Oscar Wao*, the *künstlerroman*, see Monica Hanna, "A Portrait of the Artist as a Young Cannibalist: Reading Yunior (Writing) in *The Brief Wondrous Life of Oscar Wao*," in *The Brief Wondrous Life of Oscar Wao: Junot Díaz and the Decolonial Imagination*, ed. Monica Hanna, Jennifer Harford Vargas, and José David Saldívar (Durham, N.C.: Duke University Press), 89–111.

5. María Josefina Saldaña-Portillo, *The Revolutionary Imagination in the Americas and the Age of Development* (Durham, N.C.: Duke University Press, 2003), 264.

6. Alvarez, *In the Name of Salomé*. Following Dixa Ramírez, I refer to Salomé Ureña the historical figure as Ureña and Salomé the character in the novel as Salomé. Ureña's work is woefully understudied. Though I would love to be able to speak more to Ureña's formative role in education in the Dominican Republic, as April J. Mayes observes, there is a lack of material on this topic; Mayes, "Why Dominican Feminism Moved to the Right: Class, Colour and Women's Activism in the Dominican Republic 1880s–1940s," *Gender & History* 20, no. 2 (2008): 367n20. Moreover, as Alvarez posits in *Salomé*, Ureña's work is always framed by her husband and especially her son, Pedro, both of whom were committed to promoting a specific view of the poet, one that, according to Alvarez, diminishes Ureña's blackness and censors her personal poetry.

7. Díaz, *Brief Wondrous Life of Oscar Wao*, 5.

8. Franco Moretti, *The Way of the World: The Bildungsroman in European Culture* (New York: Verso, 1987), vii, emphasis his.

9. See Jed Esty, *Unseasonable Youth: Modernism, Colonialism, and the Fiction of Development* (Oxford: Oxford University Press, 2012), 4.

10. Oscar further complicates Dominican American identities as he "liv[ed] in the DR for the first couple of years of his life and then abruptly wrenchingly relocate[ed] to New Jersey – a single green card shifting not only worlds (from Third

to First) but centuries (from almost no TV or electricity to plenty of both)"; Díaz, *Brief Wondrous Life of Oscar Wao*, 21–22n6.

11. See Ignacio López-Calvo, "A Postmodern Plátano's Trujillo: Junot Díaz's *The Brief Wondrous Life of Oscar Wao*, More Macondo Than McOndo," in *Trujillo, Trauma, Testimony: Mario Vargas Llosa, Julia Alvarez, Edwidge Danticat, Junot Díaz and Other Writers in Hispaniola*, Special Issue, *Antípodas* 20 (2009): 75–90, for a discussion of Díaz as a native informant.

12. In this chapter, I read positivism generously, as *Salomé* focuses on the practice of positivism as a pedagogy of curiosity and inquiry. However, positivist thought also espoused the very same ideas that undergirded the dictatorial regime of Porfirio Díaz in Mexico, which followed a reductive scientific method that granted legitimacy to eugenics.

13. For example, in "Why Dominican Feminism Moved to the Right," the article I reference here, Mayes outlines the centrality of Hostos's thought to the right-wing shift of Dominican women.

14. Lorgia García Peña, *Translating Blackness: Latinx Colonialities in Global Perspective* (Durham, N.C.: Duke University Press, 2022), 36.

15. David Vázquez, *Triangulations: Narrative Strategies for Navigating Latino Identity* (Minneapolis: University of Minnesota Press, 2011), 3.

16. See Maia Gil'Adí for a compelling discussion of how Latinx Studies scholars' investment in promoting social justice narratives comes at the expense of ignoring how authors like Díaz "perpetuat[e] gendered violence"; Gil'Adí, "'I Think about You, X—': Re-Reading Junot Díaz after 'The Silence,'" *Latino Studies* 18 (2020): 515. See both Gil'Adí and Ruth McHugh Dillon ("'Let Me Confess': Confession, Complicity, and #MeToo in Junot Díaz's *This Is How You Lose Her* and 'The Silence: The Legacy of Childhood Trauma,'" *MELUS* 46, no. 1 [Spring 2021]: 24–50) for an insightful discussion of how Díaz wields his own authorial voice to the exclusion of other voices.

17. Alvarez, *In the Name of Salomé*. While Erica Edwards examines the charismatic leadership of the Black Civil Rights Movement in *Charisma and the Fictions of Black Leadership* (Minneapolis: University of Minnesota Press, 2012), her discussion in the introduction of the role of women in the movement vis-à-vis charismatic male leaders is particularly instructive.

18. Raphael Dalleo and Elena Machado Sáez, *The Latino/a Canon and the Emergence of Post-Sixties Literature* (New York: Palgrave Macmillan, 2007), 133. David Vázquez takes issue with this characterization of Alvarez's work, noting that "nearly every major character in her work is from the elite—a fact that is treated as transparent in her novels"; Vázquez, *Triangulations*, 139. That said, Vázquez acknowledges that "she combats the historical silence enforced by the [Trujillo] regime" (140) and that her work produces "generative contradictions" (140).

19. Dixa Ramírez, *Colonial Phantoms: Belonging and Refusal in the Dominican Americas, from the 19th Century to the Present* (New York: NYU Press, 2018), 78.

20. Maya Socolovsky compellingly argues that "because the mother and daughter's stories are presented in alternating chapters, but never merged, the experience of reading is already haunted for the reader"; Socolovsky, "Patriotism, Nationalism, and the Fiction of History in Julia Alvarez's *In the Time of the Butterflies* and *In the Name of Salomé*," *Latin American Literary Review* 34, no. 68 (2006): 12. Socolovsky also observes that because "Alvarez structures the text so that the past and present continually lie alongside one another, she shows the connections of history across time and place, and emphasizes the past's disruption of the present" (13).

21. Ramírez, *Colonial Phantoms*, 102.

22. Dalleo and Machado Sáez analyze the use of the third-person perspective in the Camila sections of *Salomé*, noting that how odd it is, given that Camila and Dedé (from *In the Time of the Butterflies*) are "the ones left behind, [so] they are ostensibly also the ones telling the story"; Dalleo and Machado Sáez, *Latino/a Canon*, 147.

23. Elena Machado Sáez, *Market Aesthetics: The Purchase of the Past in Caribbean Diasporic Fiction* (Charlottesville: University of Virginia Press, 2015), 90.

24. Machado Sáez, *Market Aesthetics*, 91. She also compellingly reads Camila's queer love interest, Marion, as a stand-in for the reader. She writes, "Camila's sexuality is subsumed so that the pedagogical thrust of the narrative can become primary, emphasizing an *ethical* teacher-student relationship" (94). Machado Sáez elaborates: "As the novel travels further back into Camila's past, we learn that this teaching technique of erasing her self [*sic*] is tied to a romantic encounter with Marion that originated in the classroom. This trauma of intimacy informs Camila's conception of herself as a teacher, and by extension sexuality emerges as a metaphor for the challenges to the pedagogical imperative" (96). While my focus here is on the split bildungsroman between Salomé and Camila, the way that the novel seemingly suppresses Camila's queerness is quite convincing. The wrinkle in this reading is that the novel is so critical of the suppression of Salomé's personal, intimate life, that although it replicates this structurally in terms of Camila's queerness, I suggest that it does so to *not* reflect the structure of the novel in terms of content. In other words, the treatment of Camila's queerness acts as a pedagogical exercise in which students either learn the lesson and *don't* suppress Camila's queerness or fail to do so in exactly the way Machado Sáez describes.

25. In the same way that I refer to Salomé and Ureña separately, I discuss the fictional character of Francisco as "Pancho" or "Papancho" and reserve "Francisco" for the historical figure.

26. Alvarez, *In the Name of Salomé*, 13.

27. Ramírez, *Colonial Phantoms*, 119.

28. Alvarez, *In the Name of Salomé*, 25. In *We Dream Together: Dominican Independence, Haiti, and the Fight for Caribbean Freedom* (Durham, N.C.: Duke University Press, 2016), Anne Eller compellingly argues against the common idea that Dominican identity coalesced around an anti-Haitian, anti-Black identity. As Eller points out, this was commonly an elite ideology that "sprang from their disdain

for the very formation of the Dominican peasantry itself, which was born, in many areas, from an independent rural maroon population who worked on the margins of cattle society or entirely for their own subsistence" (14). Indeed, in the years leading up to the so-called Haitian occupation of the Dominican Republic, "Dominican conspirators regularly appealed to Haitian rulers for arms and support for the many revolts and conspiracies that ensued, and pro-unification plans emerged. Dominican residents of center-island towns held ceremonies that celebrated Haitian independence" (5). The period that led up to the War of Restoration (1863–65), in which Dominicans fought over Spanish rule, began with President Pedro Santana's invitation in 1861 for recolonization. As Eller notes, during this period, "someone raised Haitian colors" (118), illuminating the resonance that Haiti continued to have for liberation in the Dominican Republic.

29. Alvarez, *In the Name of Salomé*, 27.

30. Ramírez, *Colonial Phantoms*, 18.

31. Alvarez, *In the Name of Salomé*, 138.

32. Salomé Ureña, *Salomé Ureña: Selected Poems*, trans. Matt Wirzburger (Rescate, 2019), 1–4.

33. Ramírez, *Colonial Phantoms*, 45.

34. Translation in ibid., *Colonial Phantoms*, 38. In the acknowledgments at the end of *Salomé*, Alvarez admits that her translations "are approximations/improvisations in English of her own words in Spanish" (357), so we should read them as riffs on Ureña's poetry rather than direct translations.

35. Alvarez, *In the Name of Salomé*, 3.

36. Ramírez, *Colonial Phantoms*, 49.

37. I focus on the representation of "Sombras" in *Salomé* as Alvarez's depiction of the poem ignores the hopeful last stanza in which the speaker of the poem awakens to light and hope, thus signaling the connection between "Sombras" and "Luz" ("Light") (1880). "Luz" is a much more inspiring patriotic song that includes lines such as "yo soy la voz que canta" ("I am the voice that sings") (Ureña, *Salomé Ureña*, 82–83; translation by Matt Wirzburger) and points to a light-filled future.

38. Ureña, *Salomé Ureña*, 1–4.

39. Ureña, *Salomé Ureña*, 7–8.

40. Alvarez, *In the Name of Salomé*, 118.

41. Dalleo and Machado Sáez, *Latino/a Canon*, 151.

42. Alvarez, *In the Name of Salomé*, 122.

43. As Dalleo and Machado Sáez sympathetically argue, novels like *Salomé* "dramatize how these near-mythical figures cast daunting shadows over their potential heirs, demanding a heroism that seems only to reinforce the hopelessness of the postcolonial, post-Civil Rights present"; *Latino/a Canon*, 144.

44. Alvarez, *In the Name of Salomé*, 125.

45. In her examination of Salomé's and Pancho's relationship, Ramírez argues that "Alvarez's fictional biography of Ureña points precisely to the failure of marriage as a conciliatory institution that can fix political turmoil"; *Colonial Phantoms*, 104.

As we can see through my discussion of Pancho's whitening of Salomé that follows, Ramírez's point is particularly apt, given that not only can marriage not fix political turmoil, but it is also complicit in the erasure of Salomé's legacy.

46. Alvarez, *In the Name of Salomé*, 44, emphasis Alvarez's.

47. Ramírez, *Colonial Phantoms*, 108.

48. For a beautiful reading of this moment as ekphrastic, see Marion Rohrleitner, "Not in Our Mother's Image: Ekphrasis and Challenges to Recovering Afro-Mestizaje in Contemporary Latina/Chicana Historical Fiction," in *Dialogues across Diasporas: Women Writers, Scholars, and Activists of Africana and Latina Descent in Conversation*, ed. Marion Rohrleitner and Sarah E. Ryan (Lanham, Md.: Lexington, 2013), 37–55.

49. Ramírez, *Colonial Phantoms*, 84.

50. Alvarez, *In the Name of Salomé*, 177. Of this scene, Dalleo and Machado Sáez note that Salomé "comes to the conclusion that she is submerging her own voice in sounding the epic calls for the nation to throw off the shackles of Spanish rule"; *Latino/a Canon*, 153.

51. This detail appears to be something Alvarez added. According to Julee Tate, "This characterization shocked some members of the Cuban intelligentsia, not because they took issue with lesbianism but rather because this was never part of Camila's identity as a public person in Cuba"; Tate, "My Mother, My Text: Writing and Remembering in Julia Alvarez's *In the Name of Salomé*," *Bilingual Review/La Revista Bilingüe* 28, no. 1 (January 2004–April 2007): 61.

52. Alvarez, *In the Name of Salomé*, 35.

53. Dalleo and Machado Sáez, *Latino/a Canon*, 155.

54. Harford Vargas, *Forms of Dictatorship: Power, Narrative, and Authoritarianism in the Latina/o Novel* (Oxford: Oxford University Press, 2017), 6.

55. Roberto Gonzalez Echevarría, *The Voice of the Masters: Writing and Authority in Modern Latin American Literature* (Austin: University of Texas Press, 1985), 77.

56. Echevarría suggests that a scriptor is a secretary freed from the dictator. I use the term "scriptor" moving forward to maintain this interpretation while underscoring the process of collecting stories and writing them down; ibid.

57. Elena Machado Sáez, "Dictating Desire, Dictating Diaspora: Junot Díaz's *The Brief Wondrous Life of Oscar Wao* as Foundational Romance," *Contemporary Literature* 52, no. 3 (2011): 546.

58. Junot Díaz, *The Brief Wondrous Life of Oscar Wao* (New York: Riverhead, 2007). See also Ignacio López-Calvo's *God and Trujillo: Literary and Cultural Representations of the Dominican Dictator* (Gainesville: University Press of Florida, 2005), 4, and Echevarría, *Voice of the Masters*, 67–68. For more on how characters in dictator novels exist in relation to the dictator as well as the historical underpinnings of dictator novels, see Daynali Flores-Rodríguez, "Addressing the Fukú in Us: Junot Díaz and the New Novel of Dictatorship," in *Trujillo, Trauma, Testimony: Mario Vargas Llosa, Julia Alvarez, Edwidge Danticat, Junot Díaz and Other Writers in Hispaniola*, Special issue, Antípodas 20 (2009): 93.

59. As Harford Vargas observes, Yunior functions as a dictator "because he controls and orders representation and because he collects, writes down, and reshapes a plethora of oral stories that have been recounted to him"; *Forms of Dictatorship*, 35. Of three paradigmatic dictator novels, López-Calvo remarks, "Following a trend set off by the 1974 publication of Augusto Roa Bastos's *I, the Supreme* and Alejo Carpentier's *Reasons of State*, the Patriarch's inability to feel guilt for his hideous actions may open the door, after the nostalgic presentation of the pathetic autumn of his life, to the perhaps dangerously sympathetic understanding of the readers"; *God and Trujillo*, 55 (the third book alluded to but not named is Gabriel García Márquez's *The Autumn of the Patriarch* [New York: Harper & Row, 1975]).

60. See Harford Vargas, *Forms of Dictatorship*, 11.

61. Flores-Rodríguez also makes a similar point to Harford Vargas's about the role of footnotes in the novel, contending that Yunior "effectively displac[es] the traditional signifiers of power and oppression to the margins of the story. In this sense Junot Díaz erodes the sense of complacency that assigns all of the responsibility to the dictator by highlighting the underlying structures of power in a dictatorial regime, such as the complex relationship between power and writing"; "Addressing the Fukú in Us," 95. Meanwhile, Rune Graulund argues that the novel "turns all of his [Díaz's] registers into minor discourses" ("Generous Exclusion: Register and Readership in Junot Díaz's *The Brief Wondrous Life of Oscar Wao*," MELUS 39, no. 3 [Fall 2014]: 37) rather than reinforcing the majority/minority dynamics regarding "English/ Spanish, American/Dominican, and non-migrant/migrant" (37).

62. Machado Sáez, "Dictating Desire," 544.

63. For an insightful discussion of how the Trujillo regime impacted notions of masculinity in the Dominican Republic, see Maja Horn, *Masculinity after Trujillo: The Politics of Gender in Dominican Literature* (Gainesville: University Press of Florida, 2014).

64. Echevarría, *Voice of the Masters*, 84–85. Such deconstructions are fashioned from the proliferation of textualities: editor's notes, annotations, lists, records (78).

65. As Harford Vargas explains, Latina/o dictator novels "give narrative space to second-generation perspectives as they grapple with dictatorships and the afterlives of these regimes in Latin America and the United States. The residues of authoritarian pasts thus mark Latina/o fiction across national origin groups, generating a pan-Latino and transamerican dictatorship novel tradition"; "Dictating a Zafa," 25.

66. Graulund, "Generous Exclusion," 44.

67. Ibid., 39. Graulund continues, "a specificity that, contrary to its seemingly exclusivist intent, in fact achieves the very opposite by presenting a text that relies on a mix of registers so eclectic as to transcend specific places (New Jersey and Santo Domingo), specific politics (American foreign policy and Dominican dictatorships), and specific national languages (English and Spanish)" (39).

68. Machado Sáez, "Dictating Desire," 546.

69. Díaz, *Brief Wondrous Life of Oscar Wao*, 5.

70. Machado Sáez, "Dictating Desire," 545.

71. As Harford Vargas reiterates, "The cane field is a primal site where violence is perpetrated against African-origin subjects: slaves, Haitian laborers, Dominican subjects (Beli), and transnational subjects (Oscar)"; "Dictating a Zafa," 15–16.

72. Robin (Lauren) Derby writes, "If blackness in this context was a metaphor for social inequality, the Era of Trujillo thus promised to make whiteness available to all Dominicans by incorporating them into the modern nation"; Derby, *The Dictator's Seduction: Politics and the Popular Imagination in the Era of Trujillo* (Durham, N.C.: Duke University Press, 2009), 24.

73. Díaz, *Brief Wondrous Life of Oscar Wao*, 82.

74. López-Calvo further ties Beli to blackness by linking her to Haiti: "As a result, she ends up being a sort of child servant or slave (known in Haitian Creole as *restavek* or *restavec*) for a poor family that abuses her and burns her back with acid when she insists on going to school"; "Postmodern," 76.

75. Harford Vargas similarly notes Beli's connection to slavery by noting that the description of Beli's scar to the sea and her bra as a sail "calls forth a slave ship in the Middle Passage," which "establish[es] intersectional resonances between the violence enacted on Beli, Oscar, and the slaves and laborers in the cane fields"; "Dictating a Zafa," 16.

76. Díaz, *Brief Wondrous Life of Oscar Wao*, 52.

77. Machado Sáez, "Dictating Desire," 547.

78. Díaz, *Brief Wondrous Life of Oscar Wao*, 215n24.

79. See Derby, *Dictator's Seduction*, 114.

80. During the massacre of 1937 (sometimes referred to as the Parsley Massacre), Trujillo had his men kill anyone who looked Haitian (read: Black) who couldn't pass the perejil (parsley) test. Presumably, the word would determine racial difference based on linguistic difference, as Ricardo Ortiz observes in "Edwidge Danticat's *Latinidad: The Farming of Bones* and the Cultivation (of Fields) of Knowledge," in *Aftermaths: Exile, Migration, and Diaspora Reconsidered*, ed. Marcus Bullock and Peter Y. Paik (New Brunswick, N.J.: Rutgers University Press, 2009). While it may be apocryphal that Dominican soldiers actually asked people to pronounce "perejil," the idea, nevertheless, is that the test would determine whether one's language was French, thus marking the person as Black, or Spanish, thus marking the person as Dominican and therefore white-adjacent. For a nuanced reading of the massacre and anti-Haitianism, see Robin (Lauren) Derby, "Haitians, Magic, and Money: Raza and Society in the Haitian-Dominican Borderlands, 1900 to 1937," *Comparative Studies in Society and History*, vol. 36, no. 3 (July 1994): 488–526.

81. Díaz, *Brief Wondrous Life of Oscar Wao*, 321.

82. Sandra Cox's reading of this scene emphasizes Oscar's blackness, "the paradox of his *prieto* features and his *norteamericano* privilege" (Cox, "The Trujillato and Testimonial Fiction: Collective Memory, Cultural Trauma and National Identity in Edwidge Danticat's *The Farming of Bones* and Junot Díaz's *The Brief Wondrous Life of Oscar Wao*," *Trujillo, Trauma, Testimony: Mario Vargas Llosa, Julia Alvarez, Edwidge Danticat, Junot Díaz and Other Writers in Hispaniola*, Special issue of

Antípodas 20 [2009]: 121), particularly in relation to Haiti. As she observes, "The two policemen who abduct Oscar also participate in a dialogue that reveals the enduring quality of the antihaitianismo Trujillo used in his 'Dominicanization' program; 'Didn't you grow up around here' one of the men asks 'his darker-skinned pal' as they approach the cane fields, and notes, 'You look like you speak a little French to me'" (121).

83. Díaz, *Brief Wondrous Life of Oscar Wao*, 322.

84. Or, as Monica Hanna observes, "Yunior often explicitly rejects the possibility of recovering an original, whole story because so much of the history he wishes to recover has been violently suppressed and shrouded in silence"; Hanna, "'Reassembling the Fragments,'" 498.

85. Ibid., 508.

86. Harford Vargas, *Forms of Dictatorship*, 54.

87. Díaz, *Brief Wondrous Life of Oscar Wao*, 3n1.

88. As Hanna observes, "He includes the reader in this process of reconstruction; there is much that is explicitly left up to the reader's interpretation" (501). She continues, "This is another strategic move on the narrator's part; by emphasizing the constructed nature of all histories and narratives in general, the narrative compels readers to examine the power structures behind the act of telling"; Hanna, "'Reassembling the Fragments,'" 501.

89. As Yunior explains his identification with the Watcher, "It's hard as a Third Worlder not to feel a certain amount of affinity for Uatu the Watcher; he resides in the hidden Blue Area of the Moon and we DarkZoners reside (to quote Glissant) on '*la face cachée de la Terre*' (Earth's hidden face)"; Díaz, *Brief Wondrous Life of Oscar Wao*, 92n10.

90. Ramón Saldívar, "Imagining Cultures: The Transnational Imaginary in Postrace America," *Journal of Transnational American Studies* 4, no. 2 (2012): 12–13.

91. Alvarez, *In the Name of Salomé*, 8.

92. Homi Bhabha, "Foreword," in *The Wretched of the Earth*, by Franz Fanon (New York: Grove, 2021), xi.

93. Julia Alvarez, *In the Time of the Butterflies* (Chapel Hill, N.C.: Algonquin Books of Chapel Hill, 1994), 324.

4. Retconning Revolution: The Solidarity of Form in García, Barnet, and Avellaneda

1. Cristina García, *Monkey Hunting* (New York: Ballantine, 2003).

2. Miguel Barnet, *Biography of a Runaway Slave* (1966), trans. W. Nick Hill (repr. Evanston, Ill: Curbstone, 1994). Both Ignacio López-Calvo and Ana Zapata-Calle have briefly noted the similarities between *Monkey Hunting* and *Biography of a Runaway Slave*. See López-Calvo, *Imagining the Chinese in Cuban Literature and Culture* (Gainesville: University Press of Florida, 2005), 43–44, and Ana Zapata-Calle, "El Mundo de Chen Pan en 'Monkey Hunting' de Cristina García: Chinos,

Africanos y Criollos en la Diáspora Cubana," *Chasqui* 41, no. 1 (May 2012): 174. Note that Zapata-Calle also remarks upon other intertextual references, such as the resemblances between Chen Fang and Sor Juana Inés de la Cruz, as well as Ana María Simo, the codirector of El Puente, the same group of which Miguel Barnet was a part (174). As Zapata-Calle observes of Simo, "Como Chen Fang en China, fue apresada y reprimida por su orientación sexual y acusada formalmente de tener contactos con extranjeros [Like Chen Fang, she was arrested and suppressed for her sexual orientation and formally accused of having contact with foreigners]" (174).

3. García, *Monkey Hunting*, 32.

4. In fact, according to Raquel Puig, "Maroonage in Cuba's Chinese population began as soon as the first Chinese arrived to the island. It is estimated that the proportion was five to seven times higher than in the African population"; Puig, "The Imagined Nation in Cristina García's *Monkey Hunting*," in *Caribbean Without Borders: Literature, Language, and Culture*, ed. Dorsia Smith, Raquel Puig, and Ileana Cortés Santiago (Newcastle upon Tyne: Cambridge Scholars, 2008), 239.

5. Citing Cécile Leclercq's *El lagarto en busca de una identidad*, Manuel Martínez notes, "She asserts that the use of the mestizo, in the Cuban case, African and European, serves to advance a hegemonic vision in which the white component is dominant, the black subordinated, and the 'other' is non-existent. In this view then, *mestizaje* is not a celebration of cultural plurality, but rather a pretext for hegemonic homogeneity. The effect is that the African component is not recognized as a separate and valued identity"; Martínez, "Chinese-Cuban Identity in Cristina Garcia's *Monkey Hunting* and Daína Chaviano's *La isla de los amores infinitos*," *Caribe: Revista de Cultura y Literatura* 10, no. 2 (2007): 102.

6. Michael J. Bustamante, *Cuban Memory Wars: Retrospective Politics in Revolution and Exile* (Chapel Hill: University of North Carolina Press, 2021), 10.

7. Ibid., 6. For more on the Cuban Revolution as the culmination of 100 years of struggle, see ibid., 6–10.

8. Antonio López, *Unbecoming Blackness: The Diaspora Cultures of Afro-Cuban America* (New York: NYU Press, 2012), 5.

9. Ada Ferrer, *Insurgent Cuba: Race, Nation, and Revolution, 1868–1898* (Chapel Hill: University of North Carolina Press, 1999), 8.

10. Danielle Pilar Clealand, *The Power of Race in Cuba: Racial Ideology and Black Consciousness during the Revolution* (Oxford: Oxford University Press, 2017), 83.

11. López, *Unbecoming Blackness*, 7.

12. For a fuller discussion of José Martí's rhetoric of racelessness, see Ada Ferrer's "The Silence of Patriots: Race and Nationalism in Martí's Cuba," in *José Martí's "Our America": From National to Hemispheric Cultural Studies*, ed. Jeffrey Belnap and Raúl Fernández (Durham, N.C.: Duke University Press, 1998). For a more in-depth reading of the uneasy relationship between race and the fight for Cuban independence, read Ferrer's *Insurgent Cuba*. For an elaboration of how the rhetoric of racelessness was used during the Cuban Revolution, see Clarence Lusane, "From

Black Cuban to Afro-Cuban: Researching Race in Cuba," *Souls* 1, no. 2 (Spring 1999): 73–79. See Safa, "Commentary on Race and Revolution in Cuba," *Souls* 1, no. 2 (Spring 1999): 86–91 for a discussion of how the rhetoric of mestizaje reinforced white supremacy.

13. Ricardo Ortiz, *Cultural Erotics in Cuban America* (Minneapolis: University of Minnesota Press, 2007), 221.

14. Joshua Clover, "*Retcon*: Value and Temporality in Poetics," *Representations* 126, no. 1 (2014): 14. Yu-Fang Cho formulates *Monkey Hunting*'s relationship to history slightly differently, arguing that it is "a piece of imaginative critical historiography" that features a "creative reconceptualization of the structure of history—and the social relations that produces and regulates [*sic*]—that García's narrative puts forward a radical vision of imaginary and epistemological emancipation" (2–3).

15. Andrew J. Friedenthal's work, meanwhile, illuminates the connections between retconning and historiography as he examines how retconning "foster[s] a sense of history itself as a constructed narrative"; Friedenthal, *Retcon Game: Retroactive Continuity and the Hyperlinking of America* (Jackson: University Press of Mississippi, 2017), 3. However, rather than making a conservative argument about retconning, Friedenthal insists that such "shifting sources and interpretations" foreground how our understanding of history requires "a questioning of just *whose* America, and *whose* values, have been valorized in the first place" (160), thus illuminating how retconning challenges dominant historical narratives.

16. Elgin Frank Tupper, quoted in Clover, "*Retcon*," 14–15.

17. Ortiz, *Cultural Erotics*, 40. My thanks go to Justin Mann for pointing out the centrality of continuity errors in retconning.

18. In this way, I build on Elzbieta Sklodowska's point that "testimonio is constructed in such a way as to, unwittingly, direct our attention to its own fissures"; Sklodowska, "Spanish American Testimonial Novel: Some Afterthoughts," in *The Real Thing: Testimonial Discourse and Latin America*, ed. Georg M. Gugelberger (Durham, N.C.: Duke University Press, 1996), 97.

19. For another analysis of *Monkey Hunting* as a neo-slave narrative, see Marta Lysik, "Multiple Trajectories of Slavery: Cristina García's *Monkey Hunting* as a Transnational Neo-Slave Narrative," in *Revisiting Slaves Narratives II: Les Avatars contemporains des récits d'esclaves II*, ed. Judith Misrahi-Barak (Montpellier: Presses universitaires de la Méditerranée, 2007): 275–95.

20. Charles T. Davis and Henry Louis Gates Jr., *The Slave's Narrative* (Oxford: Oxford University Press, 1985), xii.

21. John Beverley, *Testimonio: On the Politics of Truth* (Minneapolis: University of Minnesota Press, 2004), 31.

22. See Rosemary Geisdorfer Feal, "Spanish American Ethnobiography and the Slave Narrative Tradition: 'Biografía de un cimarrón' and 'Me llamo Rigoberta Menchú,'" *Modern Language Studies* 20, no. 1 (1990): 100–11.

23. Ashraf H. A. Rushdy, "The Neo-Slave Narrative," in *Cambridge Companion to the African American Novel*, ed. Maryemma Graham (Cambridge: Cambridge University Press, 2004), 93.

24. Although writing about the British slave trade, Lisa Lowe remarks that "the importation of this newly, and differently, 'raced' Chinese labor was a solution to both the colonial need to suppress Black slave rebellion and the capitalist desire to expand production" (Lowe, *The Intimacies of Four Continents* [Durham, N.C.: Duke University Press, 2015], 23), a point that Evelyn Hu-DeHart extends into the Cuban context by remarking that because of "the British embargo on the slave trade" in the mid-1840s, "the Comisión [de la Población Blanca, the Commission on White Settlement] followed the British example and turned to China for contract labor, commonly known as coolie labor"; Hu-DeHart, "Race Construction and Race Relations: Chinese and Blacks in Nineteenth-Century Cuba," in *Alternative Orientalisms in Latin America and Beyond*, ed. Ignacio López-Calvo (Newcastle upon Tyne: Cambridge Scholars, 2007), 82.

25. José Esteban Muñoz, "Feeling Brown: Ethnicity and Affect in Ricardo Bracho's *The Sweetest Hangover (and Other STDs)*," *Theater Journal* 52, no. 1 (March 2000): 67–79.

26. Gertrudis Gómez de Avellaneda, *Sab* and *Autobiography* (1841 and 1839, respectively) (Austin: University of Texas Press, 1993).

27. Jennifer Harford Vargas, "Novel Testimony: Alternative Archives in Edwidge Danticat's *The Farming of Bones*," *Callaloo* 37, no. 5 (Fall 2014): 1163.

28. Miguel Barnet, *Biografía de un cimarrón* (1966), (La Habana: Editorial Letras Cubanas, 2016), 5. Throughout this chapter, I use "Biografía" to refer to the Spanish version of the text and "Biography" to refer to the English version.

29. William Luis, "The Politics of Memory and Miguel Barnet's *The Autobiography of a Run Away Slave*," *MLN* 104, no. 2 (1989): 484.

30. Ibid., 486.

31. As Luis also notes, regarding Barnet's discussion of the Ten Years' War in the English introduction, "Barnet forces the issue and writes that Montejo was a fugitive between 1868 and 1878. But if we reconstruct the chronology provided, the parenthetical reference to the war is somewhat misleading, since Montejo must have escaped towards the end of the war. Born around 1860, Montejo was only eight at the start of the war. More importantly, there appears to be information missing from Montejo's conversation with Barnet. In the same paragraph and referring to the same war, Barnet provides information not contained in the text"; Luis, "Politics of Memory," 483.

32. Abraham Acosta, *Thresholds of Illiteracy: Theory, Latin America, and the Crisis of Resistance* (New York: Fordham University Press, 2014), 130.

33. Marta Caminero-Santangelo, *On Latinidad: U.S. Latino Literature and the Construction of Ethnicity* (Gainesville: University Press of Florida, 2009), 115.

34. Further emphasizing the connections between *Monkey Hunting* and *Beloved*, Marta Lysik reads the descriptions of the scars on the backs of enslaved Cubans as reminiscent "of the scar on Sethe's back. After being whipped with a cowhide, Sethe has 'a tree on [her] back . . . A chokecherry tree. Trunk, branches, and even leaves. Tiny little chokecherry leaves'"; Lysik, "Multiple Trajectories of Slavery," 113, brackets and ellipses hers.

35. Barnet, *Biografía de un cimarrón*, 22, emphasis in original.
36. Barnet, *Biography of a Runaway Slave*, 27.
37. Barnet, *Biografía de un cimarrón*, 35.
38. Barnet, *Biography of a Runaway Slave*, 88.
39. Barnet, *Biografía de un cimarrón*, 72.
40. Barnet, *Biography of a Runaway Slave*, 89.
41. García, *Monkey Hunting*, 64.
42. Barnet, *Biography of a Runaway Slave*, 90.
43. García, *Monkey Hunting*, 243.
44. Yu-Fang Cho, "Reimagining 'Tense and Tender Ties' in García's *Monkey Hunting*," *CLCWeb: Comparative Literature and Culture* 14, no. 5 (2012): 2.
45. A key difference between Montejo and Chen Pan remains, however, as Ann Marie Alfonso-Forero points out in her discussion of African enslaved people and Chen Pan, arguing that the latter "participates in white Cuban society after freeing himself from indentured servitude. Although he is unable and unwilling to fully assimilate, he does choose to adopt the particular criollo characteristics that facilitate his success as a merchant in Havana"; Alfonso-Forero, "'A Whole New Race': Chinses Cubans and Hybrid Identities in Cristina García's *Monkey Hunting*," *Anthurium: A Caribbean Studies Journal* 7, no. 1 (April 2010): 4.
46. García, *Monkey Hunting*, 41.
47. Michelle D. Commander, *Afro-Atlantic Flight: Speculative Returns and the Black Fantastic* (Durham, N.C.: Duke University Press, 2017), 3.
48. García, *Monkey Hunting*, 19–20.
49. John Beverley, *Testimonio: On the Politics of Truth* (Minneapolis: University of Minnesota Press, 2004), 27.
50. According to Sklodowska, "Most critics [of testimonio] did not read testimonial texts—they read the official voices of these texts, confusing the tongues of the editor and his/her surrogates"; Elzbieta Sklodowska, "Spanish American Testimonial Novel: Some Afterthoughts," in *The Real Thing: Testimonial Discourse and Latin America*, ed. Georg M. Gugelberger (Durham, N.C.: Duke University Press, 1996), 98.
51. García, *Monkey Hunting*, 189.
52. For an alternate reading of this scene, see Silvia Schultermandl, "'What Did Any of It Have to Do with Race?': Raced Chronotopes in Cristina García's *Monkey Hunting*," *Atlantic Studies* 8, no. 1 (2011): 93–107. She argues that "while he is fearful for his Chino-Afro-Cuban son Lorenzo, whose skin features 'accommodations of three continents' (192), a fact that might incriminate him as a potential participant

in the Afro-Cuban uprising, Chen Pan is unable to grasp the biological dimensions of race and the social implications that result from the discourse of racism. His conception of race displays a more optimistic attitude towards racial hybridity by evoking the early modern concept of racial creolization. In fact, Chen Pan echoes the very optimism of the early years of Cuban's nationhood" (98). However, given that the description of the three hanged men follows the question in the title of her article—what did any of it have to do with race?—I suggest that the scene of witnessing is an answer to this question that boils down to: everything. In other words, this scene rehearses the racelessness theory to disprove it without question.

53. Chanette Romero, *Activism and the American Novel: Religion and Resistance in Fiction by Women of Color* (Charlottesville, Virginia: University of Virginia Press, 2012), 76.

54. The *Cuba Commission Report* was never published in Spanish; the report was first published in English in 1876 and Chinese in 1877, but it did not gain a wider circulation until the 1993 edition, which was also in English.

55. Romero, *Activism and the American Novel*, 76.

56. Abraham Acosta suggests one reason Beverley may shy away from *Biography* in his discussion of the differences between how Beverley and Barnet theorize testimonio: "Whereas Beverley conceives of testimonio as an unclassifiable ('protean'), antiliterary ('demotic'), textual form of expression by and from subalternity, Barnet saw it as a pliable, stylized, and ethnographically sound narrative form serving a foundational literary role ('obra de fundación') in national consolidation"; Acosta, *Thresholds of Illiteracy: Theory, Latin America, and the Crisis of Resistance* (New York: Fordham University Press, 2014), 139. Fascinatingly, this then leads Acosta to observe, "In fact one can make the case that Beverley's mythology of the testimonio form in 'The Margin at the Center' (subaltern expression, emancipatory ideological horizon) works quite well as a prequel to the state's subsequent appropriation of testimonio as an institutionalized narrative form for Cuban nationalism that we see in Barnet. Despite the historical moments marking their enunciations, it is ultimately Barnet who represents the conceptual limit to Beverley's notion of testimonio" (140).

57. Beverley, *Testimonio*, 43.

58. For more on the Cuban prison memoir, see Ortiz, *Cultural Erotics in Cuban America* (Minneapolis: University of Minnesota Press, 2007), 62–90.

59. For a critique of *Monkey Hunting*'s orientalizing tendencies, see Igartuburu García, "Too Chinese/Too Cuban: Emotional Maps and the Quest for Happiness in Cristina García's *Monkey Hunting*," in *Diasporic Constructions of Home and Belonging*, ed. Florian Kläger and Klaus Stierstorfer (Berlin: De Gruyter, 2015), 447–63, who compellingly argues that "Cuba is turned into this happy object, into what is good. Meanwhile, China is stripped of any possible goodness, demonized in a signifying move that seeks to agree with western capitalist orientalizing ideologies" (454). For a contrasting view of Igartuburu García's argument, see Jennifer Ann Ho, "The Place of Transgressive Texts in Asian American Epistemology," *MFS*:

Modern Fiction Studies 56, no. 1 (Spring 2010): 205–25. Ho goes so far as to claim that *Monkey Hunting* is "a uniquely Asian-American text" (213). In terms of *Monkey Hunting*'s relationship to Asian American literature, it's also significant that Jade Tsui-yu Lee sees the novel as "echo[ing] Maxine Hong Kingston's 1990 novel, *Tripmaster Monkey: His Fake Book*" (129); Lee, "(Im)migration and Cultural Diasporization in García's *Monkey Hunting*," in *Perspectives on Identity, Migration, and Displacement*, eds. Steven Tötösy de Zepetnek, I-Chun Wang, and Hsiao-Yu Sun (Kaohsiung: National Sun Yat-sen University, 2010), 127–38.

60. García, *Monkey Hunting*, 223.

61. As Antonio Benítez-Rojo remarks in his examination of the Menocal reference in the Cuban poet Nicolás Guillén's poem "Macheteros" ("Cane Cutters") in *Sol de domingo* (1982), in which Menocal is figured as an enslaver or overseer "cracking his whip" (146), "We're really dealing here with a *remembrance of the future*, since in Cuba sugar always holds the same power, and the macheteros are always the same downtrodden ones" (146); Benítez-Rojo, *The Repeating Island: The Caribbean and the Postmodern Perspective* (Durham, N.C., and London: Duke University Press, 1996). While Chen Pan was an actual machetero, Chen Fang is a figurative one, and their elegies for a lost Cuba ultimately mourn the cycles of repetition that the island experiences.

62. Steven Palmer, José Antonio Piqueras, and Amparo Sánchez Cobos, eds., *State of Ambiguity: Civic Life and Culture in Cuba's First Republic* (Durham, N.C.: Duke University Press, 2014), 3.

63. As Amy Parziale argues, such references have "important potential influence over the cultural memory of ever-receding times and places. Of course, not every reader will decide to learn more about these chronotopic contexts (nor will every reader need to); but for those who do, the novel acts as a catalyst for archival research. Readers will most likely turn to the Internet or encyclopedias for quick historical shortcuts that may enrich their reading of *Monkey Hunting* through an appreciation of the civil unrest continually playing out in the background" (949); Parziala, "Counter-Archives of Trauma in Cristina García's *Monkey Hunting*," *Revista de Estudios Hispánicos* 52, no. 3 (October 2018): 937–58.

64. Along similar lines, Yu-Fang Cho reads Chen Fang as "a composite of Chen Pan's and Domingo's stories"; "Reimagining 'Tense and Tender Ties,'" 7.

65. Lorna Valerie Williams, *The Representation of Slavery in Cuban Fiction* (Columbia and London: University of Missouri Press, 1994), 18.

66. Indeed, it is important to consider Avellaneda's work outside of the Del Monte group, given Del Monte's conservative politics. That said, scholars such as José Gomariz have argued for reading Avellaneda within the context of the Del Monte circle, noting that "la intelectualidad criolla agrupada en torno a Del Monte se mostraba favorable al cese de la trata, a la abolition gradual de la esclavitud, a la deportación de los libertos, a la transición del trabajo esclavo al asalariado y, sobre todo, al fomento de la inmigración blanca, lo cual con tribuiria tanto al fin progresivo de la esclavitud como al blanqueamiento de la sociedad [the Creole

intellectuals grouped around Del Monte favorably viewed the cessation of the slave trade, the gradual abolition of slavery, the deportation of freed slaves, the transition from slave labor to wage labor, and above all, the promotion of white immigration, which would contribute to both the progressive end of slavery and to the whitening of society]"; Gomariz, "Gertrudis Gómez de Avellaneda y la intelectualidad reformista cubana: Raza, blanqueamiento e identidad cultural en 'Sab,'" *Caribbean Studies* 37, no. 1 (January–June 2009): 99. For Gomariz, "la comunidad imaginada de la novel se blanque con la desaparición de las culturas subalternas [the imagined community of the novel is whitened by the disappearance of subaltern cultures]" (115). There is also one distinction between Del Monte's group and Avellaneda that does not rule in her favor: as Debra Rosenthal acknowledges, because Avellaneda wrote *Sab* in Spain, she "did not pen her antislavery story while witnessing daily the human toll of bondage, nor did she try to counter slavery's ills from within the country"; Rosenthal, *Race Mixture in Nineteenth-Century U.S. and Spanish American Fictions: Gender, Culture, and Nation Building* (Chapel Hill: University of North Carolina Press, 2004), 77. That said, Rosenthal concedes that Avellaneda "wrote a more penetrating critique of racist ideology and the institution of slavery itself" (78) than her peers in Del Monte's group.

67. As Jerome Branche observes, "In spite of the celebration of Del Monte as nationalist and humanitarian, for example, on the question of race he was decidedly non-egalitarian. For him the unfortunate Africans who happened to be enslaved, had no place in a future Cuban republic"; Branche, "Ennobling Savagery? Sentimentalism and the Subaltern in 'Sab,'" *Afro-Hispanic Review* 17, no. 1 (Fall 1998): 13; further, no member of the Del Monte group freed the enslaved people who worked their plantations (17).

68. Branche, for example, notes, regarding how Avellaneda likens the role of being a wife to that of an enslaved person, that "the slave-wife analogy had been an integral part of women's abolitionist discourse since the turn of the century"; ibid., 14. For this reason, Branche sees it as all the more striking that in *Sab*, "no text of sisterhood or sympathy emerges to vindicate the enslaved Black women in their hapless conditions" (14). Additional critics who see *Sab* as an abolitionist text include Stacey Schlau and Jeremy L. Cass, the latter of whom contends that the reference to the Haitian Revolution "bolsters the work's abolitionist capacity"; Cass, "Deciphering Sedition in *Sab*: Avellaneda's Transient Engagement with Abolitionism," *Romance Quarterly* 57 (2010): 186. Critics who concede that *Sab* is an antislavery text but disagree that it's also an abolitionist one include Debra Rosenthal, José Gomariz, and Marta Miquel Baldellou, who argues that *Sab* cannot be considered an abolitionist text because "even though it manifests the injustice of slavery, neither abolition nor any alternative solution to placate the situation is ever mentioned"; Baldellou, "Transatlantic Growth through Slavery and Freedom in Harriet Beecher Stowe's *Uncle Tom's Cabin* and Gertrudis Gómez de Avellaneda's *Sab*," *Odisea* 7 (2006): 137. In a compelling take on this issue, Susan Kirkpatrick points out that "the issue of slavery was from the start secondary to that of women";

Kirkpatrick, *Las Románticas: Women Writers and Subjectivity in Spain, 1835-1850* (Berkeley: University of California Press, 1989), 156, thus blunting the force of *Sab*'s abolitionist and even antislavery messaging. Critics such as Kirkpatrick and Lucía Guerra also point to Sab's privileged status as a mayoral (foreman) as yet another element that works against the novel's antislavery and abolitionist messaging. As Guerra observes, "Como en *Oroonoko*, Sab no es enteramente negro, sino mulato, con ancestros africanos de sangre real, una educación similar a la de los blancos y la vivencia de sentimientos que no lo distinguen en absoluto en su condición de integrante de un grupo cultural marginalizado [As in *Oroonoko*, *Sab* is not entirely black, but mixed, with African ancestry of royal blood, an education similar to that of whites and the experiences of feelings that do not distinguish absolutely from his condition as a member of a marginalized cultural group]"; Guerra, "Estrategias Femeninas en la Elaboración del Sujeto Romántico en la Obra de Gertrudis Gómez de Avellaneda," *Revista Iberoamericana* 51, no. 132 (April 1985): 710.

69. Edith L. Kelly, "La Avellaneda's *Sab* and the Political Situation in Cuba," *Americas* 1, no. 3 (1945): 306. Kelly summarizes the file on the novel in the National Archives of the Republic of Cuba, which includes "seven letters and an extra memorandum" from July 1844 to January 1845 (306).

70. Judie Newman, "Harriet Beecher Stowe's Cuban Characters: *Uncle Tom's Cabin* and Gertrudis Gómez de Avellaneda's *Sab*," in *(Re)Mapping the Latina/o Literary Landscape: New Works and New Directions*, ed. Cristina Herrera and Larissa M. Mercado-López (New York: Palgrave Macmillan, 2016): 21–34.

71. Johnny Zevallos offers a contrasting view of the relationship between *Sab* and *Uncle Tom's Cabin*, arguing that "consideramos que la novel no es un antecedente de *La cabaña del tío Tom*, sino que perpetúa el sistema esclavista [we consider that the novel is not an antecedent of *Uncle Tom's Cabin* but rather that it perpetuates the slave system]"; Zevallos, "Etnicidad y Género en *Sab* (1841) de Gertrudis Gómez de Avellaneda," *Boletín de la Academia Peruana de la Lengua* 64, no.64 (Julio-Diciembre): 90.

72. Colleen O'Brien, *Race, Romance, and Rebellion: Literatures of the Americas in the Nineteenth Century* (Charlottesville and London: University of Virginia Press, 2013), 57.

73. Anna Brickhouse, *Transamerican Literary Relations and the Nineteenth-Century Public Sphere* (Cambridge: Cambridge University Press, 2004), 173.

74. Doris Sommer, *Foundational Fictions: The National Romances of Latin America* (Berkeley: University of California Press, 1991), 114–15.

75. Stacey Schlau, "Stranger in a Strange Land: The Discourse of Alienation in Gómez de Avellaneda Abolitionist Novel *Sab*," *Hispania* 69, no. 3 (1986): 497.

76. Sommer, *Foundational Fictions*, 117.

77. Avellaneda, *Sab and Autobiography*, 2.

78. As Debra Rosenthal argues, "While white U.S. writers were themselves free, Cuban writers could insert themselves in the place of their slave protagonists. The Cuban slave novel conjoins racial liberation with creole political liberation in a way

unimaginable in U.S. fiction" (72); Rosenthal, *Race Mixture in Nineteenth-Century U.S. and Spanish American Fictions*. That said, Rosenthal later acknowledges that Avellaneda "'colonized' a slave subjectivity to express her own anguish" (94), thus illuminating how Rosenthal does not equate the two forms of subjugation; that said, speaking for both groups does seem to be Avellaneda's project.

79. John Beverley, "The Margin at the Center: On *Testimonio* (Testimonial Narrative)," *MFS: Modern Fiction Studies* 35, no. 1 (Spring 1989): 15.

80. Avellaneda, *Sab* and *Autobiography*, 144–45.

81. Susan Kirkpatrick offers a contrasting take on this moment in the novel as she argues that "in general the voice of protest is more concerned with society's blighting of Sab's ambitions and talents than with the oppression of a general class of human beings"; Kirkpatrick, *Románticas*: 157. Kirkpatrick continues, "In the imagined expression of a slave's outrage speaks, in fact, the anger of a young colonial woman who aspired to pour out her own subjectivity in writing capable of captivating the great centers of civilization and culture, but who was told to be silent and resign herself to the self-abnegating virtues of the angel of the hearth" (*Románticas*, 157). Kirkpatrick's comment here points to the difficulty in adjudicating whether *Sab* is an antislavery novel or a feminist one (with Kirkpatrick staunchly in the latter camp), as Carlota's status as a *colonial* young woman suggests a level of subjugation not equal to that of slavery, of course, but also not simply equivalent to that of women in the metropole.

82. Jacobson notes that "Cubitas, the little Cuba, is a microcosm of the nation Avellaneda presents and its symbolic value is emphasized in being the country's most interior space"; Jenna Leving Jacobson, "Nation, Violence, Memory: Interrupting the Foundational Discourse in Sab," *Hispanic Issues Series* 18 (2017): 177.

83. Jacobson, "Nation, Violence, Memory," 174.

84. Avellaneda, *Sab* and *Autobiography*, 146.

85. Reina Barreto, "Subversion in Gertrudis Gómez de Avellaneda's *Sab*," *Decimonónica* 3, no. 1 (2006): 5.

86. Rogelia Lily Ibarra offers a contrasting reading of Martina and indigeneity in *Sab*, noting that "Martina is given authorial legitimacy . . . in telling the story of Camagüey and the Indigenous past, she also 'rewrites' Cuban colonial history"; Ibarra, "Gómez de Avellaneda's *Sab*: A Modernizing Project," *Hispania* 94, no. 3 (September 2011): 392.

87. Avellaneda, *Sab* and *Autobiography*, 127.

88. Sommer, *Foundational Fictions*, 121.

89. Kirkpatrick, *Románticas*, 126.

90. Julia C. Paulk, "A New Look at the Strains of Allegory in Gertrudis Gómez de Avellaneda's 'Sab,'" *Revista Hispánica Moderna* 55, no. 2 (December 2000): 229.

91. Avellaneda, *Sab* and *Autobiography*, 107.

92. Bustamante, *Cuban Memory Wars*, 6.

93. David Scott, *Conscripts of Modernity: The Tragedy of Colonial Enlightenment* (Durham, N.C.: Duke University Press, 2004), 8.

5. Speculative Revolutions: Otrxs Latinidades in Delany and Silko

1. Martin R. Delany, *Blake; or, the Huts of America* (Cambridge, Mass.: Harvard University Press, 2017).

2. Leslie Marmon Silko, *Almanac of the Dead* (New York: Penguin, 1991).

3. I refer to the character Placido in *Blake* without an accent, since that is how his name is spelled in the novel; however, I distinguish between this Placido and the historical Plácido by keeping the accent. For a broader discussion of how the figure of Plácido circulated in abolitionist writings, see R. J. Boutelle, "'Great Still in Death': Race, Martyrology, and the Reanimation of Juan Placido," *American Literature* 90, no. 3 (September 2018): 461–93.

4. Ifeoma Kiddoe Nwankwo, *Black Cosmopolitanism: Racial Consciousness and Transnational Identity in the Nineteenth-Century Americas* (Philadelphia: University of Pennsylvania Press, 2005), 27.

5. Katy Chiles, "Within and without Raced Nations: Intratextuality, Martin Delany, and *Blake; or the Huts of America*," *American Literature* 80, no. 2 (June 2008): 336.

6. Jennifer C. Brittan, "Martin R. Delany's Speculative Fiction and the Nineteenth-Century Economy of Slave Conspiracy," *Studies in American Fiction* 46, no. 1 (Spring 2019): 80.

7. Eric J. Sundquist, *To Wake the Nations: Race in the Making of American Literature* (Cambridge, Mass.: Belknap Press, 1993), 184.

8. Chiles draws out the implications of this compression of time, noting that "with this insertion of the 1857 court decision into the 1853 setting of the novel, the past continues into the present; similarly, what will happen (in the 1857 court decision) already exists (in the historical setting of the novel)"; Chiles, "Within and without Raced Nations," 334.

9. As Joni Adamson tells us, "It should come as no surprise, Silko observed, when a people who have experienced some of the harshest repression in Central America but who have always exhibited a 'strong fighting spirit' arise once again to resist oppression. Stopping short of claiming that her novel predicts the rebellion, Silko acknowledged that, at the very least, it anticipates the issues brought to the table by the Zapatistas"; Adamson, *American Indian Literature, Environmental Justice, and Ecocriticism* (Tucson: University of Arizona Press, 2001), 129. For Chanette Romero, "it seems more likely that the historical significance of this region to ancient Mayan culture and its current devastating poverty made it a primary staging ground for both fictious and material revolutions"; Romero, "Envisioning a 'Network of Tribal Coalitions': Leslie Marmon Silko's *Almanac of the Dead*," *American Indian Quarterly* 26, no. 4 (Fall 2002): 637. See also Deborah Horvitz, "Freud, Marx and Chiapas in Leslie Marmon Silko's *Almanac of the Dead*," *Studies in American Indian Literature* 10, no. 3 (Fall 1998): 47–48.

10. George A. Collier and Elizabeth Lowery Quaratiello, *Basta! Land and the Zapatista Rebellion in Chiapas*, 3rd ed. (Oakland, Calif.: Food First, 2005), 1.

11. Leslie Marmon Silko, "Listening to the Spirits: An Interview with Leslie Marmon Silko," in *Conversations with Leslie Marmon Silko*, by Ellen L. Arnold (Jackson: University Press of Mississippi, 2000), 174.

12. Jerome McGann, "Introduction," in *Blake; or, the Huts of America*, by Martin R. Delany (Cambridge, Mass.: Harvard University Press, 2017), xxv.

13. Romero, "Envisioning a 'Network,'" 623.

14. Along similar lines, Shari M. Huhndorf argues, "Confounding the nationalist paradigms that have dominated Native literary studies, *Almanac* rewrites the history of the Americas from a transnational perspective that unites imperialism, slavery, and class struggle in a single, ongoing story of land conflicts, and it attempts to negotiate a collective revolutionary identity based on histories shared by Native peoples across cultural and national boundaries"; Huhndorf, "Picture Revolution: 'Tribal Internationalism' and the Future of the Americas in Leslie Marmon Silko's *Almanac of the Dead*," in *Mapping the Americas: The Transnational Politics of Contemporary Native Culture* (Ithaca, N.Y.: Cornell University Press, 2009), 141.

15. Simón Ventura Trujillo, *Land Uprising: Native Story Power and the Insurgent Horizons of Latinx Indigeneity* (Tucson: University of Arizona Press, 2020), 44.

16. Romero, "Envisioning a 'Network,'" 634.

17. Domingo Faustino Sarmiento, *Facundo: Or, Civilization and Barbarism* (1845), trans. Kathleen Ross (Berkeley: University of California Press, 2004).

18. Joni Adamson, "'¡Todos Somos Indios!' Revolutionary Imagination, Alternative Modernity, and Transnational Organizing in the Work of Silko, Tamez, and Anzaldúa, *Journal of Transnational American Studies* 4, no. 1 (2012): 6, https://escholarship.org/uc/item/2mj3c2p3, accessed October 10, 2021.

19. Delany, *Blake*, 238.

20. For an in-depth discussion of the role of Exodus in the novel, particularly Blake as a Moses-like figure, see Grant Shreve, "The Exodus of Martin Delany," *American Literary History* 29, no. 3 (Fall 2017): 449–73.

21. For a counterargument to this claim, see Christopher Castiglia, *Bound and Determined: Captivity, Culture-Crossing, and White Womanhood from Mary Rowlandson to Patty Hearst* (Chicago: University of Chicago Press, 1996), 227–28.

22. Delany first published chapters 28–30 to give his audience a taste of the novel before starting publication from the beginning.

23. Robert S. Levine, *Martin Delany, Frederick Douglass, and the Politics of Representative Identity* (Chapel Hill: University of North Carolina Press, 1997), 179; hereafter *Politics*.

24. McGann, "Introduction," In *Blake; or, the Huts of America*, by Martin R. Delany. Cambridge, Mass.: Harvard University Press, 2017, xxxiii–xxxiv.

25. Levine, *Politics*, 179.

26. Sundquist, *To Wake the Nations*, 185.

27. Chiles contends that the contradictions found in Delany's political writings and *Blake* stem from the fact that he "composed *Blake* over the same period of time that the focus of his emigration work was changing from South and Central

America and the West Indies to the Niger Valley in Africa"; Chiles, "Within and without Raced Nations," 338. Moreover, she argues that "concomitant with both this transformation and the novel's composition was the decline in Delany's rhetorical use of Haiti as an exemplary all-black republic; his early praise for Haiti gave way to disapproval" (338).

28. Martin R. Delany, *The Condition, Elevation, Emigration and Destiny of the Colored People of the United States: Martin R. Delany: A Documentary Reader*, ed. Robert S. Levine (Chapel Hill: University of North Carolina Press, 2003), 194; hereafter *Documentary*.

29. Delany, *Blake*, 262.

30. Ibid., 262. Compare with Delany's argument in *The Condition*: "To establish the equality of the African with the European race, establishes the equality of every person intermediate between the two races. This established beyond contradiction, the general equality of men" (194–95).

31. Robert S. Levine, ed., *Martin R. Delany: A Documentary Reader* (Chapel Hill: University of North Carolina Press, 2003), 15. Elsewhere, Levine goes so far as to suggest "that something similar to the racial dynamic troubling Delany's relationship with Douglass is enacted in Delany's portrayal of Placido"; Levine, *Politics*, 205.

32. Martin R. Delany, *Official Report of the Niger Valley Exploring Party: Martin R. Delany; A Documentary Reader*, ed. Robert S. Levine (Chapel Hill: University of North Carolina Press, 2003), 356, emphasis Delany's.

33. In contrast to my argument, Brittan contends that "Delany specifically doesn't give us a practical guide to revolution, he doesn't make black futurity dependent on the conspiracy plot"; "Martin R. Delany's Speculative Fiction," 96. Similarly, though I outline *Blake*'s tactics to show the range of revolutionary strategies and possibilities the novel offers, Castiglia argues that "much effort goes into limiting its outcomes. The novel's hero works tirelessly to replace revolution with institutionalism"; Castiglia, *Bound and Determined*, 226.

34. Levine points to the imperialism of Blake's plan, particularly in light of his status as an Afro Cuban, writing, "Delany's view of land and nation is just as problematic in *Blake*, despite the fact that he presents Blake as a native Cuban, for by the end of the novel Delany espouses the providential notions set forth in *Condition* and 'Political Destiny': that blacks' destiny lies in the Americas, a notion that, while posing a significant challenge to U.S. Manifest Destiny, shares its colonizing and imperialistic assumptions"; Levine, *Politics*, 211.

35. Nwankwo, *Black Cosmopolitanism*, 7.

36. Delany wrote explicitly about his anxieties concerning annexation in his essay "Annexation of Cuba" (1849), in Levine, *Martin R. Delany: A Documentary Reader*.

37. Quoted in Sundquist, *To Wake the Nations*, 183.

38. Aisha Finch, *Rethinking Slave Rebellion in Cuba: La Escalera and the Insurgencies of 1841–1844* (Chapel Hill: University of North Carolina Press, 2015), 127.

39. Andy Doolen, "'Be Cautious of the Word "Rebel"': Race, Revolution, and

Transnational History in Martin Delany's *Blake; or, The Huts of America*," *American Literature* 81, no. 1 (March 2009): 161.

40. Doolen argues, "Delany's critique defines the Revolution as a failure that cannot serve as the ideological origin for a black independence struggle that exceeds national time and space"; ibid., 157.

41. Delany, *Blake*, 113.

42. Doolen, "'Be Cautious,'" 160. See also Judith Madera, *Black Atlas: Geography and Flow in Nineteenth-Century African American Literature* (Durham, N.C.: Duke University Press, 2015), 114.

43. Delany, *Blake*, 288.

44. Orihuela argues that "seemingly, in Cuba the slave has at least the right to demand property of the self" (Sharada Balachandran Orihuela, "The Black Market: Property, Freedom, and Piracy in Martin Delany's *Blake; or, The Huts of America*." *J19: Journal of Nineteenth-Century Americanists* 2, no. 2 [Fall 2014]: 287), as they "are allowed to participate in an economic discourse where they can value, and ultimately purchase, their own bodies by demanding the price of freedom" (287).

45. Chiles, "Within and without Raced Nations," 388.

46. Grégory Pierrot, "Writing over Haiti: Black Avengers in Martin Delany's *Blake*," *Studies in American Literature* 41, no. 2 (Fall 2014): 176.

47. Ibid. Pierrot mentions the curious place of Haiti in *Blake*, since "the massive, organized black uprising presented in *Blake*'s plot is connected with—if not rooted in—the Haitian Revolution. Yet Haiti is mentioned all but twice in the entire novel, only once by name" (175–76). Madera, meanwhile, argues that "while Delany's novel obscures genealogies of black representative struggle, making Haiti into a kind of closure, Cuba evolves as a space of openings"; Madera, *Black Atlas*, 130.

48. As Pierrot explains, *Blake* "borrows details and even characters from the most renowned, most revered black uprisings of the hemisphere"; "Writing over Haiti," 193.

49. Finch, *Rethinking Slave Rebellion in Cuba*, 5.

50. Delany, *Blake*, 42.

51. John Harvard argues that, "for Delany, elevation involved an upward mobility that required culture, correct speech, sound morals, and self-reliant rather than inert religious practice"; Harvard, "Mary Peabody Mann's *Juanita* and Martin R. Delany's *Blake*: Cuba, Urban Slavery, and the Construction of Nation," *College Literature* 43, no. 3 (Summer 2016): 527. Harvard contends that "Havana offers an elevated group of blacks with whom Blake can strategize regarding how to promote uplift and eventually rebellion among less fortunate slaves" (529). Moreover, Delany himself argues in *The Condition* that "the duty of the Free, to elevate themselves in the most speedy and effective manner possible; as the redemption of the bondman depends entirely upon the elevation of the freeman; therefore, to elevate the free colored people of America, anywhere upon this continent; forebodes the speedy redemption of the slaves" (214). Much like we saw in his discussion of those of pure African

blood, here Delany once again creates a hierarchy, this time between those who are free and those who are enslaved. For additional sources on Delany's promotion of Black political consciousness as a way to think outside of identity, especially in terms of biology, see Levine's *Politics*, 211. Paul Gilroy, meanwhile, argues that "the version of black solidarity *Blake* advances is explicitly anti-ethnic and opposes narrow African-American exceptionalism in the name of a truly pan-African, diaspora sensibility. This makes blackness a matter of politics rather than a common cultural identity"; Gilroy, *The Black Atlantic: Modernity and Double Consciousness* (Cambridge, Mass.: Harvard University Press, 1993), 27. While Pierrot also argues that *Blake* offers a vision of "a black race understood as a political choice rather than mere biological accident" ("Writing over Haiti," 193), he focuses on the trope of the black avenger, especially in depictions of Haiti, and how *Blake* revises this trope from one of individual to collective action. In contrast, I focus on La Escalera and its influence on Blake's revolutionary tactics, particularly how such tactics offer a model of coalitional politics that's useful for examining how Latinx revolutionary horizons can be expanded.

52. Delany, *Blake*, 127.

53. Ibid. In meeting enslaved people where they are at, Blake is able to "mobilize local knowledges within national space" (Madera, *Black Atlas*, 83) and build "a collective counterintelligence" (84) through his conversations with enslaved people in which "he makes pointed inquiries to assess the value of their labor specializations and field-based understandings" (84).

54. Delany, *Blake*, 39.

55. Pierrot, "Writing over Haiti," 189.

56. Delany, *Blake*, 40.

57. Finch, *Rethinking Slave Rebellion in Cuba*, 180.

58. While Blake's actions in Africa are a bit of a mystery—he goes into the forest (Delany, *Blake*, 214), but we don't see his actions once there—Pierrot reminds us that Blake "somehow made contact with Mendi and Abyssa, military and spiritual leaders for the new slaves, who later on appear as members of the Grand Council [in Cuba]"; Pierrot, "Writing over Haiti," 189. Pierrot argues that "Blake rigs the market: he agrees with African chiefs to stack the group of slaves destined for the *Vulture* with warriors" (190).

59. Delany, *Blake*, 239–40.

60. That La Escalera represented a solidarity among Afro Cubans across a range of statuses (from skin color to enslaved or free) was particularly shocking to government officials. According to Nwankwo, "As the sentence meted out by the Cuban government shows, the groups (*pardos libres, morenos,* and *negros esclavos*) were conceptualized as separate, with differences between the expectations for behavior for each group and the group's level of access to freedom and status. The level of surprise expressed by the authorities at the groups' uniting suggested an expectation of separateness on the authorities' part"; Nwankwo, *Black Cosmopolitanism*, 54. Indeed, Nwankwo suggests that "Delany chose Plácido and

Cuba, at least in part, because the fact that those class and color boundaries were so institutionalized in Cuba would make their transgression, as represented in the text, even more dramatic" (54).

61. Delany, *Blake*, 239.

62. Nwankwo, *Black Cosmopolitanism*, 64.

63. See Ferrer, *Insurgent Cuba*, 170–94.

64. Rebecca Skidmore Biggio argues that Delany "embellishes recent historical accounts to illustrate the prominent role of whites in creating and enabling insurrection panic to produce the insurrection"; Biggio, "The Specter of Conspiracy in Martin Delany's *Blake*," *African American Review* 43, nos. 3–4 (Fall–Winter 2008): 441.

65. Delany, *Blake*, 298.

66. For a more in-depth discussion of speculators—as well as their connections to speculative fiction—see Brittan, "Martin R. Delany's Speculative Fiction." Also note that Count Alcora is most likely based on the real-life Captain-General Federico Roncali, "whose title was Conde de Alcoy"; Sundquist, *To Wake the Nations*, 218.

67. Delany, *Blake*, 304.

68. McGann, "Introduction," xx.

69. Delany, *Blake*, 287.

70. As Levine points out, "Grouping the 'Indians' with blacks as a unified 'colored race' allows Blake and his compatriots to ignore the distinctive claims of the native inhabitants, thereby enabling an untroubled assertion of 'black' Manifest Destiny in the Western Hemisphere"; Levine, *Politics*, 211. See also Madera, *Black Atlas*, 99.

71. For example, Levine suggests that "Delany actually ended the novel with a series of relatively nonviolent scenes that enable Blake to emerge at the helm of a regenerated society in which blackness is seen not as an exclusive or essential good but as equally worthy (or unworthy) as whiteness. The ascent to leadership of a 'pure-blooded' black, as Blake and Placido suggest at the coronation scene at Madame Cordora's, would serve as a daily refutation of whites' racist beliefs in black inferiority. Occurring in such close proximity to the United States, Blake's ascent would therefore provide U.S. whites with an image not of black homicidal fury but of responsible black leadership"; Levine, *Politics*, 216.

72. McGann, "Introduction," xxiv.

73. Orihuela points out, "Part of what makes this revolution possible is the now-freed slave population that Blake helped procure"; Orihuela, "Black Market," 293.

74. Pierrot, "Writing over Haiti," 193.

75. For a radical reframing of Benedict Anderson's notion of the imagined community and *Blake*, see Chiles, "Within and without Raced Nations," 333–37.

76. Biggio, "Specter of Conspiracy," 450.

77. Biggio suggests that "the ultimate goal for Delany is a cohesive separatist community prepared to command its own destiny" (ibid., 444); however, I suggest that in proposing blackness as a political formation and the ideas Delany puts forward in *Blake* about a broader concept of "a colored race" (287) in the Americas

offer a glimmer of coalitional politics that extend beyond blackness. Of course, this stands in marked contrast to Delany's quest for "possible locations for separatist black settlements, first within the new territories of the expanding United States and later in Central and South America and West Africa"; Brittan, "Martin R. Delany's Speculative Fiction," 97. That said, as this chapter illuminates, I am interested in the revolutionary imaginaries *Blake* makes available exactly because I find some of these imaginaries to be at odds with his stated political views.

78. Brittan, "Martin R. Delany's Speculative Fiction," 82. R. J. Boutelle argues, in focusing on the characters Madame Cordora and Gofer Gondolier, the Captain General's caterer, Delany "radically democratizes emancipation and restores black men and women from throughout the African diaspora into imaginative, organizational, and functional roles within the project of determining the forms and objectives of their own liberation"; Boutelle, "'Great Still in Death,'" 484. In so doing, Delany "shift[s] the power to actualize a revolution away from the novel's black male leaders" (484). Building on Boutelle, I suggest that Delany offers a revolutionary imaginary that can be taken up by anyone and that *not* representing the revolution leaves open capacious possibilities for what such a revolution would look like—and who should lead it.

79. Ricardo Ortiz, *Latinx Literature Now*, xvIII.

80. Ferrer, *Insurgent Cuba*, 15.

81. Finch, *Rethinking Slave Rebellion in Cuba*, 48.

82. Silko, *Almanac of the Dead*, 261.

83. For more on this practice, see Ann Twinam, *Purchasing Whiteness: Pardos, Mulattos, and the Quest for Social Mobility in the Spanish Indies* (Stanford, Calif.: Stanford University Press, 2015).

84. As Horvitz points out regarding Menardo's relationship with his grandfather, it's as if "his visionary grandfather, who 'recognized evil, whatever name you called it' (A 259), 'knew' that Menardo could be seduced by greed; the old man tells him the powerful tale of the 'orphan people' to alert his grandson to the critical weakness that will kill him"; Horvitz, "Freud, Marx and Chiapas," 58–59; however, in rejecting his grandfather and his heritage, Menardo gives into the greed and becomes "an influential and rich Destroyer" (58).

85. My reading of the Latinx revolutionary horizon in *Almanac* complements Trujillo's as he states that the novel "conjures an Indigenous horizon of anticapitalist insurgency that deposes the overlapping antiblack and settler colonial logics of dispossession in the Americas"; Trujillo, *Land Uprising*, 51. I propose Latinx revolutionary horizons as both a textual phenomenon and utopian imaginary and Trujillo's thought is central for sketching the contours of such imaginaries, while María Josefina Saldaña-Portillo's argument that "the Indian is the horizon of inclusion" (*Indian Given*, 40) points to the racialized boundaries that police such horizons.

86. Trujillo, *Land Uprising*, 90.

87. For example, rather than tying this plotline to the revolutionary vision of the novel, Huhndorf merely states that "the characters in Seese's story, then, are a focal point of *Almanac*'s critique of colonial and capitalist violence as they herald the collapse of European society under the weight of its own vices"; Huhndorf, "Picture Revolution," 164. When critics do consider this plotline, it's primarily to examine Silko's "vindictive" portrayal of homosexuality; Dorothea Fischer-Hornung, "'Now We Know That Gay Men Are Just Men After All': Abject Sexualities in Leslie Marmon Silko's *Almanac of the Dead*," in *The Abject of Desire: The Aestheticization of the Unaesthetic in Contemporary Literature and Culture*, ed. Konstanze Kutzbach and Monika Mueller (Amsterdam: Rodopi, 2007), 114. Particular attention is paid to the Eric, David, and Beaufrey dynamic (and Serlo to a certain extent); however, singling out this dynamic as indicative of a "vindictive" portrayal ignores the rampant sexual violence in *Almanac*, which ranges from the watching and creating of torture porn videos to bestiality and rape. For scholarship on Silko's depiction of homosexuality, see Fischer-Hornung, "'Now We Know.'"

88. For a useful discussion of how Seese converts from being a Destroyer to being part of the people, see Horvitz, "Freud, Marx and Chiapas," 55–56.

89. That said, Silko not only equates Montezuma with Cortés, but suggests that the former brought on the destruction of his own people as well as the Indigenous people in the Americas more broadly. I thank María Josefina Saldaña-Portillo for pointing out this problematic comparison.

90. There is a slight narrative confusion about the location of the finca—in most of the descriptions, the finca seems to be located in Colombia. The references in the text to the llanos (plains in Colombia) rather than the pampas (plains in Argentina) support this claim, as does the fact that Serlo owns the finca and that he competed internationally on equestrian teams for Colombia, with Beaufrey competing for Argentina; Silko, *Almanac of the Dead*, 544. However, in the chapter where we learn about the finca—and the eugenicist science that goes on there—titled "Alternative Earth Units," we learn that "years before they had all the mestizos and Indians relocated to work on their ranching operations in Argentina. The *finca* was to become a stronghold for those of *sangre pura* as unrest and revolutions continued to sweep through" (541). That said, on the next page, as we learn more about the stronghold, we are told that Serlo "had made a generous research grant to a young scientist from Geneva, who had traveled to Colombia and lived on the *finca* for a year" (542), which suggests that the finca is located in Colombia, not Argentina. Still later, we learn that Serlo's grandfather owned multiple fincas (547), which offers the possibility that Serlo inherited several fincas dedicated to the same mission even as he seems to only be describing one.

91. Sharon P. Holland observes that Silko "invert[s] the hierarchy of civilized/primitive" ("'If You Know I Have a History, You Will Respect Me': A Perspective on Afro-Native American Literature," *Callaloo* 17, no. 1 (Winter 1994): 343) and in so doing "deconstruct[s] Western European notions of binary oppositions" (343).

Holland also speaks in general terms rather than thinking with the intellectual traditions of the Americas that I suggest inform Silko's novel.

92. Katherine A. Gordy, "No Better Way to Be Latin American: European Science and Thought, Latin American Theory?," *Postcolonial Studies* 16, no. 4 (2013): 359.

93. Juliet Hooker, *Theorizing Race in the Americas: Douglass, Sarmiento, Du Bois, and Vasconcelos* (Oxford: Oxford University Press, 2019), 69.

94. Vasconcelos, José. *The Cosmic Race/La raza cósmica* (1925; repr. Baltimore: John Hopkins University Press, 1948, 1997), 25.

95. José Enrique Rodó, *Ariel* (1900), trans. Margaret Sayers Peden (1974; repr. Austin: University of Texas Press, 1988; Roberto Fernández Retamar, "Caliban: Notes Toward a Discussion of Culture in Our America" (1971), in *Caliban and Other Essays*, trans. by Edward Baker, 3-45 (Minneapolis: University of Minnesota Press, 1989).

96. Rodó, *Ariel*, 31.

97. For a generous reading of Retamar and Caliban's potential, see José David Saldívar's chapter "The School of Caliban," in his *The Dialectics of Our America: Genealogy, Cultural Critique, and Literary History* (Durham, N.C.: Duke University Press, 1991).

98. Rodó, *Ariel*, 99.

99. The circumstances of Retamar's writing of the essay are complex and directly linked to the historical conditions in Cuba at the time. Where Retamar details these circumstances in his "Caliban Revisited" essay (see Retamar, *Caliban and Other Essays*, trans. Edward Baker [Minneapolis: University of Minnesota Press, 1989]), Ricardo Ortiz, in *Cultural Erotics*, offers a more cogent description of these conditions, which take into account Retamar's own biases toward a heterosexual, masculine revolution. See Ortiz, *Cultural Erotics in Cuban America* (Minneapolis: University of Minnesota Press, 2007), particularly 91–101, though the entire chapter is a useful reading of Retamar.

100. Ortiz, *Cultural Erotics in Cuban America*, 96.

101. María Josefina Saldaña-Portillo, *The Revolutionary Imagination in the Americas and the Age of Development* (Durham, N.C.: Duke University Press, 2003), 87.

102. Retamar, "Caliban," 6.

103. Although a number of scholars discuss the importance of remembering our histories and stories, Trujillo offers a particularly compelling reading. See Trujillo, *Land Uprising*, 89–99, in which he discusses *Almanac* as a fugitive text.

104. For a discussion of Silko's use of Marx, see Horvitz, "Freud, Marx and Chiapas," 50–53. Significantly, Horvitz goes so far as to say that Silko's "task is identical to the one she ascribes to Marx" (52). See also Huhndorf, "Picture Revolution," 148–49, and Amanda Walker Johnson, "Silko's *Almanac*: Engaging Marx and the Critique of Capitalism," in *Howling for Justice: New Perspectives on Leslie Marmon. Silko's Almanac of the Dead*, ed. Rebecca Tillett (Tucson:

University of Arizona Press, 2014), 91–103. For a discussion of Silko's use of Freud, see Horvitz, 51. For an examination of how Silko uses Freud in her representation of homosexuality, see Fischer-Hornung, "'Now We Know,'" 112–13.

105. Silko, *Almanac of the Dead*, 535.

106. While I do not mean to equate harboring war criminals with offering refuge to a persecuted people who were the target of a systematic genocidal pogrom, I do contend that countries such as Argentina and the Dominican Republic make these whitening strategies equivalent. This is because of the logic of blanqueamiento (whitening) in Latin America most often practiced through the idea of mejorar la raza (to improve the race) through marriage to people of lighter skin. On Nazi immigration to Argentina, see Uki Goni, *The Real Odessa: How Perón Brought the Nazi War Criminals to Argentina* (London and New York: Granta, 2003); on Jewish refugees in the Dominican Republic, see Allen Wells, *Tropical Zone: General Trujillo, FDR, and the Jews of Sosúa* (Durham, N.C.: Duke University Press, 2009).

107. As Huhndorf observes, "*Almanac*, then, does not merely recount various Native histories and spiritual practices for similar purposes; she rewrites the Popul Vuh story about the quest of hero twins to defeat the lords of death, which is echoed by the two sets of twins in Silko's novel who battle 'the Destroyers'"; Huhndorf, "Picture Revolution," 160.

108. "The Haitian Revolution thus entered history with the peculiar characteristic of being unthinkable even as it happened," Michel-Rolph Trouillot argues (*Silencing the Past: Power and the Production of History* [Boston: Beacon, 1995], 73), adding that the French "could read the news only with their ready-made categories, and these categories were incompatible with the idea of a slave revolution" (73).

109. Holland offers an analysis of how Clinton—whose thinking we might call undisciplined—offers a "reprisal of history [that] seems to stand in complete contradiction to Western methodologies employed by scholars in the various fields; his discourse is not confined to 'departments' of knowledge, but constitutes a hodge-podge of information reflective of his own multifaceted heritage"; Sharon P. Holland, "'If You Know I Have a History, You Will Respect Me': A Perspective on Afro-Native American Literature," *Callaloo* 17, no. 1 (Winter 1994): 346. In other words, rather than having a line of thought disciplined by institutions such as the university, Clinton's undisciplined mind is able to make wide-ranging connections that would possibly elude specialists in a particular field. For an insightful discussion of Clinton's anticapitalist thought in relation to indigeneity and fugitivity, see Trujillo, *Land Uprising*, 51–53.

110. Kyle Bladow reminds us that "critics have suggested the ending leaves the book open for optimistic interpretations about the potential for progressive social and environmental change. However, this ending also suits the reading of the novel as an almanac, especially the kind from which Silko drew inspiration: Mayan codices that represent cyclical time"; Bladow, "Timely Objects and the Revolutionary Formerly Known as Marcos: Rereading *Almanac of the Dead*," *Studies in American Indian Literatures* 29, no. 2 (Summer 2017): 4.

111. Huhndorf observes that women in *Almanac* "serve instead as the most militant revolutionary leaders," with the characters Zeta and Lecha "number[ing] among the female characters who challenge the centrality and conventional meanings of Indigenous women's reproduction, in both the cultural and biological senses"; Huhndorf, "Picture Revolution," 158. Meanwhile, the novel "positions its male characters, such as the Barefoot Hopi, Tacho, and El Feo, as the bearers of culture (a role that is less confining for men in a patriarchal society), while the women in various ways refuse motherhood and use their sexuality in the service of revolution" (158).

112. "Leslie Marmon Silko," in *Conversations with Leslie Marmon Silko*, by Laura Coltelli (Jackson: University Press of Mississippi, 2000), 132.

113. Nwankwo, *Black Cosmopolitanism*. Robert Reid-Pharr counters this interpretation somewhat by arguing that Blake seeks "to liberate his own 'manhood' from the taint of effeminacy—and bestiality—engendered by slavery" ("Violent Ambiguity: Martin Delany, Bourgeois Sadomasochism, and the Production of a Black National Masculinity," in *Representing Black Men*, ed. Marcellus Blount and George P. Cunningham [New York: Routledge, 1995], 78) as Blake and Delany view enslavement as a "weak, effeminate, and (sexually) submissive" (86) condition.

114. Nwankwo, *Black Cosmopolitanism*, 56–59.

115. Delany, *Blake*, 195.

116. Placido's central role, particularly as mentor and teacher, stands in sharp contrast to Christopher Castiglia's reading of *Blake* in which he argues that "Blake *becomes* an institution" such that "leadership and institutionality become one and the same, whereas the majority of 'followers' become bound by their partial knowledge, their historical and regional specificity, to a locality and an embodiment that Blake himself transcends"; Castiglia, *Bound and Determined: Captivity, Culture-Crossing, and White Womanhood from Mary Rowlandson to Patty Hearst.* (Chicago: University of Chicago Press, 1996), 227. I differ from Castiglia's argument, as I suggest that Placido's conversations with others in the seclusion, particularly his discussion with Madame Cordora, shows how organizing means sharing information and ideas with the other revolutionaries so that they are not inhibited by either "partial knowledge" or "historical and regional specificity;" Placido's vast knowledge of Africa in Delany, *Blake*, 262–63, illustrates this kind of knowledge-sharing.

117. Nwankwo, *Black Cosmopolitanism*, 64.

118. Delany, *Blake*, 112.

119. Silko, *Almanac of the Dead*, 529.

120. José Esteban Muñoz, *The Sense of Brown* (Durham, N.C.: Duke University Press, 2020), 2.

Coda: Is the X a Commons?

1. Lazaro Lima, *Being Brown: Sonia Sotomayor and the Latino Question* (Berkeley: University of California, 2019), 5.

2. I read Simón Ventura Trujillo's *Land Uprising: Native Story Power and the Insurgent Horizons of Latinx Indigeneity* (Tucson: University of Arizona Press, 2020) and Lorgia García Peña's *Translating Blackness: Latinx Colonialities in a Global Perspective* (Durham, N.C.: Duke University Press, 2022) as two texts that do the work of restoring Latinx kinships and uncovering forms of latinidad not grounded in whiteness.

3. Karla Cornejo Villavicencio, *The Undocumented Americans* (New York: One World, 2020); Juan Felipe Herrera, *Akrílica* (1989; repr. Noemi Press, 2022); and Joseph Cassara's *The House of Impossible Beauties* (New York: Ecco, 2018).

4. Cornejo Villavicencio, *Undocumented Americans*, xv.

5. Farid Matuk, "Introduction," in Herrera, *Akrílica*, 9.

6. Ana Patricia Rodriguez, "The Fiction of Solidarity: Transfronterista Feminisms and Anti-Imperialist Struggles in Central American Transnational Narratives," *Feminist Studies* 34, nos. 1/2, (2008): 199–226.

7. Thank you to Gabriela Valenzuela for confirming my suspicion and giving me a historical perspective on fincas in El Salvador.

8. Cassara, *House of Impossible Beauties*, 54. When referring to the fictional character Hector Valle, I use "Hector," and when discussing the historical figure, I use "Valle."

9. In actuality, the House of Xtravaganza was spelled "Extravaganza" until 1989.

10. Livingston, Jennie, dir., *Paris Is Burning: A Conversation* (Criterion Collection, 1990).

11. Gloria Anzaldúa, *Borderlands/La Frontera: The New Mestiza*, 3rd ed. (San Francisco: Aunt Lute, 1987), 42.

Bibliography

Acosta, Abraham. *Thresholds of Illiteracy: Theory, Latin America, and the Crisis of Resistance*. New York: Fordham University Press, 2014.
Acosta, Oscar Zeta. *Revolt of the Cockroach People*. New York: Vintage, 1989.
Adamson, Joni. *American Indian Literature, Environmental Justice, and Ecocriticism*. Tucson: University of Arizona Press, 2001.
———. "'¡Todos Somos Indios!' Revolutionary Imagination, Alternative Modernity, and Transnational Organizing in the Work of Silko, Tamez, and Anzaldúa." *Journal of Transnational American Studies* 4, no. 1 (2012). https://escholarship.org/uc/item/2mj3c2p3. Accessed October 10, 2021.
Aguilar, Filomeno V. Jr. "Filibustero, Rizal, and the Manilamen of the Nineteenth Century." *Philippine Studies* 59, no. 4 (2011): 429–69.
Aguilar-San Juan, Karin. *The State of Asian America: Activism and Resistance in the 1990s*. Boston: South End, 1994.
Alcaraz, Lalo. "Princess Lupe." 2016. *Lalo Alcaraz Art Shop*. https://lalo-alcaraz-art-shop.myshopify.com/products/princess-lupe-print-by-lalo-alcaraz.
Alemán, Jesse. "Citizenship Rights and Colonial Whites: The Cultural Work of María Amparo Ruiz de Burton's Novels." In *Complicating Constructions: Race, Ethnicity, and Hybridity in American Texts*, edited by David S. Goldstein and Audrey B. Thacker, 3–30. Seattle: University of Washington Press, 2015.
———. "'Thank God, Lolita Is Away from Those Horrid Savages': The Politics of Whiteness in *Who Would Have Thought It?*" In *María Amparo Ruiz de Burton: Critical and Pedagogical Perspectives*, edited by Amelia María de la Luz Montes and Anne Elizabeth Goldman, 95–111. Lincoln: University of Nebraska Press, 2004.
Alfonso-Forero, Ann Marie. "'A Whole New Race': Chinese Cubans and Hybrid Identities in Cristina García's *Monkey Hunting*." *Anthurium: A Caribbean Studies Journal* 7, no. 1 (April 2010): 1–9.

Alvarado, Leticia. *Abject Performances: Aesthetic Strategies in Latino Cultural Productions.* Durham, N.C.: Duke University Press, 2018.

Alvarez, Julia. *In the Name of Salomé.* Chapel Hill, N.C.: Algonquin Books of Chapel Hill, 2000.

———. *In the Time of the Butterflies.* Chapel Hill, N.C.: Algonquin Books of Chapel Hill, 1994.

Anderson, Benedict. "Cacique Democracy in the Philippines: Origins and Dreams." In *Discrepant Histories: Translocal Essays on Filipino Cultures,* edited by Vicente L. Rafael, 3–47. Philadelphia: Temple University Press, 1995.

———. "Forms of Consciousness in *Noli Me Tangere.*" *Philippine Studies* 51, no. 4 (2003): 505–29.

———. *Imagined Communities: Reflections on the Origin and Spread of Nationalism.* London and New York: Verso, 1983.

———. *The Specter of Comparisons: Nationalism, Southeast Asia and the World.* London and New York: Verso, 1998.

———. *Under Three Flags: Anarchism and the Anti-Colonial Imagination.* London and New York: Verso, 2006.

Anonymous. "El Plan Espiritual de Aztlán." In *Aztlán: Essays on the Chicano Homeland,* edited by Rudolfo A. Anaya and Francisco A. Lomelí, 1-5. Albuquerque: University of New Mexico Press, 1989.

Anzaldúa, Gloria. *Borderlands / La Frontera: The New Mestiza.* 3rd ed. San Francisco: Aunt Lute, 1987.

Apostol, Gina. *Gun Dealers' Daughter.* Manila: Anvil, 2010.

Aranda, José. "Contradictory Impulses: María Amparo Ruiz de Burton, Resistance Theory, and the Politics of Chicano/a Studies." *American Literature* 70, no. 3 (1998): 551–79.

———. "When Archives Collide: Recovering Modernity in Early Mexican American Literature." In *The Latino Nineteenth Century,* edited by Rodrigo Lazo and Jesse Alemán, 146–67. New York: NYU Press, 2016.

Arcilla, Jose. S. "Rizal and Poltergeists in Dapitan." *Philippine Studies* 49, no. 1 (2001): 94–112.

Arenas, Reinaldo. *Before Night Falls: A Memoir.* New York: Penguin, 1994.

Arendt, Hannah. *On Revolution.* New York: Penguin, 1963.

Arnold, L. Ellen, ed. *Conversations with Leslie Marmon Silko.* Jackson: University Press of Mississippi, 2000.

Avelar, Idelber. *The Untimely Present: Postdictatorial Latin American Fiction and the Task of Mourning.* Durham, N.C.: Duke University Press, 1999.

Balce-Cortes, Nerissa. "Imagining the Neocolony." *Critical Mass: A Journal of Asian American Cultural Criticism* 2, no. 2 (1995): 95–120.

Baldellou, Marta Miquel. "Transatlantic Growth through Slavery and Freedom in Harriet Beecher Stowe's *Uncle Tom's Cabin* and Gertrudis Gómez de Avellaneda's *Sab.*" *Odisea* 7 (2006): 127–38.

Balestrini, Nassim. "Transnational and Transethnic Textures; or, 'Intricate Interdependencies' in Sandra Cisneros's *Caramelo*." *Amerikastudien / American Studies* 57, no. 1 (2012): 67–89.
Barnet, Miguel. *Biografía de un cimarrón*. 1966. Havana: Editorial Letras Cubanas, 2016.
———. *Biography of a Runaway Slave*. Translated by W. Nick Hill. Evanston, Ill: Curbstone, 1994.
Barreto, Reina. "Subversion in Gertrudis Gómez de Avellaneda's *Sab*." *Decimonónica* 3, no. 1 (2006): 1–10.
Bascara, Victor. *Model-Minority Imperialism*. Minneapolis: University of Minnesota Press, 2006.
Beezley, William H., and Colin M. MacLachlan. *Mexicans in Revolution, 1910–1946: An Introduction*. Lincoln: University of Nebraska Press, 2009.
Belnap, Jeffrey, and Raúl Fernández, eds. *José Martí's "Our America": From National to Hemispheric Cultural Studies*. Durham, N.C.: Duke University Press, 1998.
Beltrán, Cristina. *The Trouble with Unity: Latino Politics and the Creation of Identity*. Oxford: Oxford University Press, 2010.
Benítez-Rojo, Antonio. *The Repeating Island: The Caribbean and the Postmodern Perspective*. Durham, N.C.: Duke University Press, 1996.
Beverley, John. "The Margin at the Center: On *Testimonio* (Testimonial Narrative)." *MFS: Modern Fiction Studies* 35, no. 1 (Spring 1989): 11–28.
———. *Testimonio: On the Politics of Truth*. Minneapolis: University of Minnesota Press, 2004.
———. "'Through All Things Modern': Second Thoughts on Testimonio." *boundary 2* 18, no. 2 (Summer, 1991): 1–21.
Bhabha, Homi. "Foreword." In *The Wretched of the Earth*, by Franz Fanon, vii–xli. New York: Grove, 2021.
Biggio, Rebecca Skidmore. "The Specter of Conspiracy in Martin Delany's *Blake*." *African American Review* 43, nos. 3–4 (Fall–Winter 2008): 439–54.
Blackwell, Maylei, Floridalma Boj Lopez, and Luis Urrieta Jr., eds. *Critical Latinx Indigeneities*. Special Issue of *Latino Studies* 15 (2017).
Bladow, Kyle. "Timely Objects and the Revolutionary Formerly Known as Marcos: Rereading *Almanac of the Dead*." *Studies in American Indian Literatures* 29, no. 2 (Summer 2017): 1–25.
Blanco, John D. "Bastards of the Unfinished Revolution: Bolívar's Ismael and Rizal's Martí at the End of the Nineteenth Century." In *Imagining Our Americas: Toward a Transnational Frame*, edited by Sandhya Shukla and Heidi Tinsman, 63–87. Durham, N.C.: Duke University Press, 2007.
Bonetti, Kay. "An Interview with Jessica Hagedorn." *Missouri Review* 18, no. 1 (1995) 89–114.
Bonner, Raymond. *Waltzing with a Dictator: The Marcoses and the Making of American Policy*. New York: Times, 1987.

Boutelle, R. J. "'Great Still in Death': Race, Martyrology, and the Reanimation of Juan Placido." *American Literature* 90, no. 3 (September 2018): 461–93.
Branche, Jerome. "Ennobling Savagery? Sentimentalism and the Subaltern in 'Sab.'" *Afro-Hispanic Review* 17, no. 2 (Fall 1998): 12–23.
Brands, H. W. *Bound to Empire: The United States and the Philippines*. Oxford: Oxford University Press, 1992.
Brittan, Jennifer C. "Martin R. Delany's Speculative Fiction and the Nineteenth-Century Economy of Slave Conspiracy." *Studies in American Fiction* 46, no. 1 (Spring 2019): 79–102.
Brickhouse, Anna. *Transamerican Literary Relations and the Nineteenth-Century Public Sphere*. Cambridge: Cambridge University Press, 2004.
Brown, Jeffrey. "Conversation: Esmeralda Santiago, Author of 'Conquistadora.'" *PBS News Hour*, August 12, 2011. https://www.pbs.org/newshour/arts/conversation-esmeralda-santiago-author-of-conquistadora. Accessed September 15, 2021.
Burns, Lucy Mae San Pablo. *Puro Arte: Filipinos on the Stages of Empire*. New York: NYU Press, 2012.
Bushnell, David. "Introduction." In *El Libertador: Writings of Simón Bolívar*, translated by Frederick H. Fornoff, xxvii–lii. Oxford: Oxford University Press, 2003.
Bustamante, Michael J. *Cuban Memory Wars: Retrospective Politics in Revolution and Exile*. Chapel Hill: University of North Carolina Press, 2021.
Caminero-Santangelo, Marta. "Contesting the Boundaries of 'Exile' in Latino/a Literature." *World Literature Today* 74, no. 3 (Summer 2000): 507–17.
———. *On Latinidad: U.S. Latino Literature and the Construction of Ethnicity*. Gainesville: University Press of Florida, 2009.
Caminero-Santangelo, Marta, and Roy C. Boland Osegueda, eds. *Trujillo, Trauma, Testimony: Mario Vargas Llosa, Julia Alvarez, Edwidge Danticat, Junot Díaz and Other Writers in Hispaniola*. Special issue of *Antípodas* 20 (2009).
Campilongo, Xiomara. "A 'Chino' in Cuba: Cristina García's *Monkey Hunting*." In *Alternative Orientalisms in Latin America and Beyond*, edited by Ignacio López-Calvo, 113–23. Newcastle upon Tyne: Cambridge Scholars, 2007.
Campomanes, Oscar V. "Filipinos in the United States and Their Literature of Exile." In *Reading the Literatures of Asian America*, edited by Shirley Lim and Amy Ling, 49–78. Philadelphia: Temple University Press, 1992.
———. "The New Empire's Forgetful and Forgotten Citizens: Unrepresentability and Unassimilability in Filipino-American Postcolonialities." *Critical Mass: A Journal of Asian American Cultural Criticism* 2, no. 2 (Spring 1995): 145–200.
———. "New Formations of Asian American Studies and the Question of U.S. Imperialism." *Positions* 5, no. 2 (Fall 1997): 523–50.
Caronan, Faye C. "Colonial Consumption and Colonial Hierarchies in Representations of Philippine and Puerto Rican Tourism." *Philippine Studies* 53, no. 1 (2005): 32–58.

Carpentier, Alejo. "On the Marvelous Real in America." In *Magical Realism: Theory, History, Community*, edited by Lois Parkinson Zamora and Wendy B. Faris, 75–108. Durham, N.C.: Duke University Press, 1995.
Casper, Leonard. "Four Filipina Writers: Recultivating Eden." *Amerasia Journal* 24, no. 3 (1998): 143–59.
———. "Minoring in History: Rosca as Ninotchka." *Amerasia* 16, no. 2 (1990): 201–10.
Cass, Jeremy L. "Deciphering Sedition in *Sab*: Avellaneda's Transient Engagement with Abolitionism." *Romance Quarterly* 57 (2010): 183–204.
Cassara, Joseph. *The House of Impossible Beauties*. New York: Ecco, 2018.
Castiglia, Christopher. *Bound and Determined: Captivity, Culture-Crossing, and White Womanhood from Mary Rowlandson to Patty Hearst*. Chicago: University of Chicago Press, 1996.
Chang, Juliana. "Masquerade, Hysteria, and Neocolonial Femininity in Jessica Hagedorn's *Dogeaters*." *Contemporary Literature* 44, no. 4 (2003): 637–63.
Chiles, Katy. "Within and without Raced Nations: Intratextuality, Martin Delany, and *Blake; or the Huts of America*." *American Literature* 80, no. 2 (June 2008): 323–52.
Cho, Yu-Fang. "Reimagining 'Tense and Tender Ties' in García's *Monkey Hunting*." *CLCWeb: Comparative Literature and Culture* 14, no. 5 (2012): 1–9.
Chuh, Kandice. *Imagine Otherwise: On Asian Americanist Critique*. Durham, N.C.: Duke University Press, 2003.
Cisneros, Sandra. *Caramelo*. New York: Vintage, 2002.
Clealand. Danielle Pilar. *The Power of Race in Cuba: Racial Ideology and Black Consciousness during the Revolution*. Oxford: Oxford University Press, 2017.
Clover, Joshua. "*Retcon*: Value and Temporality in Poetics." *Representations* 126, no. 1 (2014): 9–30.
Collier, George A., and Elizabeth Lowery Quaratiello. *Basta! Land and the Zapatista Rebellion in Chiapas*. 3rd ed., Oakland, Calif.: Food First, 2005.
Commander, Michelle D. *Afro-Atlantic Flight: Speculative Returns and the Black Fantastic*. Durham, N.C.: Duke University Press, 2017.
Cook-Lynn. Elizabeth. "American Indian Intellectualism and the New Indian Story." *Writing about (Writing about) American Indians*. Special issue of *American Indian Quarterly* 20, no. 1 (Winter 1996): 57–76.
Cornejo Villavicencio, Karla. *The Undocumented Americans*. New York: One World, 2020.
Coronado, Raúl. *A World Not to Come: A History of Latino Writing and Print Culture*. Cambridge, Mass.: Harvard University Press, 2016.
Cotera, María Eugenia, and María Josefina Saldaña-Portillo. "Indigenous but Not Indian? Chicanas/os and the Politics of Indigeneity." In *The World of Indigenous North America*, edited by Robert Warrior, 549–68. New York: Routledge, 2015.
Cox, Sandra. "The Trujillato and Testimonial Fiction: Collective Memory, Cultural Trauma and National Identity in Edwidge Danticat's *The Farming of Bones* and

Junot Díaz's *The Brief Wondrous Life of Oscar Wao*." *Trujillo, Trauma, Testimony: Mario Vargas Llosa, Julia Alvarez, Edwidge Danticat, Junot Díaz and Other Writers in Hispaniola*. Special issue of *Antípodas* 20 (2009): 107–26.

Cruz, Denise. *Transpacific Femininities: The Making of the Modern Filipina*. Durham, N.C.: Duke University Press, 2012.

Dalleo, Raphael, and Elena Machado Sáez. *The Latino/a Canon and the Emergence of Post-Sixties Literature*. New York: Palgrave Macmillan, 2007.

Davis, Andrea. *Horizon, Sea, Sound: Caribbean and African Women's Cultural Critiques of Nation*. Evanston, Ill.: Northwestern University Press, 2022.

Davis, Charles T., and Henry Louis Gates Jr. *The Slave's Narrative*. Oxford: Oxford University Press, 1985.

Davis, Rocio G. "Postcolonial Visions and Immigrant Longings: Ninotchka Rosca's Versions of the Philippines." *World Literature Today* 73, no. 1 (1999): 62–70.

Dayan, Colin. *Haiti, History, and the Gods*. Berkeley: University of California Press, 1995.

DeFronzo, James. *Revolutions and Revolutionary Movements*. 5th ed. Boulder: Westview Press, 2015.

Delany, Martin. R. "Annexation of Cuba." In *Martin R. Delany: A Documentary Reader*, edited by Robert S. Levine, 160–66. University of North Carolina Press, 2003.

———. *Blake; or, the Huts of America*. Cambridge, Mass.: Harvard University Press, 2017.

———. *The Condition, Elevation, Emigration and Destiny of the Colored People of the United States*. In *Martin R. Delany: A Documentary Reader*, edited by Robert S. Levine, 189–216. Chapel Hill: University of North Carolina Press, 2003.

———. *Official Report of the Niger Valley Exploring Party*. In *Martin R. Delany; A Documentary Reader*, edited by Robert S. Levine, 336–57. Chapel Hill: University of North Carolina Press, 2003.

Delmendo, Sharon. *The Star-Entangled Banner: One Hundred Years of America in the Philippines*. New Brunswick, N.J.: Rutgers University Press, 2004.

Derby, Robin (Lauren). "The Dictator's Seduction: Gender and State Spectacle during the Trujillo Regime." *Callaloo* 23, no. 2 (2000): 1112–46.

———. *The Dictator's Seduction: Politics and the Popular Imagination in the Era of Trujillo*. Durham, N.C.: Duke University Press, 2009.

———. "Haitians, Magic, and Money: Raza and Society in the Haitian-Dominican Borderlands, 1900-1937." *Comparative Studies in Society and History* 36, no. 3 (July 1994): 488–526.

Derrida, Jacques. *Edmund Husserl's Origin of Geometry: An Introduction*. Lincoln: University of Nebraska Press, 1989.

———. *The Politics of Friendship*. London and New York: Verso, 1997.

Derrida, Jacques, and Elisabeth Roudinesco. *For What Tomorrow . . .: A Dialogue*. Translated by Jeff Fort. Stanford, Calif.: Stanford University Press, 2004.

Derounian, Kathryn Zabelle. "The Publication, Promotion, and Distribution of

Mary Rowlandson's Indian Captivity Narrative in the Seventeenth Century." *Early American Literature*, 23, no. 3 (1988): 239–61.
Derounian-Stodola, Kathryn Zabelle. "The Indian Captivity Narratives of Mary Rowlandson and Olive Oatman: Case Studies in the Continuity, Evolution, and Exploitation of Literary Discourse." *Studies in the Literary Imagination* 27, no. 1 (1994): 33–46.
Díaz, Jaquira. *Ordinary Girls: A Memoir*. Chapel Hill, N.C.: Algonquin Books of Chapel Hill, 2019.
Díaz, Junot. *The Brief Wondrous Life of Oscar Wao*. New York: Riverhead, 2007.
———. "The Brief Wondrous Life of Oscar Wao (Excerpt)." Genius. https://genius.com/Junot-diaz-the-brief-wondrous-life-of-oscar-wao-excerpt-annotated. Accessed November 11, 2021.
———. *Drown*. New York: Riverhead, 1996.
———. "The Silence: The Legacy of Childhood Trauma." *The New Yorker*, April 9, 2018. https://www.newyorker.com/magazine/2018/04/16/the-silence-the-legacy-of-childhood-trauma. Accessed November 11, 2021.
———. *This Is How You Lose Her*. New York: Riverhead, 2012.
Dizon, Alma Jill. "Rizal's Novels: A Divergence from Melodrama." *Philippine Studies* 44, no. 3 (1996): 412–26.
Doolen, Andy. "'Be Cautious of the Word "Rebel"': Race, Revolution, and Transnational History in Martin Delany's *Blake; or, The Huts of America*." *American Literature* 81, no. 1 (March 2009): 153–79.
Dussel, Enrique. *The Invention of the Americas: Eclipse of the Other and the Myth of Modernity*. Translated by Michael D. Barber. New York: Continuum, 1995.
Echevarria, Roberto Gonzalez. *The Voice of the Masters: Writing and Authority in Modern Latin American Literature*. Austin: University of Texas Press, 1985.
Edelman, Lee. *No Future: Queer Theory and the Death Drive*. Durham, N.C.: Duke University Press, 2005.
Edwards, Erica. *Charisma and the Fictions of Black Leadership*. Minneapolis: University of Minnesota Press, 2012.
Edwards, Gareth, dir. *Rogue One: A Star Wars Story*. Lucasfilm, 2016.
Eller, Anne. *We Dream Together: Dominican Independence, Haiti, and the Fight for Caribbean Freedom*. Durham, N.C.: Duke University Press, 2016.
Eng, David, Jack Halberstam, and José Esteban Muñoz. "What's Queer About Queer Studies Now?" *Social Text* 23, nos. 3–4 (2005): 1–17.
Esty, Jed. *Unseasonable Youth: Modernism, Colonialism, and the Fiction of Development*. Oxford: Oxford University Press, 2012.
Evangelista, Susan. "Jessica Hagedorn and Manila Magic." *MELUS* 18, no. 4 (1993): 41–52.
Feal, Rosemary Geisdorfer. "Spanish American Ethnobiography and the Slave Narrative Tradition: 'Biografía de un cimarrón' and 'Me llamo Rigoberta Menchú.'" *Modern Language Studies* 20, no. 1 (1990): 100–111.

Ferrer, Ada. *Insurgent Cuba: Race, Nation, and Revolution, 1868–1898*. Chapel Hill: University of North Carolina Press, 1999.

———. "The Silence of Patriots: Race and Nationalism in Martí's Cuba." In *José Martí's "Our America": From National to Hemispheric Cultural Studies*, edited by Jeffrey Belnap and Raúl Fernández, 228–49. Durham, N.C.: Duke University Press, 1998.

Finch, Aisha. *Rethinking Slave Rebellion in Cuba: La Escalera and the Insurgencies of 1841–1844*. Chapel Hill: University of North Carolina Press, 2015.

Fischer-Hornung, Dorothea. "'Now We Know That Gay Men Are Just Men After All': Abject Sexualities in Leslie Marmon Silko's *Almanac of the Dead*." In *The Abject of Desire: The Aestheticization of the Unaesthetic in Contemporary Literature and Culture*, edited by Konstanze Kutzbach and Monika Mueller, 107–27. Amsterdam: Rodopi, 2007.

Fisher, Beth. "The Captive Mexicana and the Desiring Bourgeois Woman: Domesticity and Expansionism in Ruiz de Burton's *Who Would Have Thought It?*" *Legacy* 16, no. 1 (1999): 59–69.

Fishkin, Shelley Fisher. "The Crossroads of Culture: The Transnational Turn in American Studies—Presidential Address to the American Studies Association." *American Quarterly* 57, no. 1 (2005): 17–57.

Flaubert, Gustave. *Sentimental Education*. London and New York: Penguin, 2004.

Flores, Tatiana. "Latinidad Is Cancelled: Confronting an Anti-Black Construct." *Latin American and Latinx Visual Culture* 3, no. 3 (July 2021): 58–79.

Flores-Rodríguez, Daynali. "Addressing the Fukú in Us: Junot Díaz and the New Novel of Dictatorship." *Trujillo, Trauma, Testimony: Mario Vargas Llosa, Julia Alvarez, Edwidge Danticat, Junot Díaz and Other Writers in Hispaniola*. Special issue, edited by Marta Caminero-Santangelo and Roy C. Boland Osegueda. *Antípodas* 20 (2009): 91–106.

Foran, John. *Taking Power: On the Origins of Third World Revolutions*. Cambridge: Cambridge University Press, 2005.

———, ed. *Theorizing Revolutions*. London and New York: Routledge, 1997.

Freeman, Elizabeth. *Time Binds: Queer Temporalities, Queer Histories*. Durham, N.C.: Duke University Press, 2010.

Freire, Paolo. *Pedagogy of the Oppressed*. London and New York: Bloomsbury Academic, 2014.

Friedenthal, Andrew J. *Retcon Game: Retroactive Continuity and the Hyperlinking of America*. Jackson: University Press of Mississippi, 2017.

Gairola, Rahul K. "Deterritorialisations of Desire: 'Transgressive' Sexuality as Filipino Anti-Imperialist Resistance in Jessica Hagedorn's *Dogeaters*." *Philament* 7 (2005): 22–41.

Galíndez, Jesús de. "A Report on Santo Domingo." In *Dictatorship in Spanish America*, edited by Hugh M. Hamill, 174–87. New York: Knopf, 1965.

Gamalinda, Eric. *The Empire of Memory*. Manila: Anvil, 1992.

García, Cristina. *King of Cuba: A Novel*. New York: Scribner, 2013.

———. *The Lady Matador's Hotel.* New York: Scribner, 2010.
———. *Monkey Hunting.* New York: Ballantine, 2003.
García, Emily. "On the Borders of Independence: Manuel Torres and Spanish American Independence in Filadelphia." In *The Latino Nineteenth Century*, edited by Rodrigo Lazo and Jesse Alemán, 71–89. New York: NYU Press, 2016.
García Márquez, Gabriel. *The Autumn of the Patriarch.* New York: Harper & Row, 1975.
García Peña, Lorgia. *The Borders of Dominicanidad: Race, Nation, and Archives of Contradiction.* Durham, N.C.: Duke University Press, 2016.
———. *Translating Blackness: Latinx Colonialities in Global Perspective.* Durham, N.C.: Duke University Press, 2022.
Garza, Ernesto. *Barrio Boy.* Notre Dame, Ind.: University of Notre Dame Press, 2011.
Gasché, Rodolphe. "Piercing the Horizon." *Journal of French Philosophy* 17, no. 2 (2007): 1–12.
Gibby, Kristina S. "Ghostly Narrators in Zoé Valdés's *Te di la vida entera* and Sandra Cisneros's *Caramelo: or Puro Cuento*." *Chiricú Journal* 2, no. 1 (2018): 83–100.
Gil'Adí, Maia. "'I Think about You, X—': Re-Reading Junot Díaz after 'The Silence.'" *Latino Studies* 18 (2020): 507–30.
Gilroy, Paul. *The Black Atlantic: Modernity and Double Consciousness.* Cambridge, Mass.: Harvard University Press, 1993.
Goldman, Anne E. "'Who Ever Heard of a Blue-Eyed Mexican?': Satire and Sentimentality in María Amparo Ruiz de Burton's *Who Would Have Thought It?*" In *Recovering the U.S. Hispanic Literary Heritage*, edited by Erlinda Gonzales-Berry and Charles Tatum, 2:59–78. Houston: Arte Público, 1995.
Goldstone, Jack A. *Revolutions: Theoretical, Comparative, and Historical Studies.* 3rd ed. Independence, Ky.: Cengage Learning, 2002.
———. "Theories of Revolution: The Third Generation." *World Politics* 32, no. 3 (1980): 425–53.
Gomariz, José. "Gertrudis Gómez de Avellaneda y la intelectualidad reformista cubana: Raza, blanqueamiento e identidad cultural en 'Sab.'" *Caribbean Studies* 37, no. 1 (January–June 2009): 97–118.
Gómez, Alan Eladio. *The Revolutionary Imagination of Greater Mexico: Chicana/o Radicalism, Solidarity Politics, and Latin American Social Movements.* Austin: University of Texas Press, 2016.
Gómez, Laura E. *Manifest Destinies: The Making of the Mexican American Race.* 2nd ed. New York: NYU Press, 2018.
Goni, Uki. *The Real Odessa: How Perón Brought the Nazi War Criminals to Argentina.* London and New York: Granta, 2003.
González, John M. "Romancing Hegemony: Constructing Racialized Citizenship in María Amparo Ruiz de Burton's *The Squatter and the Don*." In *Recovering the U.S. Hispanic Literary Heritage*, edited by Erlinda Gonzales-Berry and Chuck Tatum, 2:23–39. Houston: Arte Público, 1996.
Gonzalez, Rodolfo. "I Am Joaquín" (1967). In *Literatura Chicana, 1965–1995: An Anthology in Spanish, English, and Caló*, edited by Manuel de Jesús

Hernández-Gutiérrez and David William Foster, 207–22. New York and London: Garland, 1997.

Gonzalez, Xochitl. *Olga Dies Dreaming*. New York: Flatiron, 2021.

Goodwin, Jeff. "State-Centered Approaches to Social Revolutions: Strengths and Limitations of a Theoretical Tradition." In *Theorizing Revolutions*, edited by John Foran, 9–35. London and New York: Routledge, 1997.

Gordy, Katherine A. "No Better Way to Be Latin American: European Science and Thought, Latin American Theory?" *Postcolonial Studies* 16, no. 4 (2013): 358–73.

Goyal, Yogita. *Runaway Genres: The Global Afterlives of Slavery*. New York: NYU Press, 2019.

Graulund, Rune. "Generous Exclusion: Register and Readership in Junot Díaz's *The Brief Wondrous Life of Oscar Wao*." *MELUS* 39, no. 3 (Fall 2014): 31–48.

Gruesz, Kirsten Silva. *Ambassadors of Culture: The Transamerican Origins of Latino Writing*. Princeton, N.J.: Princeton University Press, 2001.

———. "The Errant Latino: Irisarri, Central Americanness, and Migration's Intention." In *The Latino Nineteenth Century*, edited by Rodrigo Lazo and Jesse Alemán, 20–48. New York: NYU Press, 2016.

———. "The Once and Future Latino: Notes Toward a Literary History *todavía para llegar*." In *Contemporary U.S. Latino/a Literary Criticism*, edited by Lyn Di Iorio Sandín and Richard Perez, 115–42. New York: Palgrave Macmillan, 2007.

Guerra, Lucía. "Estrategias Femeninas en la Elaboración del Sujeto Romántico en la Obra de Gertrudis Gómez de Avellaneda." *Revista Iberoamericana* 51, no. 132 (April 1985): 707–22.

Gugelberger, George M., ed. *The Real Thing: Testimonial Discourse and Latin America*. Durham, N.C.: Duke University Press, 1996.

Guidotti-Hernández, Nicole M. "Affective Communities and Millennial Desires: Latinx, or Why My Computer Won't Recognize Latina/o." *Cultural Dynamics* 29, no. 3 (2017): 141–59.

Hagedorn, Jessica. *Dogeaters*. New York: Penguin, 1990.

———. "The Exile Within/The Question of Identity." In *The State of Asian America: Activism and Resistance in the 1990s*, edited by Karin Aguilar-San Juan, 173–82. Boston: South End, 1994.

Hagimoto, Koichi. *Between Empires: Martí, Rizal, and the Intercolonial Alliance*. New York: Palgrave Macmillan, 2013.

Halberstam, Jack. *In a Queer Time and Place: Transgender Bodies, Subcultural Lives*. New York: NYU Press, 2005.

———. *The Queer Art of Failure*. Durham, N.C.: Duke University Press, 2011.

Hamill, Hugh M., ed. *Dictatorship in Spanish America*. New York: Knopf, 1965.

Hanna, Monica. "A Portrait of the Artist as a Young Cannibalist: Reading Yunior (Writing) in *The Brief Wondrous Life of Oscar Wao*." In *The Brief Wondrous Life of Oscar Wao: Junot Díaz and the Decolonial Imagination*, edited by Monica

Hanna, Jennifer Harford Vargas, and José David Saldívar, 89–111. Durham, N.C.: Duke University Press.

———. "'Reassembling the Fragments': Battling Historiographies, Caribbean Discourse, and Nerd Genres in Junot Díaz's *The Brief Wondrous Life of Oscar Wao*." *Callaloo* 33, no. 2 (Spring 2010): 498–520.

Harford Vargas, Jennifer. "Dictating a Zafa: The Power of Narrative Form in Junot Díaz's *The Brief Wondrous Life of Oscar Wao*." *MELUS* 39, no. 3 (2014): 8–30.

———. *Forms of Dictatorship: Power, Narrative, and Authoritarianism in the Latina/o Novel*. Oxford: Oxford University Press, 2017.

———. "Novel Testimony: Alternative Archives in Edwidge Danticat's *The Farming of Bones*." *Callaloo* 37, no. 5 (Fall 2014): 1162–80.

Harris, Cheryl. "Whiteness as Property." *Harvard Law Review* 106, no. 8 (1993): 1707–91.

Harrison, Rebecca L., and Emily Hipchen, eds. *Inhabiting La Patria: Identity, Agency, and Antojo in the Work of Julia Alvarez*. Albany: SUNY Press, 2013.

Harvard, John C. "Mary Peabody Mann's *Juanita* and Martin R. Delany's *Blake*: Cuba, Urban Slavery, and the Construction of Nation." *College Literature* 43, no. 3 (Summer 2016): 509–40.

Hau, Caroline S. "*Dogeaters*, Postmodernism and the 'Worlding' of the Philippines." In *Philippine Post-Colonial Studies: Essays on Language and Literature*, edited by Cristina Pantoja-Hidalgo and Priscelina Patajo-Legato, 113–27. Quezon City: University of the Philippines Press, 1993.

———. *Necessary Fictions: Philippine Literature and the Nation, 1946–1980*. Manila: Ateneo de Manila University Press, 2000.

———. *On the Subject of the Nation: Filipino Writings from the Margins, 1981–2004*. Quezon City: Ateneo de Manila University Press, 2004.

Herrera, Juan Felipe. *Akrílica*. Noemi Press, 2022.

———. *Akrílica*. Santa Cruz, Calif.: Alcatraz Editions, 1989.

Hickman, Trenton. "Hagiographic Commemorafiction in Julia Alvarez's *In the Time of the Butterflies* and *Salomé*." *MELUS* 31, no. 1 (Spring 2006): 99–121.

Ho, Jennifer Ann. "The Place of Transgressive Texts in Asian American Epistemology." *MFS: Modern Fiction Studies* 56, no. 1 (Spring 2010): 205–25.

Holland, Sharon P. "'If You Know I Have a History, You Will Respect Me': A Perspective on Afro-Native American Literature." *Callaloo* 17, no. 1 (Winter 1994): 334–50.

Hooker, Juliet. *Theorizing Race in the Americas: Douglass, Sarmiento, Du Bois, and Vasconcelos*. Oxford: Oxford University Press, 2019.

Horn, Maja. *Masculinity after Trujillo: The Politics of Gender in Dominican Literature*. Gainesville: University Press of Florida, 2014.

Horne, Gerald. *The Counter-Revolution of 1776: Slave Resistance and the Origins of the United States of America*. New York: NYU Press, 2014.

Horvitz, Deborah. "Freud, Marx and Chiapas in Leslie Marmon Silko's *Almanac of the Dead*." *Studies in American Indian Literature* 10, no. 3 (Fall 1998): 47–64.

Hu-DeHart, Evelyn. "Latin America in Asia-Pacific Perspective." In *What Is in A Rim? Critical Perspectives on the Pacific Region Idea*, edited by Arif Dirlik, 251–78. Boulder: Westview, 1993.

———. "Race Construction and Race Relations: Chinese and Blacks in Nineteenth-Century Cuba." In *Alternative Orientalisms in Latin America and Beyond*, edited by Ignacio López-Calvo, 82–94. Newcastle upon Tyne: Cambridge Scholars, 2007.

Hudson, Renee. "Guerrilla Conversions in Jessica Hagedorn and José Rizal: The Queer Future of National Romance." *MFS: Modern Fiction Studies* 62, no. 2 (Summer 2016): 330–49.

Huhndorf, Shari M. "Picture Revolution: 'Tribal Internationalism' and the Future of the Americas in Leslie Marmon Silko's *Almanac of the Dead*." In *Mapping the Americas: The Transnational Politics of Contemporary Native Culture*, 140–71. Ithaca, N.Y.: Cornell University Press, 2009.

Ibarra, Rogelia Lily. "Gómez de Avellaneda's *Sab*: A Modernizing Project." *Hispania* 94, no. 3 (September 2011): 385–95.

Igartuburu García, Elena. "Too Chinese/Too Cuban: Emotional Maps and the Quest for Happiness in Cristina García's *Monkey Hunting*." In *Diasporic Constructions of Home and Belonging*, edited by Florian Kläger and Klaus Stierstorfer, 447–63. Berlin: De Gruyter, 2015.

Ileto, Reynaldo Clemeña. *Pasyon and Revolution: Popular Movements in the Philippines, 1840–1910*. Quezon City: Ateneo de Manila University Press, 1979.

Irizarry, Ylce. *Chicana/o and Latina/o Fiction: The New Memory of Latinidad*. Urbana: University of Illinois Press, 2016.

Irwin, Robert McKee. "Almost-Latino Literature: Approaching Truncated Latinidades." In *The Latino Nineteenth Century*, edited by Rodrigo Lazo and Jesse Alemán, 110–23. New York: NYU Press, 2016.

Jacobs, Margaret D. "Mixed-Bloods, Mestizas, and Pintos: Race, Gender, and Claims to Whiteness in Helen Hunt Jackson's 'Ramona' and María Amparo Ruiz de Burton's 'Who Would Have Thought It?'" *Western American Literature* 36, no. 3 (2001): 212–31.

Jameson, Fredric. *The Political Unconscious: Narrative as a Socially Symbolic Act*. Ithaca, N.Y.: Cornell University Press, 1981.

Jerng, Mark C. *Racial Worldmaking: The Power of Popular Fiction*. New York: Fordham University Press, 2017.

Jiménez Román, Miriam, and Juan Flores, eds. *The Afro-Latin@ Reader: History and Culture in the United States*. Durham, N.C.: Duke University Press, 2010.

Joaquin, Nick. *The Aquinos of Tarlac: An Essay on History as Three Generations*. Metro Manila: Cacho Hermanos, 1983.

John W. Kluge Center at the Library of Congress. "How Mexican Immigration to the U.S. Has Evolved." *Time*, March 12, 2015. https://time.com/3742067/history-mexican-immigration/. Accessed July 30, 2021.

Johnson, Amanda Walker. "Silko's *Almanac*: Engaging Marx and the Critique of Capitalism." In *Howling for Justice: New Perspectives on Leslie Marmon Silko's Almanac of the Dead*, edited by Rebecca Tillett, 91–104. Tucson: University of Arizona Press, 2014.

Johnson, Kelli Lyon. *Julia Alvarez: Writing a New Place on the Map*. Albuquerque: University of New Mexico Press, 2005.

Kaplan, Amy. *The Anarchy of Empire in the Making of U.S. Culture*. Cambridge, Mass.: Harvard University Press, 2002.

Kelly, Edith L. "La Avellaneda's *Sab* and the Political Situation in Cuba." *Americas* 1, no. 3 (1945): 303–16.

Kenworthy, Eldon. *America/Américas: Myth in the Making of U.S. Policy toward Latin America*. University Park: Pennsylvania University Press, 1995.

King, Tiffany Lethabo. *The Black Shoals: Offshore Formations of Black and Native Studies*. Durham, N.C.: Duke University Press, 2019.

Kirkpatrick, Susan. "Gómez de Avellaneda's *Sab*: Gendering the Liberal Romantic Subject." In *In the Feminine Mode: Essays on Hispanic Women Writers*, edited by Noel Maureen Valis and Carol Maier, 115–30. Lewisburg, Pa.: Bucknell University Press, 1990.

——. *Las Románticas: Women Writers and Subjectivity in Spain, 1835–1850*. Berkeley: University of California Press, 1989.

Koselleck, Reinhart. *Futures Past: On the Semantics of Historical Time*. Translated by Keith Tribe. Cambridge, Mass.: MIT Press, 1985.

——. *The Practice of Conceptual History: Timing History, Spacing Concepts*. Translated by Todd Samuel Presner. Stanford, Calif.: Stanford University Press, 2002.

Krakow, Stanley. *In Our Image: America's Empire in the Philippines*. New York: Random House, 1989.

Krupat, Arnold. *Red Matters: Native American Studies*. Philadelphia: University of Pennsylvania Press, 2002.

Kuhn, Helmut. "The Phenomenological Concept of 'Horizon.'" In *Philosophical Essays in Memory of Edmund Husserl*, edited by Marvin Farber, 3rd ed., 106–23. Cambridge, Mass.: Harvard University Press, 2014.

Lamas, Carmen. *The Latino Continuum and the Nineteenth-Century Americas: Literature, Translation, and Historiography*. Oxford: Oxford University Press, 2021.

Laurel, R. Kwan. "A Hundred Years after the Noli: The Three Centennial Novels in English." *Philippines Studies* 51, no. 4 (2003): 599–643.

Lazo, Rodrigo. "Los Filibusteros: Cuban Writers in the United States and Deterritorialized Print Culture." *American Literary History* 15, no. 1 (Spring 2003): 87–106.

——. *Writing to Cuba: Filibustering and Cuban Exiles in the United States*. Chapel Hill: University of North Carolina Press, 2005.

Lazo, Rodrigo, and Jesse Alemán, eds. *The Latino Nineteenth Century*. New York: NYU Press, 2016.

Lee, Jade Tsui-yu. "(Im)migration and Cultural Diasporization in García's *Monkey Hunting*." In *Perspectives on Identity, Migration, and Displacement*, edited by Steven Tötösy de Zepetnek, I-Chun Wang, and Hsiao-Yu Sun, 127–38. Kaohsiung: National Sun Yat-sen University, 2010.

Lee, Rachel. *The Americas of Asian American Literature: Gendered Fictions of Nation and Transnation*. Princeton, N.J.: Princeton University Press, 1999.

Le-Khac, Long. *Giving Form to an Asian and Latinx America*. Stanford, Calif.: Stanford University Press, 2020.

Levander, Caroline F., and Robert S. Levine, eds. *Hemispheric American Studies*. Brunswick, N.J.: Rutgers University Press, 2008.

Levine, Robert S., ed. *Martin R. Delany: A Documentary Reader*. Chapel Hill: University of North Carolina Press, 2003.

——. *Martin Delany, Frederick Douglass, and the Politics of Representative Identity*. Chapel Hill: University of North Carolina Press, 1997.

Leving Jacobson, Jenna. "Nation, Violence, Memory: Interrupting the Foundational Discourse in Sab." *Hispanic Issues Series* 18 (2017): 173–91.

Lifshey, Adam. "Indeterminancy and the Subversive in Representations of the Trujillato." *Hispanic Review* 76, no. 4 (2008): 435–57.

——. "The Literary Alterities of Philippine Nationalism in José Rizal's *El Filibusterismo*." *PMLA* 123, no. 5 (2008): 1434–47.

Lim, Shirley Geok-lin, and Amy Ling, eds. *Reading the Literatures of Asian America*. Philadelphia: Temple University Press, 1992.

Lima, Lazaro. *Being Brown: Sonia Sotomayor and the Latino Question*. Berkeley: University of California, 2019.

Livingston, Jennie, dir. *Paris Is Burning: A Conversation*. Criterion Collection, 1990.

López, Antonio. *Unbecoming Blackness: The Diaspora Cultures of Afro-Cuban America*. New York: NYU Press, 2012.

López, Iraida H. "'. . . And There Is Only My Imagination Where Our History Should Be': An Interview with Cristina García." *Michigan Quarterly* 33, no. 3 (1994): 605–17.

López, Marissa K. *Chicano Nations: The Hemispheric Origins of Mexican American Literature*. New York: NYU Press, 2011.

López-Calvo, Ignacio, ed. *Alternative Orientalisms in Latin America and Beyond*. Newcastle upon Tyne: Cambridge Scholars, 2007.

——. "Chinesism and the Commodification of Chinese Cuban Culture." In *Alternative Orientalisms in Latin America and Beyond*, edited by Ignacio López-Calvo, 95–112. Newcastle upon Tyne: Cambridge Scholars, 2007.

——. *God and Trujillo: Literary and Cultural Representations of the Dominican Dictator*. Gainesville: University Press of Florida, 2005.

——. *Imagining the Chinese in Cuban Literature and Culture*. Gainesville: University Press of Florida, 2005.

——. "A Postmodern Plátano's Trujillo: Junot Díaz's *The Brief Wondrous Life of Oscar Wao*, More Macondo than McOndo." In *Trujillo, Trauma, Testimony*:

Mario Vargas Llosa, Julia Alvarez, Edwidge Danticat, Junot Díaz and Other Writers in Hispaniola. Special issue. *Antípodas* 20 (2009): 75–90.
Lowe, Lisa. "Heterogeneity, Hybridity, Multiplicity: Marking Asian American Differences." *Diaspora: A Journal of Transnational Studies* 1, no. 1 (Spring 1991): 24–44.
———. *Immigrant Acts: On Asian American Cultural Politics*. Durham, N.C.: Duke University Press, 1996.
———. *The Intimacies of Four Continents*. Durham, N.C.: Duke University Press, 2015.
Luis, William. *Literary Bondage: Slavery in Cuban Narrative*. Austin: University of Texas Press, 1990.
———. "The Politics of Memory and Miguel Barnet's *The Autobiography of a Run Away Slave*." *MLN* 104, no. 2 (1989): 475–91.
Lusane, Clarence. "From Black Cuban to Afro-Cuban: Researching Race in Cuba." *Souls* 1, no. 2 (Spring 1999): 73–79.
Lye, Colleen. "Racial Form." *Representations* 104, no. 1 (Fall 2008): 92–101.
Lynch, John. *The Spanish American Revolutions: 1808–1826*. 2nd ed. New York: W. W. Norton, 1986.
Lysik, Marta. "Multiple Trajectories of Slavery: Cristina García's *Monkey Hunting* as a Transnational Neo-Slave Narrative." In *Revisiting Slave Narratives II: Les Avatars contemporains des récits d'esclaves II*, edited by Judith Misrahi-Barak, 275–95. Montpellier: Presses universitaires de la Méditerranée, 2007.
Machado Sáez, Elena. "Dictating Desire, Dictating Diaspora: Junot Díaz's *The Brief Wondrous Life of Oscar Wao* as Foundational Romance." *Contemporary Literature* 52, no. 3 (2011): 522–55.
———. *Market Aesthetics: The Purchase of the Past in Caribbean Diasporic Fiction*. Charlottesville: University of Virginia Press, 2015.
Madera, Judith. *Black Atlas: Geography and Flow in Nineteenth-Century African American Literature*. Durham, N.C.: Duke University Press, 2015.
Maleuvre, Didier. *The Horizon: A History of Our Infinite Longing*. Berkeley: University of California Press, 2011.
Manuel, Dolores de. "Decolonizing Bodies, Reinscribing Souls in the Fiction of Ninotchka Rosca and Lynda Ty-Casper." *MELUS* 29, no. 1 (2004): 99–118.
———. "Marriage in Philippine-American Fiction." *Philippine Studies* 42, no. 2 (1994): 210–16.
Marez, Curtis. *Farm Worker Futurism: Speculative Technologies of Resistance*. Minneapolis: University of Minnesota Press, 2016.
Martí, José. *Ismaelillo*. 1882. Translated by Tyler Fisher. Chicago: Wings Press, 2007.
———. *José Martí Reader: Writings on the Americas*. New York: Ocean Press, 2006.
———. *Selected Writings*. New York: Penguin Classics, 2002.
Martínez, Manuel. "Chinese-Cuban Identity in Cristina García's *Monkey Hunting* and Daína Chaviano's *La isla de los amores infinitos*." *Caribe: Revista de Cultura y Literatura* 10, no. 2 (2007): 95–112.

Marx, Karl. *Surveys from Exile: Political Writings*. London and New York: Verso, 2010.

Matibag, Eugenio. "'El Verbo del Filibusterismo': Narrative Ruses in the Novels of José Rizal." *Revista Hispánica Moderna* 48, no. 2 (1995): 250–64.

Mayes, April J. *The Mulatto Republic: Class, Race, and Dominican National Identity*. Gainesville: University Press of Florida, 2014.

———. "Why Dominican Feminism Moved to the Right: Class, Colour and Women's Activism in the Dominican Republic 1880s-1940s." *Gender & History* 20, no. 2 (2008): 349–71.

McCoy, Alfred W. *An Anarchy of Families: State and Family in the Philippines*. Madison, Wisc.: Center for Southeast Asian Studies, 1993.

McCracken, Ellen. "Beyond Individualism: Collective Narration, History, and the Autobiographical Simulacrum." In *New Latina Narrative: The Feminine Space of Postmodern Ethnicity*, 65–94. Tucson: University of Arizona Press, 1999.

———. *New Latina Narrative: The Feminine Space of Postmodern Ethnicity*. Tucson: University of Arizona Press, 1999.

———. "Postmodern Ethnicity in Sandra Cisneros' *Caramelo*: Hybridity, Spectacle, and Memory in the Nomadic Text. *Journal of American Studies in Turkey* 12 (2000): 3–12.

McCullough, Kate. *Regions of Identity: The Construction of America in Women's Fiction, 1885–1914*. Stanford, Calif.: Stanford University Press, 1999.

McGann, Jerome. "Introduction." In *Blake; or, the Huts of America*, by Martin R. Delany, ix–xxxii. Cambridge, Mass.: Harvard University Press, 2017.

McHugh-Dillon, Ruth. "'Let Me Confess': Confession, Complicity, and #MeToo in Junot Díaz's *This Is How You Lose Her* and 'The Silence: The Legacy of Childhood Trauma.'" *MELUS* 46, no. 1 (Spring 2021): 24–50.

Menchaca, Martha. *Recovering History, Constructing Race: The Indian, Black, and White Roots of Mexican Americans*. Austin: University of Texas Press, 2002.

Menchú, Rigoberta. *I, Rigoberta Menchú*. London and New York: Verso, 2010.

Mendible, Myra. "Dictators, Movie Stars, and Martyrs: The Politics of Spectacle in Jessica Hagedorn's *Dogeaters*." *Genders* 36, no. 3 (2002). https://www.colorado.edu/gendersarchive1998-2013/2002/12/01/dictators-movie-stars-and-martyrs-politics-spectacle-jessica-hagedorns-dogeaters. Accessed November 11, 2021.

———. "The Politics and Poetics of Philippine Festival in Ninotchka Rosca's *State of War*." *International Fiction Review* 29, no. 1 (2002). https://journals.lib.unb.ca/index.php/IFR/article/view/7714. Accessed November 11, 2021.

Mendoza, Victor. "A Queer Nomadology of Jessica Hagedorn's *Dogeaters*." *American Literature* 77, no. 4 (2005): 815–45.

Mignolo, Walter D. *The Darker Side of Western Modernity: Global Futures, Decolonial Options*. Durham, N.C.: Duke University Press, 2011.

———. *The Idea of Latin America*. Malden, Mass., and Oxford: Blackwell, 2005.

"The Many Faces of Cosmo-polis: Border Thinking and Critical Cosmopolitanism." In *Cosmopolitanism*, edited by Carol A. Breckenridge, Sheldon Pollock, Homi K.

Bhabha, and Dipesh Chakrabarty, 157–88. Durham, N.C.: Duke University Press, 2002.

Milian, Claudia. *Latining America: Black-Brown Passages and the Coloring of Latino/a Studies.* Athens: University of Georgia Press, 2013.

———. *LatinX.* Minneapolis: University of Minnesota Press, 2019.

Miller, Stuart Creighton. *Benevolent Assimilation: The American Conquest of the Philippines, 1899–1903.* New Haven, Conn.: Yale University Press, 1982.

Moiles, Sean. "Search for Utopia, Desire for the Sublime: Cristina García's *Monkey Hunting.*" *MELUS* 34, no. 4 (2009): 167–86.

Mojares, Resil B. *Origins and Rise of the Filipino Novel: A Generic Study of the Novel until 1940.* Quezon City: University of the Philippines Press, 1998.

Molina, Natalie. "The Power of Racial Scripts: What the History of Mexican Immigration to the United States Teaches Us about the Relational Notions of Race." *Latino Studies* 8, no. 2 (2010): 156–75.

Montes, Amelia María de la Luz. "María Amparo Ruiz de Burton Negotiates American Literary Politics and Culture." In *Challenging Boundaries: Gender and Periodization*, edited by Joyce W. Warren and Margaret Dickie, 202–25. Athens: University of Georgia Press, 2000.

Montes, Amelia María de la Luz, and Anne Elizabeth Goldman. *María Amparo Ruiz de Burton: Critical and Pedagogical Perspectives.* Lincoln: University of Nebraska Press, 2004.

Moraga, Cherríe. *Loving in the War Years.* 2nd ed. Boston: South End, 2000.

Moretti, Franco. *The Way of the World: The Bildungsroman in European Culture.* London and New York: Verso, 1987.

Morrison, Toni. *Beloved.* New York: Knopf, 1987.

———. *Playing in the Dark: Whiteness and the Literary Imagination.* Cambridge, Mass.: Harvard University Press, 1992.

Muñoz, José Esteban. *Cruising Utopia: The Then and There of Queer Futurity.* New York: NYU Press, 2009.

———. *Disidentifications: Queers of Color and the Performance of Politics.* Minneapolis: University of Minnesota Press, 1999.

———. "Feeling Brown: Ethnicity and Affect in Ricardo Bracho's *The Sweetest Hangover (and Other STDs).*" *Theatre Journal* 52, no. 1 (March 2000): 67–79.

———. *The Sense of Brown.* Durham, N.C.: Duke University Press, 2020.

Murphy, Gretchen. "A Europeanized New World: Colonialism and Cosmopolitanism in *Who Would Have Thought It?*" In *María Amparo Ruiz de Burton: Critical and Pedagogical Perspectives*, edited by Amelia María de la Luz Montes and Anne Elizabeth Goldman, 135–52. Lincoln: University of Nebraska Press, 2004.

Newman, Judie. "Harriet Beecher Stowe's Cuban Characters: *Uncle Tom's Cabin* and Gertrudis Gómez de Avellaneda's *Sab.*" In *(Re)Mapping the Latina/o Literary Landscape: New Works and New Directions*, edited by Cristina Herrera and Larissa M. Mercado-López, 21–34. New York: Palgrave Macmillan, 2016.

Nguyen, Viet Thanh. *Race and Resistance: Literature and Politics in Asian America.* Oxford: Oxford University Press, 2002.

Nwankwo, Ifeoma Kiddoe. *Black Cosmopolitanism: Racial Consciousness and Transnational Identity in the Nineteenth-Century Americas.* Philadelphia: University of Pennsylvania Press, 2005.

Ocampo, Anthony. *The Latinos of Asia: How Filipino Americans Break the Rules of Race.* Stanford, Calif.: Stanford University Press, 2016.

O'Brien, Colleen. *Race, Romance, and Rebellion: Literatures of the Americas in the Nineteenth Century.* Charlottesville and London: University of Virginia Press, 2013.

O'Gorman, Edmundo. *The Invention of America: An Inquiry into the Historical Nature of the New World and the Meaning of Its History.* Bloomington: Indiana University Press, 1961.

Olguín, B. V. "Raza." In *Keywords for Latina/o Studies*, edited by Deborah R. Vargas, Nancy Raquel Mirabal, and Lawrence La Fountain-Stokes, 188–92. New York: NYU Press, 2017.

———. *Violentologies: Violence, Identity, and Ideology in Latina/o Literature.* Oxford and New York: Oxford University Press, 2021.

Ontiveros, Randy J. *In the Spirit of a New People: The Cultural Politics of the Chicano Movement.* New York: NYU Press, 2013.

Orihuela, Sharada Balachandran. "The Black Market: Property, Freedom, and Piracy in Martin Delany's *Blake; or, The Huts of America.*" *J19: The Journal of Nineteenth-Century Americanists* 2, no. 2 (Fall 2014): 273–300.

Ortiz, Ricardo. "Burning X's: Critical Futurities within Latinx Studies' Disidentifying Present." *Latinx Temporality as a Time of Crisis*, dossier of *Aztlán: A Journal of Chicano Studies* 45, no. 2 (Fall 2020): 201–11.

———. *Cultural Erotics in Cuban America.* Minneapolis: University of Minnesota Press, 2007.

———. "Edwidge Danticat's *Latinidad*: The Farming of Bones and the Cultivation (of Fields) of Knowledge." In *Aftermaths: Exile, Migration, and Diaspora Reconsidered*, edited by Marcus Bullock and Peter Y. Paik, 150–72. New Brunswick, N.J.: Rutgers University Press, 2009.

———. *Latinx Literature Now: Between Evanescence and Event.* Cham, Switzerland: Palgrave Macmillan, 2019.

Palmer, Steven, José Antonio Piqueras, and Amparo Sánchez Cobos, eds. *State of Ambiguity: Civic Life and Culture in Cuba's First Republic.* Durham, N.C.: Duke University Press, 2014.

Pantoja-Hidalgo, Cristina, and Priscelina Patajo-Legato, eds. *Philippine Post-Colonial Studies: Essays on Language and Literature.* Quezon City: University of the Philippines Press, 1993.

Parziale, Amy. "Counter-Archives of Trauma in Cristina García's *Monkey Hunting.*" *Revista de Estudios Hispánicos* 52, no. 3 (October 2018): 937–58.

Paulk, Julia C. "A New Look at the Strains of Allegory in Gertrudis Gómez de Avellaneda's 'Sab.'" *Revista Hispánica Moderna* 55, no. 2 (December 2000): 229–41.

———. "Nothing to Hide: *Sab* as an Anti-Slavery and Feminist Novel." *Hispanic Issues Series* 18 (2017): 134–52.
Pérez, Emma. *The Decolonial Imaginary: Writing Chicanas into History.* Bloomington: Indiana University Press, 1999.
Pérez-Torres, Rafael. *Mestizaje: Critical Uses of Race in Chicano Culture.* Minneapolis: University of Minnesota Press, 2006.
Phelan, John Leddy. *The Hispanization of the Philippines: Spanish Aims and Filipino Responses 1565–1700.* Madison: University of Wisconsin Press, 1959.
Pierrot, Grégory. "Writing over Haiti: Black Avengers in Martin Delany's *Blake*." *Studies in American Literature* 41, no. 2 (Fall 2014): 175–99.
Ponce, Martin J. *Beyond the Nation: Diasporic Filipino Literature and Queer Reading.* New York: NYU Press, 2012.
Pratt, Mary Louise. *Imperial Eyes: Travel Writing and Transculturation.* London and New York: Routledge, 1992.
Puig, Raquel. "The Imagined Nation in Cristina García's *Monkey Hunting*." In *Caribbean Without Borders: Literature, Language, and Culture*, edited by Dorsia Smith, Raquel Puig, and Ileana Cortés Santiago, 236–45. Newcastle upon Tyne: Cambridge Scholars, 2008.
Rafael, Vicente L., ed. *Discrepant Histories: Translocal Essays on Filipino Cultures.* Philadelphia: Temple University Press, 1995.
———. "Language, Identity, and Gender in Rizal's *Noli*." *Review of Indonesian and Malaysian Affairs* 18 (1984): 110–40.
———. "Nationalism, Imagery, and the Filipino Intelligentsia in the 19th Century." In *Discrepant Histories: Translocal Essays on Filipino Cultures*, edited by Vicente L. Rafael, 133–58. Philadelphia: Temple University Press, 1995.
———. *White Love and Other Events in Filipino History.* Durham, N.C.: Duke University Press, 2000.
———. "White Love: Surveillance and National Resistance in the U.S. Colonization of the Philippines." In *Cultures of United States Imperialism*, edited by Amy Kaplan and Donald E. Pease, 185–218. Durham, N.C.: Duke University Press, 1991.
Rama, Angel. *The Lettered City.* Durham, N.C.: Duke University Press, 1996.
Ramírez, Catherine. "Afrofuturism/Chicanafuturism: Fictive Kin." *Aztlán* 33, no. 1 (Spring 2008): 185–94.
———. "Cyborg Feminism: The Science Fiction of Octavia E. Butler and Gloria Anzaldúa." In *Reload: Rethinking Women + Cyberculture*, edited by Mary Flanagan and Austin Booth, 374–402. Cambridge, Mass.: MIT Press, 2002.
———. "Deus ex Machina: Tradition, Technology, and the Chicanafuturist Art of Marion C. Martinez." *Aztlán* 29, no. 2 (Fall 2004): 55–92.
Ramírez, Dixa. *Colonial Phantoms: Belonging and Refusal in the Dominican Americas, from the 19th Century to the Present.* New York: NYU Press, 2018.
Rannard, Georgina, and Eve Webster. "Leopold II: Belgium 'Wakes Up' to Its Bloody Colonial Past." *BBC News*, June 13, 2020. https://www.bbc.com/news/world-europe-53017188. Accessed July 30, 2021.

"Recovering the U.S. Hispanic Literary Heritage." *Arte Público Press.* https://artepublicopress.com/recovery-program/. Accessed July 30, 2021.

Reid-Pharr, Robert. "Violent Ambiguity: Martin Delany, Bourgeois Sadomasochism, and the Production of a Black National Masculinity." In *Representing Black Men*, edited by Marcellus Blount and George P. Cunningham, 73–94. New York: Routledge, 1995.

Retamar, Roberto Fernández. *Caliban and Other Essays.* Translated by Edward Baker. Minneapolis: University of Minnesota Press, 1989.

———. "Caliban: Notes Toward a Discussion of Culture in Our America" (1971). In *Caliban and Other Essays*, Translated by Edward Baker, 3-45. Minneapolis: University of Minnesota Press, 1989.

Reyes, Raquel A. G. *Love, Passion and Patriotism: Sexuality and the Philippine Propaganda Movement, 1882–1892.* Singapore: NUS Press, 2008.

Riofrio, John D. "Rio." *Continental Shifts: Migration, Representation, the Struggle for Justice in Latin(o) America.* Austin: University of Texas Press, 2015.

Rivera, John-Michael. *The Emergence of Mexican America: Recovering Stories of Mexican Peoplehood in U.S. Culture.* New York: NYU Press, 2006.

Rizal, José. *El Filibusterismo.* 1891. New York: Penguin, 2011.

———. *Noli Me Tangere.* 1887. New York: Penguin, 2006.

Rodó, José Enrique. *Ariel.* 1900. Translated by Margaret Sayers Peden. Austin: University of Texas Press, 1988. Original translation in 1974.

Rodríguez, Ana Patricia. *Dividing the Isthmus: Central American Transnational Histories, Literatures, and Cultures.* Austin: University of Texas Press, 2009.

———. "The Fiction of Solidarity: Transfronterista Feminisms and Anti-Imperialist Struggles in Central American Transnational Narratives." *Feminist Studies* 34, nos. 1–2 (2008): 199–226.

Rodríguez, Ileana. *Women, Guerrillas, and Love: Understanding War in Central America.* Minneapolis: University of Minnesota Press, 1996.

Rodríguez, María Cristina. "Political Authority Figures as Distant Memories of a Forgotten Past: Julia Alvarez's *In the Time of the Butterflies* and *In the Name of Salomé* and Cristina García's *The Agüero Sisters.*" *Journal of Caribbean Literatures* 6, no. 2 (Fall 2009): 55–63.

Rodriguez, Ralph E. *Latinx Literature Unbound: Undoing Ethnic Expectation.* New York: Fordham University Press, 2018.

Rodríguez-Silva, Ileana M. *Silencing Race: Disentangling Blackness, Colonialism, and National Identities in Puerto Rico.* New York: Palgrave Macmillan, 2012.

Rogin, Michael. *Subversive Genealogy: The Politics and Art of Herman Melville.* New York: Knopf, 1983.

Rohrleitner, Marion. "Not in Our Mother's Image: Ekphrasis and Challenges to Recovering Afro-Mestizaje in Contemporary Latina/Chicana Historical Fiction." In *Dialogues across Diasporas: Women Writers, Scholars, and Activists of Africana and Latina Descent in Conversation*, edited by Marion Rohrleitner and Sarah E. Ryan, 37–55. Lanham, Md.: Lexington, 2013.

Román, Elda María. "The Future of Demographobia, Latinxs, and the Realist-Speculative Convergence." *Latinx Temporality as a Time of Crisis*, dossier of *Aztlán: A Journal of Chicano Studies* 45, no. 2 (Fall 2020): 185–99.

Romero, Chanette. *Activism and the American Novel: Religion and Resistance in Fiction by Women of Color*. Charlottesville, Virginia: University of Virginia Press, 2012.

———. "Envisioning a 'Network of Tribal Coalitions': Leslie Marmon Silko's *Almanac of the Dead*." *American Indian Quarterly* 26, no. 4 (Fall 2002): 623–40.

Roorda, Eric. *The Dictator Next Door: The Good Neighbor Policy and the Trujillo Regime in the Dominican Republic, 1930-1945*. Durham, N.C.: Duke University Press, 1998.

Rosaldo, Renato. "Imperialist Nostalgia." *Representations* 26 (1989): 107–22.

Rosca, Ninotchka. *Monsoon Collection*. St. Lucia: University of Queensland Press, 1983.

———. "Myth, Identity and the Colonial Experience." *World Englishes* 9, no. 2 (1990): 237–43.

———. *State of War*. New York: W. W. Norton, 1988.

Rosenthal, Debra J. *Race Mixture in Nineteenth-Century U.S. and Spanish American Fictions: Gender, Culture, and Nation Building*. Chapel Hill: University of North Carolina Press, 2004.

Roth, Russell. *Muddy Glory: America's 'Indian Wars' in the Philippines 1899–1935*. Hanover, Mass.: Christopher, 1981.

Ruiz, Julie. "Captive Identities: The Gendered Conquest of Mexico in *Who Would Have Thought It?*" In *María Amparo Ruiz de Burton: Critical and Pedagogical Perspectives*, edited by Amelia María de la Luz Montes and Anne Elizabeth Goldman, 112–32. Lincoln: University of Nebraska Press, 2004.

Ruiz de Burton, María Amparo. *The Squatter and the Don*. 1885. Houston: Arte Público, 1992, 1997.

———. *Who Would Have Thought It?* 1892. Houston: Arte Público, 1995.

Rushdy, Ashraf H. A. "The Neo-Slave Narrative." *Cambridge Companion to the African American Novel*, edited by Maryemma Graham, 87-105. Cambridge: Cambridge University Press, 2004.

———. *Neo-Slave Narratives: Studies in the Social Logic of a Literary Form*. Oxford: Oxford University Press, 1999.

Sae-Saue, Jayson Gonzales. *Southwest Asia: The Transpacific Geographies of Chicana/o Literature*. New Brunswick N.J.: Rutgers University Press, 2016.

Safa, Helen I. "Commentary on Race and Revolution in Cuba." *Souls* 1, no. 2 (Spring 1999): 86–91.

Said, Edward W. *Culture and Imperialism*. New York: Vintage, 1993.

Saldaña-Portillo, María Josefina. *Indian Given: Racial Geographies across Mexico and the United States*. Durham, N.C.: Duke University Press, 2016.

———. "Indians Have Always Been Modern: *Roma*, the Settler Colonial Paradigm, and Latinx Temporality." *Latinx Temporality as a Time of Crisis*, dossier of *Aztlán: A Journal of Chicano Studies* 45, no. 2 (Fall 2020): 221–40.

———. "'No Country for Old Mexicans': The Collision of Empires on the Texas Frontier." *Interventions* 13, no. 1 (2011): 67–84.

———. *The Revolutionary Imagination in the Americas and the Age of Development.* Durham, N.C.: Duke University Press, 2003.

———. "Who's the Indian in Aztlán? Re-Writing Mestizaje, Indianism, and Chicanismo from the Lacandón." In *The Latin American Subaltern Studies Reader*, edited by Ileana Rodríguez, 402–23. Durham, N.C.: Duke University Press, 2001.

Saldívar, José David. *Border Matters: Remapping American Cultural Studies.* Berkeley: University of California Press, 1997.

———. "Conjectures on 'Americanity' and Junot Díaz's 'Fukú Americanus' in *The Brief Wondrous Life of Oscar Wao*." *Global South* 5, no. 1 (2011): 120–36.

———. *The Dialectics of Our America: Genealogy, Cultural Critique, and Literary History.* Durham, N.C.: Duke University Press, 1991.

———. *Trans-Americanity: Subaltern Modernities, Global Coloniality, and the Cultures of Greater Mexico.* Durham, N.C.: Duke University Press, 2012.

Saldívar, Ramón. "Imagining Cultures: The Transnational Imaginary in Postrace America." *Journal of Transnational American Studies* 4, no. 2 (2012): 1–18.

Saldívar-Hull, Sonia. "Introduction to the Second Edition." In *Borderlands / La Frontera: The New Mestiza*, by Gloria Anzaldúa. 3rd ed., 1–15. San Francisco: Aunt Lute, 2007.

Salman, Michael. *The Embarrassment of Slavery: Controversies over Bondage and Nationalism in the American Colonial Philippines.* Berkeley: University of California Press, 2001.

San Buenaventura, Steffi. "The Colors of Manifest Destiny: Filipinos and the American Other(s)." *Amerasia Journal* 24, no. 3 (1998): 1–26.

Sánchez, María Carla. "Whiteness Invisible: Early Mexican American Writing and the Color of Literary History.' In *Passing: Identity and Interpretation in Sexuality, Race, and Religion*, edited by María Carla Sánchez and Linda Schlossberg, 64–91. New York: NYU Press, 2001.

Sánchez, Rosaura, and Beatrice Pita, eds. *Conflicts of Interest: The Letters of María Amparo Ruiz de Burton.* Houston: Arte Público, 2001.

San Juan, E. Jr. "Configuring the Filipino Diaspora in the United States." *Diaspora: A Journal of Transnational Studies* 3, no. 2 (Fall 1994): 117–33.

———. *Crisis in the Philippines: The Making of a Revolution.* South Hadley, Mass.: Bergin and Garvey, 1986.

———. "Filipino Writing in the United States: Reclaiming Whose America?" *Philippine Studies* 41, no. 2 (1993): 141–66.

———. "Mapping the Boundaries: The Filipino Writer in the U.S.A." *Journal of Ethnic Studies* 19, no. 1 (Spring 1991): 117–31.

———. *Racial Formations/Critical Transformations: Articulations of Power in Ethnic and Racial Studies in the United States.* Atlantic Highlands, N.J.: Humanities, 1992.

———. *Rizal in Our Time: Essays in Interpretation.* Manila: Anvil, 2011.

———. *Ruptures, Schisms, Interventions: Cultural Revolution in the Third World*. Manila: De La Salle University Press, 1988.

———. "Transforming Identity in Postcolonial Narrative: An Approach to the Novels of Jessica Hagedorn." *Post Identity* 1, no. 2 (1998): 5–28.

Santiago, Esmeralda. *Conquistadora*. New York: Vintage, 2012.

Sarmiento, Domingo Faustino. *Facundo: Or, Civilization and Barbarism*. 1845. Translated by Kathleen Ross. Berkeley: University of California Press, 2004.

Schlau, Stacey. "Stranger in a Strange Land: The Discourse of Alienation in Gómez de Avellaneda Abolitionist Novel *Sab*." *Hispania* 69, no. 3 (1986): 495–503.

Schultermandl, Silvia. "'What Did Any of It Have to Do with Race?': Raced Chronotopes in Cristina García's *Monkey Hunting*." *Atlantic Studies* 8, no. 1 (2011): 93–107.

Scott, David. *Conscripts of Modernity: The Tragedy of Colonial Enlightenment*. Durham, N.C.: Duke University Press, 2004.

Sedgwick, Eve Kosofsky. *Between Men: English Literature and Male Homosocial Desire*. New York: Columbia University Press, 1985.

See, Sarita E. *The Decolonized Eye: Filipino American Art and Performance*. Minneapolis: University of Minnesota Press, 2009.

Shalom, Stephen Rosskamm. *The United States and the Philippines: A Study of Neocolonialism*. Philadelphia: Institute for the Study of Human Issues, 1981.

Shawcross, Edward. *France, Mexico and Informal Empire in Latin America, 1820–1867: Equilibrium in the New World*. Cham, Switzerland: Palgrave Macmillan, 2018.

Shields, David. *Oracles of Empire: Poetry, Politics, and Commerce in British America 1690–1750*. Chicago: University of Chicago Press, 1990.

Shreve, Grant. "The Exodus of Martin Delany." *American Literary History* 29, no. 3 (Fall 2017): 449–73.

Sieminski, Greg. "The Puritan Captivity Narrative and the Politics of the American Revolution." *American Quarterly* 42, no. 1 (1990): 35–56.

Silko, Leslie Marmon. *Almanac of the Dead*. New York: Penguin, 1991.

———. "Leslie Marmon Silko." In *Conversations with Leslie Marmon Silko*, by Laura Coltelli, 52–68. Jackson: University Press of Mississippi, 2000.

———. "Listening to the Spirits: An Interview with Leslie Marmon Silko." In *Conversations with Leslie Marmon Silko*, by Ellen L. Arnold, 162–96. Jackson: University Press of Mississippi, 2000.

Simón, Yara. "Princess Leia's Iconic Buns Were Inspired by These Revolutionary-Era Revolutionary Women." *Remezcla*, December 28, 2016. https://remezcla.com/culture/princess-leia-hair-buns/. Accessed July 30, 2021.

Sklodowska, Elzbieta. "Spanish American Testimonial Novel: Some Afterthoughts." In *The Real Thing: Testimonial Discourse and Latin America*, edited by Georg M. Gugelberger, 84–100. Durham, N.C.: Duke University Press, 1996.

Skocpol, Theda. *States and Social Revolutions*. 2nd ed. Cambridge: Cambridge University Press, 2015.

Socolovsky, Maya. "Patriotism, Nationalism, and the Fiction of History in Julia Alvarez's *In the Time of the Butterflies* and *In the Name of Salomé*." *Latin American Literary Review* 34, no. 68 (2006): 5–24.

Sohn, Stephen Hong. "From Discos to Jungles: Circuitous Queer Patronage and Sex Tourism in Jessica Hagedorn's *Dogeaters*." *MFS: Modern Fiction Studies* 56, no. 2 (2010): 316–48.

Sommer, Doris. *Foundational Fictions: The National Romances of Latin America*. Berkeley: University of California Press, 1991.

Soto, Shirlene. *Emergence of the Modern Mexican Woman: Her Participation in Revolution and Struggle for Equality, 1910–1940*. Denver: Arden, 1990.

Spoturno, María Laura. "Thresholds of Writing: Text and Paratext in Sandra Cisneros' *Caramelo or Puro Cuento*." In *The Landscapes of Writing in Chicano Literature*, edited by Imelda Marín-Junquera, 47–58. New York: Palgrave Macmillan, 2013.

Stanley, Peter W. *A Nation in the Making: The Philippines and the United States, 1899–1921*. Cambridge, Mass.: Harvard University Press, 1974.

Stevenson, Pascha A. "Reader Expectation and Ethnic Rhetorics: The Problem of the Passing Subaltern in *Who Would Have Thought It?*" *Ethnic Studies Review* 28, no. 2 (January 2005): 61–74.

Stoler, Ann Laura. *Carnal Knowledge and Imperial Power: Race and the Intimate in Colonial Rule*. Berkeley: University of California Press, 2010.

Streeby, Shelley. *American Sensations: Class, Empire, and the Production of Popular Culture*. Berkeley: University of California Press, 2002.

Sumsky, Victor V. "The Prophet of Two Revolutions." *Philippine Studies* 49, no. 2 (2001): 236–54.

Sundquist, Eric J. *To Wake the Nations: Race in the Making of American Literature*. Cambridge, Mass.: Belknap Press, 1993.

Szeghi, Tereza M. "Weaving Transnational Cultural Identity through Travel and Diaspora in Sandra Cisneros's *Caramelo*." *Gender, Transnationalism, and Ethnic American Identity*. Special issue. *MELUS* 39, no. 4 (Winter 2014): 162–85.

Tate, Julee. "My Mother, My Text: Writing and Remembering in Julia Alvarez's *In the Name of Salomé*." *Bilingual Review/La Revista Bilingüe* 28, no. 1 (January 2004–April 2007): 54–63.

Testa-de Ocampo, Anna Melinda. "The Afterlives of *Noli Me Tangere*." *Philippine Studies* 59, no. 4 (2011): 495–527.

Thoma, Pamela. "Of Beauty Pageants and Barbie." *Genders* 29, no. 1 (1999). www.colorado.edu/gendersarchive1998-2013/1999/01/10/beauty-pageants-and-barbie-theorizing-consumption-asian-american-transnational-feminism. Accessed November 11, 2021.

Tillett, Rebecca, ed. *Howling for Justice: New Perspectives on Leslie Marmon Silko's Almanac of the Dead*. Tucson: University of Arizona Press, 2014.

Tilly, Charles. *From Mobilization to Revolution*. Reading, Mass.: Addison-Wesley, 1978.

Tinnemeyer, Andrea. "Rescuing the Past: The Case of Olive Oatman and Lola Medina." In *María Amparo Ruiz de Burton: Critical and Pedagogical Perspectives*, edited by Amelia María de la Luz Montes and Anne Elizabeth Goldman, 169–83. Lincoln: University of Nebraska Press, 2004.
Tofiño-Quesada, Ignacio. "José Rizal's Ghost." *Anclajes* 5, no. 5 (2001): 89–106.
Tolentino, Rolando B. "Positioning *positions* in the Writing to the Future." *positions* 20, no. 1 (2012): 159–71.
Trouillot, Michel-Rolph. *Silencing the Past: Power and the Production of History*. Boston: Beacon, 1995.
Trujillo, Simón Ventura. *Land Uprising: Native Story Power and the Insurgent Horizons of Latinx Indigeneity*. Tucson: University of Arizona Press, 2020.
Twelbeck, Kristen. "Beyond a Postmodern Denial of Reference: Forms of Reference in Jessica Hagedorn's Dogeaters." *American Studies* 51, no. 3 (2006): 425–37.
Twinam, Ann. *Purchasing Whiteness: Pardos, Mulattos, and the Quest for Social Mobility in the Spanish Indies*. Stanford, Calif.: Stanford University Press, 2015.
Ty-Casper, Linda. *Dream Eden*. Seattle: University of Washington Press, 1996.
Ureña, Salomé. *Salomé Ureña: Selected Poems*. Translated by Matt Wirzburger. Las Vegas: Rescate, 2019.
Vargas Llosa, Mario. *The Feast of the Goat*. Translated by Edith Grossman. New York: Farrar, Straus, and Giroux, 2001.
Vasconcelos, José. *The Cosmic Race/La raza cósmica* (1925). Repr. Baltimore: John Hopkins University Press, 1948, 1997.
Vázquez, David. *Triangulations: Narrative Strategies for Navigating Latino Identity*. Minneapolis: University of Minnesota Press, 2011.
Viego, Antonio. *Dead Subjects: Toward a Politics of Loss in Latino Studies*. Durham, N.C.: Duke University Press, 2007.
Vigil, Ariana. *War Echoes: Gender and Militarization in U.S. Latina/o Cultural Production*. New Brunswick N.J.: Rutgers University Press, 2014.
Villarreal, José Antonio. *Pocho*. New York: Anchor, 1970.
Weiser, Frans. "The Hidden Archivist; Or, Julia Alvarez's Historical Fiction Beyond the Borders." In *Inhabiting La Patria: Identity, Agency, and Antojo in the Work of Julia Alvarez*, edited by Rebecca L. Harrison and Emily Hipchen, 213–33. Albany: SUNY Press, 2013.
Wells, Allen. *Tropical Zone: General Trujillo, FDR, and the Jews of Sosúa*. Durham, N.C.: Duke University Press, 2009.
Werrlein, Debra T. "Legacies of the 'Innocent' Frontier: Failed Memory and the Infantilized Filipina Expatriate in Jessica Hagedorn's *Dogeaters*." *Journal of Asian American Studies* 7, no. 1 (2004): 27–50.
Wexler, Laura. *Tender Violence: Domestic Visions in an Age of U.S. Imperialism*. Chapel Hill: University of North Carolina Press, 2000.
Wickham-Crowley, Timothy P. "Structural Theories of Revolution." In *Theorizing Revolutions*, edited by John Foran, 36–70. London and New York: Routledge, 1997.

Williams, Lorna Valerie. *The Representation of Slavery in Cuban Fiction*. Columbia and London: University of Missouri Press, 1994.

Woloch, Alex. *The One vs. the Many: Minor Characters and the Space of the Protagonist in the Novel*. Princeton, N.J.: Princeton University Press, 2003.

Yu, Hope S. "Memory, Nostalgia, and the Filipino Diaspora in the Works of Two Filipina Writers." *Philippine Quarterly of Culture and Society* 36, no. 1 (2008): 103–23.

Zamora, Maria. "Female Embodiment and the Politics of Representation in Jessica Hagedorn's *Dogeaters*." *Atenea* 26, no. 2 (2006): 167–82.

Zapata-Calle, Ana. "El Mundo de Chen Pan en 'Monkey Hunting' de Cristina García: Chinos, Africanos y Criollos en la Diáspora Cubana." *Chasqui* 41, no. 1 (May 2012): 170–86.

Zevallos, Johnny. "Etnicidad y Género en *Sab* (1841) de Gertrudis Gómez de Avellaneda." *Boletín de la Academia Peruana de la Lengua* 64, no. 64 (Julio-Diciembre): 87–109.

Index

abolition: in *Blake* (Delany), 168, 173–4, 176–7, 239n68, 242n3; in *Conquistadora* (Santiago), 19; in Cuba, 168, 173–4; and Domingo del Monte, 150; and Eugenio Maria de Hostos, 103; in Haiti, 168; and *Monkey Hunting* (García), 146; *Sab*, 137, 150–1, 155, 239n68; and *Salomé* (Alvarez), 108; and Simón Bolivar, 12; in *Who Would Have Thought It?* (Ruiz de Burton), 48–9; and women's rights, 150–1, 239n68
Acosta, Abraham, 140, 237n56
Acosta, Oscar Zeta, 43
Adamson, Joni, 163, 242n9
Afro Cubans: in *Blake* (Delany), 159–60, 164–5, 168, 171–4, 176–7, 185, 244n34; and Chinese Cubans, 146; Cuba's unresolved relationship with, 134; and Domingo del Monte, 150; in *Monkey Hunting* (García), 144–48; and the Race War of 1912, 139, 208n45; and *Sab* (Avellaneda), 151; and Ten Years' War, 172; and white Cubans, 171–3
Afrofuturism, 9
Afro Latinx: exclusion of, 12, 46, 65; and *Salomé* (Alvarez), 28
Aguilar, Filomeno V. Jr., 221n14
Alcaraz, Lalo: and browning, 34, 37–8; and indigeneity, 34; and the speculative, 33–4. See also "Princess Lupe"
Alemán, Jesse, 50, 216n27, 216n29, 217n37
Alfonso-Forero, Ann Marie, 236n45
Almanac of the Dead (Silko): and anticipation of Zapatista uprising, 158, 160–1; and Black Indians, 189–90; and brownness, 189–90; and civilization/barbarism binary, 163, 180–2, 191; and critique of Marxism, 186, 191; and indigeneity, 30, 161–3, 178–9; and speculative fiction, 30, 159; and transnational perspective, 243n14; and tribal internationalism, 161
Alvarado, Leticia, 203
Alvarez, Julia: and the dictator novel, 29, 117; and elitism, 28, 225n3, 226n18; and guerrilla conversion narrative, 99, 105; and *In the Time of Butterflies*, 26, 129, 227n22; and political consciousness, 100, 127; and the revolutionary bildungsroman, 104, 106, 109, 126–7, 227n24; and translation, 109–10; as unlikely contributor to revolutionary horizons, 27. See also *In the Name of Salomé*
Americas: as Asian, 13; and genre, 14–15, 21; as Latin, 70
American Revolution: and *Blake* (Delany), 166–7, 175; and captivity narrative, 47–48; inspiration from Latinx revolutions, 7–8; as unfinished, 167,175
Anderson, Benedict: and cacique democracy, 72; and the "First Filipino," 75, 222n17; and imagined community, 74, 176, 247n75; and national exclusion, 12; and "specter of comparisons," 98; and viewing Philippines through Latin American perspective, 73, 97, 221n13

Anglo-Saxon: and Delany, 165; and genre, 46; and imperialism, 39, 46, 216n29; and whiteness, 2, 39, 45, 49–50, 54; and *Who Would Have Thought It?* (Ruiz de Burton), 2, 39, 45–6, 49–50, 52, 54, 61

anti-blackness: and *Akrílica* (Herrera), 196, 197; and *Almanac* (Silko), 190, and Cuba, 146, 156, 160; in the Dominican Republic, 113; and indigeneity, 113; and latinidad, 1–2, 11, 196; and Puerto Rico, 18; and *Monkey Hunting* (García), 146, 156; and *Sab* (Avellaneda), 155; and the U.S., 160

anticolonialism: and *Almanac* (Silko), 186, 189, 251n109; and *Blake* in Cuba, 165–77, and La Escalera, 168–9; and *Salomé* (Alvarez), 105, 112; and *State of War* (Rosca), 82–3; and Rizal, 75–6, 79; and Ten Years' War, 168–9; and Vasconcelos, 214n14; and Zapatista uprising, 158, 160

Anzaldúa, Gloria, 43, 199, 214n19, 253n11

Aponte Rebellion, 177

Aranda, José, 43, 216n25–26, 218n51

Arenas, Reinaldo, 199

Arnold, L. Ellen, 160

Asian American: and Filipinx literature, 69, 73, 75, 208n49

Asian Latinxs: erasure of, 4, 13–4; and failures of solidarity, 12; and García, 23, 29, 157; and latinidad, 11, 14, 29; in the Philippines, 73, 75, 157, 208n49, 221n12. *See also* Chinese Cubans

Avellaneda, Gertrudis Gómez de: and the accidental, 137–8, 166; and *Autobiography*, 151–4; and Del Monte circle, 149–50, 238n66; and retcon, 137, 150–4, 156; and *Sab* as autobiography 138, 151–3, and testimonio, 29, 138, 151, 153; and women's rights, 29, 150–3, 155, 239n68. *See also Sab*

Aztlán, 3, 42

Baldellou, Marta Miquel, 239n68

Balestrini, Nassim, 62

barbarism/civilization binary: in *Almanac* (Silko), 180–3; in *Ariel* (Rodo), 180–1; in *Caliban* (Retamar), 180; as colonial rhetoric, 103–183–4; in *Facundo* (Sarmiento), 103, 163, 180

Barreto, Reina, 154

Batista, Fulgencio, 107, 116, 134, 139

Beloved (Morrison), 121, 141, 236n34

Benítez-Rojo, Antonio, 238n61

Beverley, John: definition of testimonio, 21–2, 136, 145; failure to discuss Miguel Barnet, 146, 237n56

Bhabha, Homi, 128, 206n22, 232n92

Biggio, Rebecca Skidmore, 247n64, 247n76, 248n77; and "the community of conspiracy," 176

bildungsroman: and dictator novel, 105, 119; European, 102, 119; immigrant, 29, 193; künstlerroman, 225n4; and *Monkey Hunting* (García), 29, 148; and *Oscar Wao* (Díaz), 29, 102, 105, 117, 119, 125–6; revolutionary, 98, 100–6, 119, 126, 148, 150; and *Sab* (Avellaneda), 150; and *Salomé* (Alvarez), 104, 106, 109, 126–7, 227n24; split, 109, 119, 148, 158, 227n24; and *The Undocumented Americans* (Cornejo Villavicencio), 193

Biography of a Runaway Slave (Barnet): and censorship in Revolutionary Cuba, 139–40; and *Monkey Hunting* (García), 23, 29, 133, 136–8, 140–6, 232n2; as testimonio, 21, 146

blackness: in *Almanac* (Silko), 179, 189–90; in *Blake* (Delany), 163, 171, 176, 188, 189, 245–6n50, 247n71, 247n77; and brownness, 189; in Cuba, 134, 171; in *Dogeaters* (Hagedorn), 94; in the Dominican Republic, 113, 121, 231n72; and Haiti, 107–9, 231n74; and indigeneity, 65, 113; and latinidad, 13, 19, 65; and *Oscar Wao* (Díaz), 121, 122–23, 231n74, 231n82; as political choice, 171, 176, 245–6n50, 247–8n77; in Puerto Rico, 18; and *Salomé* (Alvarez), 107–9, 113–14, 225n3, 225n6; and Vasconcelos, 42; in *Who Would Have Thought It?* (Ruiz de Burton), 45, 49–50, 65

Bladow, Kyle, 251n110

Blake (Delany): and abolition, 168, 173–4, 176–7, 239n68, 242n3; as alternative view of the Cuban Wars of independence, 177; and the American Revolution, 166, 167, 175; and Black imperialism, 165, 244n34; and Black political consciousness, 169; and blackness, 163, 171, 176, 188, 189, 245–6n50, 247n71, 247n77; and compression of time, 160; and diaspora, 245–6n51, 248n78; and enslaved people, 163, 169–70, 252n113; and Exodus, 164, 243n20; and the Haitian Revolution, 166,

INDEX

168, 245n47; and hemispheric revolutionary history, 162, 168; and imagined community, 176, 190; and latinidad, 30, 158, 162–3; and La Escalera, 159, 160, 166, 167, 168–9, 170, 175–7; and levels of narration, 173; and missing chapters, 164; and relationship between brownness and blackness, 188–90; and revolutionary organizing tactics, 165–6, 170, 172, 176; as speculative fiction, 30, 159–60, 190; and whiteness, 162–3, 165, 171–2, 174–5, 247n71
Blanco, John, 73, 212n94, 222–3n132
blanqueamiento: and the Del Monte Group, 238n66; and latinidad, 42; and Jewish refugees, 183, 251n106; and national identity, 13; and Silko 161, 177–84, 249n90; and Salomé Ureña, 113, 228n45
Bolívar, Simón: and Confederation of Spanish American Nations, 40; and Haiti, 12, 207–8n40, 209n58; and the importance of the literary to revolution, 3; as inspiration of Simoun in *Fili* (Rizal), 79; treatment of Indigenous people, 12–13, 21
Bourbons, 51–2, 218n51: Bourbon Reforms, 53
Boutelle, R.J., 242n3, 248n78
Branche, Jerome, 239n67–8
Brands, H.W., 222n25
The Brief Wondrous Life of Oscar Wao (Díaz): and charismatic leadership, 109; and diaspora, 119–23; and the dictator novel, 29, 105, 114, 116–19, 124, 126–7, 229n58, 230n59; and footnotes, 124, 126; and guerrilla conversion narrative, 99, 105, 119; and kinship, 102, 105, 117, 120, 127; and künstlerroman, 225n4; as pedagogical project, 100, 103, 105, 116; and queerness, 117, 120, 122, 199; and revolutionary bildungsroman, 100–3, 105, 117, 119, 126; and *Salomé* (Alvarez), 29; and split bildungsroman, 109, 120, 123
Brittan, Jennifer C., 160, 176, 247n66, 248n77–78, 255n33
Brickhouse, Anna, 151
Brown, Jeffrey, 210n72
brown commons, 192–3, 197, 199; as theorized by José Esteban Muñoz, 190, 192
Burns, Lucy Mae San Pablo, 69
Bushnell, David, 207n40
Bustamante, Michael, 134, 157

cacique democracy, 72–3, 80, 93, 96–7, 117; as theorized by Benedict Anderson, 72
Caminero-Santangelo, Marta, 15, 24, 27, 140, 209n55
captivity narrative: and the guerrilla conversion narrative, 65, 97; in *Mrs. Mary Rowlandson* (Rowlandson), 47–8, 217n41; in *Who Would Have Thought It?* (Ruiz de Burton), 46–8, 53, 216–17n32. *See also* Puritan captivity narrative
Caramelo (Cisneros): and anti-blackness, 28; and brownness, 28; and the Chicano Movement, 218–19n189; as Chicanx literature, 54, 2018n59; cover of, 63–4; footnotes, 7, 57–8; and history of colonization of Mexico, 7; and indigeneity, 28, 42, 54–6, 58, 63, 215n22; and mestizaje, 40, 215n21; and temporal displacement, 7; and Vasconcelos, 41, 44; and *Who Would Have Thought It?* (Ruiz de Burton), 2, 39–42, 55, 58, 65
Carpentier, Alejo, 230n59
Casper, Leonard, 223n41
Cassara, Joseph, 192, 252n8
Castiglia, Christopher, 47, 244n33
Castro, Fidel, 133, 199
Chang, Juliana, 76, 224n56
chicanidad: and Cisneros, 28, 40, 42, 55, 215n22; and indigeneity, 28, 42, 55
Chicano Movement: and Cisneros, 40, 41, 56, 191; and conservative ideology, 38, 54; and "El Plan Espiritual de Aztlán," 42; and Gloria Anzaldúa, 214n19; and indigeneity, 55, 214n15, 252n116; key texts of, 43; and la raza, 42
Chicanx: and Chicano Studies, 14; and Cisneros, 41, 215n22; literature, 43; and the Recovery Project, 43
Chinese Cubans: and Afro Cubans, 146; and *Biography* (Barnet), 141–2; erasure from revolutionary history, 133, 135, 143, 156; as indentured servants, 23, 133, 137, 141, 162, 235n24; in *Monkey Hunting* (García), 23, 133, 137, 141–6, 156
Chiles, Katy, 160
Cho, Yu-Fang, 142, 234n14
Cisneros, Sandra: and chicanidad, 40, 42; and the Chicano Movement, 41–2, 54, 191; as gatekeeper in publishing industry, 215n22; and history of French colonization of Mexico, 7

Civil Rights Movement, 2, 47, 226n17, 238n64
Clealand, Danielle Pilar, 134
Clover, Joshua, 135, 234n14
Cobos, Amparo Sánchez, 238n62
Collier, George A., 242n10
colonialism: and *Conquistadora* (Santiago), 19; French colonization of Mexico, 7; and genre, 21–22; legacy of, 85, 90; Mexican, 54; perversion of family, 98; shared histories of, 7, 9, 11, 24, 27, 171; Spanish, 25, 54, 71–3, 134, 136; U.S., 54
Columbus, Christopher, 13, 209n58
Commander, Michelle, 143
Congress of Panama, 207n40
Conquistadora (Santiago), 18–21
Cornejo Villavicencio, Karla, 192–194
Coronado, Raúl, 17, 52
Cox, Sandra, 231n82
Cruz, Denise, 78
Cuba: and *Almanac* (Silko), 184; and Afro Cubans, 134, 139, 144–6, 148, 150–1, 159–60, 164–5, 168; 171–4, 176–7, 185, 208n45, 246n60; and anti-slave narrative, 149–50; and *Blake* (Delany), 160, 164, 166–8, 170–4, 176–7, 185; Chinese in, 23, 133, 135, 137, 141–6, 148, 156, 162, 233n4; and communism, 135, 147, 149; and Domingo Del Monte, 150; history as unfinished, 157; and *Monkey Hunting* (García), 23, 133–7, 141–8, 156–7, 191; and *Noli* (Rizal), 79; and prison memoir, 147, 237n58; and racelessness, 134–5, 146, 151, 233n12, 236–7n52; and *Sab* (Avellaneda), 137–8, 150–7; and *Salomé* (Alvarez), 26, 104, 114–16; and The Dismal Swamp, 167. *See also* Fidel Castro; Fulgencio Batista; La Escalera; Plácido
Cuban Revolution: and *Blake* (Delany), 30; and *Biography*, 139–40; impact on Latinx studies, 25; and *Monkey Hunting* (García), 29, 133–7, 140; as needing testimonio, 140; and *Salomé* (Alvarez), 26, 104, 106, 108; and racism, 29; and violence, 188

Dalleo, Raphael, 15, 209n55, 216n18
Davis, Andrea, 9
Davis, Charles T., 136
Davis, Rocio G., 82
decolonization: and Homi Bhabha, 128; and latinidad, 12; as unfinished, 4, 8, 12

DeFronzo, James, 5, 206n11
Delany, Martin R.: and anxiety about annexation movement in Cuba, 244n36; and Black emigration, 173–5, 247–8n77; and "colored race," 174, 247n70, 247–8n77; and the incongruity of political writings and novels, 163, 164–5, 174–5; ideas of racial superiority, 169–70, 245–6n51; and latinidad, 30, 158, 162–3, 177; and Niger Valley trip, 161; and *Official Report of the Niger Valley Exploring Party* (1861), 165, 173; and pure African blood, 161, 165, 171, 174, 245–6n51, 247n71. *See also Blake*
Delgado, Martín Morúa, 13
Delmendo, Sharon, 75
Derby, Robin (Lauren), 231n72, 231n80
Derrida, Jacques, 6, 88, 206n15
Derounian, Kathryn Zabelle, 217n39, 217n41
diaspora: Black, 142; in *Blake* (Delany), 245–6n51, 248n78; curse of, 101, 121; Dominican, 101; in *Monkey Hunting* (García), 142; in *Oscar Wao* (Díaz), 119–3
Díaz, Jaquira, 198
Díaz, Junot: inconsistency between stated and practiced politics, 27–8; and the failure of solidarity, 104, 226n16; and investment in charismatic leadership, 104
Díaz, Porfirio, 39, 226n12
dictator novel: and the author/scriptor dynamic, 117, 127; and *Facundo* (Sarmiento), 21; as genre, 116–17; in *Oscar Wao* (Díaz), 29, 116–19, 124, 126–7, 230n59; and the revolutionary bildungsroman, 105, 119; in *Salomé*, 29, 117; as theorized by Jennifer Harford Vargas, 21, 116–18, 230n65; as theorized by Roberto González Echevarría, 117, 119
dictatorship: and Bolívar, 12; and the Dominican Republic, 100–1; and *Oscar Wao* (Díaz), 29, 100–1, 116–19, 124, 126–7; and the Philippines, 95; and *Salomé* (Alvarez), 100–1, 107; and violent revolution, 188. *See also* dictator novel
Dogeaters (Hagedorn): and guerrilla conversion narrative, 28, 70–1, 73, 81, 88, 96; and homosociality, 88; and a Latinx perspective, 69, 72–3; and queerness, 87–9; revision of José Rizal, 87–88, 90, 95; and revolutionary kinship, 71–2, 81, 87, 89, 96; and the role of women in revolution, 71, 81, 88, 95–6

Dominican Republic: and anti-blackness, 113–4, 227–8n28; and blackness, 121–3, 225n3; in *Conquistadora* (Santiago), 18; and Haiti, 105, 107–9, 123, 227–8n28; and Jewish refugees, 183; in *Oscar Wao* (Díaz), 100, 102, 120–6; and revolutionary bildungsroman, 98; and revolutionary pedagogy, 29; in *Salomé* (Alvarez), 26, 100–1, 104, 106–9, 128, 225n3; and the U.S., 29, 113–4; and the War of Restoration (1863–65), 227–8n28; and whiteness, 104, 105, 251n106; and the 1965 Revolution, 25. *See also* Hostosianismo; Salomé Ureña; Trujillo regime

Doolen, Andy, 167–168, 245n40

Dred Scott Decision, 160

Dussel, Enrique, 13

Echevarría, Roberto González, 117, 119, 126, 229n56, 229n58

Edwards, Erica, 226n17

El Cobre, 177

El Filibusterismo (Rizal): and critique of Spanish colonialism, 74; and cyclical time, 81; and guerrilla conversion narrative, 70, 75, 96; and the homosocial, 76, 79; and love triangle, 77; and nationalist romance, 89; and role of women, 77, 84. *See also* José Rizal

Eng, David L., 222n28

Esty, Jed, 225n9

Feal, Rosemary Geisdorfer, 136

Ferrer, Ada, 134, 171, 177, 233n12

filibustering, *See Rodrigo Lazo*

filibustero, 74, 79, 221n14

Filipino People Power Revolution, 4, 24–5, 28, 71, 72

Filipinx: and colonization, 85, 95; erasure from Latin America, 65, 97, 208n49, 221n12; and Filipinx American, 27, 69, 73, 96–7; Filipinx women, 85; literary tradition, 27, 70, 73, 97; and mixed races, 93; and U.S. rhetoric of, 76, 89

finca: in *Akrílica* (Herrera), 197; in *Almanac* (Silko), 179–182, 184, 249n90; and exploited labor, 180, 182, 197

Finch, Aisha, 167

Fischer-Hornung, Dorothea, 249n87

Fisher, Beth, 49, 53, 216n32

Fishkin, Shelley Fisher, 24

Flaubert, Gustave, 125

Flores, Juan, 207n35

Flores, Tatiana: on anti-blackness, 1, 11; bias towards U.S. political projects, 2; and the whiteness of latinidad, 1–2, 5; and the "x" in Latinx, 5

Flores-Rodríguez, Daynali, 230n61

Foran, John, 205n11

Freire, Paolo, 106

Friedenthal, Andrew J., 234n15

Fugitive Slave Law, 160

futurity: Black, 176, 244n33; and demographobia, 17; as former futures, 10, 17, 55, 157, 191; and horizon, 9; and indigeneity, 55, and kinship, 9, 97, 126; latinidad, 17, 210n62; and whiteness, 54; and the "X" in Latinx, 9, 15

Gairola, Rahul K, 224n49

García, Cristina: and *Biography of a Runaway Slave*, 23, 29, 133, 136–8, 140–6, 232n2; and connection between testimonio and neo-slave narrative; 129, 136–7, 143–4, 146, 148, 234n19; and critique of racelessness in Cuba, 134–5; and genealogies of revolutionary history, 129; and immigrant bildungsroman, 29; and retconning, 135–7, 140, 142–4, 148–9, 156–7; and slave narrative, 129, 136–7, 143–4, 146, 149, 234n19; and solidarity of form, 29, 129; speculative criticism, 147; 157; and speculative fiction, 144–5; and testimonio, 23, 29, 140, 142, 144, 146–7, 199. See also *Monkey Hunting*

García, Emily, 7

García Márquez, Gabriel, 230n59

García Peña, Lorgia, 13, 103, 203, 209n58, 253n2

Garza, Ernesto, 43

Gasché, Rodolphe, 6, 206n15. *See also* horizon

Gates Jr., Henry Louis, 136

Gibby, Kristina S., 57

Gil'Adí, Maia, 203, 226n16

Gilroy, Paul, 245n51

Goldman, Anne E., 48, 214n11, 216n31, 218n51

Goldstone, Jack A., 207n11

Gomariz, José, 238n66, 239n68

Gómez, Alan Eladio, 212n97
Gómez, Laura E, 210n65
Goni, Uki, 251n106
González, John M., 215n24
Gonzalez, Rodolfo "Corky," 3, 205n6
Gonzalez, Xochitl, 198
Goodwin, Jeff, 205n11
Gordy, Katherine, 180
Goyal, Yogita: and definition of slave narrative, 21; and form, 22, 209n51; and genre as world-view, 22
gracias al sacar, 177, 179
Gran Legión del Águila Negra conspiracy, 177
Graulund, Rune, 120, 230n61, 230n67
Gruesz, Kirsten Silva, 15, 17, 203, 210n62
Guerra, Lucía, 239–40n68
guerrilla conversion narrative: in *Dogeaters* (Hagedorn), 28, 70–3, 81, 88–9, 93, 95–7; as genre, 70, 74–5, 220n6; and homosociality, 70–2, 75, 78; in *Oscar Wao* (Díaz), 99, 105, 117; and the revolutionary bildungsroman, 97; and Rizal, 70–1, 73–8, 88, 95–7, and the role of women, 28, 71, 76, 81, 95, 98; in *Salomé* (Alvarez), 99, 105; in *State of War* (Rosca), 29, 70–2, 84–5, 87, 97–8, 105
Gugelberger, George, 234n18, 236n50

Habsburgs, 52, 53, 55, 56, 61
Hagimoto, Koichi, 69–71, 73, 79, 212n94
Haiti: and *Almanac* (Silko), 189; and blackness, 105, 107–9, 122, 227n28, 231n74, 231n84; and *Blake* (Delany), 166, 168, 173, 243n27, 245n47, 245n51; and Cuba, 168; in *Conquistadora* (Santiago), 18; and Dominican Republic, 105, 108–9, 122–2, 227n28, 231n80; and Latinx studies, 209n58; and *Oscar Wao* (Díaz), 122–4; as represented in *Monkey Hunting* (Hagedorn), 142; in *Salomé* (Alvarez), 107–9
Haitian Revolution: in *Almanac* (Silko), 184, 189; in *Blake* (Delany), 168, 245n47; fear of, 12, 19, 166; French perspective of, 185, 251n108; in *Sab* (Avellaneda), 239n68
Halberstam, Jack, 222n28
Hanna, Monica, 225n4, 232n84, 232n88
Harford Vargas, Jennifer: and character-space, 49; and footnotes, 124, 224n2, 230n61; and Latinx dictator novel, 22, 116, 118–19, 230n65; and testimonio, 138

Harvard, John, 245n51
Hau, Caroline S., 76
Herrera, Juan Felipe: and *Akrílica* 192, 194–8; and emphasis on Central American experience, 197; exclusion from U.S. poetry, 195; and hemispheric latinidad, 198; and translation of, 195–6; 198
hemispheric: consciousness, 99; and hegemony, 8; and latinidad, 162, 197, 211n91; and Latinx literature, 23–4, 30, 175; as methodology, 2, 7, 23–4, 30, 97; and revolution, 7, 167–8; and splitting, 102
heteronormativity: in *Dogeaters* (Hagedorn), 88, 98, 223n49; in *Noli* (Rizal), 77; and *Oscar Wao* (Díaz), 119
Ho, Jennifer Ann, 237n59
Holland, Sharon P., 249n91, 251n109
homosociality: in *Dogeaters* (Hagedorn), 87–8, 191, 224n56; and the guerrilla conversion narrative, 70; and love triangle, 71, 76, 84, 87; and Rizal, 28, 70, 72, 75–81, 87, 191; in *State of War* (Rosca), 84, 191; as theorized by Derrida, 88
Hooker, Juliet, 180, 214n14
horizon: as dissatisfaction, 10; as expanding, 7–9, 28, 63, 73, 156, 140–1, 144, 151, 156, 163, 190, 215n22, 245n51; and futurity, 102, 200; as hemispheric project, 2; and indigeneity, 12, 248n85; and latinidad, 6, 9–11, 15–17, 21–22, 27, 190, 192, 215n22, 225n13; as limit, 10, 54, 75, 89, 91, 118, 128, 150, 181, 225n13; as method, 192; and moments of rupture, 7, 15, 44, 143, 149, 159; puncturing of, 28, 57–8, 75, 82; and revolutions, 6, 8; theory of, 2, 9–10, 206n15; and utopia, 29; and "x" in Latinx, 9, 15, 65, 219n11
Horn, Maja, 230n63
Horvitz, Deborah, 242n9, 248n84, 248n88, 250n104
Hostos, Eugenio María, 103–4, 110, 111, 226n13
Hostosianismo, 103–4, 110–11, 226n13
Hu-DeHart, Evelyn, 13, 235n24
Huhndorf, Shari M, 243n14, 249n87, 250n104, 251n107, 252n111

Ibarra, Rogelia Lily, 241n86
Igartuburu García, Elena, 237n59
imperialism: Black, 165, 173–4, 244n34; and genre, 21; and the novel, 22; Spanish, 78; U.S., 14, 128

INDEX   287

In the Name of Salomé (Alvarez): and blackness, 113–14, 225n13; and Camila's sexuality, 227n24; and chronology, 106, 227n20;
 and guerrilla conversion narrative, 99,
 105; and dictator novel, 29, 117; and history of revolutions in Latin America, 29;
 and la patria, 107, 109–11; and pedagogical
 project, 29, 103–4, 106, 110, 115–16, 226n12;
 and political consciousness, 100, 127; and
 positivism, 104, 115–16, 127, 226n12; and
 the revolutionary bildungsroman, 104,
 106, 109, 126–7, 227n24; and role of
 displacement in revolutions, 26; and role
 of women in revolutions, 104–5; and the
 subjunctive, 114–15; 176; and triangulation, 104; and whiteness, 105–6, 109, 113,
 225n13
indigeneity: and *Blake* (Delany), 174, 178;
 in *Caramelo* (Cisneros), 28, 40, 42, 55,
 56, 58, 60–3, 65, 215n22; and Chicano
 Movement; 3, 214n15; and chicanidad, 28,
 40, 42, 55; and disappeared relations, 11–2;
 and Dominican Republic, 113; as held
 captive, 58, 63, 65, 134; and latinidad, 11,
 34, 40, 140; and Marx, 186; and Mexico,
 12, 33–8, 41–2, 54, 58–60, 63, 161; and
 Monkey Hunting (Hagedorn), 140, 157; in
 Oscar Wao (Díaz), 124; and Philippines,
 78, 222n16; and Rizal, 75, 78–9, 93; in
 Sab (Avellaneda), 152, 154–5, 241n86;
 in *Star Wars*, 33–4, 37–8, 63; in *State of
 War* (Rosca), 85, 90; and Silko, 30, 161–3,
 178–9, 181, 190; in *Who Would Have
 Thought It?* (Ruiz de Burton), 40, 45, 47,
 49–50, 58, 65
Irizarry, Ylce, 15, 203, 209n52
Irwin, Robert McKee: and the "almost
 Latino," 16

Jacobs, Margaret D., 216n31, 241n82
Jerng, Mark, 3, 22, 205n9, 211n82
Johnson, Amanda Walker, 205n104
Juárez, Benito, 43, 51, 58

Kelly, Edith L., 240n69
kinship: and colonial legacy, 98; in
 Dogeaters (Hagedorn), 29, 71–2, 81, 89,
 93, 95–8, 103; and *Fili* (Rizal), 81; and futurity, 9, 97, 126; and guerrilla conversion
 narrative, 70, 72–3, 78, 83–4, 87, 98; and
 Noli (Rizal), 80; and *Oscar Wao* (Díaz),
 102, 105, 117, 120, 127; and queerness, 71–2,
 89, 98, 103, 117; and Rizal, 70, 71–3, 78,
 96, 97, 98, 103; and Silko, 161–2; in *State
 of War* (Rosca), 29, 71–2, 81–4, 87, 93,
 97–8, 103
Kirkpatrick, Susan, 155, 239, 240, 241n81
Koselleck, Reinhart, 10
Kuhn, Helmut, 9
The Lady Matador's Hotel (García), 199

La Escalera: and *Blake* (Delany), 159–60,
 162, 166, 168–70, 175–6, 190–1, 245n13; as
 colonial movement, 168; as revolutionary
 model, 162, 166, 169–70, 175–6, 245n13; as
 a series of smaller rebellions, 168
La Liga Filipina, 75, 78
la patria, 106–114, 127; and Dixa Ramírez,
 105, 225
la raza, 42, 206n22
Ladder Conspiracy, 159, 169. *See La Esca-
 lara*
latinidad, 3–4, and anti-blackness, 1–2, 11,
 196; and blackness, 13, 19, 65, 162, 176,
 190; and brownness, 28, 190; cancelation
 of, 1–2, 4; and citizenship, 194; and form,
 23; and futurity, 17, 210n62; and horizon,
 6, 9–11, 15–17, 21–22, 27, 190, 192, 215n22;
 and indigeneity, 11, 34, 40, 65, 140, 190; as
 political commitment, 14–15, 30, 162–3;
 as speculative, 4; 9, 11, 15, 63, 141; and
 whiteness, 1–2, 4–5, 21, 38–40, 42, 54, 63,
 65, 162–3, 192, 225n13, 253n2
Latinx, 14, 17, 65, 198–9; as fiction, 15; and
 futurity, 14–15, 17, 63–5; and horizon, 6, 9,
 15, 219n1; and indigeneity, 65; as pan-ethnic term, 15; as political formation, 1, 5;
 and queerness, 198; and race, 65, 198; and
 the speculative, 138, 141, 198; as triangulation, 101, 104; and whiteness, 5, 65
Latinx Studies, 27; and anti-identitarian
 turn, 15; and Delany, 190; exclusion of
 Haiti, 209n58; and futurity, 16–7, 65,
 210n62; and Haiti, 209n58; and hemispheric, 23, 211n91; as ignoring gendered
 violence, 226n16; impact of Mexican
 Revolution on, 25; and nationalism, 11;
 and the Philippines, 69, 73; as political
 position, 11, 14–15; and resistance, 206n22;
 as resisting U.S. claims, 14; and Silko, 190
Lamas, Carmen E., 13, 203, 208n45, 211n91
Lazo, Rodrigo, 211n91, 221n14

Lee, Jade Tsui-yu, 237–8n59
Lee, Rachel, 88, 223–4n49
Le-Khac, Long, 208–9n49
Levine, Robert S., 164, 165, 244n31, 244n34, 247n70–1
Leving Jacobson, Jenna, 154, 241n82
Lifshey, Adam, 73, 221n13, 222n16
Lima, Lazaro, 192
Livingston, Jennie, 198
López, Antonio, 134
López, Marissa K., 211n91
López-Calvo, Ignacio, 13, 229n58, 230n59, 231n74, 232n2, 235n24
Los Indios Bravos, 75, 78
Loving in the War Years (Moraga), 43
Lowe, Lisa, 13, 153, 211n84, 235n24
Lucas, George: and Princess Leia design, 34, 37, 213n6; as white farm boy, 37–8
Luis, William, 139
Lusane, Clarence, 233n12
Lye, Colleen, 22
Lynch, John, 13
Lysik, Marta, 234n19, 236n34

Macondo, 226n11
Machado Sáez, Elena, 15, 106, 117–22, 203, 212n93, 226n18, 227n22–4, 228n43, 229n50
Madera, Judith, 245n47, 247n70
Maleuvre, Didier, 10
Manifest Destiny, 39, 44, 46, 244n34, 247n70
manifesto: El Plan Espiritual de Aztlán, 42; and Latinx literary studies, 194; and Latinx resistance, 3
Manuel, Dolores de, 82; 223n35
Marcos regime: and conjugal rule, 72; in *Dogeaters* (Hagedorn), 71–2, 87–8, 90–3; and Malakas and Maganda, 72; in *State of War* (Rosca), 71–2, 81–2
Marez, Curtis, 37, 38, 203
Martí, José, 3, 24, 71, 103, 133, 171, 223n42, 233n12
Martínez, Manuel, 133, 233n15
Marx, Karl, 191
Marxism, 185, 186
Matibag, Eugenio, 223n44
Matuk, Farid, 194–6; and *Akrílica* (Herrera), 192, 194–9, 204
Mayes, April J., 103, 225n6, 226n13
McCracken, Ellen, 219n71
McCullough, Kate, 217n35
McGann, Jerome, 173, 175, 176

McKinley, William, 76, 94–5
Menchaca, Martha, 210n64
Menchú, Rigoberta, 21, 148, 211n78
Mendible, Myra, 82, 90, 223–4n49
Mendoza, Victor, 223–4n49
mestizaje: and blackness, 42; and Cisneros, 40, 42, 63, 65, 215n21; holding ideas of revolution captive, 28; and indigeneity, 40, 63, 65, 134; and latinidad, 40; and Mexican Revolution, 40, 42; and racelessness, 134; and Ruiz de Burton, 42, 50, 65; and Vasconcelos, 42, 214n14; and whiteness, 42, 233n5, 233n12. See also mestizx
mestizx: and *Almanac* (Silko), 182, 183; and *Caramelo* (Cisneros), 58; and indigeneity, 38, 63; and *Monkey Hunting* (Hagedorn), 137; and "Princess Lupe" (Alcaraz), 38; and whiteness, 40
Mexico: and *Almanac* (Silko), 162, 178–9, 184; and *Caramelo* (Cisneros), 7, 55–63; colonial history of, 51–3; French colonization of, 7, 39; and indigeneity, 12, 41, 55, 60, 63, 162, 221n12; and Mexican American identity, 39; and Partido Revolucionario Institucional, 25; and "Princess Lupe" (Alcaraz), 24, 37; and rebozo, 55–6; and revolutionary context, 26, 27, 39; and U.S., 2, 216; and U.S.-Mexico Border, 17, 162; and U.S.-Mexico War, 28, 39, 44–7, 53, 193; and whiteness, 65; in *Who Would Have Thought It?* (Ruiz de Burton), 28, 44–7, 50–4, 217n35, 218n51. See also Benito Juárez; Vasconcelos
Mexican Revolution: in *Caramelo* (Cisneros), 4, 7, 40–2, 54–8, 61, 63; and the Chicano Movement, 54, 214n15; as haunting, 41, 212n96; and indigeneity, 37, 54–5, 61, 190; impact on Latinx Studies, 25; and María Cristina Mena, 45; and race, 3; as a series of revolutions, 39, 58; and soldaderas, 34, 37; and *Star Wars*, 34, 37–8; and violence, 188, 190; in *Who Would Have Thought It?* (Ruiz de Burton), 54
Middle Passage, 143–4, 162, 231n75
Mignolo, Walter D., 1–2, 39–40, 70
Milian, Claudia, 65, 211–12n91
Mirabal sisters, 101, 124, 129
Molina, Natalie, 45
Monkey Hunting (García): and Afro Cubans, 144–8; and anti-blackness, 146,

156; as Asian American text, 88, 237n59; and *Beloved* (Morrison), 236n34; and connection between testimonio and neo-slave narrative, 129, 136–7, 143–4, 146, 148, 234n19; and communism, 135, 147, 149; and critique of racelessness in Cuba, 134–5; and diaspora, 142; and immigrant bildungsroman, 29; and orientalism, 237n59; and retconning, 135–7, 140, 142–4, 148–9, 156–7; as revision of *Biography of a Runaway Slave* (Barnet), 23, 29, 133, 136–8, 140–6, 232n2; and revolutionary bildungsroman, 148; and *Sab* (Avellaneda), 156–7; and slave narrative 129, 136–7, 143–4, 146, 149, 234n19; and speculative criticism, 147, 157; and speculative fiction, 144–5; and testimonio, 23, 129, 133, 136, 140–2, 144–8; and whiteness, 133–4; 140

Montejo, Esteban: and *Biography of a Runaway Slave* (Barnet), 139–40, 235n21; and Cuban Revolution, 133, 140; and *Monkey Hunting* (García), 23, 29, 133, 136–8, 140–6, 232n2; and testimonio, 136, 140

Montes, Amelia María de la Luz, 46

Moretti, Franco, 102

Muñoz, José Esteban: and brown commons, 190, 192–3; and definition of queer, 222n28; and horizon, 9; and identity-in-difference, 137; and "the then and there," 9. *See also* utopia

Murphy, Gretchen, 52, 218n51

neocolonialism: in *Dogeaters* (Hagedorn), 89–90, 93, 95–6, 224n56; U.S., 73, 89, 95, 209n52

neo-slave narrative: as genre, 4, 21; in *Monkey Hunting* (García), 129, 136, 145, 234n19; and testimonio, 21, 129, 136, 145, 156. *See also* slave narrative

Newman, Julie, 150

Nguyen, Viet Thanh, 89, 223–4n49

Noli Me Tangere (Rizal): and critique of Spanish colonialism, 74; and cyclical time, 81; and guerrilla conversion narrative, 70, 75, 96; and the homosocial, 76; and love triangle, 77; and nationalist romance, 89; and role of women, 84. *See also* José Rizal

Nwankwo, Ifeoma Kiddoe, 160, 166, 171, 188, 189, 246n60, 252n113

Ocampo, Anthony, 208n49, 221n12

O'Brien, Colleen, 240n72

O'Gorman, Edmundo, 13

Olguín, B.V., 42, 206n22

Ontiveros, Randy J., 203, 218–9n59

Orihuela, Sharada Balachandran, 244n44, 247n73

Ostend Manifesto of 1854, 166

Ortiz, Ricardo; and the "always-already Latinx," 16; and latinidad, 11, 15–17, 176; and "x" in Latinx, 6, 14

Pact of Zanjón, 151

Palmer, Steven, 238n62

Parziale, Amy, 238n63

Paulk, Julia C., 156

Pérez, Emma, 138

Pérez-Torres, Rafael, 201, 215n21

Philippines: in Asian American context, 26, 73, 75; colonial history of, 65, 69–73, 75, 82, 90, 95, 221n12, 221n13; and *Dogeaters* (Hagedorn), 26, 87, 90, 94; and *Fili* (Rizal), 26, 74, 79–81; and homosociality, 76–7, 81; within Latin American context, 26, 28, 65, 69–71, 73, 95–8, 220n5, 221n12, 221n13; and *Noli* (Rizal), 26, 74, 77, 79; and *State of War* (Rosca), 26, 82–4, 87; and the U.S., 69, 73, 76, 89, 95, 221n12, 224n56. *See also* cacique democracy; Marcos Regime

Philippine-American War, 76

Philippine Revolution: as failure, 25; and Rizal, 25, 74–5, 90, 212n97; in *State of War*, 82

Pierrot, Grégory, 168, 170, 176, 245n47–8, 245–6n51, 246n58

Pita, Beatrice, 39

Piqueras, José Antonio, 238n62

Plácido (Gabriel de la Concepción Valdés), 159–60, 162, 164–5, 167–71, 173, 175, 188–90, 242n3, 244n31, 246n60, 247n71, 252n116

Platt Amendment, 134

Ponce, Martin J., 77, 222n28

positivism: and *Blake* (Delany),171; in Dominican Republic, 104, 115; and Hostosianismo, 103; and Ruiz de Burton, 43; and *Salomé* (Alvarez), 104, 115–16, 127, 226n12

postcolonialism: and Chicanafuturism, 9; and colonial pasts, 157; and Latinx identity, 1, 40; in the Philippines, 69

"Princess Lupe" (Alcaraz): and browning, 34, 37–8; and indigeneity, 34; and Princess Leia, 33–4, 37; and the speculative, 33–4; and the Virgen de Guadalupe, 33–4, 37
Puerto Rico: and *Conquistadora* (Santiago), 18–20; and erased history of blackness, 18; and *Olga Dies Dreaming* (Gonzalez), 198; and *Oscar Wao* (Díaz), 121–2; and *Salomé* (Alvarez), 104, 108; and the Spanish-American War, 70; and *The House of Impossible Beauties* (Cassara), 198
Puig, Raquel, 233n4
Puritan captivity narrative, 48

Quaratiello, Elizabeth Lowery, 242n20
queerness: and chosen kinship networks, 71–2, 89, 98, 103, 117; definition of, 77, 222n28; in *Dogeaters* (Hagedorn), 81, 87–9, 96, 97, 223n49; and Latinx commons, 192; in *Oscar Wao* (Díaz), 117, 120, 122; and Rizal, 71, 76–7, 84, 96, 97; and *Salomé* (Alvarez), 227n24; as not included in revolution, 199; and *The House of Impossible Beauties* (Cassara), 198–9

race: and *Almanac* (Silko), 161; and captivity narrative, 47; and *Caramelo* (Cisneros), 55, 60; and *Conquistadora* (Santiago), 19; and *Dogeaters* (Hagedorn), 93; and Dominican Republic, 104, 107, 113–4, 121; and fiction, 23; and form, 22; and latinidad, 3–4, 14, 16, 18, 27, 40, 129, 136, 163, 198; mixed-race, 93, 96, 105, 107, 121, 143, 161, 164, 189; and *Monkey Hunting* (García), 136, 142–3, 146; 236n52; and *Noli* (Rizal), 78; and *Oscar Wao* (Díaz), 121–2; racelessness, 134–135, 151, 233n12; racial scripts, 45, 46, 155; and revolutionary consciousness, 28; and *Sab* (Avellaneda), 152, 155–6; and Spanish colonialism, 77, 78, 136; Vasconcelos, 41–2, 180; visibility of, 3; and *Who Would Have Thought It?* (Ruiz de Burton), 45–7, 49, 50, 52–3
racism, 29, 49, 59, 134, 217n37, 236–7n52
Race War of 1912, 139–40, 145–6, 172, 208n45
Rafael, Vicente L., 69, 72, 76, 84
Rama, Angel, 3
Ramírez, Catherine S., 9
Ramírez, Dixa, 105–10, 113, 225n6, 226n19, 227n21, 227n27, 228n30, 228n33, 228n36, 228n45, 229n47, 229n49
Rannard, Georgina, 219n63
Reconquista, 17
Reid-Pharr, Robert, 252n113
Retamar, Roberto Fernández, 42, 180–2, 250n99
retconning: and *Almanac* (Silko), 188; definition of, 135; and historiography, 234n15; as methodology, 157; in *Monkey Hunting* (García), 135–7, 140, 142–4, 148–9, 156–7; in *Sab* (Avellaneda), 137, 150–4, 156; and "x" in Latinx, 138
revolution: and brownness, 38, 178, 190; and charismatic leadership, 116; and displacement, 26; and education, 103, 111; and genre, 7, 21–2, 24; as haunting, 5, 26, 41; hegemonic imaginaries of, 11–12; and heterosexual romance, 77; and horizon, 6, 8, 57, 75, 177–8, 191; and kinship, 29, 30; and the literary, 3; and masculinity, 188, 191; and relationality, 104, 129; and role of enslaved people in, 19; role of women in, 71, 76–7, 81, 88, 104; and speculative imaginaries, 159; theories of, 5–6, 205n11; and violence, 188
Reyes, Raquel A. G., 75
Riofrio, John D., 211–12n91
Rivera, John-Michael, 216n31
Rizal, José: and Benedict Anderson, 74; exclusion of women in revolutionary thought, 76–7, 84, 88, 95–6, 168, 190, 219n1; as Father of Filipino literature, 70; as filibustero, 74, 221n14; as "first Filipino," 75, 222n17; and the guerrilla conversion narrative, 28, 70–1, 73, 75–6, 78, 83, 93, 95–6, 98, 103, 105; Hagedorn's revision of, 25, 28, 71–2, 81, 87–88, 90, 93, 95–8, 190; and homosociality, 28, 70, 72, 75–9, 81, 87, 190; impact on Filipino as national identity, 75; and mentor-mentee model, 70, 77, 87–8, 96, 105; Rosca's revision of, 25, 28, 71–2, 81, 83–6, 97–8, 190
Rodó, José Enrique, 42, 180–2
Rodríguez, Ana Patricia, 197, 211–12n91
Rodríguez, Ileana, 77, 215n20, 222n27
Rodriguez, Ralph E., 22–3
Rodriguez, Richard, 54
Rodríguez-Silva, Ileana M., 18, 210n67
Rogin, Michael, 39
Rohrleitner, Marion, 203, 229n48

Román, Elda María, 17
Romero, Chanette, 146, 149, 161, 242n9
Rosca, Ninotchka: and alternative kinships, 29, 71–2, 81–4, 87, 93, 97–8, 103; and heterosocial, 72; and inclusion of women in revolutionary project, 84–5, 88; 223n35; revisions to the guerrilla conversion narrative, 29, 70–2, 84–5, 87, 97–8, 105; and *The Monsoon Collection*, 81; revisions to Rizal, 25, 28–9, 71–2, 77, 81, 83–6, 97–8, 190–1. See also *State of War*
Rosenthal, Debra J., 238–9n66, 239n68, 240–1n78
Ruiz, Julie, 52, 214n11
Ruiz de Burton, María Amparo: and the accidental, 45, 50, 53, 137, 166; biography of, 43–4; and the captivity narrative, 46–8, 53, 216n32; critique of U.S. eastern culture, 46–7; 54; and Chicano Movement, 215n24; and elitism, 39–40; French influence on, 39; and hegemonic latinidad, 42–3; and Mexican American literature, 43, 216n26; and positivism, 43; and *The Squatter and The Don*, 43, 45; and whiteness, 2, 39–42, 45–6, 49–50, 54, 63, 214n11, 216n29. See also *Who Would Have Thought It?*
Rushdy, Ashraf H. A, 235n23

Sab (Avellaneda): as abolitionist novel, 137, 150–1, 155, 239n68; and the accidental, 137–8, 166; as anti-slavery novel, 241n81; as autobiography, 138, 151–3; 240n78; and Del Monte circle, 149–50; 238n66; and failure of solidarity, 155; and indigeneity, 52, 154–5, 241n86; and *Monkey Hunting* (García), 156–7; and race, 152, 155–6; and retcon, 137, 150–4, 156; and revolutionary bildungsroman, 150; as slave narrative, 138; as testimonio, 29, 138, 151, 153; and *Uncle Tom's Cabin* (Beecher Stowe), 150, 240n71; and women's rights, 29, 150–3, 155, 239n68
Sáez, Elena Machado, 15, 106, 117–22, 203, 226n18, 227n22, 227n24, 228n43, 229n50
Safa, Helen I., 233–4n12
Said, Edward W., 22
Saldaña-Portillo, María Josefina: and future-perfect temporality, 12; and the guerrilla subject, 220n6; and indigeneity, 12, 248n85, 249n89; and Marxism, 186, 206n54; and the meliorist theory of subjectivity, 8–9; and transcendental model of revolutionary conversion, 101
Saldívar, José David, 211–21n91, 225n4, 250n97
Saldívar, Ramón, 127
Saldívar-Hull, Sonia, 214–15n19
Sánchez, María Carla, 216n28
Sánchez, Rosaura, 39
San Juan, E. Jr., 75
sangre limpia, 161, 178–9
sangre pura, 161, 182, 184, 249n90
Santiago, Esmeralda: and *Conquistadora*, 18–21; refusal to identify as Black, 20–1
Sarmiento, Domingo Faustino: and civility/barbarism binary, 103; and dictator novel, 21; and eugenics, 180, 183; and *Facundo* (Sarmiento), 21, 103, 163, 180; influence on Vasconcelos, 180; Silko's revision of, 163, 180–1
Schlau, Stacy, 152, 239n68
Schultermandl, Silvia, 236n52
Scott, David: and colonial pasts, 157
Second French intervention: in *Caramelo* (Cisneros), 56, 58; in *Who Would Have Thought It?* (Ruiz de Burton), 39, 40, 43, 46
Sedgwick, Eve Kosofsky: and the love triangle, 71, 76, 81, 83–4
See, Sarita E., 89
Shawcross, Edward, 53
Shreve, Grant, 243n20
Sieminski, Greg, 48
Silko, Leslie Marmon: and anticipation of Zapatista uprising, 158, 160–1; and Black Indians, 189–90; and brownness, 189–90; and civilization/barbarism binary, 163, 180–2, 191; and critique of Marxism, 186, 191; and indigeneity, 30, 161–3, 178–9; and speculative fiction, 30, 159; and transnational perspective, 243n14; and tribal internationalism, 161
Simón, Yara, 213n4
Sklodowska, Elzbieta, 145, 234n18, 236n50
Skocpol, Theda, 205n11
slave codes of 1842, 18
slave narrative: in Cuba, 149; and the Del Monte Circle, 149–50; as genre, 21, 136; in *Monkey Hunting* (García), 136–8, 143–6, 148–9; in *Sab* (Avellaneda), 138; and testimonio, 23, 136–7, 145–6, 148; in U.S., 149. *See also* neo-slave narrative

Socolovsky, Maya, 227n20
Sohn, Stephen Hong, 88, 89
Sommer, Doris: and national consolidation, 13, 78–9, 155–6; and national romance, 28, 70–1, 75, 77, 154; and *Sab*, 151–2
soldaderas, 34, 37
Soles y Rayos de Bolívar conspiracy, 177
Spanish-American War, 25, 70, 74, 133, 139, 171
speculative criticism: and critical fabulation, 157; in *Monkey Hunting* (García), 147, 157
speculative fiction: in *Almanac* (Silko), 159, 161, 190; in *Blake* (Delany), 159–60, 190; and latinidad, 9, 15; in *Monkey Hunting* (García), 144–5; and *Star Wars*, 33–4
Spoturno, María Laura, 219n64
Star Wars: and Princess Leia, 33, 37; and Tatooine, 37; and whiteness, 37
State of War (Rosca): and alternative kinships, 29, 71–2, 81–4, 87, 93, 97–8, 103; within Asian American context, 69; and cyclical model of time, 81–2; within Filipinx context, 69, 73; and the heterosocial, 72; and friarocracy, 82, 85; and homosociality, 84, 191; and inclusion of women in revolutionary project, 84–5, 88; 223n35; and nationalist romance, 89; revisions to the guerrilla conversion narrative, 28–9, 70–2, 84–5, 87, 97–8, 105; revisions to Rizal, 25, 28, 71–2, 77, 81, 83–6, 97–8, 190–1
Stevenson, Pascha A, 216n28
Stowe, Harriet Beecher: and accommodationist stance, 161; and *Uncle Tom's Cabin*, 150, 239n68
Streeby, Shelley, 39, 201; and critique of the American 1848, 39
subaltern: and revolution, 8–9, 206n22; and testimonio, 140, 145, 237n56
subjunctive: and *Blake* (Delany), 176; and *Salomé* (Alvarez), 114–15, 176; as theorized by Brittan, 176
Sundquist, Eric J., 160, 164
Szeghi, Tereza M., 219n67

Taft, William Howard, 76
Tate, Julee, 229n51
Ten Years' War: and *Biography of a Runaway Slave* (Barnet), 139–40, 235n31; in *Blake* (Delany), 177; and the Cuban Wars of independence, 168; and Fidel Castro's one hundred years of revolution, 134; in *Monkey Hunting* (García), 5, 145; and *Salomé* (Alvarez), 108
testimonio: and *Before Night Falls* (Arenas), 199; and *Biography of a Runaway Slave* (Barnet), 21, 23, 133, 139–42; and Cuban Revolution, 140; definition of testimonio, 21–2, 136, 138, 145; and *I, Rigoberta Menchú*, 21, 148; and *The Lady Matador's Hotel* (García), 199; limitations of definition, 145, 234n18, 236n50; in *Monkey Hunting* (García), 23, 129, 133, 136, 140–2, 144–8; and neo-slave narrative, 21, 129, 136, 145, 156; in *Sab* (Avellaneda), 29, 138, 151, 153; in *Salomé* (Alvarez), 109; and slave narrative, 23, 136–7, 145–6, 148; and *The Undocumented Americans* (Cornejo Villavicencio), 194; as theorized by Jennifer Harford Vargas, 138; as theorized by John Beverley, 21–2, 136, 145–6, 237n56; in *Who Would Have Thought It?* (Ruiz de Burton), 44, 51
Tillett, Rebecca, 250n104
Tilly, Charles, 205–6n11
Tinnemeyer, Andrea, 47, 217n39
Trouillot, Michel-Rolph, 185, 209n58, 251n108
Trujillo regime: and familial forms, 121; and Haitian genocide, 101, 122, 124, 231n80; and *Oscar Wao* (Díaz), 101, 118, 121–2, 124, 231n82; and representations of masculinity, 230n63; and *Salomé* (Alvarez), 226n18; and sexual politics, 97, 121; and whiteness, 231n72
Trujillo, Simón Ventura, 9, 11, 73, 161, 221n12; and disappeared relations, 11–12, 73, 97, 161, 179, 192, 221n12
Trump, Donald J., 4, 17, 33–4, 54, 194
Twinam, Ann, 279n83

United States: and Anglo-Saxon, 49; and anti-blackness, 160; and *Blake* (Delany), 160, 164, 166–8, 172, 244n34, 247n71; and the captivity narrative, 47–8, 53; and Cuba, 134, 164, 166–8, 172, 240n78; and *Dogeaters* (Hagedorn), 73, 93; and Dominican Republic, 29, 100, 102, 113–14, 125; as drawing inspiration from Latinx revolutionaries, 4, 7–8, 189; and fear of reconquista, 17; and imperialism, 7, 14, 128–9; and *Monkey Hunting* (García), 29; and *Oscar Wao* (Díaz), 100, 102, 120–1,

125, 128; and Philippines, 69, 73, 76, 89, 95, 221n12, 224n56; and the Puritan captivity narrative, 48; and *Salomé* (Alvarez), 102, 104, 128; and slavery, 121, 166–7, 172, 197; and *The Undocumented Americans* (Cornejo Villavicencio), 194; and U.S.-based latinidad, 2, 4, 9, 16, 40; and U.S. reader, 99–100, 102, 117, 120, 125, 128–9; and whiteness, 49, 113; and *Who Would Have Thought It?* (Ruiz de Burton), 46–50, 53

Ureña, Salomé: and "A Mi Patria," 109–11; and ambivalence about revolution, 104, 111–2; and Dominican national identity, 101, 105; and education, 103–6, 111, 115, 225n6; erasure of blackness, 113–14, 225n6, 228n45; and Hostosianismo, 103, 110; and "Mi Pedro," 111–12; and "Quejas," 113; and "Sombras," 109–11, 115, 228n37

U.S.-Mexico Border, 17, 162, 193

U.S. Civil War, 39, 46, 54; in *Who Would Have Thought It?* (Ruiz de Burton), 39, 46, 54

U.S.-Mexico War, 44; in *Who Would Have Thought It?* (Ruiz de Burton), 44

utopia: and desire, 127; and indigeneity, 154, 248n85; and José Esteban Muñoz, 207n25; and latinidad, 4, 17, 29

Vargas Llosa, Mario, 226n11, 229n58, 231n82

Vasconcelos, José: and the Chicano Movement, 41–2; drawing from Sarmiento, 180; and eugenics, 41, 180; and Gloria Anzaldúa, 214n19; and indigeneity, 41–2, 54, 60, 214n19; and la raza, 41–2, 180

Vázquez, David, 15, 23, 27, 104, 203, 209n55, 218n59, 226n18; and triangulation, 104, 152, 209n55, 218n59, 226n18

Viego, Antonio, 210n62

Vigil, Ariana, 203, 211–12n91

Villarreal, José Antonio, 43

Virgin of Guadalupe, 33–4, 37–8, 213n2; and Lalo Alcaraz, 33

Wars of Independence: and Cuba, 108, 135, 168, 177; and the dictator novel, 21; as elite revolutions, 177; and failure to address women's rights, 151; as limitation on latinidad, 10, 18–19, 162; and national identity, 39

Webster, Eve, 219n63

Wells, Allen, 251n106

Weston, Edward, 63, 64

whitening, *See blanqueamiento*

whiteness: and *Almanac* (Silko), 162–3, 177–8; in *Blake* (Delany), 162–3, 165, 171–2, 174–5, 247n71; in *Caramelo* (Cisneros), 54–55, 56, 58–61, 65; and *Conquistadora* (Santiago), 21; in Cuba, 133–4, 171–2, 233n15; and the Dominican Republic, 104–5, 109, 113–14, 231n72, 251n106; and latinidad, 1–2, 4–5, 19, 21, 38–40, 42, 54, 63, 65, 162–3, 192, 225n3, 253n2; in *Monkey Hunting* (Hagedorn), 133–4, 140; in *Oscar Wao* (Díaz), 109, 122; proximity to, 4, 17; in *Salomé* (Alvarez), 105–6, 109, 113, 225n3; and *Star Wars*, 37; in *Who Would Have Thought It?* (Ruiz de Burton), 2, 39–42, 45–6, 49–50, 52, 54, 63, 65, 214n11, 216n29

Who Would Have Thought It? (Ruiz de Burton): as abolitionist novel, 48–9; and blackness, 45, 49–50, 65; and *Caramelo* (Cisneros), 2, 39–42, 55, 58, 65; and captivity narrative, 46–8, 53, 216n32; critique of U.S. eastern culture, 46–7; 54; and French influences, 39; and indigeneity, 40, 45, 47, 49–50, 58, 65; and mestizaje, 42, 65; and race, 45–6, 47, 49, 50, 52, 53; and testimonio, 44, 51; and whiteness, 2, 39–42, 45–6, 49–50, 52, 54, 63, 65, 214n11, 216n29

Wickham-Crowley, Timothy P., 5, 205n11

Williams, Lorna Valerie, 238n65

Woloch, Alex: and character-space, 49; and character-system, 49

"x" in Latinx, *See* Latinx

Zapata-Calle, Ana, 232–3n2

Zapatista uprising, 158, 160

Zevallos, Johnny, 240n71

Renee Hudson is Assistant Professor of English and Director of Latinx & Latin American Studies at Chapman University.

www.ingramcontent.com/pod-product-compliance
Lightning Source LLC
Chambersburg PA
CBHW020356080526
44584CB00014B/1043